Self-Help from the Middle Ages

Self-Help from the Middle Ages
A Journey into the Medieval Mind

PETER JONES

HUTCHINSON
HEINEMANN

HUTCHINSON HEINEMANN

UK | USA | Canada | Ireland | Australia
India | New Zealand | South Africa

Hutchinson Heinemann is part of the Penguin Random House group of companies whose addresses can be found at global.penguinrandomhouse.com

Penguin Random House UK,
One Embassy Gardens, 8 Viaduct Gardens, London SW11 7BW

penguin.co.uk

First published 2026
001

Copyright © Peter Jones, 2026

The moral right of the author has been asserted

Penguin Random House values and supports copyright. Copyright fuels creativity, encourages diverse voices, promotes freedom of expression and supports a vibrant culture. Thank you for purchasing an authorised edition of this book and for respecting intellectual property laws by not reproducing, scanning or distributing any part of it by any means without permission. You are supporting authors and enabling Penguin Random House to continue to publish books for everyone. No part of this book may be used or reproduced in any manner for the purpose of training artificial intelligence technologies or systems. In accordance with Article 4(3) of the DSM Directive 2019/790, Penguin Random House expressly reserves this work from the text and data mining exception.

Set in 13.2/16 pt Garamond Premier Pro
Typeset by Six Red Marbles UK, Thetford, Norfolk

Printed and bound in Great Britain by Clays Ltd, Elcograf S.p.A.

The authorised representative in the EEA is Penguin Random House Ireland, Morrison Chambers, 32 Nassau Street, Dublin D02 YH68

A CIP catalogue record for this book is available from the British Library

ISBN: 978–1–529–15486–3

Penguin Random House is committed to a sustainable future for our business, our readers and our planet. This book is made from Forest Stewardship Council® certified paper.

For my mother, Kim

Contents

The Seven	1
1. Pride	30
2. Envy	64
3. Anger	96
4. Sloth	132
5. Avarice	168
6. Gluttony	201
7. Lust	232
The Seven, Again	261
Acknowledgements	265
Notes	269
Bibliography	317
Picture Credits	347
Index	351

The Seven

I can't think of the word. It's not 'distant' or 'obscure', these are too cold. But it's not 'exotic' either. What's the word for this, the thing that horrifies you but then unlocks your heart?

In my hands is a book written on lambskin seven hundred years ago. It's tall, like an oversized restaurant menu. The pages are yellow, the spine has the waxy feel of dead skin, and it smells of damp gardening gloves. It weighs roughly the same as a large fresh salmon. I'm sitting with it in the Vatican Library, and under the flash of the archivist's spectacles I feel like the skinned lamb myself. Usually this book is kept in a concrete vault. You have to show your credentials at the front gate and surrender your passport to the Swiss Guards. Next you have to go through a brief interview, get your photo taken, sign several forms, and leave all your things in a digitally activated locker. Only then, after you've stripped off your modern identity, are you allowed to climb the stairs and get your hands on this, the world's only copy of the *Ark of Wisdom*.[1]

Is it worth travelling to the Vatican City for? Opening up the 650-year-old manuscript, I find every combination of anxiety and desire. And although the ink is ancient, the ideas are as fresh as if they had been written this morning. Across the 300 pages there are ecstasies and passions, rages and fantasies, procrastinations and jealousies. So many of the thoughts I imagined were mine alone – thoughts exhilarating, petty, lonely or afraid – are here, exposed in brown Gothic handwriting. There are the telltale signs of hypocrisy; the 'right' and 'wrong' kinds of personal grooming; the best remedies for depression.[2] The book pulses with energy, as if every word were written by somebody who already knew our world was coming.

I shouldn't be surprised that this manuscript feels so alive. It was structured around a sixteen-hundred-year-old system that still works; a map that continues to function as a reliable guide to the human brain. Because the *Ark of Wisdom* is really a handbook for how to live with the Seven Deadly Sins.

For most of us in the twenty-first century the Seven Deadly Sins are a bit of a joke. Not too long ago they inspired a range of ice creams, with a pink strawberry 'Lust' and a peanut-butter 'Sloth'. Graphic novels have made them into villains, and video games have made them into end-of-level bosses. It's still possible to stream *Se7en* (1995), the blockbuster movie starring Morgan Freeman and Brad Pitt, which features a serial killer who punishes people for each sin in turn (although in the wrong order).

But in the Middle Ages the Deadly Sins were more than a gimmick. They were psychological tools, keys for deciphering personality and decoding desire. They were a Periodic Table for the mind. As desert monks like John Cassian described them, the sins were a system for ordering and processing all thoughts. Every tempting idea and harmful act, in theory, could be traced back to some combination of these seven.[3]

What are their names? And what's their 'correct' order?[4] Listing them in their classic form – and in their usual ranking, from most to least 'deadly' – the seven are:

1. *Pride*: Self-obsession, to the point of dismissing the lives of others. This usually grows out of your focus on yourself.

2. *Envy*: Craving for other people to fail, or for their successes to be crushed. This usually grows out of your focus on others.
3. *Anger*: Frenzy, rage and a loss of the power of reason. This usually grows out of your impatience with others, or with yourself.
4. *Sloth*: Despair, depression, or falling out of love with life. This usually grows out of a lack of focus.
5. *Avarice*: Questing for more and better possessions. This can also cover 'wasteful' generosity, or fixation on different objects. It usually grows out of a focus on material things.
6. *Gluttony*: Excessive desire for food, alcohol, or other consumables. This can also cover total abstinence from eating, or excessive connoisseurship. It usually grows out of a focus on necessity.
7. *Lust*: Fixation on sex, but also sensory pleasure. It usually grows out of a focus on bodies.

The *Ark of Wisdom* moves through each of these seven with the precision of a sniper and the compassion of a kidney donor. Written sometime in the late 1300s, it has rarely been cited or copied since. In fact, it remained more or less unknown beyond the monastery near Milan where it was first kept. So, reading it now, in the Vatican Library, is a moving experience. But really, the *Ark of Wisdom* is only the beginning. Out there in Europe's archives are thousands of works just like this one: books that use the Seven Deadly Sins to explore temptation, frustration, fear, anxiety, grief and passion; guides for coping with rage and narcissism, and for embracing life's positives. Obstacles keep these books out of our reach. Most are inaccessible, written in obscure languages and torturous handwriting. Also, they're usually packaged under two labels – 'medieval' and 'theology' – that don't always excite the average reader.

And this is an enormous loss. Because if these guides have a true home, it isn't in the concrete vaults of a library building. And it's not in a university research seminar, either. It's in the hands of all of us, as we struggle through these labyrinths we get thrown into. The dark mazes of our lives.

A Pink Sky

A few years ago I fell into a trap that nearly swallowed me whole. It was a trench packed with unforgiving snow, and it was one I had dug all by myself.

I was teaching medieval history at a university in Siberia. Winter was approaching, and it was already bitterly cold. Below around minus 20°C my eyelashes grew tiny icicles. Beyond minus 25°C, if I stayed outside for longer than twenty minutes I could no longer feel my legs. I spent my afternoons in shopping malls, browsing leather bags and microfibre hats. I ate herring salads in cafés with pictures of the Eiffel Tower on the walls. Snow covered the pathways like fresh earth on a casket. Soon I found I no longer thought about the future. I stopped reading the news and I stopped contacting my friends. Then I stopped going outside at all. In my apartment I just stood by the window, pressed up against a radiator, watching as chimney stacks puffed smoke into a pink sky.

History can be an escape portal. It can transport you to a different life, a different heart. This was a lesson I began to learn when I was nine. One afternoon, early in the school holidays, my mother took me on the Piccadilly Line to the National Portrait Gallery in London. I stood in front of a picture of Richard III, the king who had been his mother's twelfth child and who had died at the Battle of Bosworth Field in 1485. I looked at the faded lines of his black robe, his crooked fingers with their colourful rings, and his luminous, desperate face, and I felt something inside me spike. Part of it was horror. *To live in a world so different. To be bludgeoned to death in a muddy field with a halberd axe. For this to be a plausible life outcome.* But alongside this horror was another feeling. I found I was burning to lift the veil, to cross the abyss. I wanted to discover what life was really like for the people on the other side of this window of oil and wood.

Over the next three decades I chased that mystery I'd seen in the Middle Ages wherever it led me. It was a quest that took me around the world. For a while I lived in the basement of a second-hand bookshop, absorbing shelves of books with foxed endpapers and titles like *Cistercian Monasticism*. At university I became obsessed with medieval mystics, and wrote a musical comedy about the twelfth-century lovers Abelard and Heloïse. Moving to New York to do a PhD, I found my mentor, a French scholar who taught me to look for clues to medieval psychology in obscure Latin texts. I travelled between the archives of Paris and London, and I hunted through the margins of forgotten manuscripts. I published articles in academic journals, gave papers at conferences and found teaching jobs, first in Toronto and then in London, just a few hundred yards from the National Portrait Gallery. On quiet days I sometimes went back to visit King Richard, to thank him for all the glamour he had brought me.

And then, for reasons that are still opaque to me, I moved to the city of Tyumen in Siberia. Some of my motivations were fairly rational, in hindsight. My contract in London was ending and the job advert was enticing. The challenge of the climate and language appealed to me, and I was curious to see what medieval Europe might look like to people who had grown up under Vladimir Putin. When I sat explaining these reasons to my friends, it did occur to me that they didn't amount to much, but I left these doubts behind when I arrived in my new home. At first I loved it. My days were filled with walks through silver birch forests. The snowflakes shone for me in the heavy air like diamonds. On the wall of my new apartment the landlord had hung a framed photograph of the cosmonaut Yuri Gagarin waving to a cheering crowd on a Moscow street. And most days I waved back.

But over time I stopped waving at Yuri. Over time the coldness in my life stretched beyond the hard fact of the weather. After days of heavy teaching, I would wake up with an ache that flowed from the stem of my brain into every capillary of my bloodstream. I was supposed to be researching and planning my lessons, to be getting on with my life. But I couldn't bring myself to do anything at all. Standing by the window, my spirit disappearing with the smoke in the sky, I realised I had nothing to say. I didn't want to give lectures. I didn't want to read, and I didn't want to look at any smiling cosmonauts. All I wanted to do was curl up and sleep for a thousand years.

A modern diagnosis of my condition would probably be straightforward. I was, I think, depressed. I was suffering from burnout, disillusionment, and the kind of deep melancholy that strikes around 20 per cent of the global population at some point in their lives. If I'd used my Siberian medical insurance, I would probably have been recommended either therapeutic or pharmaceutical solutions. I could have taken a CBT course, or gone through counselling sessions, or begun a regime of fluoxetine, citalopram, or sertraline, depending on how severe my doctor judged my case to be. Whatever the treatment, though, it might not have solved things for ever. According to psychiatric research, a substantial number of people who finish a course of antidepressants and do not receive further treatment relapse within twelve months.[5] Experts on the culture of burnout have even suggested that a state of depression is knotted into my generation's worldview in threads that can never be untangled.[6]

I was still immersed in medieval thought, though. And as my nights got longer I kept turning over the same inevitable question. How would my condition have been treated in the Middle Ages? How did people get through a crisis of inertia or self-doubt seven hundred years ago, before Europe became 'modern'? Although there would have been no drugs or clipboards, my depression would still have been considered a professional matter in the year 1300. In fact, an expert would have analysed how I thought, dreamed and moved through the world with an intensity that could make some modern therapy seem superficial. Because, as I discovered, the world that lay on the other side of the frame of King Richard's portrait had a curious characteristic, a feature that makes it surprisingly close to our own. This was a civilisation geared towards understanding the human mind.

When I say this, I'm not talking about the entire European Middle Ages. Conventionally, the period spans the thousand years from the end of the Western Roman Empire (c.400s) to three major transformations in European history: the invention of the printing press (c.1450), which brought mass literacy and the rapid-fire circulation of ideas; the colonisation of the Americas (c.1492), which changed the economic and political landscape for ever; and the Reformation (c.1517), which fragmented the religious unity of much of Europe. Although 'medieval' can still be a useful label for this long time span, in practice the differences between society in the 600s and society in the 1400s are often so vast they cannot be put together in the same box. And so, when I say 'medieval', I'm really talking about the four centuries I fell in love with: the period we call the High and Later Middle Ages (*c.*1100–1500).

For the sake of getting to know them a little, these four centuries can be compared to four Beatles albums.

The 1100s are *Revolver*. Full of potential and uneasy tensions, with a creativity that was not yet self-conscious. This was an era of groundbreaking innovation: the first universities in Bologna and Paris; the first crusades; the first Gothic abbeys and cathedrals in Saint-Denis and Sens; and also the first Arthurian romances (a genre that, some have claimed, invented the modern idea of love). The writing from this period was looser, more experimental, and although often cynical it was also unpredictable and fun. From this point in time, anything seemed possible.

The 1200s are *Sgt Pepper's Lonely Hearts Club Band*. More developed and sophisticated than what came before, with everything now in technicolour. The universities were in full flow, producing some of the biggest hits in the whole medieval canon. Eastern ideas exploded across the continent, with translations of the Quran and works of Arabic science, philosophy and medicine filling European libraries. The artwork was now more solid, more three-dimensional, and more emotionally expressive. But somehow everything was also becoming a parody of itself, with writers straining to hold all that creativity together without letting conflict and self-indulgence take over.

The 1300s are *The Beatles* (or the 'White Album'). Sprawling and fragmented, with a surprising amount of violence and death tying things together (from the Peasants' Revolt to the Great Plague). The major powers were now drifting apart, no longer uniting for joint crusades. And although some of the best writing of the Middle Ages survives from this period, including the *Divine Comedy* and the *Canterbury Tales*, these works somehow feel more isolated. Instead of being in the universal language of Latin, they were written in Tuscan and Middle English. And so, even though literature could now reach wider national audiences, the era of continent-wide literary hits was coming to an end.

And the 1400s are *Abbey Road*. All the powerful entities of Europe were now drifting apart, while a major conflict (the Hundred Years' War) roared between the two protagonists of England and France. There were constant scraps about finances, and by the end of the century (with the start of transatlantic colonisation) the centre of economic gravity had shifted to America. But still, this was a time of great artists (like Jan van Eyck and Rogier van der Weyden) at the peak of their powers and producing technically perfect art.

How was this a civilisation geared to understanding the human mind? For one thing, a passion for analysing thought and impulse dominated the top professions. The brightest and best brains, as sharp as the sharpest today, didn't dream of becoming entrepreneurs or hedge-fund managers after they got their education. Instead, the first university students travelled to Paris or Oxford to study Theology (which was then the most prestigious subject on offer). Armed with this degree, the best of these graduates competed to become bishops or cardinals, where the job description involved analysing the triggers of temptation and desire, giving lectures on fear and doubt, and healing the anxieties of people in crisis.[7] The whole point of the university, as Pope Gregory IX announced in 1231, was to create self-aware citizens. It was to turn students, with their 'hearts of stone', into a 'shining' army of preachers.[8]

Outside the classroom, the same message pulsed across works of literature. If medieval readers demanded one thing, it was a combination of psychological exploration and heartbreaking compassion. One of the most widely read books in these four centuries was Boethius's *The Consolation of Philosophy*, a conversation between a man condemned to death and a woman named Philosophy, who visits his prison cell and teaches him how to get through his despair. Another was the *Romance of the Rose* by Guillaume de Lorris and Jean de Meun, a book whose plot now sounds like a Pixar movie: a lover meets with a series of embodied psychological states, including Generosity, Fear, Honesty and Diversion, on a moving quest to understand the true nature of love.

But the biggest psychological initiative was just around the corner from people's homes. At the Fourth Lateran Council of 1215, the pope made it compulsory for every adult to make confession at least once a year. From then on, everyone had to undergo regular counselling sessions to take stock of their behaviour and make a spiritual pledge for the next twelve months. For these purposes, priests often ended up playing a role similar to a modern-day therapist.[9] This was tough emotional work, and the quality could vary wildly. If you were an aristocrat, you might have your own personal chaplain to counsel you.[10] But some communities had lazy parish priests, or ones who leaked secrets to neighbours, and if you were unlucky, your confession might be rushed or frantic.[11] You might be crammed into a church full of people, spaced out across the pews like students in an exam, head bowed while waiting for a whispered counselling session.[12]

Still, even people at the lower end of the economic spectrum could shop around. After 1215, ordinary people began seeking out priests with the best reputations for wisdom.[13] The difference could be night and day. If you lived in Cologne around this time, and confessed to a priest named Everard at the start of his career, it wouldn't have been a very therapeutic experience. Back then he was harsh to everyone, calling them 'disgraceful' when they confessed their sins to him. But if you caught Everard towards the end of his career, you'd have found a more sympathetic listener. By now he'd experienced many of the same temptations himself, committed many of the same sins, and this had taught him to be more forgiving, more open.[14] To be less tied to that destructive fantasy: the perfect life.

How would one of these counselling sessions work in practice? Let's follow the steps I would go through, if my listless Siberian winter had been in the fourteenth century. After I'd found my priest-therapist I'd present him with my predicament – 'Father I'm too cold, physically but also I think emotionally, to do my job' – and he'd have to come up with a constructive plan for getting my psyche back on track. As well as a schedule of prayers, he might suggest acts of penance, which he'd prescribe like a doctor handing out antibiotics.[15] For concrete actions there could be simple solutions. Lying to a loved one might be treated with one or two weeks of fasting on bread and water. For killing someone, I might need to spend ten years in exile.[16] But for my current problem – the ambiguous, psychological problem of 'emotional coldness' – a good priest would need to take a more complex approach.

Acting now in the role of spiritual adviser, he would ideally draw on a wealth of art, literature and philosophy to diagnose my problem.[17] But time is always short, and medieval priests were often quite stressed themselves. In many cases they would have dozens of confused people, just like me, who all needed their attention in one way or another. What they needed were quick guidebooks; self-help textbooks that could help them process a difficulty and its remedies as efficiently as possible. Luckily there were thousands of these books around, spread across the continent like copies of *The Da Vinci Code*. In every major European archive you can still find works like the *Ark of Wisdom*: treatises, preaching handbooks, sermons and confession guidebooks. All of them were designed for priests who tended to people in my situation, and nearly all of them are underpinned by the same organising principle: the Seven Deadly Sins.

Even without a guidebook, I have no doubt my priest would have recognised the basket of problems my own Siberian difficulty belonged to straight away. I was suffering from sloth, or as he would have known it, *acedia*. The fourth of the Seven Deadly Sins. But to understand the deeper nature of this sin – what it meant, how it manifested, and also how it might be redeemed – he would have been wise to look at one of these popular guides, designed for priests in the business of counselling sinners in distress.

And this is precisely what I did myself, a few years ago, during that coldest winter of my life, when I wanted to start tunnelling my way out.

The Rushing River

I'm in Dublin, in the manuscript library at Trinity College. On the desk in front of me is a text known as MS 306. The room is empty except for me and the archivist, and all I can hear is the distant knock of a cricket ball from the playing fields outside the window. It's surprisingly hot and I'm wearing a pair of rubber surgical gloves, so turning the pages of packed text feels like performing a dental exam. As if predicting my difficulties, the medieval scribe made this manuscript easy to navigate. At the top of each page is a red label to remind the reader which of the Deadly Sins they're reading about. The first section is labelled 'Superbia', and begins with a discussion of Lucifer. But I skip this and go straight to the one I'm most interested in. The one labelled 'Acedia', deep in the heart of the book.

Reading through the Latin, I immediately see how I might digest this advice for a person in distress, if I were a priest-therapist in the 1300s. As a university teacher I've been trained to sugar-coat bad news. This is what my colleagues used to call the 'shit sandwich' approach. First you give the student a cause for hope. 'Your essay has a fantastic idea at its heart, and you write with so much energy!' That's the bread, the wholesome-tasting outer shell. But now comes the filling. 'I did wonder, though, if you couldn't have structured this with more care. In a way, it reads like a list of fragments. I suppose it doesn't really have an argument either, does it?' At the first sign of disappointment you then pat down this criticism with another slice of bread. 'I'm confident that this is your first step to writing history from the heart.' This is university teaching at its finest, and precisely the skill that landed me my job in Siberia.

But as slothful as my heart has become, this 800-year-old shit sandwich in the archive is still able to work its magic on me. *Acedia*, the guide tells me, is the sin of 'coldness' (*frigidis*, in the Latin). Although as it turns out, this isn't so bad. Being cold is a typical consequence of getting lost in work or in the mechanical demands of life. And coldness is much better, the guide says, than being 'lukewarm' (*tepidus*). When you are lukewarm you are complacent. Mindlessly satisfied with your small efforts, you stop questioning or challenging yourself, and soon you grow insensitive and cruel. But to feel real coldness – to be on the point of depression; to live each day as if you will never love anything again – is to be stripped down to the essentials of life. And that coldness can clear the decks, making you ready for an awakening that will be sharper, more beautiful and more alive than anything you knew before. *A field which, after thorns and thistles, gives abundant fruit is more loved than a field that, although it never had any thorns or thistles, never really gave much fruit at all.*[18]

I lean forward in my chair. Does this old handbook know something about my life? If I was suffering from *acedia*, it told me, I would find that all the things that used to please me leave me feeling nothing at all. I would be cynical and sometimes heartless. I would feel like I was *standing in the middle of a rushing river, facing a current that froths and beats at my legs, but without the energy to move forward.* I can't think of a more perfect description of how it felt looking out through my apartment window at that pink sky [19]

But what to do about it? If I think I can simply be cured of my gloom, the guide says, I'm approaching things the wrong way. *Whether you like it or not, the Jebusites live within your borders. You can subjugate them, but you cannot exterminate them.* These 'Jebusites' were an ancient tribe that once invaded Jerusalem. Although the Judeans in the city didn't want them there, the Jebusites refused to leave, and so the Judeans' only choice was to learn to live alongside them. And this, the medieval guide is telling me, is what I need to do with my emotional coldness. I need to accept it and not let it master me. Because real human strength is not destroying the things that upset you. It's living with your scars and failures, moving with your blisters and your pains, and finding a way to turn everything – the whole hulking mess of you – in a direction that does some good.[20]

It's unusual to feel moved while wearing ill-fitting rubber gloves. Also, the chairs in this manuscript library are bizarrely tiny, like they were constructed for small children to swivel on. But none of this matters. Sitting here I can feel a hand reaching out from across the centuries; my priest, wise and discreet, leaning in for an embrace. Or maybe, in all seriousness, what I'm feeling is the exhilarating sense that I'm not alone. That people in different centuries have been in my position and found inspiration and hope in things I thought I couldn't see, in scents I thought I couldn't inhale, in surfaces I thought I couldn't touch. Reading this handbook, and sitting in this child's seat with these surgeon's gloves on, I feel I'm catching these images on my eyelashes, these fragrances in my throat, these textures through my fingertips. A strange language is speaking to me, and it's the language of the past and present crashing together as one. Living with my coldness will always be difficult. But at least I can move forward with an expanded heart. Because the surprising thing about medieval self-help is that it still punches hard.

From the Desert to the Valley

Where did this system of the Seven Deadly Sins begin? How did it enter Western culture, and how did it evolve? And what, after all, was it supposed to be?

My brief escape to Dublin had sparked something inside me. Returning to Siberia, with an idea of designing a course for my students, I found I was burning to dig into all of these questions, to get to the bottom of how this system came to exist. And the thrill of the search reminded me why I had wanted to become a historian in the first place. It involved hunting down clues and following leads, watching an idea expand and contract backwards through time. The journey was long and full of sharp turns. Over the centuries the names of some of the sins got substituted a few times. Once there were eight of them, and their original language was not Latin but Greek. And every search for their origins led me back to the Egyptian desert in the 300s CE. To a network of young radicals who lived in a cluster of isolated communities. To a man named Evagrius Ponticus, who once conducted an experiment to discover the inner negative workings of the human mind.

When Evagrius began his brain experiment he was standing naked and alone, up to his thighs in a freezing well of water. He was then coming up to forty years old, a tall man with dark hair, soulful eyes and a deep mellow voice. Evagrius had grown up in a wealthy family on the Turkish coast of the Black Sea, and his journey to this well in the desert had been complicated. Once, he'd been a young politician in Constantinople, and he'd had a dazzling reputation. Walking the streets at night, he used to mouth the speeches he hoped he'd make one day as city premier. But then he fell in love with a colleague's wife, and after the scandal broke he was forced into exile. Now in his late thirties, jobless and without a home, Evagrius started to question the point of everything he'd ever done. Hadn't his whole life been a waste of time? He'd worked so hard to get more out of the world. More recognition, more money, more power. Why had he never managed to get more out of himself?[21]

Maybe it was inevitable that Evagrius would drift down to the Egyptian desert. Because here, around two days' walk south of Alexandria, a network of bright but frustrated people had set up a community designed precisely for individuals like him.[22] These drifters were inspired by a legendary figure who had come to this same patch of desert a few generations before. That man, Anthony, had been tortured by a set of inner demons, and he had defeated those demons through a regime of isolation, prayer and meditation. Only in the desert could he have done this, Anthony said, because just as 'fishes, exposed on the dry land, die', so the mind also shrivels when it stays in ordinary society too long.[23] Inspired by Anthony's example, hundreds of men and women of Evagrius's generation – some of them in their teens, many more in middle age, and a few in their nineties – made the same journey across the sands, hoping to fight their own demons in the same way.[24]

Although they were together in their loneliness, these desert drifters were also lonely in their togetherness. They arranged themselves in a constellation of mud cells, stretched out across the landscape, and other than sharing meals on Sundays they hardly ever saw each other. Their 'cells are at such a distance', one visitor noticed, 'that nobody can be recognised by another or be seen with ease; neither can one's voice be heard'.[25] Instead, they spent all their time weaving baskets. Watching the sun rise and set across the sands, they waited and hoped that tomorrow would bring them closer to self-understanding.[26]

Basket-weaving wasn't always enough, though. Many, in time, sought out more extreme challenges to stretch their mental endurance. When Evagrius stood naked in his freezing well, it was part of a last-ditch assault against himself. Haunted, still, by the same dark thoughts that had brought him to the desert, he had devised a series of brutal physical tests to jump-start his life. At night he slept outside, until his body was overrun by ticks and lice. He never took a bath, and chanted a set of repetitive mantras from morning to night. His only food was a single loaf of bread a day, divided out across the hours, with some oil that he rationed to a single teaspoon with every slice. Slowly, he found, his skin was beginning to dry up.[27]

But Evagrius's most intense challenge was his attempt to rewire the brain itself. Elite athletes trained their bodies through punishment and pain, so shouldn't elite thinkers train their minds in the same way? With this goal, Evagrius began a wildly ambitious mental experiment. He decided to record every troubling thought that came into his head, at any hour of the day. If at night he craved to be back with his lover in Constantinople, he would write this down. If he cringed at something he had said once to a friend, he would write that down too. Evagrius vowed to document everything: all the fantasies, urges, desires and jealousies that passed through his mind. His goal was to get to the root of his own suffering, and in the process to get to the heart of negativity and fear itself.

The published result of this experiment was an enormous book, *Antirrhêtikos* (or 'Talking Back'), which has been compared to a collection of magic spells. Inside it Evagrius lists all of his tempting thoughts, from the most generic ('the thought that thinks up treachery against a brother') to the most specific ('the thought that remembers pleasant wines and the cups we used to hold in our hands'). Next to these he produces a set of answers, using a different passage from the Bible (verses he calls the 'weapons of the spirit') for each one. As a handbook, the *Antirrhêtikos* was intimate yet universal, and it remains one of the most probing accounts of human temptation ever written.[28]

And it's here, in this unusual desert memoir, that the idea that became the Seven Deadly Sins first entered into culture. Because, as he was writing, Evagrius realised that all the impulses he was recording really belonged in eight distinct categories. He called these the eight 'generic thoughts' (*genikōtatoi logismoi*), and in the order he devised them they were:

1. Gluttony (*gastrimargia*)
2. Lust (*porneia*)
3. Avarice (*philargyria*)
4. Sadness (*lype*)
5. Anger (*orge*)
6. Sloth (*akedia*)
7. Vainglory (*kenodoxia*)
8. Pride (*hyperphania*)

For the rest of his life, Evagrius pledged to deal with these negative patterns of thought, not only for himself but for anybody else who might listen. By inviting his readers to reflect on their own thoughts he wanted them to make themselves 'athletes' in a 'battle of the intellect'; urging them to find a path to mental clarity by exercising 'self-control in all things.'[29]

Maybe it reflects the emptiness of Evagrius's desert life that 'envy' wasn't one of his eight demons. He doubled up on thoughts of self-obsession, though, listing both 'pride' (delusions of one's own power) and 'vainglory' (boasting or attention-seeking). Given his intense loneliness, it's no surprise that he identified two depressive patterns of thought: 'sloth' and 'sadness'. More significant is the general label he gave to these eight weaknesses. Rather than 'deadly sins' he described them as 'generic thoughts', and this is the biggest difference with the system that developed later. Because whereas a 'deadly sin' sounds like something rare and dangerous, a 'generic thought' sounds like something commonplace. Evagrius believed that lust and anger and pride don't just creep into the minds of 'evil' people. They're undiscriminating and universal, as unstoppable as the common cold in a crèche.

Where did this idea come from? Numbered sets of psychological challenges had been a familiar trope in the deserts north-east of Egypt for at least a thousand years before Evagrius. Ancient Babylonian poets talked about seven evil spirits that haunted every mind. 'The first is the South Wind . . . The second is a dragon, whose mouth is opened . . . The third is a grim leopard, which carries off the young . . . The fourth is a terrible shibbu [a horned snake] . . . The fifth is a furious wolf, who knows not to flee. The sixth is a rampant [beast] . . . which marches against god and king . . . The seventh is a storm, an evil wind, which takes vengeance.'[30] Later, worshippers of the god Mithras gave this same motif a redemptive twist, arguing that souls travelled to seven different planets after death, to purge themselves of the seven different vices they lapsed into in their lives on earth.[31]

Closer to home for Evagrius would have been ideas from the Jewish world. The *Testament of Reuben*, a Hebrew text from the second century CE, listed eight 'corruptible' human faculties, or natural gifts that could all warp into something destructive. With their negative flip sides in brackets, these were:

1. *The Spirit of Sex and Love (Fornication)*
2. *The Spirit of Taste (Greedy Appetite)*
3. *The Spirit of Speech (Fighting)*
4. *The Spirit of Smelling (Trickery)*
5. *The Spirit of Teaching (Arrogance)*
6. *The Spirit of Sight (Lying)*
7. *The Spirit of Life (Injustice)*
8. *The Spirit of Sleep (Fantasy)*

It's an evocative list, and suggestive of some of the paths not taken by the system that developed. But as close as these are to Evagrius's eight thoughts, it's unlikely he knew this text directly.[32]

As somebody with a Greek and Latin education, Evagrius was more likely influenced by the world of classical antiquity. He would have known the Eight Olympian Gods – Zeus, Poseidon, Dionysus, Hera, Apollo, Hermes, Athena and Artemis – who each symbolised different patterns of thought, from love to wisdom and war. Equally, he may have read Virgil's classic poem the *Aeneid*, which described how the five planets represented five destructive human passions: 'Saturn's torpor, Mars' wrath, Venus' lust, Mercury's covetousness and Jove's ambition for power.'[33] Other parallels include Aristotle's *Nicomachean Ethics*, which sketched out how to fight anger and other vices, and the works of the theologian Origen, which described combatting demons in similarly vivid terms.[34] As Evagrius was obsessed with eradicating his own negative thoughts, another major influence would have been Stoicism (the ancient philosophy of resilience and acceptance). Like Seneca, after all, he wanted to cultivate 'a secure and calm mind', and like Epictetus he believed that 'people are disturbed not by things, but by the principles and notions which they form concerning things.'[35]

All the same, Evagrius's precise formula of 'eight generic thoughts' was unique. And so, in time, was his solution to them. First he completed all his challenges, defeating his lust and egotism by starving himself and standing in those wells of cold water. By all accounts, his life then had a fairy-tale ending (at least, if the goal of fairy tales is to achieve 'mindfulness'). After fifteen years in the desert, Evagrius achieved a state he called *apatheia*. Unlike the cold detachment of *acedia* (and unlike the similar English word, 'apathy'), *apatheia* was blissful, enlightened and warm. It was a way of existing in perfect harmony with himself, with all aggression and pain and frustration dissolved into a sensation of total peace. At night, the time when images of his lover in Constantinople used to come to him, he now felt at peace. When he sat weaving baskets, the time he used to remember his old political career, he felt nothing but contentment. And as he walked to get water, he no longer pined after his family's olive grove. Evagrius believed he'd reached the pinnacle of existence: a life free from anxiety and pain.[36]

With this idea, a global phenomenon was born. Shortly after Evagrius died, a wandering monk named John Cassian visited the same desert community in Egypt. He was under pressure from a bishop who wanted him to write a preaching guide for peasants in the French countryside, and Evagrius's thought experiments sounded like a perfect fit. But Cassian added an extra dimension of his own. Dropping the label 'generic thoughts', he rebranded them as the eight 'deadly sins'. He also added an extra, dramatic edge. 'Your body has been subdued and conquered,' he said in *The Institutes*, the guide he ended up writing, by 'swarms of foes' and 'hosts of enemies'. Now was the time to fight them all, not through empty gestures but by getting serious and bringing our bodies 'into subjection'.[37]

Eight sins didn't become seven until two hundred years later, with the intervention of a pope. While trying to write a type of encyclopaedia for lost souls, Pope Gregory the Great hit upon Cassian's deadly sins and thought they would be the perfect tool for mapping out the troubles of the mind. For the sake of his readers, though, Gregory decided to do some editing of his own. He removed 'Sadness' (merging it with 'Sloth'), and he rolled 'Vainglory' into 'Pride'. He also added 'Envy', a sin he described as 'hatred, whispering, and detraction'. In the process, Gregory came up with the ranking that has more or less stuck to the sins ever since:

1. Pride
2. Envy
3. Anger
4. Sloth (or Sadness)
5. Avarice
6. Gluttony
7. Lust

Gregory justified this order by aligning each sin to a different part of the body. Pride was the chief sin, he said, because it arose from the head. And lust, which was generated low down in the groin, was the least deadly.[38]

Until the 1200s, when priest-therapists began using Gregory's updated system in confession, these Deadly Sins were mainly a topic of intellectual debate, more likely to show up in works of theology than art or literature.[39] But scholarly discussions added new layers to how the system was imagined, to how it was believed to work. A treatise by the Parisian writer Hugh of Saint Victor described the sins as a chain, which dismantled the soul piece by piece.

> Through pride the heart swells; through envy it dries up; through anger it cracks; through sadness it is crushed and reduced as if to dust; through greed it is scattered; through gluttony it is infected; through lust it is trampled and reduced to mud.[40]

Around the same time a network of educated preachers began bringing the idea to a wider public, telling audiences in Europe's larger towns about the need to fight the sins for themselves. 'We are at war with an enemy' that lives inside our minds, Robert Pullen – a theologian and preacher who was one of the first to teach at the University of Oxford – said in one of his sermons. People needed to take up weapons: to destroy the three highest-ranking sins – 'Pride, Envy and Anger' – as they met them, in their most basic daily thoughts.[41]

It wasn't until after the Lateran Council of 1215 – when the energetic young Pope Innocent III launched a series of outreach schemes to counsel and console ordinary people – that the popularity of this system exploded.[42] As priests and preachers now needed to get the public to confront the inner workings of their own minds, the sins emerged as an ideal tool. Dozens of manuscripts appeared, with lines of tiny text that readers could follow, like a telephone directory, to explore the branches of each Deadly Sin through passages of scripture. In most of these directories, for some reason, avarice and gluttony had the largest entries.[43] Diagrams showed the sins as winged demons, each with their own children and grandchildren (plate 1). 'Hatred' was a son of anger, while 'Homicide' was anger's grandson. Writers also began speculating about which Deadly Sin belonged to which nation (one manuscript described 'the gluttony of the French', 'the lust of the Gascons' and 'the anger of the Britons').[44] Soon, there were so many treatises on the sins in circulation that they could be used as scrap, pasted into the boards of manuscripts to bind the endpapers together.[45]

By the mid-thirteenth century, as universities began to expand across Europe, thinkers developed a deeper philosophy of what this system was really about. Up to this point writers had tended to see the sins in a harsh and one-dimensional way. They were 'the cause and origin of all evils', the theologian Peter Damian said, and needed to be met with a zero-tolerance policy.[46] But now writers found a more forgiving angle. Each of the Deadly Sins, according to the Parisian master of theology Jean de la Rochelle, is a form of distorted love. We all desire good things, Jean said, but this desire turns into sin when we feel it too strongly. Gluttony and lust are when we love 'lesser goods' (food and sex) to excess. Avarice and anger come when we love 'exterior goods', such as material objects or winning a fight, too much. Our excessive love for two 'interior' goods – the talents that bring us success, and the joy of the success itself – is what produces pride and envy. The exception in this system, for Jean, was sloth. Instead of excess, this is the result of a love that stutters and fails. It's the product of a malfunctioning heart, which leaves a cynical weariness in its place.[47]

Then, building on this tradition, came the most popular guidebook of them all. Vast, complex and compassionate, William Peraldus's *Summa of Vices* (c.1236) gained a huge following because it was so user-friendly.[48] Alongside Bible verses it drew together sparky anecdotes and insights from classical authors like Cicero and Seneca, walking through each of the sins with humour and warmth.[49] Best of all, Peraldus offered his readers hope. Incorporated into later editions of his handbook was a companion work, the *Summa of Virtues*, which suggested the qualities needed for combatting each sin. For pride there was 'humility', for anger there was 'patience', and for sloth there was 'fortitude'. So, any priest-therapist reading through the problem of *acedia* in Peraldus's book could now flick through to the corresponding section on virtues and learn about the different ways their 'patients' could practise courage, hope, or faith, which would help them get through another dark winter of the soul.[50]

Peraldus's book was useful for priests, but its forbidding length and Latin complexity meant it wasn't digestible by ordinary readers. For the wider public, the capstone of the Deadly Sins as a forgiving system came in the early 1300s with Dante's *Commedia*. The landmark poem of the Italian language, and arguably the greatest literary work of the medieval millennium, this was a trilogy that encouraged readers to confront their sins and reconcile themselves to the darkness inside us all. In the *Inferno*, Dante's pilgrim meets sinners like Francesca (whose lust made her treat her lover like a toy) and Pietro della Vigna (whose *acedia* drove him to suicide). Next he travels to Purgatory, an enormous mountain where souls atone for the sins one by one, carrying heavy rocks on their backs for their pride and being doused in thick smoke for their anger. Dante's pilgrim is only permitted to enter Paradise once he's learned to recognise all seven of the sins within himself (and the reader, ideally, has done the same). And then, once he's made peace with each of them, the pilgrim is finally able to reach the pinnacle of the universe, to feel the 'love that moves the sun and all the other stars'.[51]

Dante's template was one of compassionate confrontation.

The souls in his Hell are united by a single common flaw: they're all unable to acknowledge their sins, and unable to own the negative impulses that move inside them. Francesca and Pietro consider themselves perfect, and blame their actions on someone or something else. By contrast, the souls on Dante's Mount Purgatory are saved because they recognise their own flaws. More than that, by confronting the Deadly Sins and working through them one by one they learn to love themselves for who they really are. And so, the only way to get out of a midlife crisis of despair, Dante said, is to confront our own inner darkness in all its horror. We must first tunnel down through Hell (which is a frozen landscape), and then up through the tortures of Mount Purgatory. We must listen to all the tragic and hopeful stories of the damned and saved until we begin to see how precious it is to embrace the life we already have.

Many great medieval literary and artistic works appeared after this, bringing this message to wider audiences across the continent. The *Canterbury Tales* (*c*.1380s), Geoffrey Chaucer's Middle English masterpiece, dramatised the sins through a set of comic and satirical stories. The psychedelic paintings of the Dutch artist Hieronymus Bosch (fl.*c*.1500) showed the seven sins in all their grotesque horror. As modernity dawned, though, this system gradually lost its shine.[52] Renaissance and Reformation combined to interrupt the original spirit that had flowed from Evagrius to Dante – the sense that the sins were inescapable human feelings, to be respected and limited rather than denied or annihilated.[53] With the 1800s, what had once been a guide to self-acceptance had morphed beyond recognition, used only as a tool for demonising people and policing behaviour. By the late twentieth century, all seven sins were reimagined as virtues. Pride was now self-esteem and envy was now appreciation. Anger was assertiveness, sloth was relaxation, avarice was enterprise, gluttony was gusto, and lust was libido.⁵⁴ And you could indulge all of them in those seven ice creams, launched by Magnum in 2003.

Only this is not quite the end of their story. In the second decade of the twenty-first century, the spirit of the desert began to be resurrected in Silicon Valley, as the Californian tech community embraced the insights that understanding the Seven Deadly Sins can bring. The resurgence began when Reid Hoffman, the founder of LinkedIn, made a speech claiming all his successes were thanks to his knowledge of this medieval system. Think of any top tech company, Hoffman said. Wasn't it true that they were only popular because they exploited at least one of the seven sins? Tinder thrives on lust, Yelp on gluttony, LinkedIn on greed, Netflix on sloth, Twitter on anger, Facebook on envy and Instagram on pride. Many people in Silicon Valley (like the investor Tim Chang) believed Hoffman was on to something, and began using the '7DS system' of commercial development to build their products with these seven impulses in mind.⁵⁵

All of this may sound like just another ice-cream-style gimmick. But Hoffman, at least, seems to have been serious. He argued that the Deadly Sins identified the 'deep universal, psychological structure' of the mind, and like John Cassian or Gregory the Great he wanted to be evangelical about it. Good tech companies shouldn't just feed the sins, he said; they should try to reform them. They should harness the urge for envy or anger and find a way to plug it into something that's better for society, better for the individual.⁵⁶ Where could this design idea lead? Would it one day produce social media algorithms that train envious eyes on compassionate content? Would it make games that force otherwise lazy people to engage with the world around them? Hoffman, as yet, wasn't clear. But as he later co-founded a company called Inflection AI, with the stated mission of developing a more compassionate digital mind, it's possible he wanted to use the Seven Deadly Sins as a guide for programming a new generation of Artificial Intelligence.

This book will explore a thousand years of expertise on depression, fear, anxiety, grief, narcissism, temptation and passion. The medieval sources will include poems and maps, treatises and chronicles, medical textbooks and saints' lives, as well as dozens of unpublished manuscripts from the libraries of Rome, London, Oxford, Cambridge, Paris and Dublin. There will be confessions of espionage, works of 'anti-pornographic' erotic literature, murder mysteries and accounts of midlife breakdown, all showing the self-help of the Middle Ages in the technicolour it deserves. Medieval readers loved rankings and listicles, countdowns and steps, so there will be plenty of these as well, from the twelve steps of pride to the five types of tears and the six signs of poisonous envy. Along the way, we'll encounter different shades of the sins through a set of images, most of which (because medieval art was rarely supposed to be taken as straight representation) are puzzles to solve.

Confronting the sins one by one, we will move through them in their classical medieval order: Pride, Envy, Anger, Sloth, Avarice, Gluttony, Lust. But as the medieval users of preaching handbooks would have advised, it's always okay to skip ahead to our own special sins when we feel the need. The exploration of each includes a close examination of an artefact or a life, or else a story of somebody who struggled with these impulses themselves and symbolised that sin in the medieval imagination. Some of these stories are inspiring and some repulsive, some comic and many tragic. All of them, though, carve a path towards the same enormous question: *What can an ancient map of human psychology tell us about the way we think and feel now?*

THE SEVEN

If this is a self-help guide, it's also a self-help journey. A story of how I escaped Siberia, not so much the physical landscape itself (which in the end wrapped itself around my heart), but the emotional Siberia I made for myself there. My journey was a typical modern-day career adventure: a quest to follow my passion that sometimes plunged me into an abyss of heartlessness and despair. But the solution I found was uniquely medieval. Over the centuries, attempts to deal with the Deadly Sins have usually come in four different varieties. Some have ignored them. Others have given in to them, or embraced them and tried to make them into strengths. But many have tried to annihilate them, which strikes me as unwise. Because if there's one thing I learned from studying the sins in the Middle Ages, it's that we need to learn to forgive ourselves. These seven are the habits that make us who we are. They're in our midst, and we have no choice but to live with them. To live with ourselves and to live with our flaws, even as we try to push our lives towards the place of greater generosity, of greater love, that we all deserve.

CHAPTER 1

Pride

It's the second week of classes, and even the students from further north in Siberia are now saying it's okay to call this 'winter'. In these conditions our university building becomes a type of submarine, a glowing tube of steel and glass rocked by squalls of ice. We have an entrance, but for practical purposes no exit. By the thick double doorway the cloakroom staff hold our coats hostage and stack our thawing boots on steel racks. At lunchtime we go to the *stolovya* on the ground floor, a traditional canteen that serves beetroot fritters and frankfurters. Next to that is a coffee counter, where two men in plaid shirts sell lattes and lavender macarons, and further down the corridor is a bookshop that specialises in works of Russian literature and graphic novels. Sometimes recently, passing the doors, I've thought about stepping out into the snow and leaving this job for good. But this morning, as I catch my reflection in the glass, I turn straight around and begin to climb the stairs up to the classrooms.

Pride, as any medieval priest-therapist would tell you, is both the first and the worst of the Seven Deadly Sins. It's 'the queen of the vices', a force that 'delivers' the brain to all other forms of corruption, hatred and hurt.[1] This may be surprising to readers now, because it contradicts everything this word has come to mean. Pride today is self-esteem, ambition, dignity and respect. People say they're proud of their children, or proud of their work, or proud of their sexuality. It's difficult to find negative views of pride in modern scientific literature, either. According to the psychologists Lisa Williams and David DeSteno, pride is simply an 'appropriate response' to achievements. In most cases it's 'a functional social emotion with important implications for leadership and the building of social capital'.[2]

Pride didn't carry much social capital in the Middle Ages, though. In fact, it was a codename for the darkest side of humanity. Emerging in tyranny, in self-absorption, or in what we would today call narcissism, pride was a cancer in the organs of the social body, an impulse that captured your heart before paralysing it.[3] As the desert monk John Cassian said, this sin is an infection that opens the door to all other forms of corruption and self-destruction. When it takes hold, it kills even the slightest 'shadow of freedom' in your soul.[4]

How was pride supposed to do this, precisely? What's the danger that all these medieval writers saw but apparently we don't?

Vocabulary is an important place to start. If I wanted to talk with a medieval confessor about my pride, the Latin word I'd be using would be *superbia*. With the same 'super' as 'supersede' or 'superman', this word implies going above or beyond something. But above or beyond what? First, according to many medieval poets and theologians, *superbia* takes us beyond *our own capacities*. It's a form of self-delusion, they said, in which we trick ourselves into believing we're special. It's when we think we're superior or unique, or in extreme cases that we have super-human powers. Connected to this, the other thing *superbia* goes beyond is *other people*. We'll know pride has got its teeth into us, as one twelfth-century handbook put it, when we feel an uncontrollable urge 'to transcend all those around' us; to outdo everyone we know in everything we do.[5]

For the *Ark of Wisdom* – the obscure, oversize fourteenth-century manuscript I visited in the Vatican Library – pride is really a failure to see other people, and a failure to see ourselves.[6] According to the *Ark*, *superbia* operates in four distinct ways. First is when we look around at our friends or colleagues and decide we're better than them. Next, convinced that we're special, we start to pick and choose the rules we want to follow. Pride's third stage is when, ignoring all feedback or criticism, we become close-minded and rigid in our principles.[7] But the most destructive operation, according to the *Ark*, is *superbia*'s fourth. This is when, with our hearts now anaesthetised against the lives of others, our self-belief slips into heartlessness and we begin to feel we can manipulate other people like toys.

And this, really, is why *superbia* was the chief Deadly Sin for nearly a thousand years. Pride, in its medieval formation, isn't just egotism. It's a way of thinking that makes you want to ignore, refute and refuse. It's when you set yourself apart from your family and friends and insulate yourself from your colleagues. It means taking all the credit, ignoring all the advice, and comforting yourself with five little words. *I. Don't. Need. Other. People.*

The reason I'm climbing this narrow stairway this morning is because I've received an email. *Could you please come up to the fourth floor? Shakhlo would like to arrange some photographs.* Shakhlo works in the university's administration, and in this building she's universally loved. Last year she announced she was leaving to take up a new job in Moscow. The students held a party, and put up a banner with the words 'We love you! Don't go!' I remember watching her step out to take a taxi to the airport, her eyes glowing and her face determined. But then a few months later she returned. At first she had loved the freedom of living in Moscow. It was even bigger and more beautiful than she could remember. But somehow she couldn't resist the call of

Siberia. She missed her family and she missed her friends, but most of all she missed this life, marooned from the world and crashing against the elements, on board our little submarine.

Why would Shakhlo need me to be in any photographs? Recently these things have been happening more often. I published my first book a few months ago and our university's publicity machine went into maximum gear. Our boss encouraged me to make a video describing my 'intellectual journey'. I was invited to give talks at art gallery receptions and cultural festivals, where my name was advertised on posters. People I had never met began coming up to me in the streets of Tyumen, telling me they'd seen me speak, or watched videos of my lectures. My classes filled with students, and I was told I was now the university's model professor. 'Look at him,' our director said in one faculty meeting. 'Try to be more like that.'

But really I want to be more like Shakhlo. Arriving on the fourth floor I see her smiling behind a camera and tripod, comfortable in her own skin. 'We're doing a photoshoot for our website,' she says. They want to publicise my class (which is a lecture series on the Seven Deadly Sins), and they've decided the best way to do it is with my face. 'Couldn't we use artworks instead?' But Shakhlo laughs nervously. 'I think it needs to be photos.' There's a pause. 'We thought you could pose like you're doing each of the sins. So maybe an angry face for "Anger"?' Behind her I can see a plate of cakes, prepared for me to put in my mouth for 'Gluttony'. And I begin to feel sick. What is she going to ask me to do for 'Lust'?

Lust, it turns out, isn't the most difficult pose. Actually, the hardest is 'Pride'. In front of the camera I lift up my chin and try to look superior. But reviewing the photo with Shakhlo afterwards, we decide it just looks like my normal face. And because I'm wearing the same clothes, it's more or less identical to the faculty profile picture of me already on the website. Is this because pride, as a sin, is invisible? Or is it because this is now the only face I can do? We need to get this photo right, because 'Pride' will be the first lecture and they want to post links and videos straight away. We take twenty, thirty more shots. But looking at them, I can't see anything but a bland face. A smug professor who's delighted to be getting so much of the camera's attention.

Lucifer's Shoes

So, what does *superbia* really look like? How should I have posed to embody medieval pride at its worst? What are the ancient giveaways of a dangerous ego in the wild?

Years ago, when I was working in a second-hand bookshop in Bristol, I came across the face I needed. A professor at a local

The Garden *Lucifer, dazzling and very much in command.*

college had died and his widow wanted us to buy his book collection. While packing up the crates, I noticed a grey volume at the top of the first pile. *Hortus Deliciarum*, it was called. *The Garden of Delights*. Turning my back slightly, I opened it up, and what I saw caught me by surprise. It was a technicolour angel with enormous wings. It was Lucifer himself.

I didn't know it at the time, but what I was looking at was one of the rarest images in medieval art. Only a few pictures of Lucifer in this situation are known to exist, and none of them can be found in the world's art galleries. Instead, they're all hidden away in manuscript archives. Maybe medieval artists found it too uncomfortable to show? *The team before the betrayal. The high-school photo before the tragedy.* It's a picture of Lucifer when he was still a seraph, one of the six-winged angels who occupied the highest point of heaven. Lucifer, before he turned away from God and persuaded a group of rebel angels to worship him instead.

This Lucifer is one of the great lost treasures of Western art. Illustrated in the late 1100s by Abbess Herrad of Landsberg, it was part of the first encyclopaedia made by and for women in history.[8] The only way to see it now is in a modern copy, as the original manuscript was destroyed in 1870 during the Franco-Prussian War. Still, even in the stark colours of the Victorian facsimile I saw in that copy of *The Garden of Delights*, this Lucifer shimmers. Shrugging with a sceptre in one hand and an orb in the other, he's the unapologetic master of all he sees. Everything in the image – from the golden halo to the robe studded with precious gemstones – asserts his superiority. He's imperious, a self-appointed leader seizing command of everyone and everything around him.

As *superbia* so often is, the *Garden* Lucifer is both magnetic and beautiful. According to the art historian Danielle Joyner, this was a deliberate strategy of the artist. Herrad made Lucifer more gorgeous than the other angels, she says, because she wanted to work a type of counter-magic on the nuns who would look at this page. *Beware men who try to dazzle you*, she was warning them. *Beneath their curls and their charms they're all the same.*⁹ Whatever Herrad was trying to do, the point is that she made Lucifer's beauty a superficial illusion. His tiny upgrades – the playful kink of his hairstyle, the sequined robes – show his desperation to set himself apart. Take these away, and wouldn't he be more or less identical to all the other angels around him?

Years after my initial encounter with that little grey book I tracked down three more of these rare pre-fall Lucifers. Each

The Munich Lucifer (left), standing beside God and Saint Michael. Look at their feet . . .

of them was just as surprising; it's always unusual to see Satan, smiling and powerful, without any horns. Although they share so many characteristics, each of these Lucifers also possesses its own distinct characteristic of *superbia*. Together, they reveal the three giveaways for identifying an ego that's taken itself to a dangerous place.

Finding pride in the second Lucifer, who appears in a manuscript from Munich, is like playing a game of spot-the-difference. You have to look for the features that separate the nearly-fallen angel from his counterpart, Saint Michael, on the right. Some of these differences are obvious. First, this Lucifer is more dazzling, his jewelled robe far more impressive than the clothes worn either by Michael or the enthroned God. Just as clear is the contrast in the objects they're holding. While God has a book and Michael has a spear, Lucifer has an orb and a sceptre. The way he's drawn, carrying these two symbols of kingship, it's almost as if he's the real lord of the universe, a conclusion he seems to have reached for himself. In contrast to Michael, with his gentle bow of the head, Lucifer's face is upright, his smudged eyes staring ahead in self-satisfaction.[10]

Beyond these obvious signs, there's another component of *superbia* in this picture. Another clue to Lucifer's pride, which the artist has hidden in plain sight. With this one, the devil really is in the detail. Some might get it immediately, although it's also possible to stare at this image for ages without seeing it. The answer is to look at the feet. While the toes of both God and Michael are exposed, Lucifer's aren't. He's wearing a pair of shoes.

If we want to identify pride, in ourselves or in others, this is the first of its calling cards. *Superbia* is somebody who, like this Munich Lucifer, sees the dress code but decides it shouldn't apply to him. It's the person who walks into a room and insists on announcing his superiority in every thread of fabric, every flashing buckle, every colourful sash. Clothes, though, are just the tip of the problem. By flouting the no-shoe rule the Munich Lucifer shows that he is also the colleague who doesn't check his emails, the one who ignores the small print or takes a pass on the latest company agreement. Whereas others concern themselves with solving collective problems – in the picture, Saint Michael has even crushed a demon beneath his feet – Lucifer's priority is his own comfort. And this is one of the ways pride was understood in medieval literature and art. It was stepping out, stepping on and stepping away. It was making sure that you do things, always, your own special way.

For the people who first owned this manuscript, all of this would have been instantly clear. Lucifer was a star of so many medieval stories, and his fall was a lesson for everyone, everywhere. According to medieval legends, Lucifer was originally supreme among all the angels: the fastest flyer, the most sublime singer and the possessor of the most incredible beauty.[11] He flew around wearing a set of robes, just like those of the Munich Lucifer, covered in shimmering topaz, diamonds, onyx, jasper, sapphire, emeralds and gold.[12]

But then something stirred in his mind. He looked at the perfection of God and decided he didn't want to join it. Instead, he wanted to be better than it. Hypnotised by his own dazzling light, he stirred up a rebellion and persuaded a group of angels to worship him instead of God. But this was a mistake. 'The whole kingdom was terrified,' as the thirteenth-century mystic Mechthild of Magdeburg imagined it, 'and the pillars of heaven shook.'[13] God threw Lucifer and the other rebels to the ground so violently that their bodies shattered straight through the earth's crust. Dante, the great Italian poet, claimed they gouged a crater so deep that it made a cavern in the earth, a hollow that formed the enormous funnel-shaped Kingdom of Hell. And somewhere

PRIDE

The Bamberg Lucifer. Note the smug smile, the wagging finger and the generous leg-spreading.

at the bottom of that crater Lucifer is still reeling, stuck in a pool of ice at the earth's core.[14]

Where the *Garden* Lucifer is seductive and groomed, and the Munich Lucifer is defiant and individualistic, the third pre-fall Lucifer is just plain obnoxious. Preserved in a prayer book made in thirteenth-century Bamberg, in Northern Bavaria, this one turns the *superbia* up to the point of suffocation. Because, alongside a studded crown and a flowing cloak, the artist has given this Lucifer another of pride's telltale signs, and one that can often be its most unbearable symptom. *A smug smile.*

Why is smugness so irritating? Everybody will have their own answer to this, but one is that it accepts no vulnerability and receives no criticism. Analysing Lucifer's sins, the theologian

Peter of Poitiers hit on this trait precisely. Lucifer knew he wasn't God's 'equal', Peter said. Yet, unable to tolerate feeling inferior, he found a conclusion that suited him. Lucifer decided that although he wasn't as powerful as God he had an 'equality of knowledge' with him. This assumption allowed him to justify everything else he did,[15] including ignoring the talents of others and blocking out alternative points of view. Sealing himself in the nutshell of his narrow mind, he was free to imagine that he was the king of infinite space.

How to spot this trait in others? With this Bamberg Lucifer, the smugness overflows in a combination of micromanagement, leg-spreading and condescension. Looking both sumptuous and dangerous, with a pair of green swords at his belt, he's turning towards God to offer him a word of advice. But although his lips are pursed and his finger is wagging, it's impossible to read what he's trying to say. Whatever words once looped across the scroll at his chest have all worn away. Maybe the original owner of

The Holkham Lucifer (centre top), with co-conspirators on the right and scandalised angels on the left.

this prayer book got tired of seeing them and decided to smudge them out? Or maybe what he said was never that important, it was that he was saying it at all. Because, in contrast to Lucifer's flurry of words, God's scroll beside him is totally silent. Which is fitting, as this is one of the main symptoms of smugness, and of pride more generally. It doesn't listen. It only talks.

So far we have seen two of *superbia*'s telltale signs – *ignoring the dress code*, and *smugness* – which are both easy enough to spot in isolation. But the third and final sign often appears only in busy social situations. We can usually spot it best in the reactions of other people, in the ripple of bad feeling that a sufferer of extreme pride often leaves in their wake.

There's no clearer case of this than the Holkham Lucifer, and the splinter party he's hosting at the top of a manuscript page. On a folio from a fourteenth-century Bible, just above a picture of the architect God holding a compass, is a semicircle of angels. Right at their centre is Lucifer, sitting on a throne and pointing at his own heart. It seems he's causing a stir among the team of angels of which he's supposed to be a part. While those to his right are talking nervously behind their hands, the ones on his left are all transfixed in worship, with one of them holding up a crown. As soon as that crown touches Lucifer's head, we know, God is going to put down his enormous compass and strike the rebel to Hell. But in this instant we're allowed to see Lucifer's nanosecond of triumph, and the infighting that enabled it.

Anybody who's ever been part of a disruptive work environment will recognise this scene straight away. The pride of the Holkham Lucifer, really, is the pride of the colleague (or boss) who destroys any team they join. This is the kind of *superbia*, as the twelfth-century philosopher Hugh of Saint Victor put it, that manifests in refusing either to cooperate or to depend on anyone else. Pride is the 'small stream' that 'separates itself from its source', Hugh wrote, the 'ray' that 'turns itself away from the sun'.[16] It's the team member who ignores the project's objective because he has ideas of his own, the brother who drives a wedge between family members. It's the cold-blooded employee who gets a thrill out of manipulating everyone else in the office.

In medieval folklore, the devil's *superbia* never kept him happy for long. Although these four pre-fall Lucifers are all so full of confidence – dwelling in the 'delights of paradise', as the caption above the *Garden* Lucifer puts it – really, they're all on borrowed time. These are just the flickering moments before that confidence will plunge the angel into disaster. And yet in each of these snapshots Lucifer's fall from grace is not inevitable.[17] He still has all that beauty and drive, all that intellectual brilliance, to share. Like the faces in childhood photos, he has a self-belief that hasn't been punctured by self-consciousness, a joy in success that hasn't been swallowed by ambition. Suspended in this moment, the pendulum of his pride could still have swung either way.

The way it ended up swinging, though, appears on a later page in *The Garden of Delights* (plate 2). In this Manga-style illustration Lucifer sits in the bottom right-hand corner of Hell, now too hot to wear his full sequined robe. His skin has turned blue and his head has sprouted horns, but he's still enthroned, presiding in majesty. Nestled alongside a tableau of flames and tortures, this smirking Lucifer has been exposed for the monster his choices have made him. As an angel, his problem was that he'd been obsessed with beautiful images and not with beautiful principles. He'd wanted to be 'glorious', to be commanding and impressive, but in the process he'd made the mistake of believing glory flows from power alone.[18]

The fall of Lucifer may seem extreme. But at the heart of this story is a single basic idea about pride, one that's as true for us now as it was for the people who painted these Satans seven hundred years ago. *Superbia* emerges, most of all, when we turn our backs on other people. As Abbess Hildegard of Bingen put it, Lucifer's problem wasn't that he couldn't see what was good in the universe. It was that he saw it but decided to walk away from it.[19] And these four Lucifers show four different ways we can turn our backs:

1. We can be the *Garden* Lucifer, pampering ourselves and fussing over the tiny differences that we hope can make us different from, and better than, other people.
2. We can be the Munich Lucifer, wearing shoes while others are in their bare feet, abandoning the codes others abide by and caring only for our comfort.
3. We can be the Bamberg Lucifer, patronising, condescending and smothering the oxygen out of a conversation.
4. Or, we can be the Holkham Lucifer, cutting ourselves off from our team, our family or our friends, and sowing discord in every room we walk into.

Can any of us ever be immune to the devil's *superbia*? When we're trapped in a situation we find frustrating – like a silly photo shoot, or a difficult day in a Siberian classroom – it can be tempting to walk away, to feel we're somehow 'above' it all. Does this make us a Lucifer, in some way? If it does, a forgiving medieval priest-therapist would be able to tell us that this isn't necessarily a problem. A dose of medieval pride can be normal, healthy even. If we have something that's worth sharing, like a good idea or maybe a decent lecture series on the Deadly Sins, then it would be 'weak spirited' not to advertise it.

The key, though, is that we recognise what we *do* have, but also what we *don't*. *Superbia* isn't just an appetite for excellence, as one thirteenth-century theologian said, it's an 'appetite for excellence *in excess of right reason*'.[20] Pride emerges in the gap between what we are and what we think we are. When our self-belief matches the talents we possess, there's no reason we shouldn't be proud of ourselves. The real trouble begins when we stretch or overestimate what we can do, and the specialness we think is ours alone. It begins, in other words, when we forget how to use a mirror properly.

The Two Ways of Looking in a Mirror

According to one medieval theory, the Seven Deadly Sins are all symptoms of love. A love that's run wild. Gluttony is an uncontrolled desire for food or drink, and anger is a passion for justice that's curdled into violence. If this theory is correct then what's the love that produces pride? With Lucifer in the rearview mirror, it may seem we've already answered this question. Isn't pride an overwhelming love of self? But this diagnosis is a little too simple. Pride doesn't necessarily arise when we love ourselves too much. In fact, it can be at its strongest when we love ourselves *too little*.

Stumbling across a rare Lucifer in the pages of a second-hand book was a lucky find. Even with modern search tools, it's often impossible to find the best medieval sources. Back when I was a graduate student at New York University, if you wanted to exit the library after hours you had to go through a separate security check, showing your books so the guard could see they were all stamped properly. One night I handed over two leatherbound volumes to a man with a clicking radio and a name badge that said 'G. Downs'. As he looked at them he laughed out loud. 'The *Rolls Series*, yes indeed. You'll have fun with those!' I smiled, but this was strange. Because the words 'Rolls Series' aren't written anywhere on those books. Their official title is *The Chronicles and Memorials of Great Britain and Ireland*, which is what's marked on their spines. The *Rolls Series* is their secret name, the name known to medievalists alone. So how did officer 'G. Downs' know that?

Gerry, it turned out, had once been in my shoes. Decades before me, he'd studied as a graduate student in medieval history here at the same university. Obsessed with twelfth- and thirteenth-century popes, he'd known the contents of every papal declaration, the name of every cardinal, the design of every Roman chapel. He'd started to write a PhD thesis under the supervision of one of the legends of the field, but other things got in the way. Gerry was never able to finish his degree, but he didn't lose his passion for the Middle Ages. During my time in Manhattan he acted as my informal adviser, and every time I left the library late we'd discuss the books I was taking. Then he'd give me recommendations, telling me about obscure Latin treatises and forgotten legal records, and where to find them up in the stacks.

It was during one of these counselling sessions that I first came to look at the Fournier Register, and the private confessions of the shepherds who lived and died in southern France. Gerry had been telling me about these texts for months, calling them a 'goldmine' of cultural history. Then one evening, scribbling a call number on a sheet of scrap paper, he told me to turn back around and climb the stairs to find three volumes on the fourth floor. For the next few hours, as night edged towards day, I sat with these books in the library's overnight study centre, trying to reconstruct a tragic story of two fourteenth-century lives. Part romance and part spy thriller, it was a story of two men and the flawed self-love that led one of them to be burned at the stake. A story of *superbia*, and the two ways we can look in the mirror.

Pierre Maury looked after sheep in the green mountains between Andorra and Carcassonne, and before he was arrested in the early 1320s he had enjoyed a nomadic life.[21] Every night he dined with whichever friends he met along the road, he drank the local wine and slept under the stars. Behind his good spirits, though, Pierre was always a little tense. He kept alert to the news that came south along the roads from Paris, as he knew that one day the authorities would come to get people like him. Because as well as being a shepherd, Pierre was a member of a sect. A group of believers that called themselves the 'good people'.

Being one of the 'good people' in fourteenth-century France meant rejecting a major portion of mainstream culture. At a practical level, you had to become a vegetarian and totally abstain from sex. You also had to believe in reincarnation, and claim the existence of two deities: a 'God of Evil', who created all the things we can see and touch, and a 'God of Goodness', who created the spirit and all the things we cannot see.[22] While historians can't be sure how organised the 'good people' were – and one has even claimed they never existed – it's clear that, from the early 1200s on, the Catholic Church treated them as an existential threat.[23] In 1235, Pope Gregory IX sent bands of friars from town to town to catch anyone suspected of being a member of the sect. As well as asking questions, these inquisitors were licensed to use force, so long as they neither 'killed' nor 'broke the arms or legs' of anyone.[24] After interrogation, around 5–10 per cent of those convicted would be executed.[25]

Pierre's best friend was a younger man called Guillaume Bélibaste. Although he lived a similar nomadic life and adopted identical views, Bélibaste had a far darker streak. After killing a man in a fight, he had been exiled from his parents' wealthy farming community and was forced to make his own living.²⁶ Then, while he was working as a shepherd, he came to the town of San Mateo in the Pyrenees, and the house of an entrepreneur named Guillelma. With her large property in the heart of the wine slopes, Guillelma was the lynchpin of a community of drifting radicals. She ran a commune of 'good people', who all gathered to debate the meaning of existence in the daytime and drink wine throughout the night.²⁷ Bélibaste was thrilled to join, and signed himself up as a member.

Superbia, though, rarely accepts the rules as they are given. Rather than simply following this commune's ideas, Bélibaste wanted to become a master of them. He underwent a ritual known as the *consolamentum*, bending down on his knees and renouncing the 'false' ideas of the mainstream church, before receiving blessings and kisses from others who'd followed the same path.²⁸ From that moment on he demanded to be treated as a 'perfected spirit': someone who had purified himself of pride and all the other Deadly Sins.²⁹ He set himself up as the commune's spiritual leader, giving lectures, instructing people on the horrors of eating meat, and leading tirades against the corruption of the organised church.³⁰

It was desperation, ultimately, that brought Pierre and Bélibaste together. One day in 1308 the news networks finally brought the message Pierre had always feared. A team of inquisitors was sweeping through the mountain villages of southern France, looking for heretics just like him. When they caught him, his friends joked, they would rip off his fingernails, one by one. Wasting no time, Pierre fled over the hills into Catalonia, and then San Mateo.³¹ And although he liked this new community, most of all he loved the new friend Bélibaste he met there. 'I love Guillaume more than any of my brothers,' he said. 'Whatever we possess we pool, half and half.' It seemed to Pierre like an unbreakable bond, and even if Bélibaste asked him to hand over his only personal luxury – his pair of Spanish leather boots – he would have obeyed. Yet the other man exploited Pierre with a chilling ruthlessness. Bélibaste refused to pay back money he had lent him, denying it had ever been a loan at all. 'You didn't lend it to me,' he said, 'you paid it to me out of the love of God.' Another time, when they made a deal to buy six sheep together, Bélibaste forced Pierre to pay on his behalf, and then took the sheep for himself without acknowledging the debt.[32]

These weren't Bélibaste's worst deceptions, though. By a long distance, that title goes to the marriage plot he cooked up over the course of a drunken week. Bélibaste knew that Pierre never wanted to settle down with anybody. Still, he began urging him to consider marrying a young woman named Raymonde Piquier. It's true that Raymonde had slept in Bélibaste's own bed many times, but this was no reason to worry. Their sleeping ritual was just a 'cover', he said. It was a trick to divert the wider community from unmasking Bélibaste as a sex-denying heretic. Pierre refused, but Bélibaste kept pestering him. So, after another night of drinks, he gave in. 'Since you're so anxious, I'll do as you wish.' Bizarrely, though, after just three days of marriage Bélibaste intervened again, forcing Pierre and Raymonde to annul their relationship. Then, when Raymonde gave birth a few months later, Bélibaste was the first to tell everyone that the baby must be Pierre's.

Was this *superbia* in the raw? Was it 'cover' for a manipulative trick, a way for Bélibaste to hide a pregnancy that would have destroyed his reputation as a 'perfected spirit'? As I found in those volumes recommended by Gerry, many people around the two men guessed that it was. One witness testified that she came upon Bélibaste and Raymonde in bed together one afternoon, in the months before the birth. She saw Bélibaste raised over Raymonde, she said, 'with his knees bent' in what she could only see as a sexual act. 'You wicked woman!' Bélibaste shouted back. 'You've disturbed the work of the Holy Church!'[33]

It's easy, thinking back to pre-fall Lucifer, to see all of the telltale signs of pride in Bélibaste's character. Preaching against the evils of sex while sleeping with his girlfriend Raymonde, he was clearly somebody who felt the dress codes didn't apply to him. His desperate need to be different practically oozes from the page. Thriving on conspiracy and intrigue, he seems to have revelled in being the biggest fish in a small pond. And it doesn't take much to imagine Bélibaste, on that night of the marriage plot, patronising his friend Pierre with a smug smile.

Even so, there was another mental ingredient that set Bélibaste apart. *His tendency to hide from himself.* Or rather, his deficiency in self-love. Pierre, for all his flaws, knew precisely who he was. He was a shepherd following his beliefs, and no amount of coercion could make him change. Bélibaste, on the other hand, constructed an identity that was false to the core. He split himself in two, calling himself a 'perfected spirit' even while cheating his friends. But in this way, his self-love could only ever be flawed and hollow, his self-knowledge remote and narrow. Obsessed with the persona of the all-powerful Bélibaste that he'd created, he neglected to love the real Guillaume, the runaway farmer and confused shepherd that he'd always been underneath.

To be a narcissist in the Middle Ages was not the same thing as it is today. Modern clinical psychologists tell us that narcissism comes in two main varieties: *grandiose* (an exploitative arrogance, built on high self-esteem); and *vulnerable* (a paranoid manipulation of others, built on low self-esteem). Binding these two types together is a single core trait: *antagonism*. A modern narcissist will always see you as an enemy to be beaten, a rival to be surpassed, or a threat to be extinguished. Because, like the ancient mythical figure who gave his name to the condition, modern narcissists are self-obsessed. They stare at their own reflections and – believing what they see is superior, or obsessing over making it so – disregard everyone and everything else.[34]

This is not how writers in the Middle Ages saw narcissism. Instead of antagonism or vanity, the fatal flaw of the medieval Narcissus was actually his lack of self-recognition. In John Gower's *Confessio Amantis* (a poem written in the late 1300s), when Narcissus looked into the water his mistake wasn't that he fell in love with himself. It was that he mistook his own reflection for the face of somebody else. His failure, despite basking for hours in his own image, was that he couldn't actually recognise himself at all.[35] And if the medieval conception of pride has a single essence, then this is it. It's *failing to see yourself for who you really are.*

Bélibaste's downfall came when his cell was infiltrated by an outsider. In 1320, a local shoemaker named Arnaud Sicre joined their little community at San Mateo. His arrival in the doorway was initially met with suspicion, and Guillelma tested him. 'Would you like to be shown an understanding of *the good*?' she asked, using a well-known code for the beliefs of the 'good people'.[36] Arnaud recoiled. 'I wouldn't,' he said. 'My father's house has suffered a great deal because of the heretics.' Returning two weeks later, though, Arnaud dropped his caginess and explained away his initial reluctance as a ruse. He'd only been testing whether he could trust their little cell, he said, and these enquiries had proved that he could. So he revealed to Guillelma that he already had an 'understanding of the good'; that he'd always been a true member of their sect. And she let him in, and told him he could stay for as long as he needed.[37]

At first Bélibaste and Pierre were delighted to make a new

friend. They sat up late into the night sharing stories, drinking the wine that had been made in the fields near Guillelma's house. Bélibaste did his wacky impersonations of local priests, and the newcomer Arnaud was a good sport, laughing along. But not everyone in the community was convinced. The first time he'd entered the house in San Mateo and met them all, Arnaud hadn't remembered to make the usual greeting the 'good people' made to each other, which was worrisome.[38] So Pierre – who was less self-absorbed than Bélibaste, and more alert to the comings and goings in San Mateo – decided to test Arnaud's faith.

The plan was devious. Stopping at a riverside tavern one night, Pierre mixed two strong wines together in secret, and urged the newcomer to drink as much as he could. When Arnaud fell under the table drunk, Pierre carried him off to the bed upstairs. Just as Arnaud was dozing off, Pierre set a trap for him. That man Bélibaste is a 'heretic', and 'speaks nothing but evil', he said. So, how about handing him over to the authorities and getting 'fifty or a hundred Turonian pounds for him'? Arnaud was shocked. 'Oh, Pierre,' he said, 'I can't believe you're the sort of person who'd want to sell him. No, I won't do it . . .' They all drifted off to sleep, but in the morning the test continued. 'What was it we were speaking about last night?' Pierre asked Arnaud. 'And who put you to bed?' Again, Arnaud was steadfast. 'I can't remember. I put myself to bed, didn't I?'[39] So Pierre and Bélibaste stopped harassing him, certain he was genuine.

Sadly for them, they had it all wrong. Arnaud really was a spy, and at that moment he was being paid by Bishop Jacques Fournier (the overseer of the inquisition) to infiltrate their cell. Arnaud's own motivations were complex. His mother had been a heretic, who when Arnaud was still young had been caught and burned at the stake, and the family property had been confiscated by the inquisitors. By bringing down heretics like Bélibaste, Arnaud was hoping not only to clear his family's reputation, but to win back his family home as a reward. Concocting the plan himself, Arnaud had gone to see Bishop Fournier and volunteered to perform this undercover operation. He would need to play a role, he said, 'pretending to be a believer' before luring Bélibaste and his followers to their arrest.

So this, in the summer of 1321, was precisely what happened.[40] Secure after passing Pierre's mixed-wine test (all along he'd avoided getting drunk, only pretending to stumble and pass out), Arnaud tricked the group into taking a mission over the border to Carcassonne, where they were met by an ambush. For Pierre there would be no more pastures and no more sheep, no more sleeping outside beneath the moon. After an interrogation he was condemned to a prison cell for the rest of his life. But for Bélibaste, the spy's original target, things were much worse. His fate, following trial, was to be burned at the stake, just like Arnaud's mother had been all those years ago.

If Bélibaste had taken the chance to look into a mirror in the days before his execution, what would he have seen? What does any acute sufferer of *superbia* ever see? According to the poem *Li dis dou miroir*, written by Jean de Condé in the early 1300s, there are actually two ways we can look at our reflections. One of them can help build self-understanding and growth, but the other can lead to self-loathing and moral decay. When people like Bélibaste peer into the mirror they see a reflection that is both 'dark and scattered'. Sometimes they only see their faults, and at other times they only see their own good looks. But eventually they become so confused with all this 'honour' and 'shame' that the two become almost indistinguishable. What they miss in this oscillation – what these sufferers of pride always miss – is the face that's really there.

PRIDE

By contrast, people like Pierre Maury, 'gentle hearts', look in the mirror for both positive attributes *and* faults. In fact, they hoover up every tiny detail. Instead of only seeing 'honour' or 'shame', they see a set of behaviours to repeat and a set of behaviours to work on. They see themselves as works in progress. By looking this way, these people come to understand that the best way to move forward is to balance self-criticism with forgiveness. 'These mirrors give you the example,' as the poem put it, 'to see what it is that your heart indulges, and in which manner and which form they can help you to change your life.'[41]

Guarding against medieval pride, counterintuitively, doesn't mean we need to look at ourselves *less*. Rather, we have to look at ourselves even more. Ideally, as the poem says, we should keep a mirror with us 'night and day', so the lessons we learn about ourselves 'stay in the heart' for ever. The important thing, though, is to pay attention. While Bélibaste shied away from the truth behind his own flattering image, we have to stare until we begin to see the skeleton beneath the skin. Looking at ourselves in photographs – like my own pose for 'Pride', which Shakhlo has now uploaded to our college's website – we have to look not only with criticism and delight, but also with compassion and honesty. We have to strain until we see ourselves as the chalky, shivering things we are. Then, seeing that fragile face, we have to find a way to love it.

And this, it turns out, is how medieval *superbia* can transform into self-aware modern pride. It's not enough to be humble, or to avoid being self-conscious. Although valuable, these can lead to what Thomas Aquinas called 'pusillanimity': a failure to stand up for ourselves, a failure to use the talents we possess for good. Instead, the flip side of pride is to work with the grain of our self-obsession, tempering it with some honest self-awareness. And this means seeing our limitations for what they are. It means accepting that we can't always find our way in the world without a friend, a librarian, or a mentor. That we can't always do our research without the help of a watchful security guard, someone devoted enough to let us back into a locked library after hours with a call number scribbled on a scrap of paper.

How to Fly without Falling

So, how do we become properly self-aware? Not many of us will set ourselves up as an all-powerful Lucifer or a 'perfect' Bélibaste. But most of us, from time to time, can be tempted to overestimate our capacities. And the secret to preventing these slips from becoming toxic pride, as medieval theologians knew, is to make sure we catch ourselves in the moment before we start to fall.

In theory, if somebody ambushed me with a manuscript, here in our submarine-like university building, I should be able to tell them when and where it was produced just by looking at the shape of the letters and the layout of the text on the page. Fourteenth-century handwriting is usually frantic and looped, with English writers elongating their 'A's and French ones making stabbing triangular 'S's. It's easy to tell if something was written after 1220, because then (for reasons unknown) writers began leaving an empty line at the top of the page. And thirteenth-century Latin handwriting is always thorny and densely packed, coded like an early-2000s text message.

Learning these clues took a lot of work, and sometimes I tried to run before I could walk. The first manuscript I touched was in Hereford, a set of sermons from the late 1100s that had never been edited before. This meant there were no printed copies, and so the only way to read it was by sitting there, at that table, in Hereford's archive. I was thrilled, knowing that if I found anything useful I could count it as my own personal discovery. But in reality I struggled to read anything. Smothering every line were thick abbreviations, sets of dots and slashes with their own secret rules I didn't yet know: *A line over a set of letters means either an 'n' or an 'm' is missing. If there's a hook at the end of a word, then an 'us' or an 'ur' should be there. A curving sign over the letter 'l' means a vowel must have been skipped. 'P' can mean 'per' if there's a cross through the descender, or 'pro' if there's a downward loop in the tail, or 'prae' if there's a triangular wedge cutting backwards from the top.* How to read anything without knowing this? On that afternoon, as I sat alone with those coded sermons, I was no different to 90 per cent of the twelfth-century population.[42] I was illiterate.

Self-awareness, the true remedy for pride, can only begin when we recognise our deficiencies. Often this awareness will come in the moments when we're stretching ourselves too far, faking or bluffing our way through a situation. Which, really, is the third distinctive thread in *superbia*'s web. Whereas the pride of Lucifer is the pride of turning our backs, and the pride of Bélibaste is the pride of not recognising ourselves, this is the pride of the deliberate liar or fraud. It's the CEO who claims their invention is going to revolutionise industry, without letting anyone see their plans. Or it's the fundraisers for an incredible island festival that, although it exists in a shiny brochure, could never be organised in real life.

On one or two polished flagstones at the foot of the Capitoline Hill in Rome, according to one medieval writer, there are still a few spatters of ancient blood. These are the last traces of one of the greatest frauds in the city's history, somebody who learned the cold facts of his own limitations in the hardest way of all.[43] Simon Magus (according to the medieval version of his story, told by Jacobus of Voragine) was a magician and performer who arrived in Rome around the same time as Saint Peter (between 57 and 64 CE). Jealous of the apostle, Simon set himself up as a rival and boasted about his own superhuman powers. 'I can fly through the air,' he said, and 'make new trees, change stones into bread, stand in fire without injury. I can do anything I choose to do!'

Really, though, Simon was a fraud, and all of his miracles were flimsy magic tricks. Jacobus revealed that Simon used a system of ropes to pretend he could levitate, and that he performed his 'resurrections' by poking at dead bodies with sticks and claiming they had moved by themselves. His biggest trick involved staging his own death. 'Cut off my head,' he challenged the Emperor Nero, 'and I will rise from the dead'. How he managed this isn't clear, although Jacobus suggests Simon persuaded an executioner to behead a sheep in his place and sprinkle its blood on the ground. After three days in hiding he astonished Nero by appearing again. 'Have my blood, which I shed, wiped up, because, though I was beheaded, here I am, risen on the third day as I promised!' So Nero put up a statue in one of the city's squares. On it were the words 'To Simon, The Holy God'.[44]

Just like Lucifer or Bélibaste, or any of the biggest modern practitioners of narcissistic *superbia*, Simon developed his own personality cult. Building on his success with Nero he wrote a set of empowering self-help books, drawing readers in with some incredible claims. One of these, titled *The Great Announcement*, promised to unlock its readers' dazzling inner fire with a combination of mantras and prayer. Within each of us, Simon said, is a 'Boundless Power': a deep well of godlike intelligence and physical force. Because most of us are too timid to use it, this power has 'lapsed into darkness'. But if we can tap into its potential – if we can release the glorious power within our own minds – we'll harness this force to achieve miraculous feats. We'll transform ourselves, 'in essence', into 'greatness and completeness' itself.[45]

When I've not been hiding in manuscript archives, I've met my fair share of Simons in my life. I've read enough magazine articles about frauds and tricksters, listened to enough podcasts about gurus who pretend they have the power to touch the stars. And while some of these may have been outright con artists, my diagnosis now is that most of them suffered from a Lucifer complex, or a Bélibaste syndrome. That their real problem was their failure to recognise their own frail human condition, and to accept the limitations that came along with it. Still, one problem of *superbia* remains unanswered. Were these people born that way? Or could any of us go from being an ordinary social being to a narcissistic Simon Magus?

Luckily, one medieval writer thought to make a guidebook to prevent precisely this problem, an intricate database of pride and all its symptoms. This was *The Steps of Humility and Pride*, a twelfth-century text by Bernard of Clairvaux that invited readers to identify the signs of pride in themselves. And we can still use it today, to catch ourselves when we worry that we're falling deeper into *superbia*.

Superbia, according to the guide, has twelve descending stages.[46] And the first three could apply to all of us. Pride's first flicker comes with number one, *Curiosity*. This is when we look at things around us in a mildly dissatisfied way, wondering how they might be better and how, by extension, we might be better. Hovering somewhere between boredom and frustration, this curiosity may seem innocent. But really, it's a wandering restlessness, opening up the first cracks of self-hatred in our minds. Next up is number two, *Imbalance*, when we become hyperconscious of our own qualities, delighting in the things we think are excellent, and regretting all the things we feel are shortcomings. Tired with these mood swings, the tempting next step is number three, *Silliness*, which is where we stop taking things seriously and try to cheer ourselves up by making fun of other people's tiny mistakes.

It doesn't take a Lucifer or a Bélibaste to slip down these three steps. They're as universal and compulsive as scrolling down a smartphone screen. But still, according to the guidebook, these are the shallow waters where every deep ego first learns to swim.

For the next six steps we take a more serious dive down into self-obsession. At this point pride begins to announce itself in a set of bold, sometimes insufferable ways. Number four, *Boastfulness*, is when we try to impress people with our achievements, dropping CV highlights with a clang. Anyone who's ever cut somebody off mid-sentence to tell an impressive anecdote, the guide says, has probably circled around this step. Number five, *Eccentricity*, is the exhibitionist habit of doing things our own special way. And number six, *Conceit*, is the embedded belief that, underneath, we're better than anybody else we're talking to. Number seven, *Audacity*, is when we refuse to let good advice hold us back. Number eight, *Defence of wrong-doing*, is when we never admit to being wrong. And number nine, *Dishonest confession*, is when we regularly lie to people to hide a web of deceit.

Right at the bottom of these steps, according to the guidebook, are the three levels reserved for people so full of *superbia* that they've become 'spiritually dead'. Of these, the first is number ten, *Rebellion*, a type of pathological inability to cooperate, a 'shameless' refusal to live alongside others in any kind of community. Next it's number eleven, *Freedom to sin*, where we stop following social or moral codes, keeping ourselves free to do whatever feels good in the moment, no matter who we hurt. In the final step, number twelve, *Habitual sin*, the heart is now a vacuum. Flitting from pleasure to pleasure, we only care about maximum self-expression and maximum supremacy. And

PRIDE

now, unfortunately, in a kind of game, we count the lives we can destroy along the way. In this final stage of pride, if we ever get there, we'll believe we're untouchable, supreme. Godlike.[47]

Simon Magus saved his most godlike trick for last. Explaining that his time on earth was over, he announced that he was now ascending to heaven. He walked up to the Temple of Jupiter, the highest building on Rome's Capitoline Hill, and climbed to the top. As he stood on the precipice facing the breeze, an enormous crowd gathered below. To the sound of screams, Simon jumped. There was a silence. And then, although nobody could quite believe it, he seemed to be up there flying over their heads.[48]

How did Simon manage this trick? Really, there were two ways of flying in the Middle Ages. One was a method that involved an intense individual effort. Around the year 1000, a man called Eilmer climbed to the top of a tower in the town of Malmesbury in Wiltshire. On his hands and feet he'd affixed a set of homemade wings. To everyone's disbelief he jumped off the tower, just like Simon Magus, and managed to fly. Apparently he travelled through the air for at least 200 metres, which is around twice the length of the first controlled flight, by the famous Wright brothers, in 1903. But then Eilmer hit some turbulence and fell to the ground, breaking both of his legs. He struggled to walk for the rest of his life. While today we may hail Eilmer as Europe's first aviator, his contemporaries were lukewarm at best. William of Malmesbury, the greatest historian of the 1100s, spoke with monks who remembered meeting Eilmer in his later years. All he could say of him, though, is that he was guilty of *superbia*. He'd 'mistaken fable for truth', he said, and estimated his own powers a little too high.[49]

The other way of flying appears in an obscure book written by a scientist, Roger Bacon, at Oxford University in the 1200s. Among his designs for contraptions and weapons (made a full two and a half centuries before the notebooks of Leonardo da Vinci), Roger discussed his plans for a flying machine. 'It's possible,' he said, 'that a device for flying shall be made so that a person sitting in the middle of it, turning a crank, shall cause artificial wings to beat the air after the manner of a bird's flight.' Although Roger admitted that he'd never actually seen this machine, he'd once met a 'wise man' who'd designed one in detail, he said. And as well as planning to make one at the university, Roger went on to describe his own ambitious plans for other inventions, including a deep-sea diving suit, a long-distance projectile flamethrower and a mirror that would show people whatever they desired as a flickering image on a screen.[50]

Why should one of these ways of flying be 'better' than the other? Unlike Eilmer's artificial wings – and unlike Simon Magus's tricks – Roger Bacon's aviation depended on a team of experts, working together. He gathered plans by collaborating with the 'wise' scientists he met, and formulated the contraption as a project for a wider group. Even more distinct was his motive, which was not to fly for himself but to fly for his community. When humanity faced the coming apocalypse, Roger said, people would need his false mirrors, his flamethrowers and his flying machines to fight back. They were all in a cosmic arms race against evil, and Roger wanted to make sure they didn't lose.[51]

As Simon flew weightless over the squares of Rome, many watching below must have believed his boasts were real. But plunging towards the pavement beneath the Capitoline Hill, he would have felt the full scope of his limitations rushing towards him. While Simon wanted to *seem* miraculous, he wasn't ever bothered about whether the miracles were genuine or not. So he tried to fly without ever learning what flying really involves. On that point medieval moralists and twenty-first-century pilots would agree. Aviation is impossible without the hard work and support of dozens of people. When we try to sprout wings before we can walk – when we show off with medieval manuscripts, assuming we can transcribe an 800-year-old page without asking an expert for help – we risk outrunning ourselves. We flap and flap, but in all that effort we miss the opportunity to reach out, to connect, to hook ourselves up to the engines of other people.

It's not snowing, but a cloud has covered the sun. Walking away down the corridor, approaching my next class, I'm wondering if I paid enough attention to what Shakhlo needed from me when she was trying to take those photos. I thought we were both treating this as a bit of a joke, but maybe she saw something else: an arrogance, a refusal to do things somebody else's way. I can't escape the feeling that by imagining I was 'above' a silly photo shoot I was doing something worse, in terms of pride, than throwing myself into every pose.

Gerry, on one of those long nights at the university library, once gave me a piece of advice. To be a historian you need to be a good listener. You need to read and read the documents of the past, until you hear the voices speaking. Pride makes this almost impossible, because at its essence pride is a condition of selective hearing. It talks but it doesn't listen, it sends but never receives. It's Lucifer giving advice to the silent architect of the universe, or it's Bélibaste preaching to a captive community while ignoring everyone's feedback. This selective listening wouldn't be so dangerous if it wasn't twinned with pride's major strength, which is its seduction. Confronted by *superbia* in full flow – looking into the eyes of the beautiful Lucifer, hearing the speeches of a Bélibaste, or watching a Simon fly over our heads – the experience can be ravishing. Like a vortex it sucks us in, showing us a sparkling power we hope can be our own.

What these seducers usually want, though, is something that's best only for themselves. If you're a Pierre, walking into the web of somebody's *superbia* can make you lose your sheep, or your money, or your Spanish leather boots. But then if you're a Bélibaste, leaning into a hypocritical fiction of yourself, it can lead to your execution on a burning pile of wood. Either way, pride at its worst doesn't distinguish between what's 'right' and 'wrong'. It only worries about what's best for the preservation of the ego.

All this self-obsession leads to a dead end. Because pride is also a blindness to ourselves, a delusion that stands in the way of self-recognition, self-acceptance, and ultimately self-love. Surrounding himself with willing acolytes, Bélibaste couldn't see himself properly. He couldn't accept that, underneath his adopted identity as a 'perfected spirit', he was becoming a fabulist, a fraudster, a bad friend. The technicolour Lucifer may be stunning to look at but – like Simon Magus, or like any other ego who suffers from self-delusion – he was more interested in the all-powerful fantasy he'd created rather than the real seraph underneath. In either case, *superbia* is the basic thought that tempts us to substitute ourselves for a glossier version. When we try to be more perfect, or more highly regarded or respected, it's a sign that we haven't yet learned to live with the face we see in the mirror.

Still, there's a reason pride has become such a powerful virtue today. Boil off all the elements we find insufferable in a Lucifer, in a Bélibaste, or in a Simon, and we're left with a positive ethics of the ego. A user's manual that can still be valuable today, even if we're facing an embarrassing photoshoot in a Siberian university. And that manual tells us that ego can be self-love, so long as it's grounded in self-recognition rather than projection. That mirror-gazing can be valuable, when we gaze in self-scrutiny and not self-obsession. It tells us that it's okay to throw around our talents, provided they don't work against other people. All of which is a way of saying, I suppose, that I need to stop staring out of the window here by the exit doors of my university building, stop dreaming of doing something heroic and start doing something useful instead. That I need to recognise my limitations and find a way to be valuable for my students and colleagues here, in this submarine of a building, while this job is still mine.

CHAPTER 2

Envy

I can't see any green outside my office window. An overnight blizzard has covered everything, except for Lenin, whose statue on the main square has an icing of white across his shoulders and cap. Do the city authorities keep him heated, to repel the first blitz of frost? Below in the street I can hear two competing sounds: the creeping of cars across compacted snow and the scraping of metal shovels on concrete pathways. But although my body is here in Tyumen, receiving these sound waves, my mind is somewhere much warmer. Really I am in Italy. I can feel sunshine beating on the back of my linen shirt, I can taste pistachio from a half-eaten cannoli, and I can feel myself stretching out to shake the hand of a man named Francesco Montefalco.

In the snow-filtered light on the desk in front of me is my laptop.

> Dear Professor Montefalco, I hope this message finds you very well. I am writing to submit materials for the position of Professor of Medieval History in the International Program at the University of Verona. With seven years' experience teaching undergraduate students in the UK, the USA, Canada and now Siberia, I hope I can be a valuable contributor to your team. Please find attached my CV, as

well as a research plan for the projects I look forward to working on with you over the coming years.

I've never met Professor Montefalco. With each day that passes without a response, it feels less likely that I ever will. But I like to imagine him reading through these materials and smiling. Smiling about the still-young researcher he'd like to interview, with his smart linen shirts and his love of pistachio.

Envy exists somewhere between our daydreams and our paranoia. And lately I've had a lot of time to think about it. One of my friends recently posted about his new academic job on social media, and I've been scrolling back to look at it again and again. The two of us were together in the graduate programme in New York, and we hit it off straight away. In the breaks between seminars we used to buy each other paper cups of black coffee and chat about our love of British comedy. When I ran out of money once he showed me how to survive on two-dollar falafel, and when I was struggling to write my thesis his enthusiasm helped me to fall in love with research again. Now he has a position at a university in California, and I'm happy for him. But sitting here, surrounded by the snow shovels and the frost-coated Lenin, I can't help wanting a life swap.

Do I envy my friend? If I was speaking to a modern therapist, my answer would probably be 'Yes.' Even if I could hide it, why would I try? *His job in California would be a dream. I have the frosty plains, he has the beach.* But if I was talking to a medieval priest-therapist, I hope my answer would be 'No.' Because *invidia*, as this sin was known in medieval Latin, was much more disturbing than our modern concept of envy. If I had modern envy, I'd want some element of my friend's life for myself. I'd want to experience his Californian sun, to relax in his air-conditioned libraries, to feel the same confidence that tomorrow will be another step along a stable career path. If I was cruel I might fantasise about replacing him, of putting myself in the sunshine and him in the snow. And yet my main motive would still be aspirational. I'd want to achieve something for myself.

On the contrary, with medieval envy we aren't looking to achieve anything. We don't want things or experiences, and we don't want to grow either. Because medieval envy is an allergy to other people's successes. It's an impulse to spoil and wreck, a 'hatred of all things that are good'.[1] A restless obsession with things we don't have that leads to a cruel addiction to the pain of others.

As far as modern scientists understand it, envy's main engine is social comparison. Researchers today talk about the effects of 'upward contrast': browsing social media pages and perceiving somebody 'up' from us on the social or economic scale apparently doing much better in life. In these moments, they say, we feel an instant pain at being ourselves; an inadequacy that produces the spiteful side effects of 'malicious envy'.[2] Modern psychologists, likewise, tend to see envy as a symptom of powerlessness and deep insecurity. It's the feeling we have when, looking at others and feeling unable to emulate their good qualities, we sink down into a well of self-pity and resentment.[3]

But for medieval writers the key feature of envy was 'blindness'. Just as pride is the failure to understand ourselves, envy is the inability to really see *other* people for what they are. It's 'the hell of the human mind', as the preacher and theologian Alain de Lille wrote. A misdirected fixation on somebody else that makes us 'unerringly blind' to all the beauty and fortune we already possess.[4]

Why do some people suffer from this more than others?

And where, precisely, does *invidia* come from? According to the writer Jean de la Rochelle, envy (like the other Deadly Sins) is a form of perverted love. More particularly, it's a blend of two types of loving: one that goes into overdrive, and another that stutters to a halt. On the one hand it comes when we love achievements too much, and on the other it touches us when we love others too little.[5] It usually starts when we begin to desire something, like success or praise, that we think will make us feel good. But, because envious desire is selfish and paranoid, it soon turns out that we want to have this thing 'for ourselves without any companion'.[6] So, we come to feel *invidia*'s chief symptom: becoming empty and bereft at seeing another person's success, like we're seeing a lover cheating on us.

It's at this point that the frenzy really kicks in. Because once envy hooks us, it becomes impossible to resist the feel-good buzz of knocking other people down. When we overhear someone else being praised, we ignore it, carrying on as if nothing had been said. But if we overhear criticism of somebody else, we rush to join the crowd, adding our own contributions, hoping 'to darken another's shining renown with a cloud'.[7] We become addicted to the accidents, the misfortunes and the mistakes of other people. We even enjoy their pain, to the point that, when we see a rival in distress, we hope nobody comes to their rescue.[8] All of which is the essence of *invidia*, and the thing that justifies its usual ranking as the second most Deadly Sin. It's when our craving for somebody else's misery rises above our desire for our own happiness. It's not wanting what somebody else has; it's wanting them *not* to have it.

Beyond my laptop's now-darkened screen, more snowflakes fall. If only I really was in California, or in Italy. Or anywhere else but here.

The Arena Chapel Code

People often think of the Middle Ages as cold and damp. But really, up until around 1300, Europe was much warmer than it was during the Renaissance. Average temperatures were high enough for wine grapes to grow in southern Scotland and for children to swim in the Black Sea in January. Climatologists usually call this the Medieval Warm Period (MWP) or the Medieval Climate Anomaly (MCA), and from analysis of tree rings, Swiss Alpine glaciers and Greenland ice cores they have estimated it began around 1000 and lasted for nearly three hundred years.[9] There is still disagreement over the causes. Did cooler Pacific Ocean temperatures force warm air currents up to the northern hemisphere? Did a sudden decline in volcanic eruptions stop the flow of cooling aerosols into the atmosphere? Or was it all the product of a mysterious surge in solar force?[10]

But one thing everyone can agree on is that modernity, with its colonial expansions and printed books, began life in the cold spell that followed. In the 1310s successive harvests failed in much of Europe, and wine production in France slumped by as much as 80 per cent.[11] Glaciers began forming in the mountains of southern Spain, the tree line plunged, and the surface of London's River Thames froze solid every winter. A few hundred miles inland from the west coast of Greenland are the remains of a town that archaeologists have called the 'Viking Pompeii'. Between around 1000 and 1350 this had been a thriving farming community with thousands of inhabitants. One day, though, the whole population abandoned the site for good. Nobody can find any evidence for why they disappeared, other than the increasingly unbearable cold. By the 1400s the empty town was smothered by permafrost, which is how it remained until the

1980s, when our own new 'climate anomaly' began to thaw a chasm in the ice.[12]

If there's one place where we can still feel those currents of pre-modern warmth and Renaissance chill colliding, it's in Padua's Arena Chapel. A small city in the north of Italy, Padua sits in a low valley, but with a view of the soaring Alps in the distance. Although famous for its ancient university and for its stockfish stews, the city's real draw is its art. And the epicentre of it is a narrow building, surrounded by a ring of trees and crumbling walls. The Arena Chapel is this city's UNESCO World Heritage Site, and the home to the greatest masterpieces of Giotto: a Florentine artist whose imagination and skill changed the history of art.

When I first walked into the chapel, a few years ago, it felt like I was entering a vault of sunshine. They only allow small batches of visitors inside at any one time, and so the whole experience is intimate and hushed. Still, even in the silence, the chapel screams with colour and life. Shimmering like a jewellery box, its walls are covered with luminous frescoes painted in tumbling blues, greens and pinks. Overhead is a ceiling the same deep azure blue as the Italian evening sky, which leads the eye up to a freckling of golden stars. But while the art has all the warmth of a botanical garden and all the drama of a stage musical, I couldn't help feeling a chill, a cold front. Something snakelike, something deadly on those walls painted by Giotto.

Giotto di Bondone grew up in poverty, the son of shepherds in the Tuscan hills. He loved drawing from an early age, although he had neither formal training nor access to paint. But his golden opportunity arrived one day when Cimabue – the superstar artist of thirteenth-century Florence – came across him on the roadside sketching in the dirt. According to the story told by the writer Giorgio Vasari, Giotto was sitting drawing on the path with a stick when Cimabue, who was out for a stroll, stopped to look. There was something in the boy's eye, he thought. Something unique in the way he controlled his strokes. Many years later Giotto would win a commission from the pope purely on the basis of how well he drew a circle with his free hand. And here already, in the dust of the Tuscan hills, Cimabue saw the same tremendous potential. So he invited Giotto to Florence, where the shepherd boy joined Cimabue's workshop as an apprentice.[13]

Before long, Giotto was itching to outdo Cimabue. One afternoon while everyone was out to lunch he walked up to one of his master's unfinished paintings and added a tiny fly to the face. It was so realistic, Vasari said, that when Cimabue returned he spent a while trying to swat the fly away before he realised what had happened. Giotto soon moved to a more sophisticated strategy of sabotage. Cimabue had painted one of his masterworks, the *Santa Trinita Maestà*, in around 1280, not long before Giotto joined his workshop. It was a great painting in the Byzantine medieval style: solemn and imposing, with an austere Virgin Mary surrounded by two flanks of angels. Now Giotto painted the same scene himself, showing not only that he'd mastered all the tricks in Cimabue's playbook, but that he could outstrip them.

For a sense of the gulf between the two artists, it's worth comparing these two paintings (both of which are now in the Uffizi Gallery in Florence) closely. Whereas Cimabue's version is flat, Giotto's has a realistic depth. Some of the angels' faces are obscured by the throne and others are part-submerged in the crowd, just as they would be in a photograph. But it's with the central figure of Mary that Giotto really shows his greater power for evoking the deeper psychology of individuals. In Mary's face he captures a set of conflicting feelings almost impossible to describe. There's duty, but also a reluctance, a maternal instinct mashed with a rebellious streak. There's also anxiety, as anybody might understand it today. Because although Giotto's Mary seems to be smiling, her body language – the awkward shifting of weight, the tentative hand around the leg – registers a deep concern. Whereas Cimabue had painted Mary as Mother of God, Giotto painted her as mother. An ordinary parent, dealing with all the conflict of bringing a person into the world.[14]

Cimabue (left) versus Giotto (right). An enviable improvement?

Cimabue never lived to see Giotto's Arena Chapel frescoes. We can only imagine the envy he would have felt if he did, because these were unprecedented marvels of Western art. Arranged in rectangular panels, the scenes follow the life of Christ, the life of Mary and the life of her father Joachim in parallel. As beautiful as they are, their shimmer is balanced by something else. Giotto didn't like to paint joy in the raw. Instead he liked to offset it, sharpening the ecstasy of success with a shiver of jealousy. And alongside all the miracles of Jesus, Mary and Joachim, *invidia* is always lurking in the wings. It's in the halting gestures, the private glances and the ghostly stares of so many of the isolated figures at the margins of these scenes. These are figures who seem to be feeling a silent pain at all this happiness. Once you notice them, they make your blood run cold.

A servant watches from the side, in one of the scenes, as an angel gives Anne (the mother of the Virgin Mary) the life-changing news that she's going to have a daughter. Instead of showing delight, this servant's face seems to be stricken and stiff. Bathed in a pale green shadow, her eyes narrowed and her lips pursed, she clutches at a spool of thread with a curling fist.[15]

A servant overhearing the 'good news' about Anne's pregnancy, with a face of pure invidia.

Another bitter witness appears in the very next fresco. In this scene Joachim and Anne, the Virgin Mary's parents, are leaning on one another and kissing at the Golden Gate in Jerusalem. For years they'd tried and failed to conceive, but now Anne is telling Joachim she's pregnant and the two of them are kissing ecstatically. But once again there's a spectral figure in the background: a woman who doesn't want to be a part of the celebration. A black veil pulled tightly to her face, she looks away with an expression that's instantly recognisable. You can almost feel her blood draining away in horror at having to see somebody else so happy.[16]

Joachim and Anne kiss, and one onlooker can't bear to watch.

As if to join all these dots, the Arena Chapel also includes a painting of Invidia, the Deadly Sin personified. It's a fresco in which Giotto managed to condense the entire mythology of medieval envy into nine square feet of wall space. At first glance, Invidia's combination of tortures and afflictions is overwhelming. Her eyes are distorted and obscured, to the point of being extinguished. A poisonous snake has slithered through her mouth and is now coiling back to bite her in the face. Her feet are bathed in flames, her right hand is clawing out in rage and she is clutching a money bag in her left fist. Finally, a pair of horns is curling from the back of her head, cradling her enormous ears, which extend right back like those of a bat.

Giotto's figure of Invidia, complete with her seven clues about the nature of envy.

What do all these symbols mean? What can they tell us about envy? When I first stood there, in the chill of the Arena Chapel, I could barely take this image in (not least because of my overwhelming fear of snakes). It isn't meant to be absorbed in one go, though. A longer look at this fresco reveals a code, an intricate puzzle that unfolds with further analysis. *Snakes. Eyes. Flames. Claws. Money. Ears. Horns.* Unlock the mystery of these seven – plunge down through these myths, and follow them where they lead – and it's possible to unlock the intricacies of *invidia* as it existed in the medieval imagination.

I can't help but dispense with the snake first. Why did he paint it like this, creeping from mouth to eye? At one level the association with envy is an obvious one. Snakes not only wait in hiding before striking their prey, their slithering and venom capture the effect of backstabbing in the midst of a good society. Giotto, with his classical instincts, was probably familiar with the snakelike character in Ovid's *Metamorphoses*, who was also called Invidia. Crouching in the corner of a dark and frosty hovel, this character spends her days eating the flesh of poisonous snakes. But all this poison only feeds her fear of missing out. Emaciated, and with venom dripping from her tongue, she lies awake at night, panicking that other people might be enjoying the successes she isn't. And so 'she gnaws and is gnawed', Ovid said, to the point that she becomes 'herself her own punishment'.[17]

Still, that snake is coming from inside the mouth, or inside the person – and so Giotto is telling us something else. When we suffer from *invidia*, we actually *become* the snake ourselves. Somewhere behind this idea is the medieval legend of the Basilisk. A single look into its eyes, writers claimed, would be enough to kill you. Though, unlike the creature that appears in modern fantasy novels, basilisks appear in medieval bestiaries as tiny chimeras, part-bird and part-snake, with feathered bodies 'half a foot long, with white spots'. And for medieval visitors to this chapel, the transference between legendary Basilisk and ordinary envious person would have been clear. Too much *invidia* makes you see other people the way a snake sees them: as victims to be deceived, trapped, poisoned, or squeezed to death.[18]

Now, what about those eyes? Why are Invidia's shown as nothing more than tiny dark holes? Has she already been blinded by the snake? In medieval Latin the verb *invidere* could mean either 'not to see' or 'to see against'. And typically *invidia* implied two types of 'not seeing'. The first was an act of will, where you (as an envious person) *choose* not to see. By turning away from the sight of somebody else's success, you wilfully make yourself temporarily blind. 'Tormented by other people's glory and happiness,' explained the abbot Bernard of Clairvaux, envy 'strikes the eye with a proper bruise'.[19] Because in this type of *invidia* you pretend not to see someone else's good news. You put your phone into your pocket to block out the sight of someone else's happy life on social media. This is 'head-in-the-sand' envy, and it's written all over the face of the veiled woman in Giotto's *Meeting at the Golden Gate*, who tilts her veil as if she hasn't noticed the joyful couple kissing.

Invidia can also involve a second type of blindness. In some cases it can corrupt your vision, so that while you still see other people – and perhaps you look at them *compulsively* – you find you only do so in a twisted way. Envy 'cannot see good things unless it sees bad in them', the French preacher William Peraldus wrote, sometime around the year Giotto was born. In this type of envy you really *do* engage with the world. Instead of compassion, though, what you see creeps into your brain as a commentary on your own successes or failures. You still devour all the details from a friend's social media post, but instead of sharing their joy you brood on how their news might reflect on you, and your own life journey.[20]

Symbols three and four on the fresco deepen this sense of antagonism. Giotto's Invidia is shown with two acts of violence: one that hurts her (a ball of flames at her feet), and one that hurts others (the claws of her outstretched right hand). Did Giotto imagine this clawing to be a response to the pain of the flames, or its deeper cause? Although this isn't so clear, what is clear is that *invidia* was often imagined as producing symptoms of slow-burning torture. 'In a great blaze of envy,' a manuscript of sermons now in Lambeth Palace Library said, 'the sufferer bursts into flames.'[21]

What is it, exactly, that sparks all of this envy? Giotto's fifth symbol – the money bag Invidia grasps in her left hand – could apply as much to the Deadly Sin of avarice. But then, grasping after cash is also a symbol of the restlessness often cited as envy's core feature. Money is one of those 'things that delight us with its beautiful and deceptive pleasure', the scientist Roger Bacon wrote in the 1290s, while making us 'blind'. Because having money is never enough for the envious person. Instead, the impulse to fixate on the possessions of others makes even our own gold seem like 'foul dross'.[22]

With everything else that's going on in this fresco, it's easy to overlook Invidia's enormous ears. Like a social media predator, Giotto's Invidia is ready to hoover up scandals and rumours. An anonymous thirteenth-century treatise on the sins described this impulse as 'the subtraction of another's good through a pile-up of twisted words'.[23] Because envy was not just a sin of the eye but also of the ear; a mechanism for amplifying faults and spreading them to others in your local community or professional network. Baldwin of Canterbury, the twelfth-century theologian, consequently believed that a discreet silence was one of the best solutions for envy. When you are injured, it's best to stop and think: should I be stretching my ear to catch this insult? Does reporting an injury serve a good ethical social good? Or does it only satisfy my own desire for revenge?[24]

One final piece of Giotto's code remains. And for this, unfortunately, we have to jump into the depths of medieval anti-Semitism. Why does Invidia have those horns curling from the back of her head? A quick guess might be that these were associations with the devil, or else with some kind of animal. But really these horns allude to an obscure mistake in the Vulgate, the Latin Bible used in the Middle Ages. When Saint Jerome translated the Book of Exodus, he mixed up two Hebrew words: *qāran* (which means something like 'glorify' or 'dazzle'), and *qeren* (which means 'horn'). And so, instead of translating the passage as 'Moses's face appeared to dazzle,' Jerome wrote it as 'On Moses's head there appeared horns.'[25]

Over the centuries Jerome's little mistake was amplified, and writers and artists began giving horns to all of 'Moses's people'. Horned Jews multiplied rapidly through the 1200s, not only in artworks but even in legal and bureaucratic documents. At the Council of Vienna in 1267 Jews were ordered to wear 'a horned hat', so that they could be easily identified. Philip III (d.1285), King of France, enacted a law forcing Jews to wear badges with horned figures on them. And on a document from London's National Archives somebody doodled a group of horn-hatted Jews being tormented by demons with horns of their own.[26]

All of which means that Giotto probably added those horns to connect Invidia to the 'envy of the Jews', a European myth that, by the early 1300s, had once again become topical. Saint Paul (who was himself Jewish by birth) described the Jews of the Roman Levant as the 'killers of Christ'. They had acted with pure *invidia*, he suggested, because they had not been able to bear the sight of Christ's spiritual majesty. By Giotto's era, people were using this myth to justify persecution, violence and even mass murder. Pogroms occurred across Europe throughout the twelfth and thirteenth centuries, and Jewish people were expelled from England in 1290 and France in 1306 (while the paint was still drying on the Arena Chapel walls).

While we can discount the horns, what remains is a six-part message about *invidia* encoded onto the walls of this heartbreakingly beautiful Italian chapel. Beware envy, which is the venom that clouds your bloodstream. It's the impulse that depends on acute ears, the private addiction that thrives on individual ambition and drives you to strike out at others, first with the hidden cunning of a snake and then with the open lashing of claws. It's the Deadly Sin that will burn you up. Anybody who walks out of this chapel in Padua should, by rights, be so horrified by these six things envy does to us that they never obsess over the things other people have again.

When I walked away from the Arena Chapel on that day in Padua, I felt all of this chill but I still hadn't absorbed the fresco's message. Faced with those warnings about an envy that's similar to our own, I carried on walking away, daydreaming about a better life. Which is why, as I sit in my Siberian office, slipping over to social media feeds and academic job postings, I suppose I can still feel envy's flames licking at my feet.

Anthony's Green Tongue

Unfortunately for me and my phobia, Giotto's Invidia's isn't the only snakelike tongue in the city of Padua. If anything, the other one is even more macabre. Walking for twenty minutes south, through the city's underbelly of narrow paved streets, I arrived at the Basilica di Sant'Antonio di Padova, an enormous church built in the 1230s. As I emerged from the shaded streets into a blazingly white square, I could barely see; my eyelids were stitched tight by the blinding sun. Still, this building hit me like a shovel in the face. It's everything the Arena Chapel isn't: muscular instead of slim, sprawling instead of narrow, out in the open instead of half-hidden.

Inside, instead of frescoes, the basilica has dozens of tiny statues arranged in lines of shadowed alcoves. Stepping through the huge rounded arch, I saw a long queue of people lining up along the left-hand side. They slithered like an airport security line, from the centre of the nave towards a flash of golden colour set just apart from the basilica wall. What they were queuing for, I soon discovered, is maybe the most spectacular and haunting reliquary produced in the entire medieval era.

Reliquaries are boxes for the remains of saints. Often in the Middle Ages they were designed to mimic the surrounding part of the body from which the relic came, so that a reliquary for a finger might be in the shape of a golden arm, and a holy toe might be embedded in a dazzling silver foot. The one in Padua's Basilica di Sant'Antonio di Padova – which houses the relics of Anthony of Padua, a thirteenth-century preacher famous for his dazzling speeches – is the most bizarre I have ever seen. A mandible hovers in a bubble, set at the front of a golden head. A jewel necklace drapes across a golden chest, and above this, where the eyes would normally be, is a dark, latticed tiara shaped like a peacock's plumage. A bottom row of teeth judder up like stalagmites, and above them sits the tongue, a pickled lump of muscle the colour of unexpected mould. The whole effect, to modern eyes, is somewhere between space alien superspecies and billionaire's diving helmet (plate 3).

People don't just queue up to marvel at the medieval sci-fi of this reliquary. Many of the Basilica's visitors see Anthony of Padua's tongue as a miraculous organ, a nuclear weapon in the history of religious debate. These are the people who know the saint's backstory. Born in 1195 in Lisbon, Anthony built a reputation as his century's most charismatic speaker and persuader. After learning a fleet of languages he travelled to Italy and gave a sequence of sermons that were like theatrical performances. Following the kind of pacey structure you might find in a detective thriller, they were studded with comic interludes and tragic soliloquies. He could explain the power of lust by pointing to a pond full of frogs, and described the mystery of knowledge as 'a feather in the throat of a swan'.[27]

Anthony also had a lot to say about the human tongue itself, and especially how it could be twisted by *invidia*. Comparing the Deadly Sins to seven different animals, he made envy their chief: the dragon. And the problem with this dragon-envy, he said, is that it damages your deepest inner life. More than any physical damage, 'the wound made by a critical tongue' has the power to 'break the bones' that structure your sense of self. And when you start to focus on the mistakes and slips of other people, the whole habit can become a painful addiction. It's 'like a wine that inebriates the mind'; a deadly poison that strikes with 'the incurable venom of asps'.[28]

If *invidia* is such a deadly drug, how do people get addicted to it in the first place? Whenever medieval theologians wanted to solve a psychological puzzle like this, they usually turned to the Bible, though they didn't always expect to find straight answers there. Rather, they liked to wrestle with the deeper meanings of biblical stories for themselves, coming to understand something new about the human brain in the process. While the New Testament gave the most direct examples of how to live ('turn the other cheek'; 'do unto others as you would have done to yourself'), the Old Testament gave them more freedom to explore. In the story of Cain, the son of Adam and Eve who murdered his brother Abel, medieval writers found a way to confront one of the biggest questions about *invidia*. What is it that makes an otherwise happy person slip into a jealous hatred?

Lesson number one is that envy often begins with a legitimate grievance. When medieval people encountered the story of Cain and Abel in the Book of Genesis, many empathised with Cain's predicament. 'We are all the successors of Cain,' Abbot Robert of Cricklade said.[29] And really, things never were equal between the Bible's original two brothers. Cain was assigned a back-breaking regime of ploughing fields, Abel was given the more relaxing task of animal husbandry. As well as demanding unequal effort, these two tasks yielded unequal results. Abel could offer God generous cuts of meat as his sacrifice, Cain could only offer bundles of grain. So, when God praised Abel's offerings and rejected Cain's, wasn't it understandable for the older brother to feel like he'd been the victim? Feeling that the whole system was stacked against him, wasn't it reasonable to experience the first pangs of *invidia*, a 'sorrow at another's good fortune'.[30]

It seems that some of this basic sympathy for Cain spilled over into medieval artworks. Another Padua treasure, a fifteenth-century bas-relief carving, underlined just how unfair things were for earth's first older brother. The way this panel has been made, it's not obvious which of the two brothers at the centre is Cain and which is Abel. Both of them have identical haircuts, identical jawlines and identical togas. The only difference between them is the sacrifice they hold as they approach the altar (plate 4). Which raises an unsettling question: if Abel had been given the inferior job – with grain to offer instead of the lamb – would he, instead, have been overrun by *invidia*? And if so, does this mean the only real difference between a murderous envy and a serene existence is the cards we're dealt by fate?

Whether fate shines on us or not, lesson number two of envy is that it tricks the heart, right to the point that we crave the wholesale destruction of another person. A tiny image in the Alba Bible, made in the Spanish city of Toledo in the early 1400s, shows this type of ecstatic frenzy at its extreme. On a bed of spongy plants, the bloodstained Cain is pouncing on Abel's chest and ripping at his neck with a set of sharp-pointed teeth.[31] He is 'gnashing like a beast looking for a fresh kill', to use the words of another medieval writer who described *invidia*'s giddy rush.[32] If Cain's envy was awakened by his feelings of injustice, and triggered like antibodies responding to a virus, then this image shows that system roaring into overdrive. It's *invidia* surging through him like a deadly inflammatory reaction, one powerful enough to turn victim into vampire.

Given the right trigger, are we all capable of becoming envious vampires? For Robert of Cricklade, Cain's 'jealousy and contention' are still part of the fabric of human civilisation. And yet for other medieval writers the answer was a decisive 'No.' Cain was simply a human aberration, they said; a genetic one-off.[33] It wasn't just that a momentary shot of *invidia* pushed his ordinary sense of injustice over the limit. It was in the fibre of his being. Augustine of Hippo (d.430), a writer whose impact on medieval thought is comparable to Isaac Newton's impact on modern science, took this argument to its ultimate conclusion. Cain's *invidia* was neither provoked nor proportional, he said. It was a product of his own natural-born evil. Cain had always, since birth, had a 'fire of envy' kindling inside him. A sinister energy – which he had, but which the rest of us hopefully don't – that bloomed through his life like petals unfolding from a bud.[34]

Cain's frenzy – whether provoked or inborn – is one thing. This is envy as a reaction, a snap of revenge. What about the more cold-blooded side of *invidia*, though? What about treachery, or the slow-burning resentment that leads to plots, betrayal, or revenge? *Invidia*'s other medieval icon is a figure from the New Testament, and another star of Paduan art. Another jealous man who destroyed his own 'brother', and who, as Saint Anthony said, 'sold his neighbour with the kiss of flattery'. This was Judas Iscariot.

Many of the Deadly Sins could claim Judas as one of their

mascots. Avarice is one, because he was tempted to betray Christ for thirty pieces of silver. Sloth is another, because his despair, according to medieval legend, led him to die by suicide. And yet, more often than not, *invidia* was seen as his master sin. More precisely, Judas was thought to suffer from a strain of envy one step beyond the frenzied jealousy of Cain. An ambitious *invidia* that blended an intense fear of missing out with a secret craving: the urge to expunge a rival's achievements from the record completely.

If I'd stayed long enough with that snake in Padua to appreciate it, I would have seen that this type of ambitious envy is really the centrepiece of the Arena Chapel. Giotto's fresco of Judas, arguably the boldest of all the artworks on those walls, shows him betraying Christ with a kiss, with a look of cold hatred unsurpassed in medieval art (plate 5). Yet the painting includes something extra. Judas covers Jesus with his cloak, nearly obscuring him from the neck down in the folds of yellow material. As the art historian Claudio Bellinati put it, this gesture was meant as a 'symbol of abusive power'. Still, it's difficult to imagine a better rendering of *invidia* than that yellow cloak. As well as showing envy as an attempt to blot out a rival, it also marks a contrast between dullness and brightness. Compared to the gold of Christ's halo, which Judas is trying and failing to extinguish, doesn't that cloak look all the more dusty and dark?[35]

Many medieval writers decided Judas's envy, like Cain's, must have been hard-wired. In Jacobus of Voragine's popular *Golden Legend* (c.1260s), Judas received an elaborate trauma backstory, with a childhood of jealous resentment leading him to kill his brother, murder his father and (unwittingly) marry his mother.[36] Manuscript illustrations showed Judas's body deformed by envy's twin signatures: a long, curving tongue and rapacious eyes that 'swelled to such an extent that he could not see the light at all'.³⁷ And in one story, which circulated in the Early Middle Ages, Jesus met Judas in Hell and assured him that his envy would never be forgiven. The 'light of his eyes has been destroyed', he said, the 'hair of his head has been pulled out', and his 'mouth has been filled with thirty serpents to devour him'. So, as punishment, his name would have to be 'erased from the book of life' for ever.³⁸

And yet there was also a tradition in medieval art that showed Judas with a halo. In Verona's Museo di Castelvecchio, not far across the Italian countryside from Padua, is a fourteenth-century wooden altarpiece (plate 6). Artworks like this were usually hung in parish churches, either as decoration or as tools for teaching. This one has thirty square panels, tracing world history from God's creation (in the top left), through the life, crucifixion and resurrection of Christ (the central three rows), before finishing with the Last Judgement (at the bottom right). Situated in the middle of it all, at the centre of panel number sixteen, is Judas himself. And the artist must have seen Giotto's fresco in the nearby Arena Chapel, because he likewise showed Judas wearing a yellow cloak, leaning across Jesus to kiss him in betrayal.

There's a critical detail hidden in these central panels. A clue both about the nature of Judas's transformation and the effect of his envy. Typical in medieval iconography, this Judas has no halo while he's betraying Christ. But in panel number fourteen, two scenes before, we see Maundy Thursday, when Jesus washed the feet of his twelve disciples. And if we count them, we can see that all twelve of the haloes are there, and that up to this point Judas still had his halo intact.

So what was the artist trying to say? In truth, this tiny band of gold on the Verona altarpiece opens up a radical and refreshing idea. That before he acted on his *invidia*, Judas's path to salvation was still open. That he had never been doomed by his envy. That, on Maundy Thursday at least, he could still have written a fresh page in the story of his life. If only Judas had allowed himself to see that he had a halo above his head – if only his *invidia* hadn't blinded him to all the potential that was still at his fingertips – maybe he wouldn't have tried to blot out others?

When, on that day in Padua, it was my turn to look at Anthony's reliquary, all I could think about was bodily imperfection. I could see several of the saint's teeth that needed root canals, and decided the whole thing called for Invisalign. I imagined scraping patches of green off the surface of the tongue with a toothbrush. The problems weren't really with Anthony, though. They were with me, and what I was choosing to see. Anthony said in one of his sermons that there are really two kinds of tongue: the tongues that drip with poison and the tongues that heal with medicine. But aren't medicine and poison often similar? Isn't it what we do with our criticism, and how we concentrate it, that really makes the difference? And don't we all have tongues that are capable of both healing and poisoning?

Envy can sometimes feel suffocating. And seeing it in others can often draw it out in ourselves. It's tempting to write off as a monster somebody who has acted in spite, or who has betrayed their closest friends, or who has committed some selfish act of sabotage. To think of them as vampires or cannibals, rolling around in the grass with sharp and bloodied teeth. But against Augustine, the lesson this mouth of Anthony once articulated – and the lesson of that Verona altarpiece – is that envy isn't really an innate defect. It's a tide that ebbs and flows inside all of us. Instead of cursing it, we need to recognise that no matter how many acts of hatred we're responsible for, there's always a path that leads back to that halo.

ENVY

Europe's First Tourist

Checking my email has now become my compulsive default. Every six minutes my fingers twitch to my phone and I tap through again to an empty inbox. Sometimes I find the absence of messages comforting. Everything, the whole suspension of my heart, can at least remain in stasis. But at other times the emptiness of the inbox strikes me as the emptiness of myself. It feels like a confirmation that I will stay here for ever, unchanging, in the Siberian snow.

But then the silence breaks. Returning from another walk around the top floor of the building, I sit down and scroll automatically again on my phone to the email app. And this time there's a new message. It's from the University of Verona. My heart beats high in my chest. Behind the blur of the screen I can see myself again in my linen shirt, climbing the steps to meet Professor Montefalco. But the message isn't from him. It's a brief note, and it's been signed by 'HR System'.

> Thank you for your interest in the position at the University of Verona. Although we looked favourably on your application, we regret to inform you that on this occasion other candidates have been selected for interview.

Where is my speech? I am in a box in Padua. I am the detached tongue, I am the gaping mandible. I can feel my thoughts turning to *something*, although I'm not quite sure what. Is it poison, or is it medicine? Is it the cannibal instinct of Cain, or the curdled ambition of Judas? What I wouldn't give to be in California now, or back in Italy on that August afternoon, struggling to map out not just a tourist walk but also the story of my life. What I wouldn't sacrifice to have another chance for a different future, far from this landscape of laptops and Lenin and frost.

Alongside that snake from Giotto's *Invidia* and Anthony's pickled relic, Padua has a third famous medieval tongue. One with no golden reliquary, no set of colourful frescoes and no UNESCO heritage status, but maybe a greater global impact. Although Francesco Petrarch grew up near Giotto's city of Florence, he spent the last years of his life in Arqua' Parcheggio, a village just outside Padua. Along with Giovanni Boccaccio and Dante Alighieri he was one of the three crowns of Italian literature, writers considered the successors of Virgil, Horace and Cicero. Petrarch wrote poems, letters and treatises, but he was also a famous conversationalist. He's credited with coining the term 'Middle Ages', a label he invented to dismiss the thousand years of 'darkness' that separated his own enlightened era (the mid-1300s) from Ancient Rome. Ironically, most critics today think of him as part of the Middle Ages himself.

Petrarch was especially interested in how envy affects a friendship. It's a 'virus', he said, that produces a 'kind of evil' unlike any other. He first came to experience it for himself, as he told his friend Donato in a letter, one day when he was ambushed in Venice. Four of his well-connected friends – he didn't repeat their names, since Donato would 'know them all' already – had met up to discuss Petrarch's work. After private deliberation, they decided to condemn his mistakes in a series of public attacks. Holding 'a tribunal of envious friendship', they called out all the places Petrarch had made philosophical 'errors', and the points where he had supposedly contradicted 'the law of Aristotle'. His education had been somehow soft, they said, his reading rather light. He was a 'good man' but he lacked knowledge, and was too much of a performer. 'Much eloquence', they decided, but 'little wisdom'.[39]

To Petrarch, this was slander. He had no doubt, on reflection, that their condemnation was driven more by envy than any concern for philosophy. Maybe they began their criticisms with 'good intentions', but soon – as often happens with *invidia* – 'an unfortunate grudge' crept through the 'cracks' into their hearts. What was it, precisely, that they envied? It couldn't be his body, Petrarch was sure of that. And it couldn't be his wealth, as all four were richer than him. He wanted to believe they envied him his 'virtue'. But really, what these friends envied most was Petrarch's fame. This was a poet who'd been invited to instruct three successive popes. He was somebody that the emperor up in Germany regularly wrote letters to, and that King Robert of Sicily considered a close friend. Petrarch had become, in other words, a literary celebrity. And these four friends – who all considered themselves serious scholars – wanted to find a way of invalidating his success.

Invidia is a sin that thrives in the shadows. The most upsetting thing for Petrarch was not so much these four friends' condemnations, as the secretive and sniping way they went about them. Instead of bringing their problems with his work to him straight away, they chose to meet in secret. As they never considered any evidence in Petrarch's favour, these private meetings soon lapsed into full-scale character assassinations. To make things worse, even as they were conducting their private meetings, these four friends carried on visiting Petrarch, pretending nothing was going on. They made 'agreeable conversation' with 'astonishingly good manners' and 'bright faces'.[40] They practised the envious art, as another medieval writer once put it, of hiding 'anguish beneath a paralysed smile', covering 'hidden animosities with flattery'.[41]

If anything, Petrarch stayed upbeat through all this rough treatment. The best defence against *invidia*, he felt, was to stay focused on doing what's good, instead of what's popular. And his diagnosis of jealous hatred – where enjoying other people's mistakes becomes your lifeblood, and knocking down your rivals becomes a reason to exist – still feels fresh and alive. Isn't this the same experience many people go through today, in a life lived half online? But there's a good reason why a medieval writer like Petrarch was able, instinctively, to summon a culture that resonates with our own. And that's because his social system, that of the very first universities, was a lot like ours. One defined by backstabbing, shaming and revelling in the flaws of other people.

Medieval universities were powered by individual reputation and popularity. Or, to put it another way, they were powered by *invidia*. During higher education's 'start-up' era, the early 1100s, being a professor was less a professional vocation than a journey. First, just like today, you needed to get credentials. Usually – because centres of learning were scattered sparsely around the continent, and because all education took place in the international language of Latin – this involved a lot of travel. To begin, you could go to either one of the major cathedral schools (like Chartres, Metz, Reims or Würzburg), or maybe a nearby monastery. There you would learn the basic essentials of the seven liberal arts: grammar, rhetoric and dialectic, as well as music, geometry, mathematics and astronomy. This was costly, but worth the effort. By mastering these essentials you were making an investment in yourself.

To really get ahead in this ecosystem, you would have to travel to one of the new universities and study one of the three 'advanced' subjects (theology, medicine, or law). Europe's three major institutions, Bologna, Paris and Oxford, welcomed between 1,000 and 2,500 students each in these early decades, and conditions were sprawling, anarchic and provisional.⁴² Professors (or masters as they were called) hired rooms and formed their own schools. Students then had to choose between them, paying fees relative to their reputation. If a master had good reviews, he could charge more. If he had bad reviews, he would quickly find himself with no students and no livelihood. Consequently, the most famous masters of this era, like Peter Abelard, made their careers, in part, by cutting down competitors. When Abelard made a fool of his rival William of Champeaux, outperforming him in a public battle of logic, William was left 'seething with such envy' that he 'boiled' inside, feeling such a pain that 'words cannot do it justice'.⁴³

Petrarch, in his youth, had followed this same educational pathway. He studied law in Bologna, at a time when that school's population was growing. Still, he was never inclined to become a university master. Academic life always felt claustrophobic, and he claimed to regret those years as 'a waste of time'. Really, Petrarch's heart was with his poetry, and he was burning to carve a life away from education, to find a way to become 'good rather than learned'.⁴⁴

And it was this drive that led Petrarch to travel widely. Visiting villages and towns across Italy, throughout southern France and up the Rhine valley, he earned the nickname of 'Europe's first tourist'. His real passion, in all this, was for the Alps. He once climbed Mont Ventoux, and looked across at the same mountains I saw while I walked between the Arena Chapel and the Basilica di Sant'Antonio in Padua. When Petrarch climbed them, he felt 'an inexpressible longing'. There was only so far this beauty could take him, though. Descending the mountains, he decided to 'turn' his 'inward eye' on himself. Thinking about the ten years that had passed since he had finished his own studies, he reflected that he still wasn't free of his 'perverse and wicked passions'. 'I am not yet in a safe harbour,' he wrote, 'where I can calmly recall past storms.'

What, exactly, were these 'perverse and wicked passions'? What were the storms? Although Petrarch's life was complex, it seems that one of the things that tortured him was his envy. He once wrote a letter to another great Italian writer, Boccaccio, confirming that he wasn't jealous of Dante. Here, he was defending himself from an accusation that had often been thrown at him. Why had he never owned a copy of Dante's *Commedia*, people asked, even though it was the greatest work of Italian literature? Dante had once lived with Petrarch's own father, so shouldn't it be a prized work on his shelf? 'I didn't want to risk imitating it,' Petrarch said, unconvincingly.[45] In another revealing letter to Boccaccio he outlined in painful detail where the three poets (himself, Boccaccio and Dante) ranked in terms of prestige. 'I have heard that our Old Man of Ravenna [a mutual acquaintance] . . . is accustomed to assign you the third place,' he said, before protesting just a little too much. 'If you think that I prevent your attaining to the first rank – though I am really no obstacle – I willingly . . . leave you the second place.'[46]

Even as he tried to run from the accusation, Petrarch recognised the universality of envy. Just like the writers who sympathised with Judas or Cain, he believed *invidia* was really an unavoidable ingredient of every human relationship. 'I have envied my friends' one of the characters in his dialogue, *De remediis utriusque fortunae*, told his master. 'But, who hasn't?' As the master said, there was only one way to live without jealousy. And that was to *run away from society*. To 'leave public honours and offices' and 'sequester yourself as much as you can'. Petrarch's solution was to never try to 'extinguish' his *invidia*. This was naïve, and would only lead to greater misery. Instead, his answer was to learn to live with it. To soften his envy and then shape it, and to find something else to do with all that nervous energy.[47]

How to do this, exactly? How do we turn an envious grudge into something more inspiring? As Petrarch said, the first rush of *invidia* – Cain's sense of injustice, Judas's burning ambition, or even the jealousy we all often feel – shouldn't be discarded or discounted. Instead, it should be redirected and repurposed to help us achieve something great or useful. Rivalry can 'accomplish wonders',[48] Petrarch said, so long as we follow only its strengths: its burning curiosity; its obsessive interest in other people; and its restless desire for self-improvement.

So, if attention is the main tool of envy, it can also be its cure. The challenge, according to a thirteenth-century preaching guidebook from Cambridge's Corpus Christi College, is to make all this curiosity, interest and ambition into the ingredients of a more open and ethical social life. When we're envious – like Petrarch's four friends, meeting in secret to churn over and enjoy somebody else's every last flaw – the plus side is that we are at least paying an intense amount of attention to another person. All we need to do, then, is modify our attention. To bring it out in the open and, instead of sniping, try to 'feel every wound', to 'rejoice in every triumph' of our rival. Practise this long and hard enough and we'll find that our envy can wash into compassion. Then, if we've done it right, we'll discover that we understand both ourselves and the person we've been watching all the better. We'll love both them and ourselves in ways we could never have dreamed of before.[49]

How do we stop the flow of resentment? How can we stop looking with hatred and hunger at the lives of other people? Is there a cure for that feeling – disgusting to admit – that makes us sometimes want to see another person fail? Judas and Cain experienced envy as a toxic combination of two drives. A sense of injustice combines with an irrational fear that others are taking away things we want to enjoy ourselves, forming an explosive loathing. One answer to this, for medieval thinkers, is to train the eye to see differently. John Climacus, a theologian who died in the seventh century, believed the cure for envy was to see other people the way a winemaker sees a grapevine. Coming to pick the grapes, you should reach only for the good ones. The bad grapes – the ones that are rotten, or broken, or unripe – you should pass over without a glance.[50] Can we do the same with all the difficult features we encounter in another person? Ignore those, and reach out for the inspiring things instead?

And yet even medieval theologians admitted that it was impossible to live without a little resentment in your heart. As Anthony of Padua described it, *invidia* was like a strain of bacteria. We all need an amount of it in our microbiome to function; a little bitterness to help us fight injustices, a little competitive rivalry to get the best out of our talents. But when it's unchecked, *invidia* can multiply and overflow, especially when we don't deal properly with a wound. Under vulnerable conditions it can send a toxin through the bloodstream, making even relations with our friends – and maybe especially our friends – into something poisonous. So, as with any injury, it's better to seal off the wound that sparked the envy and try to build up our immunity, rather than keep the wound open, out of morbid fascination, and allow *invidia*'s infection to take hold.

And so the other answer to envy is not to fight it, but to follow it. It's to take all the elements in the Arena Chapel code and turn them towards something worthwhile. We shouldn't feed that snake that wants to grow inside us. But if it's there, we can remember that the harshest poisons, in the right doses, can be medicinal. Although we need to reduce the size of our ears, so that they don't act like satellite dishes waiting to pick up news of other people's successes or failures, we can comfort ourselves that we are at least listening. And we can embrace this as the seed of an attention that, used well, can make us good friends, better partners, good citizens. We can keep our claws, so long as they reach out in hope. We can use our horns to pierce through brambles, and make sure that ambition for money becomes philanthropical. And that flame, licking at our feet, can warm us as much as it can burn.

Most of all, though, the cure for envy is to try to see what's in front of us. To really see it, and to accept it for the beautiful and fragile thing it is. And what I see now is that I'm not shaking the hand of Professor Montefalco in Verona, and I'm not back in Padua on a warm August day. What I see is that I'm sitting here in a bright and warm office in Tyumen. And before I walk away I need to appreciate everything that's here. Judas had a halo, which he didn't seem to notice as he slipped out to betray his friends. And Cain had his own golden crops, whose worth he couldn't see because he was so wrapped up in the sight of Abel's juicy mutton. What is it I'm not letting myself see about my own life?

CHAPTER 3

Anger

We're halfway through a staff meeting. One of those long, slow ones, where somebody always has a follow-up question. A neon red clock on the wall is running nine minutes ahead, and a rancid blend of cigar smoke and leaded petrol is seeping up through the window. One of my colleagues behind me has a bad cold but no tissue, and is sniffing heavily. And our chemistry professor is making a speech about the length of the canteen lunch queue, and why we should get our students to stop using our first names and start calling us 'professor' instead.

Although everybody recognises anger as a dangerous pathology, its mechanics still remain a mystery.[1] Wellness advocates talk about it as a by-product of a poor diet and disrupted sleep rhythms.[2] For psychologists, rage is a symptom of insufficient self-awareness and unreasonable expectations.[3] One modern philosopher has understood it, more simply, as a cry for recognition.[4] Whatever its precise cause, we usually think of anger as an impulse, a passion and an emotion. As people who do unforgivable things in anger often claim, it's not always our fault.[5] It's a reflex of the brain, reacting to some overbearing pressure or stress. Or it's a symptom of an inability to unpack complexity. Or it's a response to being insulted, violated, misunderstood, or trapped.

In the Middle Ages, anger had a different identity. It was, if anything, *seductive*. When we're tempted by a blend of righteousness and revenge, writers argued, we give into our rage because it makes us feel *incredible*. First comes the trigger, which as the philosopher Thomas Aquinas said is usually some moment of 'contempt' or 'spiteful treatment' that touches us deep inside.[6] Next follows an intoxicating blast of 'sharp smoky vapour',[7] an 'oblivion' of rage that 'darkens the sight' and hits us with an astonishing power.[8] In fury, according to the thirteenth-century lawyer Albertanus of Brescia, 'we think we can do more than we can.' Struggling in a frenzy, we stretch ourselves beyond our own fragile limits.[9]

Writers believed that rage, like other seductions, can be exquisite. Some of anger's symptoms listed in the medical encyclopaedia *The Property of Things* (*c*.1240) – 'a wave of bliss'; the feeling that 'all your body heat is pumping' with direction and force through all the veins, nerves and arteries – blur the lines between agony and ecstasy.[10] Anger is always accompanied, said one thirteenth-century compilation, by a 'pleasure' that's 'sweeter than dripping honey'.[11] It's a force that 'infatuates' us even while it 'pollutes' us.[12] It's so blissful, the great theologian Augustine of Hippo said, that we want to 'cherish' it, to nurse it inside our chests.[13] Because anger's power is that it warms us with a single, glowing conviction. That this time and without question *we are right*.

And, at least in theory, the thing we're 'right' about could be something that benefits other people as well. This is what made anger less harmful, in the usual medieval rankings of the Deadly Sins, than envy. Whereas with envy you're seeking something that's good *only for you*, with anger you're reaching for something that's good *in itself*.[14] So, when you snap at someone for spilling your coffee or for refusing your visa application on a silly technicality, you're also making a pitch for a better world: a world without clumsiness or narrow-minded bureaucracy.

But no matter how well intentioned our anger is, a problem often emerges. When fury surges, it makes us rush into delicate situations like an express train ripping through a fog. With no time to take in the nuances, our rage crushes any complex issue down to a simple formula of 'right' versus 'wrong'. In its blur, as Albertanus of Brescia said, there's no space for 'mercy,' and there's no empathy for the other side of the argument.[15] There's only a single, overbearing sense of our own justification.

For the last minute or so I've been sitting forward in my seat, clenching my fists to the rhythm of the ticking neon clock. I can feel a hammering in my chest and I know I'm about to say something hostile. Our chemistry professor is a harmless man in his early forties. He collects orchids, and before he moved to Siberia he used to work in his mother's flower shop on the outskirts of Zagreb. But at the moment I don't care, I just want to stop all the sound waves that are coming out of his mouth. 'What are you talking about?' I interrupt, surprised by how loud my voice sounds in the stuffy room. 'Why should any of us force our students to call us "professor"? Is this a university or a prison camp?'

My heart is beating high in my chest and my temples are throbbing. For a second I feel exhilarated, but the bliss already seems to be burning off. The orchid-loving chemistry professor is lifting his chin, his eyebrows an apologetic arch. He says he's sorry for taking so long to make his points. And now he's explaining how studies have shown that, by enforcing the separation between students and faculty, there can be a proven educational benefit to using the term 'professor'. My adrenaline flickers, ready to launch into a second outburst. I know I need to stop. Is there a remedy for an anger like this? If there is, how do I know in the moment – with my blood already up – whether I need to use it or not?

The Miracle Drug of Montpellier

Anger in the Middle Ages was often treated as an addiction. An obscure work known as the *Septuplum*, written around 1348 by the English theologian John Ayton, explained how it affects the brain in a 'threefold disorganisation'. This is what he called *rixa*, the compulsive habit of starting fights in social situations. *Rixa* begins with an 'alertness to contention', which is when we start looking for faults in everything and everyone we come across. Next comes 'delight', when we begin getting joy – or a 'dopamine high', as we'd say now – from contradicting others, from winning arguments, or from challenging people in a hostile way. Although potentially unpleasant, in these earlier three stages our anger is still a casual hobby. Something we enjoy when we get the chance, but that we don't necessarily dedicate our lives to.

After 'alertness' and 'delight' comes Ayton's final and more chronic stage. When this hits, we need urgent intervention. Like a 'perverted spring', bubbling up in an otherwise serene landscape, this more advanced *rixa* emerges when we start looking for arguments just for the fun of them. It's when, instead of enjoying anger as and when it arrives, we set out to engineer rage in every conversation we join. It's when we 'troll' people into saying something that irritates us just so we can enjoy another disagreement, another chance for revenge, another exquisite anger fix.[16]

Today, anger addiction can be treated with a range of drugs and therapies. If it's really getting in the way of our lives, a doctor might prescribe some mood stabilisers or antidepressants. More likely, they'll suggest a course of therapy, an opportunity to sit down and assess some of our triggers and the assumptions and misplaced priorities behind them. This feels very modern, but a similar set of options was in place in the 1200s. In fact, there

SELF-HELP FROM THE MIDDLE AGES

were a number of sophisticated medieval methods for dealing with rage, some of them branching into areas of science and self-examination that have largely been forgotten today. One of the epicentres of these sciences was Montpellier in France, the home of one of the bestselling wonder drugs of the Middle Ages.

Although I once spent a summer living in Montpellier, my memories are a little blurred. Shortly after I arrived one of my molars disintegrated while I was eating an almond croissant, and I spent the next three months wandering the streets in agony. Night after night, unable to sleep, I always walked to the same building. Halfway down a hill, next to the city's botanical gardens, I found my way to a soaring Gothic turret beside a stone bridge. Beneath this was the entrance to the Faculté de Médecine, the place I also came, during the afternoons when the ibuprofen kicked in, to decipher medieval manuscripts. Back then I wasn't sure why I always walked to this spot, although reflecting now I think I found it comforting to see the door and know that soon the sun would be up and the pain would be gone, and I'd be back in the archive again.

If you wanted to study medicine, for centuries this building in Montpellier was the premier place to go in Europe. Historians don't know precisely when the city's era of healthcare dominance began, but already by the early 1100s people were calling it 'a home and a temple' of medicine.[17] By 1153, Montpellier's physicians were considered 'safe' enough for the Archbishop of Lyons to put his life in their hands (apparently paying more than he could afford). And yet the archbishop was probably ripped off. All of Montpellier's doctors at this point (as one contemporary claimed) were little more than 'failed philosophers'. Finding their studies in Paris too difficult, they were chancers who had drifted down to the southern coast to try their luck at something a little more practical.[18]

ANGER

Over time, Montpellier became a medical powerhouse. A succession of hospitals popped up on the city's outskirts, giving trainee doctors plenty of practice, and the city also began attracting a talented pool of immigrant doctors. Up until it became French in 1349, Montpellier had belonged to the Kingdom of Aragon, and by the second half of the 1100s it welcomed a stream of Jewish and Muslim medical faculty who, tired of war and economic instability in Iberia, were looking for somewhere new to teach. Sensing a chance, the city's lord William VIII backed these refugees with a raft of legislation. He ruled that no group of people should ever have a monopoly over medicine – that was 'abhorrent and contrary to what is fair and moral' – and he made a new guarantee. Anyone, 'whoever they might be and from wherever they may hail', would now have the right to teach medicine in the city, unimpeded and with permanent rights to remain.[19]

Under these conditions the medical school at Montpellier produced a golden generation of theorists and practitioners. At their pinnacle was Arnaud de Vilanova (d.1311), a Catalonian doctor known as the first person to isolate pure alcohol as an antiseptic. Arnaud had first studied in Montpellier in the 1250s, before a chequered career that skirted high highs (serving as the King of Aragon's personal physician) and low lows (getting imprisoned for heresy).[20] His medicine was deeply theoretical and book-based, and – in a move possibly aimed at clearing that reputation for being 'failed philosophers' – he even persuaded the pope to force medical students to learn Greek and Arabic. Arnaud was also a practising surgeon, and in his *Experimenta* he described performing over seventy medical procedures, including treating patients suffering from cancer.[21]

Throughout his life, Arnaud also wrestled with the problem of anger. As a professional he studied its activity and causes in the body, and even experimented with drugs that he hoped could cure it. In his personal life, though, he once had an experience that revealed an exquisite anger within himself. In 1299, Arnaud's colleagues at Paris met behind his back and decided to condemn him for heresy. His crime, they believed, was that in his spare time he'd dabbled in conspiracy theories. One of his treatises had claimed that the apocalypse, and the arrival of the Antichrist, was imminent. Even more audaciously, Arnaud had calculated the precise year this would happen: 1376.[22] Meeting to discuss his ideas, and upset that Arnaud had presumed he knew more than them, the committee of theologians came to a stark verdict. He would be suspended from his university position, and his work would be suppressed. Arnaud's written response – published in the updated text that, nevertheless, he went ahead and circulated – was wounded, shaken, and above all angry. There's only one reason the 'theologians deem this little work unworthy', he wrote. 'Because it is not written or compiled by a man of *notable authority*.'[23]

What happens inside our bodies when our anger bubbles up like this? Interested in this question himself, Arnaud laid out its usual symptoms in one of his medical texts. Rage, he said, begins when we experience a phenomenon that our brain processes as an 'injustice'. The response could then take one of two pathways in our bodies. With the first – which Arnaud called 'perfect' anger – we seek revenge. Preparing for a blissful strike, our hearts expand and contract until a thrill of heat surges through every artery, vein and capillary.[24] In this response, both body and mind are working together in harmony, with everything pulling together to express our 'perfect' fury.

With the other path, though, things are more complicated. Instead of pushing towards revenge, in this response we experience what Arnaud called an 'anger mixed with fear', with some part of our brain pouring cold water on our fury. Now, although we may have been hurt by something that deserves to be met with force, our hearts refuse to pump into action. Instead of surging with heat, our bodies remain cold. And so we tremble for a revenge that, somehow, we can't deliver.[25]

But what dictates the response our body follows? Who feels which of these strains of anger? And why does one person tend to seek revenge, while another prefers to hold back in fear?

For some of the intellectuals in Arnaud's circle, the answer to these questions lay in the zodiac, which was another sphere of professional scientific scrutiny at Montpellier's medical school. Astrology wasn't just a niche interest in the Middle Ages, it was a developed art, with a thousand off-branches and applications. Astrologers cultivated pin-sharp calculations of the stars, using elaborate machines called astrolabes, and ordinary people were encouraged to be aware of these configurations, and to consult experts to see how the stars might affect their plans. Building a water mill might be a good idea in a 'water' month (those when the sun was in Cancer, Scorpio, or Pisces), these experts might suggest, but the same plans could go awry if they were attempted in an 'earth' month (like Taurus).[26]

Making a calendar of tasks could be fun. But really, the most valuable thing about the medieval zodiac was that it could be used to examine and explain personality traits. At its best it was a tool to get people to confront their own deeper emotional mechanics. And this was encouraged, even at the highest levels of theological and philosophical thought, as good therapeutic practice.

How did this work? According to the *Speculum astronomiae*, an anonymous work written in the thirteenth century, the stars and planets shape our bodies' organs and fluids as we are born. These forces, the *Speculum* said, leave a unique stamp on our natural tendencies and personalities, and consequently our decision-making. People who are Aries, Leo and Sagittarius, because of their 'hot and dry' nature, were believed to be especially prone to irritation, while 'cold and wet' Pisces were supposed to be more laid-back.[27] Yet this wasn't a deterministic system. These personality traits were never seen as fixed, and good ethics could be defined by how well a person struggled against their astrological inheritance.[28]

How was any of this useful for dealing with a problem like anger? First of all, astrology could make people aware of their own character flaws and help them begin to work on them. A Virgo, consulting a detailed zodiac chart, would never have settled on a quick diagnosis of 'irritability'.[29] Instead, she would have explored the full range of influences the different planets weighed on her at the precise time and place she was born. She would have thought about the presence of Saturn, and what that meant for the relative sadness in her life, as well as the role of Jupiter (for joy) or Venus (for love). But she would also have reckoned with the impact of Mars (anger), which 'cycles through each sign in sixty days and twenty-one hours'.[30] Or, if she had the rising sign of Scorpio, she would have reflected on how she was sometimes stubborn, with a temper that stings. In the process of all these calculations, the final product was always a form of self-questioning. 'Is my temperament really like this?' she would have asked. 'What could I do to fight these tendencies?'

Facing a patient with chronic rage, Arnaud and his colleagues would also have turned to another of medieval popular culture's personality tools: the four humours. According to this theory, our bodies each contain four different fluids – yellow bile, black bile, blood and phlegm – all of which are in a state of imbalance, and whose precise proportions lead to different dominant character traits. Nobody could study medicine in Montpellier without studying these four humours, and Arnaud gave a detailed account of their patterns in his *Treatise on Phlebotomy*. If you have an overbalance of black bile, he said, you are 'melancholic', prone to bouts of fear, anxiety and sadness.[31] An excess of blood makes you 'sanguine', or over-excitable, impulsive and passionate.[32] Too much phlegm gives you a sluggish character, defined by a passiveness and reserve. And an excess of yellow bile gives you a 'choleric' temperament, which, as well as making you a born leader, renders you stubborn and prone to fits of sharp anger.[33]

If irritability was a bodily problem – a symptom of an overbalance of humours, generated by the positions of the stars – this opened up an intriguing possibility. Did this mean anger could have a cure, in the same way parasols could prevent sunburn or goose feathers could keep you warm in a blizzard?

Between all his surgical appointments, somewhere on the same Montpellier streets I wandered in pain on those nights of my broken molar, Arnaud experimented with developing a set of drugs that promised to do just that. In his *Liber de vinis* he described a kind of drink that could cure acute fits of anger outright. This involved taking the roots of oxtongue (*Picris*), cleaning them and then soaking them in wine overnight. Drink enough of this wine, Arnaud promised, and you would expel any excess choleric fluid in your urine. To promote his case, he described a woman in Paris who had raved with fury to the point that she had to be tied up. And the cure for her anger was a single glass of this oxtongue wine.[34]

Arnaud put even greater faith in a drug called Theriac. Regarded as a universal antidote against all poisons, Theriac was as close as the Middle Ages got to a major pharma operation. It was cited as a cure for dozens of ailments, and some even believed it to be a solution to cancer, the problem for which medieval surgeons believed there was no cure or treatment 'beyond the sharp edge of a razor'.³⁵ Over the course of the 1200s Theriac came to be used as a general tranquilliser, with advocates claiming that it could calm the body and soothe any excess anger or irritability in the process.

Theriac had been known about since antiquity. Galen (d.216 CE), the grandfather of medicine, had listed its properties and effects in texts read by every medieval medical student. Theriac's precise composition and dosage, however, were never properly isolated and documented until the circle around Arnaud in Montpellier published the definitive works in the 1200s, the *Tractatus de Tyriaca* and the *Epistola de dosibus tyriacalibus*. The drug's main ingredient, as the physician Bernard de Gordon explained, was viper's flesh, and this needed to be selected and prepared, blended with forty-nine other ingredients, and then sweetened with honey and distilled lilies. When it was ready, the solution needed to be taken at a minimum dosage of 0.92ml (to put Bernard's measurements in modern terms), extending up to a maximum of 3.7ml, depending on the condition.³⁶

How did this drug work? And how could it solve a problem like anger? According to Arnaud and his colleagues, Theriac worked by strengthening the heart and maintaining the overall balance of the body's humours. This included maintaining levels of choleric, thereby keeping to a manageable level within the bloodstream the humour that drove anger and irritability. Avicenna (d.1037), the Arabic philosopher and physician, believed in these balancing properties so much that he claimed doses of Theriac should be taken by people who were perfectly healthy, as a type of preventative tonic to maintain heart health and a balance of mood. While Arnaud himself disagreed with the idea of handing out Theriac to everyone, he accepted this basic idea about its value for irritability. When taken with decoctions of bitter herbs or sage, he said in his book of antidotes, the drug could 'bring strength' and 'expel debilitating passions'.[37] It could also 'rectify the malice' of people whose minds had grown cold and morose with resentment.[38]

These new measurements and clarifications opened the way for a big business venture. Similar to drugs like Prozac or Valium in the twentieth century, the leading doctors of the late 1200s began pushing Theriac as a kind of wonder drug. On this count, Arnaud was at least a little guilty. His treatise listed dozens of problems that he claimed the drug could help fix, from haemorrhoids to stomach pains, spells of lethargy and tinnitus. He also maintained that it could help fight different cancers, specifying tumours in the nose – which he said could be eased by rubbing Theriac around the nostrils – and other cancerous growths visible to the eye, which he advised should be treated by doses of the drug diluted with 'lots of wine'.[39]

It probably comes as no surprise that Theriac didn't really cure cancer.[40] But it turns out it couldn't really treat anger, either. William of Brescia, a doctor working in Montpellier in the decades after Arnaud had left, made revisions to the analysis of the drug, and streamlined the advertised list of the effects it offered. Although he never criticised Arnaud by name, William claimed his predecessors had been too scattershot. While he agreed the drug could work by fortifying the heart, and that it operated by attaching itself to the body's natural heat, he judged that this likely didn't give the drug any general calming qualities. Anger wasn't really a poison, after all. So it was a stretch to think that it could be neutralised by an antivenom.

Would these criticisms have bothered Arnaud? Did he even want a simple cure for anger, anyway? At the height of his scandal, after he was condemned from afar by medical colleagues in Paris, Arnaud was forced to leave Montpellier and chose to exile himself on the island of Sicily. Although there are worse places to end up, it must have frustrated him to be away from his laboratory and his students. After a lifetime of mild evenings in the breezy French Riviera, the hot climate would have itched at him too, especially as Arnaud himself believed excessive heat could bring out the worst choleric irritability in all of us.[41]

Still, Arnaud never bothered reaching for a bottle of Theriac while he was in exile. Instead of medicalising his anger problems, in the end he cultivated psychological fortitude instead. Fury pulls the mind away from reason (*ratio*), Arnaud reflected, and losing yourself in anger is like letting a puppeteer take control of your brain as well as your limbs. So the best defence, he decided, is to fortify the heart. It's to fill yourself up with compassion, and to make sure that heart keeps pumping with concern and love for the people and things you come across. Because even in the most justified revenge, anger only ever ends up 'stripping your heart bare.'[42]

My own irritability, in those Montpellier months, was always beyond my control. Or this is what I liked to believe. If only there was no tooth pain, I used to say, I would never have lost my patience. I'm tempted to think the same now, as I try to recover from my outburst in our staff meeting in Tyumen. I blame my irritation on the fumes coming through the window, the heat of the room, the barrage of grating sounds. In normal circumstances I would never snap at a colleague. But anger is never just a product of forces outside our control, and there never was a wonder drug that could switch it off whenever we needed it to. Anger is always a response to the configuration of our hearts. While the zodiac or the humours might be used today as get-out-of-jail cards to explain our anger management deficiencies, in the Middle Ages these were tools to help us self-examine and confess. Tools for examining these strange instruments inside our chests; these hearts that beat and drive us to do extraordinary things.

ANGER

Judith's Rage (Images Ranked)

Do we always need to cure anger? *Ira* is unique among the Deadly Sins, because it's a passion we often justify as 100 per cent necessary. For medieval writers, this type of forgivable *ira* was thought of as righteous anger: the rage that 'through zeal, finds good';[43] or the short and sharp fury that emerges only when we need to 'correct injustice' and then evaporates.[44] Identifying its limits can be difficult, though. Today, the boundaries of acceptable anger are policed by legal precedent or company codes of conduct. There are leaflets in doctors' waiting rooms and websites that offer ten-week online courses, designed to help us recognise when rage is toxic and when it's proportional. But what about in the Middle Ages? How did people then judge where the 'red line' between acceptable and unacceptable anger lay?

For solving a question like this, there aren't many better places to go than the Warburg Institute. Behind its modest Art Deco exterior, the Warburg is a cavern, a palace, a labyrinth. Set up in the 1930s to house the collection of the refugee German art historian Aby Warburg, it sits at the edge of a London square, surrounded by plane trees. Across four floors, labelled 'Image', 'Word', 'Orientation' and 'Action', the Warburg houses a rare collection of books, maps, plans, charts and scrolls. The corridors echo with conversations in German and Italian, although there's always an electric silence among the stacks. Everyone is absorbed in the volumes of Latin poetry, ancient tomes of magic and medicine, and leatherbound works of mysticism and geometry.

One of the unique treasures of the Warburg is its photographic collection. Located upstairs, and lined with grey filing cabinets, no computer search can substitute for an afternoon in this room.⁴⁵ Inside are photographs of nearly half a million artworks, each the result of a private research trip taken some time over the past decades, and the space is watched over by a team of experts: the keepers of this great eccentric maze, who seem to know the contents of every filing cabinet, every cardboard folder, every creaking wooden drawer. One afternoon after I returned from Montpellier – when my tooth had received root canal treatment and I could concentrate on medieval texts without pharmaceutical intervention – this is precisely where I came.

I began by opening a filing cabinet labelled 'Old Testament: Judith'. It seemed like a natural place to start, as Judith was a popular symbol of righteous anger in the Middle Ages. According to the Bible legend, Judith was a widow who lived in the city of Bethulia when it was besieged by the forces of Nebuchadnezzar, the Babylonian king. Holofernes, the invading general, tortured her community with a series of brutal tactics. First he stationed soldiers from his 170,000-strong army all along the town's perimeter, and then he cut off the city's water supply and barred any chance of escape. He was hoping the city's children would begin dying of thirst, and that Bethulia would have no choice but to surrender.⁴⁶

Judith, like the rest of her community, was furious. But instead of panicking she directed her rage into a careful plan. She began by changing her clothes, taking off her mourning outfit of sackcloth and ashes and covering herself in perfumes and jewels, and tying up her hair with a ribbon. Next she found her way into the enemy camp and talked herself into Holofernes's tent. Here, apparently, her 'dazzling' outfit helped. Inside, she convinced him that she had changed sides and was ready to betray her city. She strung him along with 'little promises until she could find the right moment'. By Judith's third visit Holofernes was infatuated, and he drank nearly his own weight in wine. And then, after the tyrant had passed out, Judith took out a sword and cut off his head.[47]

The visual life of this legend has been dazzling. For Renaissance artists it was a parable of righteous rage and the subject of several masterpieces. Donatello's austere bronze sculpture, which shows Judith in a simmering fury, is an exceptional example. Although her eyes are steady as her sword springs on a lateral behind her head, Judith's slightly pouting lower lip reveals the pulsing anger underneath. Even more famous is the painting by Caravaggio (*c.*1600), now kept in the Palazzo Barberini in Rome, which shows Judith more on the 'disgusted' end of the rage spectrum. Between all the drama of the flowing red drapes and Holofernes' gaping head (apparently the artist's own gruesome self-portrait), Judith is pulling the face you might make while reading an email about your company restructuring, or when a family of nine jumps in front of you in a festival toilet queue.

But when medieval artists made images of Judith, they often showed her anger as something more enigmatic. As I discovered in that filing cabinet in the Warburg, their choices mapped the full range of righteous anger as it existed in the premodern imagination.

First of all, every Christian commentator agreed on one thing. Judith's anger was *right*. Holofernes was an evil tyrant who had been trying to kill children, and her bloody revenge was therefore not only justified, it was divinely sanctioned. That's not to say that this was a society that usually sanctioned murder. Far from it, murder was – in the words of the theologian Peter Damian – 'the death of souls', something that would always lead its perpetrator to 'eternal damnation'.[48] But Holofernes' siege was an act of war, and in the absence of any war-crimes tribunal Judith's single targeted strike wasn't really seen as 'murder'. It was instead – as the resulting liberation of Bethulia and retreat of Nebuchadnezzar's army seemed to prove – an efficient means of conflict resolution.

But not everybody agreed that Judith should have accompanied her swipe of the blade with any anger. While some medieval artists showed her in a wild fury, others preferred to show her holding back and keeping her rage in check. Consequently, it is possible to arrange the medieval images of Judith's revenge along a spectrum. Some of them in the Warburg's photo archive show her killing Holofernes in full fury, while others show her more relaxed, more in control of her emotions. On the day of my visit I tipped the photos out of the folder and ranked them, from most to least furious, across the surface of the large wooden table.

Judith number six is the most frenzied example in the collection. Captured in a thirteenth-century illuminated French Bible, she's raking back her sword with almost drunken abandon. Her brows are knitted so tightly you can almost see them trembling. Like the Judith who appeared in an Old English poem, recorded around the year 1000, the force of her anger has pushed her into a trance. 'Avenge me, Almighty Lord,' Judith called out to God in the lines of that poem. 'Give me anger in my heart, heat in my mind.' Then she 'grabbed the heathen man hard by his hair' and plunged the sword into his throat.[49]

Although not everyone would agree with my ranking, at number five I put an image from a popular theological guide, produced in Belgium in the late 1300s. This Judith has two scorching red cheeks, the symptom of *ira* most often listed in medieval medical texts. And while her gaze seems to be fixed elsewhere, that slight crinkle between her eyes hints at a deeper-lying exasperation. She also scores extra points for the splotches of blood dripping from her blade, and for the frantic energy in her limbs as she stretches out in her pleated green dress.

ANGER

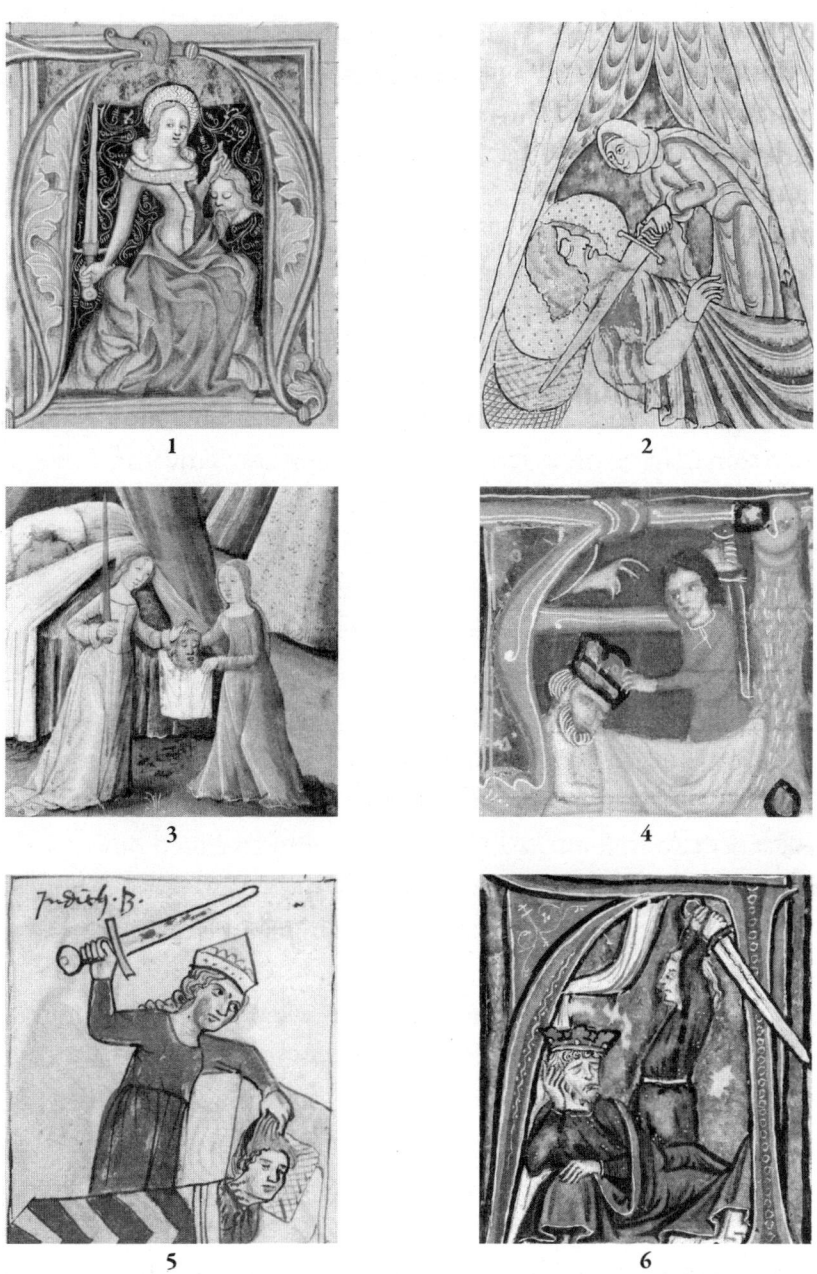

Judith's outburst, as imagined by six different medieval artists. Here they are ranked from the most serene (top left) to the most ferocious (bottom right).

Judith number four is a masterclass in tight-lipped control, although her anger is barely contained. Despite her stony face and her averted gaze, she's drawing her sword in a drastic vertical backswing. All the heat in this image is concentrated in her smouldering expression. Her red lips pop out from the page of this Bolognese Bible, channelling the rage into a single pout. Foreshadowing another artist who fixated on the hero's lips – Lucas Cranach the Elder, whose painting of this scene includes the most sarcastic thin smile in the history of Western art – this medieval artist plays with the same motif that would define Judith's image until at least the time of Gustav Klimt.[50]

The next three images showcase the more composed end of the medieval rage spectrum. Judith number three comes from a fifteenth-century book of hours now kept in Saint Petersburg in Russia. It's saturated with gore, with dark waves of blood pooling across the bedsheets and the floor. But while her accomplice looks like she's about to be sick into that laundered white sack she's holding out to collect the head, Judith herself is stern and calm. It's as though she's straining to perform this decapitation without the least ounce of excess emotion.

Now things move in a more upbeat direction. Judith number two is one of the most puzzling images in the Warburg's filing cabinet. Taken from an early twelfth-century Bible, it can only have been illustrated by somebody lucky enough to have never seen violence in real life. Holding her sword in an interlocking golfing grip, this Judith seems more relaxed than the average golfer. She's not only serene, she's smiling a distracted smile. If *ira* really was a seductive drug in medieval culture, this is somebody experiencing a blissful overdose.[51]

Even so, there's no competition for the number one spot. A tiny typed note on the back of the image card for Judith number one in the Warburg's Photographic Collection describes this one as 'somewhat indecorous'. It's true, she's posing here *after* she's cut off Holofernes's head, rather than during the actual process of decapitating him. Everything else about her, though – the playful sway of her back, the unrumpled sheen of her blue dress, the unapologetic smirk on her face – oozes composure. Decapitation, it seems, just wasn't that much of a big deal. In the time it took to withdraw a sword from the bloodied stump of the neck, she's managed to turn from vengeful rage to bashful photoshoot.

If she's anything, Judith number one is a symbol of the school of medieval thinkers who believed anger should be felt but never shown. 'Every time we restrain the turbulent emotions', as Adalbert of Metz wrote in a twelfth-century treatise, we're improving ourselves. We're fixing 'a torn mind', and struggling 'to return it to the likeness' of our better selves.[52] Even if somebody spits in our face, as one writer said, it's our challenge as good humans to find a way to make light of it.[53] According to Adalbert, the same should apply to Judith, or to the Judiths among us. He felt that we should keep our emotions in check, even when we're confronting a genocidal tyrant who has been trying to starve our community's children.

This was the Stoic school of medieval anger. And it was defined, for generations of medieval readers, by the writer Boethius (d.524) and his bestselling *Consolation of Philosophy*. Boethius was influenced by ancient writers like Seneca and Epictetus, who gave him comfort while he was in a prison cell in Pavia awaiting his execution for spurious corruption charges. The goal of life, Boethius said, was to accept whatever conditions we face. We should never let the 'fury of the oceans' nor the 'smoke and fire' of volcanoes upset us, he said. Because when we rage, we will always 'rage in ignorance'.[54]

It was an appealing message, right throughout the Middle Ages.

Although this was a society that celebrated warriors and crusaders, the shelves of the Warburg's second floor are stuffed with medieval tales featuring precisely Boethius's kind of hero. Knights, like Guigemar in the *Lais of Marie de France*, who remained patient through harrowing tortures. And saints, like Lawrence of Rome, able to smile while being burned to death on a grill.[55]

But aren't we only human? Anybody who claims they can be insulted and feel 'no mental disturbance', as the writer Guido da Pisa put it, 'is either God or a stone'.[56] Opposing the Stoic school were the 'warriors': the writers who were happy to embrace the power of anger, even when it bordered on violence. For some, this was simply because repressing your anger can do more damage than good. If you follow your fury you can at least get an apology or an explanation, the theologian John Climacus said. But if you bite your tongue, you'll always get swallowed by your own 'black gall'.[57]

Others took this idea even further, arguing that anger was not just a necessary evil but the framework for a happy life itself. According to the theologian Lactantius, our brains would collapse into misery without it. Our capacity to experience any emotional high, like joy or relief, always depends on our ability to deal with their counterforces, misery and anger, he said. If we don't exercise our capacity to rage we have no hope for any kind of meaningful existence.[58]

Judith, with her flashing sword, more naturally belonged to the 'warrior' school. When the poet Christine de Pizan (d.1430) told her story, she made it part of a longer tradition of powerful and assertive women throughout history. Judith's rage, Christine implied, was similar to the anger of the Amazons, the mythical warriors mentioned in Homer's *Iliad*. After their community was invaded and torched by the Greeks, two of these women – Menalippe and Hippolyta – took revenge. 'Boiling with the most terrible rage and fury', they attacked Hercules and Theseus, the Greeks' two greatest heroes, knocking them over along with their horses. As Christine saw it, this meant that the Amazons' 'anger bore fruit'. And this was a sign that, so long as the cause was a good one, women should never be afraid to exercise their fury even to the point of violence. 'How,' she said, 'can one praise these women highly enough?'[59]

Between the Stoics and the warriors, how to judge whether anger is ever 'right'? How to know which Judith we should be, when we're sitting in a staff meeting and get the feeling we really need to intervene?

The trick is not to ask 'should I be angry or not?' It's to ask 'which kind of anger do I feel?' Because there was not one anger, according to medieval theologians, but three. And these three ran a spectrum from dangerous frenzy to enlightening rage, from harmful pathology to productive social force.

Anger is *triplex*, according to the commentary on the Song of Songs by the Cistercian monk Thomas of Perseigne (d.*c.*1190). This is a work worth listening to because, although it's now obscure, it was popular enough in the twelfth century that seventy-eight manuscript copies survive.[60] The first – and lowest – type is 'Defective Anger', which is really an exercise in insecurity. This involves snapping in fury at the tiniest of slights, which Thomas says is like blowing on a boiling pot in the hope of extinguishing the steam.

More positive, although equally unproductive, is what Thomas called 'Affective Anger'. Like envy, this is provoked by an injustice, although it ends up consuming you more than it does the target. 'Burning' and 'melting' in rage, with this anger you 'grieve over' a set of problems that you've failed to address. And then, stuck in an enormous sulk, you become like a handful of 'flour, pan-fried in oil': all cooked up, but appetising to nobody.[61]

But after this there's anger's sweet spot. A furious state of bliss that consumes, culminates and redirects all of those deepest frustrations. 'Effective Anger' is when you channel all your pain and grievance into some kind of positive action. Whipping up 'a red heat', this is an anger that works on behalf of others, 'rebuking the restless, comforting the faint-hearted and supporting the weak'. Unlike the 'lower' forms of anger, where your fury prevents you from seeing a situation properly, 'Effective Anger' is like being given the gift of sight all over again. It's a telescopic lens, bringing the truth of a problem into the sharpest focus. And instead of keeping you fumbling around in smoky darkness, it sends up a burning sun to light the path ahead.

So, the challenge for medieval thinkers – as much as it is for us today – was to work out how to tell these three modes apart in the heat of the moment. In the case of Judith, this process would seem relatively easy. Her community had lost their water supply and children were losing their lives, and so she had every right to seize the situation, to embrace her 'Effective Anger' in whatever way she felt most useful. Maybe we can put ourselves in her shoes, or maybe we can't. The point is that she saw her situation clearly, and she saw that it was unsustainable. And, understanding this, she saw what needed to be done.

But what about here and now, in this staff meeting? How can I know if I'm experiencing 'defective' or 'effective' anger? How can I tell if my fury is 'righteous' or not? The trick, if we trust writers like Thomas of Perseigne, is to question the clarity of my vision. I have to ask whether my outburst of anger is coming from seeing the situation in the round and grasping what needs to be done, or whether it's coming from frustration at a situation I don't really understand. Maybe, in this case, I'm making a mistake. Maybe I've become like a boiling pot, here in Siberia, and snapping now is as futile as blowing at a cloud of steam.

What I need is to reduce the temperature at the source, and to get to grips with the deeper strategies of anger management that can help prevent rage from hijacking my brain.

The Burning Man

What does good anger management actually look like?

Every murderer returns to the scene of the crime. But so does every historian. We lurk like ghosts around the sites of famous assassinations, crawling across Dealey Plaza (JFK) or the Theatre of Pompey (Julius Caesar) hoping to inject some traces of an event into our bloodstreams. Approaching Canterbury Cathedral late one afternoon, I found myself wanting to do the same. Like millions of medieval pilgrims, I was visiting this building, with its honey-coloured buttresses and its echoing crypt, to make sense of one of the worst cases of political violence in English history. And in the process I was trying to uncover the mechanics of one of the great medieval experiments in anger management.

I was investigating a twelfth-century murder. Not just any murder, but a murder with the same celebrity status as the JFK assassination. The King of England ordered the killing of his former best friend, the Archbishop of Canterbury. While this sent shockwaves right across Europe, in England it carved a new path for the country's future. At the time, in the later 1100s, England was in the process of establishing the common law and the bureaucratic system on which the modern nation state was built.[62] By accelerating these changes, the murder created the DNA of English politics: Magna Carta (the charter of 1215 that imposed the first popular checks on royal power); the Reformation (the country's cutting of ties in the 1530s with the Catholic Church, and in the process with one type of European union);

and even Brexit (the exit from another type of European Union, in 2016), all in one. Because this was an event when an English ruler said a violent 'no' to European influence, in an overstep that set the state on course for parliament and democracy.

The guilty party in the murder was Henry II (r.1154–1189), the charismatic king with flame-red hair who was famous for his sharp mind and raging temper. The victim was Thomas Becket (b.*c*.1120), the archbishop who had once been Henry's closest friend. The two fell out in 1163, when Thomas made a radical political U-turn. Insisting that his own power came directly from the pope in Rome, Thomas said he didn't need to obey the king any more. Then he announced that two of Henry's bishops were excommunicated (an act somewhere between a filibuster and a magic spell). We don't know for sure who drove the events that happened next. Did the king order revenge directly or not? All we know is that Henry blazed with fury, and that a few days later four knights travelled down to Canterbury, ambushed Thomas in the cathedral and smashed his brains out all over the cold stone floor.[63]

Together Henry and Thomas went on a journey, from level-headed friendship to furious murder. Their escalating rage, as I discovered in Canterbury, fits the pattern of *ira* as a Deadly Sin. That is, the story of Henry and Thomas can be mapped onto the seven subspecies of anger – *furor, temeritas, luctus, indignatio, contumelia, blasphemia* and *clamor* – as listed by the twelfth-century theologian Hugh of Saint Victor.

Anger can be at its worst when we're frustrated by a problem of our own making. And what Henry suffered from, first of all, was *furor*, an 'unbridled rage against adversities' that 'we've conceived within our own minds'.[64] These mechanics were hard-wired into the way Henry approached his government from the very start. He inherited the English throne after two decades of civil war, and immediately set about building the

ANGER

country's biggest empire until the 1700s, conquering a region that stretched from Ireland to the Pyrenees. Managing this kind of territory, in practice, was difficult, so Henry created a brand new network of laws and codes, shaping England one reform at a time into a tightly controlled bureaucratic regime.[65]

Unfortunately, though, all this bureaucracy infuriated Henry on a daily basis. One time, while he was out walking, he learned that a young man was exploiting his new laws to push his father off his land.[66] Henry was outraged, and started reversing these cases ad hoc as he came across them. He could now barely sit through a legal procedure without threatening people. Why, if he was king, should he have to listen to the judgements of lawyers? As he warned one of his bishops, while the man was making a long speech appealing to the laws of the land, no codes and protocols should be able to stop the king 'pushing' anybody from their position.[67]

By temperament, King Henry suffered from anger's second subspecies: *temeritas*, the tendency to experience 'undisciplined outbursts' that abandon 'all rationality'. He had regular angry episodes, one of his closest aides said, and these left a panicked imprint on everyone around him. 'The anger of the king is like a roaring lion,' wrote the bishop Roger of Pontigny, and he often sent his courtiers scattering in 'horror and dread'.[68] Even worse was the evening the king was so infuriated by a piece of bad news that he fell to the ground and began rolling in agony. He was so furious, apparently, that he took off his clothes and shoved handfuls of straw into his mouth.[69]

Anger can also be a symptom of impotence. And this was the type of rage initially experienced by the murder victim, Thomas Becket. Two things defined Thomas's life: a vertical rise to the highest levels of power; and a fear that he would never be taken seriously, no matter how high he climbed. He was the son of a trader in the city of London and grew up in a family that was part of an emerging middle class: not rich themselves, but fascinated by the rich. Through a connection with a friend who worked in deliveries, Thomas got a job in the household of Theobald, the Archbishop of Canterbury. While this was quite a leap, Thomas's skill set seemed to fit. Bankrolled by his father's profits, he had been part of the world's first-ever generation of university students at Paris. Even though there's no evidence he ever graduated, this meant he could at least read and write in basic Latin.

It seems Thomas's rise 'from the dust' irritated his lungs.[70] The historian R. I. Moore has written about the frustrations of this new generation of socially mobile bureaucrats: young people, with precarious positions in powerful households, who had to compete to impress their bosses.[71] This culture was a breeding ground for *luctus*, Hugh's third subspecies of anger: 'the exasperated mind' that 'weeps' in impotence against its 'superiors'; or, the anger of somebody who feels powerless and shut out in their workplace. As hard as he tried, Thomas could never quite fit in with his new boss's inner circle. All the people who worked in the same office – people like John of Salisbury, who wrote fat works of Latin literature, and Gilbert Foliot, who conducted impressive debates with the pope in Rome – seemed so assured, so competent. It was as if they were born into this life (and, by virtue of their higher-class families, in a sense they were). How could Thomas ever compete?

But against the odds it was the rough-around-the-edges Thomas, rather than John or Gilbert, who became 'the king's chosen one, plucked out of thousands'.[72] Henry first met Thomas while he was conducting business with Theobald, and he was impressed by the young man's humour and charm. Soon the two became inseparable, spending days together drinking and hunting, and all Thomas's impotent workplace anger must have burned away to nothing. Henry loved his new friend so much he even invented a political position for him: 'chancellor', the overseer of half of the royal government. When Theobald died in 1161, Henry took an even more daring step. Although Thomas tried to refuse, Henry insisted on making him Archbishop of Canterbury, the top-ranked position in the English Church. The king 'blazed up in favour of his desire', and sent representatives straight to Montpellier, where the pope was away on business, to make the arrangement official.[73]

The fun didn't last long. Soon, both parties slipped into the fourth subspecies of anger: *indignatio*, 'a wild and malicious contempt for an inferior'. First, and to everyone's surprise, Thomas transformed himself into a puritan. Unknown to Henry he began taking private lessons in theology, and quoted the Bible in every conversation. At this time he also started wearing a hair shirt, a piece of torture clothing (popular among monks) that was hidden beneath the robes to keep the skin in constant discomfort. Worst of all, Thomas began blocking the king's policies and decisions. He said it was his own exclusive right, as archbishop, to judge priests indicted for crimes (even murders). Insisting that he represented the 'higher' authority of Rome, he also kept telling Henry he had to defer to him as the pope's representative in England.

Hugh's fifth type of anger is *contumelia*: the 'bitter grief' we feel when we're at the mercy of a 'power' we find 'disgraceful'. And this is where both these minds turned next, as Henry made a series of veiled threats and Thomas fled to France in the autumn of 1164. At a cloister in Pontigny, Thomas and a band of friends set up camp, styling themselves the *eruditi*, or 'learned ones'. Although they spent years writing letters to the pope and the King of France, seeking diplomatic solutions, Henry refused to compromise.[74] Back home, the jealous Gilbert Foliot (now Bishop of London) was busy proving he could perform the archbishop's roles in his absence. And the king, still outraged by Thomas's 'betrayal', slid into the sixth of Hugh's anger subspecies: *blasphemia*, or 'maliciously striking out at someone or something holy'.

When I arrived in Canterbury, on that autumn afternoon, I knew all too well how this conflict ended.[75] I knew how, shortly after Thomas negotiated a brief return to England in 1170, the king snapped. According to William Fitzstephen, who was well-connected enough at court to know the inside story, Henry called his barons together and gave them an exhaustive list of Thomas's crimes. He'd mistreated his bishops, he said. He'd cheated Henry's son and 'disturbed the whole realm' by making threats. Now, using the pope, Thomas was squeezing the king and all his barons, so that soon none of them would have any power left. What should he do in response? Although he was already at boiling point, Henry's rage was fed by two sycophantic barons. 'The only way to deal with such a man is to hang him on a gibbet,' one said. Even popes had been killed in the past for similar 'insolence', said the other. So Henry's anger hardened, and the assassination was set in motion.[76]

From my reading, I was able to picture so many of the details from this deadly event. I knew the names of the four men who carried out the killing itself: Reginald Fitzurse, Hugh de Morville, William de Tracy and Richard le Breton, and had seen pictures of their shields. I felt like I had smelled the saltwater as the king's supporters sank one of Thomas's ships, and heard the cries as they mutilated one of his packhorses. Still, until that day I had never stood on the spot of the murder itself. I had never soaked up the cold atmosphere where political rage once burst over the boundary into state violence.

Walking under the archway into the grounds of the cathedral, I stepped across waxy mounds of dark red leaves. A light rain was making the walls ripple in the afternoon light. Inside I wove through the stacks of Gothic columns, which seemed to flow down from the high ceiling like stone waterfalls, and came to a cold passageway, just beside a staircase up to the altar. This is where, on that December evening, Reginald, Hugh, William and Richard ambushed Thomas and bludgeoned him to death. Hanging above the spot is a sculpture, a jagged iron cross with two swords jutting from either lateral. The art of this memorial is striking, like the logo of a heavy-metal band. Looking at it, though, it was hard to get a sense of the frustrations, the clawing shrieks, the slow-burning rages of the slashes that took place underneath.

Thomas – although impotent, frustrated and defeated – was supposed to have been 'peaceful' and 'accepting' when he took his final breaths, standing on these polished flagstones.[77] But how? And how, in those difficult years leading up to the assassination, did he stop himself from being consumed by the rage of *contumelia* (the painful anger, which many of us have, when somebody we don't respect takes charge of our lives)?

I came to Canterbury armed with an extra clue. Weeks before, in the library of Trinity College Cambridge, I'd looked at a manuscript that was once owned by Herbert of Bosham, a friend of Thomas who had lived with him throughout his exile. It's a copy of the Psalms, complete with the commentary Herbert selected, edited and arranged himself. On the folios of this manuscript I was excited to find an image that never appears in Google searches, or even in the filing cabinets of the Warburg Photographic Collection. A small cartoon that captures the exiles' anger management philosophy in a series of pen strokes.

The drawing is of a naked man on fire. He has an apologetic face, red hair in a central parting and two dozen tiny tongues of orange flame coiling from his skin. Above him on the page is a tiny caption, although this doesn't explain much. 'The man is on fire,' it says. 'God is in the man.' But everything about the

The burning man, from Herbert of Bosham's Commentary on the Psalms.

cartoon's position in the manuscript makes it clear that this was meant to be a clue about what to do with our anger. Because curving around the picture is some commentary on a passage from the Psalms that deals with the same problem Thomas and his friends were facing: an angry king who had been persecuting the 'followers' of the Lord. And the commentary advises them that, like the burning man, they needed to find a way to hold their righteous anger together with a tranquil mind.

How did this work? Next to the cartoon is a story about Moses: a parable not only about the exhilaration of anger, but also about how to contain it. Moses, in this story, represents the worst frenzy of rage imaginable. He had been at the top of Mount Sinai talking to God, according to the Book of Exodus, but was away for so long that his fellow Israelites grew restless. Drifting, they turned to worship a golden calf instead. When Moses returned and saw this betrayal he flew into a violent rage. First he hurled the stone tablets with all of God's laws on them to the ground, splitting them in two. As if this wasn't enough, he plunged their golden calf into a fire and melted it down to liquid gold. Then he did something unthinkable. He poured the molten metal into jugs, and forced everyone who had worshipped the calf to drink it all down, scorching their throats and destroying their stomachs.

Moses may have been a prophet, but this didn't mean Thomas Becket and his friends were supposed to copy his behaviour. Among Hugh's seven types of anger, Moses's was the last: *clamor*, or the snap triggered by an outrage or crime. But as Herbert explained in his commentary, this *clamor* should never result in actual violence. 'The wrath of God' is no longer a physical force, Herbert said, it's 'a movement that takes place in a holy soul'. Or, to put it another way, it's a type of anger that expresses itself not through drawing blood but through constructive action. Anybody irritated enough to want to copy Moses – forcing molten liquid down somebody's throat – should take a break. They should wait patiently, and trust that the arc of justice will always favour those who are on the right side of history. 'Hold on now', the commentary said. Although your enemies 'do not yet burn', you can be sure that the laws of justice mean they will come to 'burn in the future'.[78]

So, for Thomas and his friends, this was the best way to deal with anger. Not to deny it, but to put it to work, until 'out of bitterness, sweetness' would be 'born'.[79] Like the burning man on that manuscript page, they wanted to experience two things at once. They wanted to be calm and composed, but they still wanted to feel every lick of their anger's fire. Holding both together was the secret. Because, without fury they might lose sight of the things that matter, the wrongs that need to be put right over the long term, and yet without composure they might never find any sort of lasting solution.

What about the king? Did he have any anger management techniques at all? Having left the cathedral, I took a bus to the University of Kent where, in the neat but airless aisles of the library, I hunted for a copy of a text that's hard to come across anywhere else. It's a work that has never been translated, and which is rarely mentioned in studies of Henry II, but which I had discovered by following a trail in a set of footnotes. It's an interview, recorded sometime after the murder, between the Abbot of Bonneville and King Henry himself. And in it, apparently, Henry reflects on the killing, the nature of his own emotions and his own guilt for the crime. Unlikely as it may sound that the king would ever agree to sit down for an interview like this, it was apparently based on a genuine discussion. Because the lines of dialogue attributed to Henry are simply too harsh to have been invented by any writer.[80]

Although I had known about the existence of this text for quite a while, it wasn't until I was in those Canterbury library stacks that I got my hands on it. I couldn't believe how candid it was. At first, the king makes every effort to deny his responsibility. Just like Herbert's commentary on the Psalms, he compares himself to Moses, who he said had never 'allowed evildoers to live'. Henry also defends his rage on the basis of human nature. 'Anger is a natural value,' he says, pointing to the way animals strike out at each other. 'Since I am a son of anger by nature, why shouldn't I be allowed to get angry?'[81]

But this was an interview, not a monologue. Combative in spirit, the abbot continues to poke holes in Henry's defences. Anger doesn't achieve much, he says, and he reminds the king that it's usually better to wait for justice than to strike out ourselves. Loving a neighbour is better than hating him, he explains. And knocking down the 'nature' argument, the abbot tells Henry that humans shouldn't be held to the same standards as animals. At first, none of these arguments seem to be getting through. Although Henry is on the ropes, being held to account by an interviewer who won't pull any punches, he keeps defending violent anger as a useful tool of political power. Magna Carta, at this point in the interview, seems a long way off.

As the conversation progresses, though, the abbot finds a more promising path. Anger itself isn't necessarily the problem, he says, and he agrees with Henry that it can be part of a healthy life. But the king needs at least to accept that his anger had gone in the wrong direction. What he needs to practise is 'perfect hatred': a rage that is neither self-absorbed nor personal, but which produces genuine change in the world. Luckily, the abbot says, this is actually simple to achieve. All Henry has to do is redirect his anger towards a better target. He has to 'hate the sin of the person, and not the person himself'.

As I headed for Canterbury train station, walking past rowing boats and stone houses with puffing chimney stacks, I thought about King Henry's predicament. Anger is complicated, not least because injustices often overlap. Thomas *did* provoke him, and he had a reasonable case to see the challenge from the church as an existential threat to his royal power. Unlike Judith attacking Holofernes, though, Henry lashed out at somebody who could still have offered him a dialogue. What made him snap? Was he, really, raging against the limitations of his own power? Was he an addict, suffering from the habit of *rixa*, the restless craving for new outrages to fight? Or was he a perfectionist who just couldn't cope with any challenge to his plans? Whatever made him lose his temper, it was obvious from the interview that behind his trigger-happy rage was an emptiness. As the theologian John of Fonte (d.1225) said, anyone easily 'angered by what they do' is usually a lost soul, someone who 'longs for something but never follows it'.[82] These people rage, but ultimately the ones they rage against are themselves.

For most of us, day to day, anger isn't a matter of life and death. As long as it doesn't last too long, and as long as it isn't accompanied by physical violence or personal insults, an angry snap in a staff meeting is usually forgiven. And yet it can also be a sign that there's something under the hood – a problem in our hearts that we haven't confronted – that we need to stop and take a look at. Anger, like all of the Deadly Sins, is a symptom of our love. It pulses through us when we care about something, when we love a thing enough to want to protect it or avenge it or redeem it. But it's an unfiltered passion; a one-sided love that refuses to refine itself through flexibility or dialogue. So, the problem is that it ends up drowning out our powers of judgement. It speeds up our responses, giving us no time to engage with the nuance along the way.

As I'm walking off to my shared office, my colleague the chemistry professor catches up with me in the corridor and touches me on the shoulder. 'Sorry if I upset you,' he says, and he starts to explain his point of view. It all sounds fairly reasonable: formality breeds respect, and respect breeds discipline. I can see, though, that he still hasn't grasped my point; that he still can't see why I might not like the idea of making my students call me 'professor'. Yet, in that staff meeting, wasn't I just the same as him? I didn't pause to think about why *his* idea of enforced politeness might be a good one, either. The difference between us is that, whereas he is now trying to talk through his confusion, I chose to snap my way through mine. Snapping rarely works; but then neither does sitting on our hands. In fact, if there's anything I learned from studying the murder of Thomas Becket, or from following the medics of Montpellier, or mapping Judith's spectrum of rage, it's that there's never a quick fix for the problems that lead us to our difficult anger. We can practise being a Stoic, and pretend we don't feel the fire even as it burns us. Or we can tell ourselves that our agitation is fair and proportionate, while letting it bubble over and disturb us every day. But no amount of oxtongue wine or Theriac can wash away the limitation in our brains that makes us enjoy anger in the first place. Sometimes *ira* just sends a volt through us, and it feels like there's nothing we can do to stop it.

So, the best medieval advice was never to repress our anger. Often, writers recommended feeling the fury, letting it fill our lungs and trying to make it into a fire that can warm other people around us as well. A little anger can be a beacon, as Thomas of Perseigne said: it can magnify those problems in our lives that need more love or more effort to solve. If we're a Judith, this means recognising a problem and acting fast to root it out in the most efficient way. And when there's a murderous tyrant like Holofernes around, making that anger work for our community is better than eradicating it.

But even though it's tempting to justify all our rage as vengeance against the misaligned systems we're caught in, in my case I'd be deceiving myself if I thought I could identify with Judith. Worse, I'd risk falling into the trap of *rixa*: a restless state where, thirsty for my next hit, I'd keep seeking out new and bigger outrages. To function, we need to keep our anger in proportion and perspective. Sometimes, we can be like Thomas Becket, and trust that the arc of justice will eventually bend in our favour (even if that approach didn't really work out for Thomas so much). But there will always be situations where our only option is to strike into action, to use force to make a situation right. When this happens, the key is to keep our balance. It's not necessarily a problem to be a Judith who slices off a tyrant's head. But it is a problem to be a Judith who, wiping the blood from the blade, goes out looking for a new Holofernes to kill.

CHAPTER 4

Sloth

In the middle of Gilyovskaya Roscha, one of Tyumen's forests, all the trees are blue with frost. A few minutes ago I was running along a snow-lined trail, winding through a maze of birches, when I slipped off the walkway and fell – hands outstretched – into a shallow pit of leaves. I must have hit the ground too hard while turning the corner. Or perhaps I lost my footing on an unseen patch of ice. But as I struggle to stand up, my hands thick with a mulch that's staining my gloves, I feel a sensation that seems new. After weeks of feeling numb and staring out the window at nothing, it's great to experience something for a change, even if that something is a sprained ankle.

I came to the forest today to escape *acedia*, a concept that no longer exists and yet a condition that's more alive than ever. Coined by the Greek-speaking monks in the Egyptian desert nearly two thousand years ago, *acedia* originally meant a 'lack of care'. Its significance expanded over the Middle Ages, acquiring as many as thirteen separate definitions, although with modernity this once-united set of ideas got broken apart. Our label that remains for the fourth deadly sin – 'Sloth' – is a placeholder, a term that suited a streamlined intellectual world where isolated desert monks no longer mattered.[1] So, instead of the complex *acedia* of the Middle Ages, our society has inherited a word that for most people means being unwilling to get out of bed in the morning.

When we look inside any medieval treatise on the Deadly Sins, *acedia*'s original meaning becomes clear. This sin is far richer, far more enigmatic than laziness. *Acedia* is when the heart malfunctions. It's an absence of love, a paralysis of care, a vacuum of the spirit. It's when all the things that used to light up your day now leave you cold and indifferent. It's the colour draining from your eyes, the taste dissolving from your tongue. It's when every song on your playlist sounds like a drone. It's when you talk to a friend and discover that your voice is robotic and you can't find anything new to say.

According to medieval texts, *acedia* consists of three core problems. Standing here, among the silver birches in Tyumen, these are easy for me to remember. The first is *restlessness*, or boredom. Desert monks talked about the monotony of life in their cells, how they would flit from one activity to another and pass the time by making plaits from palm leaves.[2] *Acedia*'s boredom strikes us in just the same way: we become disengaged from the moment. It's the itch that makes us want to get out of every situation we're in. It begins with a revolving set of day-dreams, conjuring new scenarios – a job back in the city, a place to live by the sea – that you think will make life better. Then it matures when you fantasise about giving up, about running away from the *taedium vitae*: the boredom of the way things seem to be in your life.[3]

And yet the problem is that you don't run. Or rather, you can't. *Acedia*'s second core characteristic is *inertia*. This can feel like you're standing, unmoving, in a freezing river that's rushing against your legs.[4] Often it involves taking 'your hand from the plough', or giving up on doing anything productive with your time.[5] It's when, in the face of difficult tasks, you crumble and shrink away. Or it's when you disconnect yourself through procrastination, pulling out of making decisions.[6] Either way, *acedia* is a torpor that freezes you somewhere between waking and sleep. Caught in its icy grasp, you want to escape but find you're unable 'to run away from the face of this cold'.[7]

What kind of cold, though? *Acedia*'s third main medieval characteristic was *tristitia*, or sadness. And with this, writers were really reaching for the thing we now call *depression*. Conrad of Hirsau, a theologian with a flair for psychology, once defined *acedia* as the moment when all 'good things now leave you bored'.[8] It's when you convince yourself that all the good in your existence has been damaged beyond repair. Your mind fluctuates between fear (of action, of making things happen), bitterness (failing to see the point of anything) and reclusiveness (hiding from the world), until all your joy is extinguished and you start to 'despair, and hate your own life'.[9]

Looking at them now, these three definitions feel bracingly modern. In fact, twenty-first-century psychologists have confirmed that medieval writers were on to something. Clinical researchers have connected boredom to attention problems, explaining how restless behaviour (like endless flicking through a phone) can make depressive episodes more likely.[10] Others have documented inertia as a symptom of negative thought patterns, identifying rumination (or dwelling on the negative aspects of a problem) as another of depression's triggers.[11] Given these parallels, it's no wonder that the psychologist Andrew Solomon once echoed the medieval approach in his bestselling book *The Noonday Demon*, calling depression 'the flaw in love'.[12]

Our understanding of clinical depression today has reached the level of the neurotransmitter, and treatments now include medications to alleviate symptoms and improve function. But medieval solutions aren't too dissimilar to some strands of modern cognitive behavioural therapy. Writers often promised to lead people out of their *acedia* with a single key, something only graspable once we appreciate *acedia*'s unique placement in the scheme of the Deadly Sins. Of the seven, Sloth sat right in the middle. It wasn't as serious as the 'spiritual' sins, Pride, Envy and Anger, which all culminate in hostility towards other people. And yet it also wasn't as innocent as the three 'bodily' sins, Avarice, Gluttony and Lust, which all fixate on material things. Sloth existed as a category apart, because it's the Deadly Sin that wants *nothing*. *Acedia* is a total failure of human engagement, a stalling of the spirit.

In the medieval world, the fix for boredom and inertia was straightforward. It was to learn to fall in love again. To escape *acedia* you had to jolt-start your heart, to fall in love with yourself and with the world and all of its contents. If this sounds simple, it also sounds impossible. Still, as the clouds of my breath float away in the glistening forest, I feel like I have to try it. Getting up from the ground, I rub the dirt from my gloves and start to run some more. But my ankle twinges and I pull up a few metres down the pathway. How do I begin, to begin to begin again?

Finding Your Mountain

Unlike the other Deadly Sins, *acedia* isn't something you *do*. Although we can show our pride, direct our envy, vent our anger, indulge our avarice, feed our gluttony, or stoke our lust, there's no active verb to go with our *acedia*. Because sloth is something that *happens to* you. Often, it feels like you have no control over it at all.

At least, this is how it felt for Elisabeth, a woman who lived near the banks of the Rhine in the 1100s.

Elisabeth was part of a community in the small German city of Schönau, alongside dozens of other nuns. Late in life she became famous for her ecstatic visions, which she recorded on sets of wax tablets, and which left her trembling with emotion. Before this she went through a period she came to see as the crucible of her life; a chasm of nothingness that nearly swallowed her whole.

It began with poor timekeeping. One day, when Elisabeth was supposed to take communion with the other nuns, she got 'detained for some reason'. Arriving late to the gathering, she found she couldn't feel any of the pleasure she usually felt at these things. Her mood dropped over the next few days. A 'certain darkness of the soul' brought with it a deluge of negative thoughts. 'All my faults rose up in my heart,' she wrote in her memoir, 'and I exaggerated each of them.' Her vision of the world snapped into a kind of black and white. 'Wherever I would turn, I felt like I was walking in shadows in comparison to the light that I used to experience.' And these shadows made her 'loathe' everything around her. She used to love praying, but she now found it 'annoying'. She couldn't get through a page of reading without throwing the book aside. Everything and everyone she used to love now left her cold. At one point, she admits, she was tempted to take her own life.[13]

How do you get out of a situation like this? At first, Elisabeth couldn't understand her condition. 'What has happened to me?' she asked over and over. But when she hit on an explanation, it helped her find a cure. Her problem, she decided, was that she was being stalked by an enemy. A type of supernatural adversary whose goal was to tempt her away from the joys of life. So, to drive this enemy away, Elisabeth found a more powerful friend. She began having visions of a spectral 'lady' who visited her in a series of waking dreams.

Elisabeth's woman appeared to her in different forms, each more thrilling than the last. Sometimes she was a spinning wheel of flame, and at other times she was a dove with wings outspread.

SLOTH

Once she even became a beam of light, shining down on a perfect city with buildings that reached above the clouds.[14] The point of these visions wasn't to show Elisabeth another world. It was to show her the same world – the world she had always loved – in a new light. Now, when Elisabeth walked around the familiar convent of Schönau, she felt 'ecstasy' instead of despair. After the darkness, her friendly guide had led her back to a life of purpose, direction and meaning.

Elisabeth's solution, although dazzling, wasn't unique. According to William Peraldus's popular medieval treatise on the Deadly Sins, *acedia* has eight cures. And although many of these could apply to her case – occupy yourself with hard work, learn to be patient, keep your thoughts future-oriented – there's one in particular that Elisabeth embraced with incredible creativity. As Peraldus said, a powerful way to get through your depressive sloth is to find yourself a 'strong mountain'. This is somebody or something that comforts you when you're at your lowest; somebody who can awaken the strengths, the qualities and the purpose inside you. Just like the Old Testament figure of Aaron, who once held up Moses's arms when he was tired, this is the friend who becomes your rock.[15] It's someone with both the patience and love to help you rediscover that strange lost thing: the person you were before *acedia* swallowed you up.

Elisabeth's 'strong mountain', when it arrived, was obvious. It was that phantom of a beautiful woman who spun for her in the shape of a flaming wheel when everything else in her life was dark. But the thing about these mountains is that we often don't recognise them, even when we're standing on top of them. We stop calling the friend whose love has always brought out our most generous side. Like the figure in Albrecht Dürer's *Melancholia*, we grow bored of all the treasures and tools stacked around us, neglecting the wings on our backs.

Albrecht Dürer's Melancholia. Bored by everything, even those wings.

If fighting *acedia* is a mountain-quest to discover ourselves anew, there was no better mountaineer in medieval literature than the Italian poet Dante. Like Elisabeth, Dante also had a crisis of despair, in the early 1300s, that nearly led him to suicide. Unlike her sudden fever, though, his was a slow-burning slide into mental disintegration. In his *Commedia*, he describes his own journey, through Hell and then up Mount Purgatory, to banish that sadness, which crept up on him during his marriage and career, and confront the demons hidden inside himself.

There have always been dozens of reasons to read Dante's *Commedia*. It's an all-time classic. It defined the Italian language. It's funny, it's terrifying, it's intricate. Parts of it, even in translation, are more beautiful than any song, any film, any artwork or photograph. But none of these reasons get to the core of why the *Commedia* is eternal. Because when Dante wrote about this journey through Hell, Purgatory and Paradise, and all the souls

SLOTH

and tortures and delights he saw there, he wasn't just creating a work of artistic beauty. What the *Commedia* was always meant to be was a code for future generations. It's a user's manual for the human heart that every individual reader needs to decipher for themselves.

More than that, the *Commedia* is a story about the experience of *acedia* and how to escape it. Because after narrating his breakdown, Dante's epic poem documents the discovery of his own 'strong mountain': a person who'd been filling up his heart since he was a child.

Dante (whose full name was Durante Alighieri) grew up in Florence, around the same time as the artist Giotto. At that time the city was full of trade and investment, and Dante's family profited from all of it. His father was a merchant and banker, and his mother was part of a local noble family, although both parents died when Dante was still very young. In their absence, his heart was always restless. When he was nine, as he was out walking on the first day of spring, he locked eyes with a girl around his own age. Her name, he later learned, was Beatrice Portinari. She was dressed in 'a subdued crimson', and with one glance he felt something powerful inside him stirring. He was confused; he thought an 'animal spirit' was beginning 'to tremble' through his body, as he later wrote in his autobiographical *La Vita Nuova*. Whatever it was, it made the world seem different. 'Now has your bliss appeared,' a voice whispered to him from somewhere deep in his brain.[16]

Acedia isn't usually a product of love. In fact, it arises precisely when our love fails to start. And Dante found this out nine years later, when he encountered Beatrice again at the age of eighteen. As she met his gaze on the street, this time Beatrice gave Dante a polite wave. This one gesture was enough to torture him. He ran home and locked himself in his bedroom, and in his restless sleep he saw a vision of Beatrice. She was naked, and being carried in the arms of a man he recognised as 'Love' himself. In this spectral man's hand he saw a flaming ball of blood and tissue. 'Behold,' Love said to the dreaming Dante. 'Your heart.'

From this point, Dante's *acedia* showed its first symptom: *tepiditas*, the cold paralysis in which you feel you can't move forward with your life. Because even though Dante soon got married to another woman – Gemma, the daughter of his landlord – he couldn't get over this one glance from Beatrice, and the unrequited possibility it seemed to open up.[17] His life now felt hollow, and even though he had children his marriage was little more than a business deal. All the while, Dante's obsession deepened. Beatrice was now married to Simone de' Bardi, the son of a banker, and whenever Dante saw her in Florence his 'natural spirit' broke down. He was so 'overcome by the force of Love' that he found he could no longer hold a proper conversation.[18]

If this was the end of Dante's love story it would be a little depressing, but hardly explosive. But soon Dante's heartache gave way to grief, and this is when his *acedia* really plunged into an abyss. Beatrice was only twenty-five years old when she passed away. How or why she died, no historian can tell. All Dante could write about the death in *La Vita Nuova* was that it took place 'in the first hour of the ninth day of the month', and in the ninth month of the year 'according to the Syrian calendar'. In the aftermath, Dante succumbed to another of *acedia*'s symptoms: *desperatio*, or despair. He was haunted by 'a desire for death', he said in his *Rime* poem number twenty-five, a desire 'so sweet' that it made his face change colour.[19] 'Pierced' with an unquenchable sorrow,[20] he was now too 'ashamed' to leave the house.[21] As his biographer Boccaccio put it, he became 'almost a wild thing to look upon.'[22]

SLOTH

Dante's *acedia* really snowballed when his career started to break down. By thirty-five he had become an influential player in Florence's city government. Elected as one of six priors in May 1300, he took difficult decisions on the exile of violent gangs and the building of new roads. As a politician, though, Dante was caught between two warring factions: the Black Guelphs (citizens loyal to the pope), and the White Guelphs (citizens loyal to popes usually, but not to Pope Boniface VIII, whom they saw as an autocrat who wanted to strip away the city's autonomy). Although he claimed to be impartial, most Florentines believed Dante was really a supporter of the White Guelphs. So when Pope Boniface sent troops into the city to support a Black Guelph coup in November 1301, Dante was one of the first officials to be condemned by the newly installed city government. Charged with corruption, he was sentenced to exile. If he ever dared return, the pope warned, he would be arrested and burned at the stake.[23]

Exile triggered the third of Dante's *acedia* symptoms. This is *dissolutio*, when you feel like a ship without an anchor, disconnected from the places and things you used to love. He would never see Florence again, and he was also forced to abandon his family. All four of his children stayed behind in the city, including the youngest, Antonia, who was then still a tiny baby. For years Dante had to move from place to place, learning 'how salt is the taste of another man's bread, and how hard is the going down and then up another man's stairs'. And this exile deepened the existential despair that had been growing inside him since he first fell in love with Beatrice. 'How I came there I cannot really tell,' his pilgrim says at the outset of the *Inferno*, while wandering towards the gates of Hell. 'I was so full of sleep when I forsook the one true way.'[24] From what he tells us in the *Commedia*, it seems Dante was close to suicide. Virgil, his guide through most of the poem, says that when he found the pilgrim in that wood, 'his time was almost at an end.'[25] And the next 'dark forest' in *Inferno*, after the opening, is in the seventh circle of Hell, surrounding the souls who have killed themselves.[26]

While Elisabeth of Schönau's *acedia* struck her down like a fever, Dante's *tepiditas*, *desperatio* and *dissolutio* grew on him like mould, as the consequences of his choices unfolded gradually through his life. Despite this difference, these two writers have a single factor in common. Before they fell into their sloth, both had built up a commitment to causes that occupied their whole hearts. Elisabeth had been a devoted nun, dedicating her life to passionate prayer, reading and singing in worship of the Virgin Mary. Dante had been a poet and public servant, and threw an incredible energy into his art. When *acedia* came for them, it was as if all that intense love had been turned upside down, inverted inside them.

And this is what's so cruel about *acedia*, the Deadly Sin. It exploits our love and turns it against us. Like a rollercoaster, it plunges us downwards into a meaninglessness that's all the more dizzying the higher we've built up our passions first. Then, in despair, *acedia* makes us carry the unbearable weight of all that hulking love; the love that no longer has wings to fly.

Over the course of my research career, twice I've sat with a manuscript and felt the same cold of *acedia* flowing from the mind of a medieval writer. Once, in a library in Cambridge, I found a Gloss on the Psalms made by the theologian Gilbert of Poitiers. While he was dealing with the line 'My soul is weary with sorrow' from Psalm 119, Gilbert captured the spirit of Elisabeth or Dante at their lowest ebb. He did this, oddly for an academic work of that time, in the first person. When I'm in danger and 'feel sloth', Gilbert wrote, even though 'I know all the training', still 'my soul does little or nothing'.[27] Sloth is when we 'sleep', and grow 'forgetful' of the knowledge inside us. It's when we have all the training to do the right thing, but still somehow avoid doing it. It's Prince Hamlet, unable to avenge his father. It's the bystander who, seeing somebody slipping on the ice, can't find the conviction to cross the road to help.

The second time I felt the same weight of *acedia* was in the Weston Library in Oxford, when I sat reading a text known as *The Dialogue between a Sinner and Reason*. This work, by the English monk Ralph of Battle (d.*c*.1124), is essentially the transcript of a counselling session.[28] Like Dante's *Commedia*, it's in the voice of a person (called 'Sinner' in the text) who's come to feel that all his love for life has been hollowed out. I have a 'putrefying mind', the Sinner says, and 'from my childhood until this hour, I have been completely corrupted and confused.' Feeling 'the end of life is near', he asks the kind of question people only ask in their most desperate moments of self-doubt: 'How have I been able to live all this time and never learned to do anything other than evil deeds?'[29]

Sitting in the silence of the manuscript library, I could feel the desperation of those words on the surface of my skin. The Sinner's shame had made him 'scarcely able to breathe', and he could no longer allow himself even the tiniest self-assurance. The sensation was so sharp, perhaps, because the rollercoaster of care had previously got so high. Ralph's 'Sinner' was a monk whose life up to then had been dedicated to love and prayer. But now, 'even when I do something with a semblance of good' a set of inner doubts come to 'corrupt and defile everything'.[30] Like Dante, the Sinner was tortured by the plunging gap between what he had once been and what he had now become. Because he knew how good things *should* feel, the bitterness was all the worse. As he discovered, *acedia* is not laziness without a direction. It's laziness *in spite of* a direction.

How to escape this trap of *acedia*? Dante explores the wrong answer in his *Commedia*, in the dangerous pathway he sketches out in Canto 19 of his *Purgatorio*, before he gives the right one. When he reaches the terrace of Sloth, Dante's pilgrim falls down to sleep, and while sleeping has a bizarre dream vision. A woman, 'stammering' and with a 'sickly pale complexion', appears to him and starts singing. Listening to her, the pilgrim is distracted but happy. The woman's voice is so beautiful that he finds it nearly impossible 'to turn aside'. But his guide, Virgil, sees what's really going on. Ripping at the siren's clothes he exposes her belly and reveals a band of rotting flesh beneath.[31] After that moment up Mount Purgatory, Dante's pilgrim never once lets himself get distracted again.

It's an unsettling dream, and it raises all kinds of questions about Dante's approach to women.[32] Like so many premodern poets, he's making distraction a feminine problem and imagining a masculine solution. At its heart, though, this vision is still a general warning about the dangers of procrastination. The siren comes to Dante's pilgrim precisely when he's at his most restless and drowsy. What she shows him, in that moment, is the *wrong* path out of *acedia*. A spiral of distractions. When we're bored, we're often vulnerable to small temptations: to things that are shiny or fun or enigmatic and spellbind us with their beauty. If we haven't sorted out our hearts, these distractions can be a trap. Without love as our guide, we have no signal or device to work out whether they're good for us or not. And so we follow them, click by click, not knowing if we're following something that's rotten at its core.[33]

What was the safe path out of *acedia*? For Dante, like for Elisabeth of Schönau, the way forward involved finding a 'strong mountain'; finding somebody or something who can give us a map and a compass, and remind us who we are beneath all our sadness and self-doubt. In Dante's life, this mountain had been there all along. As he discovered, sometimes the same energy that flips our lives into *acedia* can power our pathway out. Because Dante's mountain was also his torturer: Beatrice, still alive in his dreams, even though she was now long dead. It was her spirit that sent Virgil to collect Dante at the beginning of the poem, when he was stuck in the forest in the abyss of his miseries. And all the way through, it was only the promise of seeing Beatrice again that gave Dante the bravery to walk through Hell itself.

What Dante discovered, from that moment, is that he couldn't escape his despair by running away from it. Instead, he had to move headlong into his sadness. He had to confront all his own worst qualities, meeting all the tortured souls in Hell to see all his own lust, avarice and pride reflected back at him. And in those moments, he had to take the hard lesson that he was capable of the same sins.[34] Only then, after tough self-examination, could Dante find the joy that would defeat his *acedia*. A joy that came when Beatrice appeared to him at the top of Mount Purgatory, as inspiring to him as she had been when they were both nine, eighteen, or twenty-five.

Beatrice's message to Dante was a strong one. To paraphrase another poet, it was: *The only way out is through.*[35] When it comes, the Deadly Sin of *acedia* will always try to consume us from all sides at once. Turning away and running backwards, as Dante knew, is futile. And it's also a fallacy to try to reinvent ourselves, or to flee and think we can escape our sadness by putting thousands of miles between us and our old life. Elisabeth of Schönau beat her *acedia* by embracing the same convent, the same community, and learning to love it all again. She didn't need a new life or a new heart. All she needed was to restart the heart she'd always had.

Fifty Years of Grief

I am awake, although I shouldn't be. Two lights pop out from the darkness of my room: the pale blue diode from my laptop charger and a pair of white eyes. The eyes belong to Lenin, whose portrait was hung by my landlord on the bedroom wall. Even beneath his 'soothing' face, I find I cannot sleep. Nor can I remember how to sleep. My ankle is still sore from the run in Gilyovskaya Roscha, and I keep stretching out for a part of the mattress that doesn't feel hard. Lying on my side, with one headphone in my ceiling-side ear, I switch on the BBC World Service. British voices talk about sewage problems beneath the streets of Iraq and I try to drift away with them. And yet I can't do it. I'm brought back instead to a room in Bristol, to a blue vinyl mattress beneath a strip of fluorescent light. To an eye that can't meet my gaze and a hand that can't squeeze mine back.

My father died on a February evening, many years ago now. Every other week I flew from my new home in Toronto back to England to visit him, rescheduling my teaching. The last time I came he told me he was hoping to die before Sunday to save me having to reschedule any more. Huddled with my older brother around his narrow bed, we spent that week talking about the past. We fed him and we washed him. When he was thirsty we held a carton of apple juice to his mouth. Through the night we came in to update his morphine and to sit and talk some more. We laughed harder than we should have done at his jokes, some of them old but most of them new. And then his breathing became mechanical and abrupt and he stopped speaking. When he died it was around an hour after sunset, and only the slimmest band of light hung in the sky outside the window.

There are things we know about grief in the Middle Ages,

and things we don't. We know there were outward conventions for mourning, similar across Europe, and that these seem to have intensified from the late 1200s onwards. We know that women in fifteenth-century Iberia, for example, were expected to weep dramatically and perform public prayers.[36] We know it wasn't unusual in later medieval literature to find heroes like Sir Gawain kissing the bloodied corpse of his brother and weeping until 'his legs gave way, his heart failed, and he fell as if dead.'[37] We also know that excessive grief was seen as a strand of *acedia*, and that some of these conventions caused anxieties when taken to their extreme; that in Italian towns, such as Orvieto in the later thirteenth century, local governments even banned excessive displays of emotion at funerals.[38]

Why might the government of Orvieto have been anxious about these displays? Isn't it insensitive to try to control the pain a person feels when somebody close to them dies? Most people today might be reluctant to regard grieving as a 'Deadly Sin'. Modern society expects that, if somebody close to us dies, we'll feel a combination of profound sadness, inactivity and listlessness, and – in stronger cases – the sense that life simply cannot go on. And yet the idea that grief can turn into something destructive is not alien to us. Doctors and psychologists tend to set a time limit on grief symptoms, conscious that a loss can spin out of control if it's not processed.[39] Prolonged Grief Disorder, which was added to the World Health Organization's International Classification of Diseases in 2016, is diagnosed in cases when the debilitating effects of grief persist for more than six months after the death.[40] The WHO is vague on the nature of these symptoms, however. We'll know grief is 'pathological', they say, when it 'clearly exceeds expected social, cultural or religious norms'.[41]

How we define those 'norms' today, inevitably, reveals the

values that separate us from our medieval counterparts. For writers seven hundred years ago, grief's pathology depended less on how it stopped us 'functioning' as workers or social beings and more on how, in the pain of loss, it stopped us focusing on something *good*: the life we have, and not the one we don't. As the theologian Origen said, when we have the sadness of grief-driven *acedia* we lose our 'vigilance' and 'fall into sleep' until, like dreamers, we can no longer tell reality from the conjuring of our minds.[42] Cases of medieval *acedia* can reveal a lost red line, one that is maybe too difficult to include in the WHO's guidance. The line separating the mind that accepts a painful reality from the mind that dwells inside a tranquillising fantasy.

A dramatic nineteenth-century painting, now hanging in the Prado Museum in Madrid, shows medieval grief at its most 'pathological' (plate 7). At the centre of the enormous canvas is Queen Juana of Castile and Léon, standing in clothes of sweeping black. Her eyes are fixed on a candle flame at the foot of a coffin. Juana, who was the daughter of the 'Catholic Monarchs' Fernando and Isabella, and heir to the united Spanish crown, is being engulfed by smoke. But she doesn't notice the fire at her back, or the smoke, or the white-robed monk reading from a prayer book, or the crowd of distracted mourners behind her. Her sleep-starved eyes are held only by the flame, as it dances in a wind that will soon come to extinguish it.

Most of the Spanish visitors to the Prado know the legend of this woman, known as *Doña Juana la Loca*, or 'Joanna the Mad'. They know that countless courtiers and ambassadors in the early 1500s described her as 'unstable', 'unpredictable' and 'unhinged'. Her family were so embarrassed by her behaviour that they tried to hush it up. Shortly after this coffin scene her father locked her away in an isolated palace for nearly fifty years, citing her 'madness'. Today, historians still debate the same questions that once circulated around the courts of Valladolid and Toledo. Did Juana suffer from any genuine mental illness? Was she pushed into a self-destructive form of depression by her grief? Or was her reputation for madness part of a conspiracy designed to cheat a young woman out of inheriting an empire?[43]

To understand Juana's grief-*acedia*, it's important to know the name of the man in the coffin. This was Philippe the Archduke of Burgundy, nicknamed 'Philippe the Handsome'. Juana married him when she was around sixteen, and was smitten right from the start. Even though Philippe could be cruel and manipulative, sometimes even hitting her, nothing broke her devotion to him.[44] One time, a few years into their life together as a couple, Philippe had to travel to look after business in his native Flanders. It was just before Christmas and Juana fell into a consuming misery. She 'never lifted her spirits in joy, nor lifted her eyes from the ground' from the moment he left. Keeping her head partially covered, she thought of nothing but his absence. 'Of riches, of power, of kingdoms, of her parents themselves', she had no care. Her mind, as the gossiping courtier Pedro Mártir de Anglería put it, now became a 'whirlwind', unable to rest without him.[45]

From this point on Juana's behaviour grew erratic. Later that winter she packed her things, determined to escape the fortress of La Mota where she was staying, hoping to follow Philippe to Flanders. Although her mother begged her to stay, Juana resisted, even threatening to make the journey on foot. So her mother sent a bishop to intercept her. When Juana found this bishop had locked her exit to the grounds she refused to go back inside. She stood outside for hours instead, in a patch of mud between the gates. It was 'one of the coldest nights' of the year, yet still Juana stayed there, motionless in a web of frosty dew, until two o'clock in the morning.[46]

When Juana was finally allowed to go to Flanders the

next year, her anxieties only got worse. Her jealousy had been bubbling up for a while, and she suspected Philippe had taken a lover. Shortly after she arrived she found the evidence that seemed to prove her suspicions. According to Pedro Mártir, who was at the court when it happened, Juana found a single blonde hair on her husband's clothes and flared into violence. With a 'frenzied heart', a 'flaming face' and 'gnashing teeth', she found the girl she assumed was Philippe's new lover and hit her in the face. Then, as Pedro remembered, she forced her husband to shave off all the woman's long, blonde hair.[47]

It's possible the relationship could have weathered this rough patch. Near their tenth wedding anniversary, though, Philippe caught a fever that spiralled into a life-threatening sickness. He was still only twenty-eight years old, but it 'wilted him like a flower'. At first, eyewitnesses praised Juana for her calmness. One doctor claimed he'd never 'seen any woman of any social class' display such 'composure, touch, air and grace'.[48] Even when Philippe died, on a September afternoon, Juana kept her cool. She held a sober conversation with Cardinal Cisneros, the nation's most powerful cleric and politician, on the arrangements of her husband's will, and just days later took time to reshuffle government advisers.[49] At some point, though, she broke. According to an anonymous witness, Juana kept opening the lid of the coffin as it lay in state, ripping off the shrouds surrounding the body. And then she sat there for hours, kissing Philippe's dead feet.[50]

Nearly anything can be excused in the first rush of grief. Our mourning only tips over into *acedia*, medieval theologians believed, when we fall into a rut of self-sabotaging behaviour. Idleness, called *ignavia* in Peraldus's handbook on the Deadly Sins, is when *acedia* derails us from doing anything new, anything productive, or anything at all to help ourselves. This is when we feel like we're 'submerged' in mud, but would rather stay put

SLOTH

than fight our way out. Or it's when we feel like we're standing in a tongue of flame, yet would prefer to stay and burn than take another step forward.[51] As that word *ignavia* implied in Latin, this *acedia* makes us into a hulking lost ship: incapable of turning around and navigating our way towards something better.

If Juana did become a drifting vessel, it was on the day she ordered Philippe's coffin to be exhumed and relocated to Granada. The procession she organised was astonishing. A 400-mile route, chartered exclusively through muddy rural back roads, bringing her husband's body to its new resting place. For this mission Juana seems to have done everything she could to make things harder for herself. Movement had to take place at night, as she insisted on stopping every day to perform the funeral rites over and over again. Although she was pregnant with Philippe's child when she started, this didn't stop her. She simply paused the procession to give birth, and then carried on a few weeks later. Rumours now circulated that Juana kept women away from the coffin out of jealousy, and that she often inspected the body for signs of interference. According to her father's secretary Miguel Peréz de Almazán, who was present on the journey, 'There is no one, great or small, who does not say now that she is confused and brainless.'[52]

When our *ignavia* forces us into a rut – when we reach a point that we can no longer help ourselves – somebody may come along to stage an intervention. Eventually, Juana's father Fernando came to deliver the final blow to the procession plans. Since his wife Isabella had died in 1504, Fernando had always been a little put out by the arrangement that the throne of Castile would pass directly to Juana, as their daughter, and not to him. And now he caught up with the cortège in August 1507, while they were zigzagging between Burgos and Valladolid, and asked Juana to sign a form that would let him rule Castile in her place. Was this a manipulative move? Some observers suspected it was. King Henry VII of England (d.1509), who once met Juana and had even proposed marriage to her, expressed his deep suspicions. Maybe, King Henry wondered in a letter, Fernando 'likes to have her this way . . . in order to deprive her of everything'.[53] But whatever her father's precise motives, his intervention was decisive. A few months later, after she had completed around 105 miles of the mission from Burgos to Granada, Fernando ordered for Philippe's coffin to be forcibly removed to a convent, and for Juana to be taken to the palace of Tordesillas near Valladolid.[54] There she was kept under a type of house arrest until her death, at the age of seventy-six, in 1555.

Juana ended up spending nearly fifty years in mourning. That's almost a hundred times the period of 'debilitating' grief recommended by the World Health Organization as a healthy maximum. Still, I'm not sure I believe Juana was ever 'mad' at all. A while ago I looked at bureaucratic documents in the royal archives in Simancas in central Spain. Among the documents, I saw one Juana wrote to Manuel I of Portugal, dated 1509 (shortly before her incarceration), explaining in fluent government jargon that she wouldn't interfere with Portuguese exploration and exploitation in Africa.[55]

Many of the most scandalous stories about Juana seem pedestrian when taken in context. Who hasn't flown off the handle in jealousy, once or twice? Who wouldn't be capable of performing a cold protest outside the gates of a fortress if our partner had run to Belgium and our mother was sending a bishop to lock us in our home? Even Juana's obsessive funeral mission to Granada makes a certain kind of sense. Some have argued she was only following Philippe's dying wishes, and others have claimed the procession was really a way of asserting her political independence.[56] Although these arguments sidestep the strangeness of

SLOTH

that journey, it's true that the most outlandish rumour of her madness – the story of her kissing Philippe's dead feet – only ever appeared in a single, dubious, source.[57]

Was Juana's journey, after all, just another way to process grief? If it seemed pathological to contemporaries, it was because rather than processing her sadness in the conventional ways – through confession, or through reaching out to others – Juana seemed to switch off and shut down, sequestering herself away from her political duties on that long funeral march to Granada. Afflicted, arguably, by a classic case of *ignavia*, she couldn't find the will to turn her ship around, even as it was headed for an iceberg.

But then what was the alternative? If Juana went too far, what was the medieval model of controlled sadness in the face of unbearable loss supposed to look like?

Recently, on another listless afternoon in my apartment, I found a small book I once bought in a library sale. A book I can't remember bringing with me to Siberia, but which at some point I must have known I might need. It's called *The Pearl*, a medieval poem that describes the worst kind of grief. Written in Middle English around the era of Chaucer, it's narrated by a man who finds himself wandering through a garden of herbs. He's been driven to despair, he says, because he once lost a pearl somewhere near this place. 'She slipped from me through grass to ground, and I mourn now, with a broken heart, for that priceless pearl without a spot.' Only later, through a lot of pain, does the narrator reveal the full story. That this pearl was really his two-year-old daughter, who had died suddenly a few years ago. And that here, in this herb garden, is where it happened.[58]

Like Juana of Castile, the father in *The Pearl* is a lonely figure. He's also obsessive, returning again and again to the same spot, hoping to find his daughter resurrected among the herbs. But his grief has one critical difference: as he looks around at the garden, this father doesn't just rest in his melancholy. Actually, he stops to appreciate how even this harshest loss can open up a new space for life to blossom. 'Spices must thrive and spread in that spot,' he says, as he looks at the ground where his daughter died. 'Rot and ruin enrich the soil' and 'flower and fruit could never fade where my pearl entered the dark earth.' His reward for this optimism is an ecstatic vision of Paradise. After falling to the ground in sleep, he wakes to find himself transported to a clearing beside a forest, where he sees 'trunks of Indian blue' and 'layers of leaves like burnished silver'. And then, in his dream state, he travels along a river to the foot of a mountain, where he gets to see his lost daughter one last time.[59]

I've had a long time to reflect on the wisdom of *The Pearl*. Some lines can be difficult to digest, especially the lines where the daughter, no longer a toddler but now the grown-up woman she would have become, tells her father not to be sad because she now enjoys all the pleasures of bliss. She also tells him that he can't follow her any further. He stops to close his eyes in wonder, but when he opens them he finds he is now separated from his daughter by a flowing river. Panicking, he tries to jump to the other side. 'Nothing mattered more than being near her.' But the splash of water wakes him from his dream vision. His heart aching, he struggles again for his pearl, the girl he'd lost but thought he'd found. And although he knows she's not coming back, somehow this time he finds the strength to get back on with his life, to reconcile himself to his sadness. 'I'll happily dwell in this dungeon,' he says. Because at least now he knows his daughter's spirit will always be inside him.[60]

It's rare to feel like the father in *The Pearl*, secure that the person you miss still lives on in a paradise at the other end of sleep. But I've found that the lesson this poem teaches is also one of the core truths of *acedia*. Re-enactments are always hollow.

Instead of brooding on a body that has lost its warmth, we need to direct our love towards the presences that always stay with us: the memory of a person that's alive in the heart, in all the dreams and decisions that map the shape of our existence.

Did Juana ever learn that lesson? No historian can know what went on inside her brain. It seems all we can know for sure is how her contemporaries judged her, and how they thought she'd 'lost' her senses. But historians can still search for clues. Among the possessions she left in her palace-prison after she died were some books that suggest her state of mind. These include a songbook, the *Cantigas de los músicas*, which her mother gave her as a gift when she was a child.[61] She also had a book of hours, a lavish bespoke prayer book that included colourful pictures of Juana herself, alongside many of her favourite saints. Judging by the wear along the lower pages, she kept this book propped open at the same place for months on end – at a page decorated with spiralling flowers and a picture of a small mirror from which a skull looks back at the reader.[62]

Was Juana paralysed by her grief when she sat staring at this page? Or sitting there, did she come to the same conclusion as the *Pearl* poet? It's tempting to see the propped-open book as just another example of her *ignavia*, of her transformation into a ship that won't turn around. Or as more evidence that she suffered the kind of grief that prefers a painful fantasy to a difficult reality. Fifty years is a long time, though. And we have no idea where Juana's mind travelled to in that grief. Lying here now in Tyumen, half-listening to the BBC World Service, I'm beginning to see her point. Society may want us to stop wearing black and get on with our lives. The WHO may expect us to choreograph our grief into a neat six-month window, to remain 'functional' in our 'occupations'. But, sometimes, there just can't be any getting on.

The Five Ways We Cry

Why do we cry? What's the precise emotional chemistry we need, to make salt water start tumbling out of our eyes? And what can our tears tell us about living a good life?

In Madrid's Prado Museum, a short walk down the corridor from that enormous painting of Juana of Castile in grief, is one of the greatest works of medieval art. *The Descent from the Cross*, painted by Rogier van der Weyden in 1435, is famous for its colour and emotional power (plate 8). At the beginning of his book *Leaving the Atocha Station*, the writer Ben Lerner describes how every morning his protagonist came to the museum to stand in front of this painting before starting work. Although he felt he should be having a 'profound experience of art', he failed to feel anything much at all. One day he found a man, slimmer than him, standing in his usual place. And this man was crying,

The tears of Joseph of Arimathea.

apparently moved to a state of trembling by van der Weyden's fifteenth-century brushstrokes.[63]

The tiny, bubble-like tears on the face of Joseph of Arimathea, who looks dishevelled with a five o'clock shadow and carelessly aligned fur collar, are van der Weyden's signature. No other artist of his generation could execute lifelike pearls of salty water like this. Standing in front of the life-size painting in the Prado, anyone who isn't too busy having a 'profound experience of art' for themselves will feel they can reach out and touch those tears and feel their wetness on their fingertips.

What exactly would they be touching, though? Were medieval tears really the same as our own?

Crying, for medieval writers, was a diagnostic tool. It was a way to measure the quality and direction of our love. By showing us the contents of our deepest drives and desires, our tears reveal to us who we really are. 'Every tear proceeds from the heart,' wrote the fourteenth-century mystic Catherine of Siena. By looking into someone's eyes when they're weeping – by reaching out and touching their pearl-drop tears – we can catch sight of the real priorities of their heart. We can find out whether they've been able to order their love and point it in the right direction, or whether they've become stuck with *acedia*, and a love that falters or refuses to fire.

As usual with medieval writers, this idea was accompanied by a numbered ranking list. According to Catherine of Siena we need to look out for five different types of tears. And defining these tears can also be a way to map our journey, from self-ignorance to self-awareness; from the lovelessness and despair of *acedia* to the joy of living a better life.

The first tears we cry, Catherine said, are *tears of damnation*. These tears simply respond to the consequences of our situation, and the disastrous choices we've made. Maybe we've acted selfishly or we've been cruel, and now we're crying because people are shunning us and we don't understand why. Our love at this point is narrow and misdirected, our hearts pointed inwards. And so we cry, simply, for ourselves.

Second are the *tears of fear of punishment*. The difference with these is that they come with a degree of self-awareness, as we're now able to regret the bad things we've done, having watched their effect on others. They tell us that we've now acquired a sense of guilt. With this guilt, at least, we can be assured that we have enough love for other people to feel bad about upsetting them. Still, motivated mostly by our desire for this guilt to go away, our tears at this point remain inward-focused.

Only after this self-absorbed phase are we ready for the higher-level tears, at which stage our self-pity pivots towards self-improvement. The third way we cry is with *imperfect tears*, which is when all our fear and negativity starts to burn off. We're now more self-aware, seeing our faults for what they are, and we recognise the distance between the flawed person we have been and the better person we could still become. Ready to change our ways, we cry with compassion for others, but also compassion for ourselves and the mistakes we still need to correct.

Fourth are the *tears of sweetness*, which come only when we've ordered our love fully towards others. At this point we no longer weep for ourselves, but we weep for others and the pains we can see them going through. Our hearts are now sensitive to the human story: the struggle of people, everywhere, to get through the difficult labyrinths life has thrown them into. So, with these tears we cry for the suffering of humanity itself.

At the end of all this crying are the purest tears of all: the *tears of great peace*. As Catherine said, these flow like a river from the eyes of people who've reached enlightenment. We only cry this way when we have reached total self-knowledge and attained a comprehensive understanding of what it means to be good. Then, with hearts full of energy, our tears swell with a love – for others, for ourselves, for everything – that beats out the rhythms of the universe.[64]

Catherine of Siena died in 1380. Before that she had her own battle with the Deadly Sins, which we'll come to a little later. What she had no way of knowing when she died, though, was that there was already a child alive who would one day take her philosophy of tears and live it to the maximum. A woman from the English county of Norfolk, who confronted her sadness on a nomadic journey through love, loss, writing and redemption.

Margery Kempe is the writer of the *Boke*, the first known autobiography in the English language. And her story is one of the most tear-soaked in medieval history. She had a life riddled with paradoxes. She was a mother who gave birth to fourteen children but who then committed to a life of celibacy; an entrepreneur who built two businesses but then became a writer and recluse; a socialite from East Anglia who sailed to Venice, Jerusalem, Gdansk and Norway in search of a new life. There's also something refreshing about Margery's memoir. Because although she narrates her troubles with *acedia* – troubles that took her into stages of self-harm – her memoir is also an inspiring story of how to invert our tears, and how to redeem ourselves from the darkest recesses of *acedia*.

Margery's depression began in a midlife spin-out. She was part of a respectable family, and like many other women of her generation she wanted to have her own income, to gain a degree of economic independence from her husband and keep up with her neighbours.[65] Although Margery launched two businesses, both of them failed. First she set up a small brewery, but sales tanked when all the beer began coming out flat, no matter the adjustments she made. Next she bought a mill, acquiring two horses and paying a man to grind-up corn. This plan failed when both horses turned wild and started walking backwards instead of forwards. People in Bishop's Lynn (now known as King's Lynn) said she was cursed, or else (snobbishly) that she was getting her comeuppance for all her social climbing. Not for the last time in her life Margery stood alone, the butt of cruel jokes with nobody in her corner to support her.[66]

After she gave birth to one of her children (she doesn't tell us which), Margery plunged into her worst slump of self-hatred. She grew cynical and untrusting, she says, and began mocking her friends behind their backs. Just like Dante or Elisabeth of Schönau, nothing seemed good to her any more, and nothing could really make her happy. Voices in her head kept urging her to kill herself. One day she scratched a set of dents in her chest with her fingernails. Later she went further, biting 'her own hand so violently that the mark could be seen for the rest of her life'.[67]

Margery's tears, at this point, were still tears of self-pity. Or at least, they were tears of deep distress and confusion. Everything began to change, though, after she turned forty. Running low on money and desperate for some lift, she had the vision that shifted her life's direction. Jesus first appeared to Margery while she was lying down. He walked into her bedroom wearing a purple silk gown, sat down on the edge of her bed and flashed his beautiful brown eyes at her. When he spoke, his voice was gentle. 'Daughter, why have you forsaken me, and I never forsook you?'

Now Margery's crying graduated to the next level. Over the next months she spent her days sitting in the local church, weeping. She held her head in her hands and sat there groaning, sometimes for two hours at a time.[68] All of this was apparently spontaneous and heartfelt. But why was she doing it? At times, she said, she was crying in misery: remembering her mistakes and all 'her unkindness since her childhood' (all of which matches

SLOTH

Catherine's third type of tears). Other times she said she was crying for the suffering of others (or Catherine's fourth). One Good Friday she sat looking at the crucifix until, as she said, the feeling of Jesus's pain overwhelmed her and she sat roaring and sweating until she 'turned all blue like lead'.[69]

Had Margery finally achieved Catherine's highest type of crying, the *tears of great peace*? Not everybody in Norfolk was convinced. Many accused her of being a hypocrite, saying she switched her weeping on and off like a tap.[70] A well-respected friar who visited the town one weekend even complained about her from the pulpit of Margery's church. 'I wish this woman would leave. She's annoying people.'[71] Despite this public humiliation Margery never doubted herself. By now, after all, she had found her own 'strong mountain'. Appearing in her bedroom again one night, the ghostly Jesus told her she had nothing to worry about. 'How often have I told you that your sins are forgiven and we are united together without end?'[72]

Acedia, as we know, works by turning the full weight of our old loves against us. It inverts our hearts, torturing us with the gap between what we think we *should* be feeling and the emptiness of what we *actually* feel. When we begin fighting this problem, it can be the most exhilarating experience. Feeling the force of all that old self-love and self-belief returning is like standing by a radiator after a three-hour hike through the snow. And this, seemingly, is how it felt for Margery. At this moment in her life, her 'strong mountain' beneath her, she wept with delight. Life was moving forward again, and she wasn't scared of anything.

In all this new zeal, we only know for sure about one soul Margery ever managed to convert. That was her son who lived in Prussia, John, the only one of her fourteen children she ever mentions in her *Boke*. As a young man John had moved away to Gdansk, where he worked in shipping. He was part of an emerging trend of immigrants who, in the later Middle Ages, crossed the northern seas to switch cities.[73] A bachelor with a string of interchangeable girlfriends, John soon made enough money for all of his clothes to have fashionable slashes in the fabric. But when he came back to Norfolk to visit, Margery grew tired of all his self-centred talk at the dinner table. She began to cry, this time not for herself but for him. She wanted John to set his heart in order; to point his love towards the things that really mattered.

At first the son laughed at his mother and brushed off her advice like droplets of rain. Returning to Gdansk, though, he found that her words – and her tears – were beginning to sink in. John got married and had a child, and began making pilgrimages to Rome and other places to atone for his old life. He'd found a new moral direction, he believed, and he credited it all to his mother.

Everything from here should have been straightforward. Yet this newfound closeness only made the coming rupture – Margery's final test – even more tragic. During a family visit to introduce his new wife, John left his mother's dinner table and went to lie down. He stayed there for nearly a month, slipping into a fever that got worse and worse. Then one afternoon, upstairs in his old childhood bedroom, he died. Margery's husband, who had been terminally ill during John's final visit, died soon after. From this point on Margery was alone in the world. If she'd been put through this grief earlier in life, she might have crumbled. But instead of burrowing deeper into her *acedia* – instead of biting a chunk out of her hand – she chose to walk a different path.

Acedia's major remedy – according to the compassionate thirteenth-century treatise on the Deadly Sins by William Peraldus – is fortitude.[74] More than anything this means a bravery of spirit, a readiness to fight the core of our sadness. If this core has a label, it's usually 'fear': a fear of moving forward; a fear of living in a new way; a fear of confronting our situation in all its reality. So, we have to walk through the darkness of our lives without giving in to our terror at all.[75] And this is precisely what Margery practised, after her son died. Because even though she was now nearly sixty and had a badly injured foot, she made the dangerous voyage across the North Sea and over into the Baltic, determined to accompany her grieving daughter-in-law home. The ship nearly sank, and all the crew screamed in terror for their lives. Eventually, though, they arrived in Gdansk and Margery could marvel at the stone buildings and seaport taverns her son used to haunt, so strange yet so familiar to the world of Lynn.[76]

How did Margery see herself, standing strong on that nearly wrecked ship? At the end of all her journeying, when Margery sat down to narrate her memoirs, she didn't refer to herself by her own name. Instead, she called herself 'the creature'. Perhaps she wanted to show herself as a universal character, as a 'creature' among thousands of others. Or maybe she wanted to humble herself; to be less of a person of status and more of a simple soul. But by making herself anonymous she was following a well-worn path. Often in medieval romances heroes tried to erase their own names, especially when they were experiencing an overwhelming sense of breakdown or despair. Usually in these moments, this change of name worked as both a symbol and a confirmation of a commitment to make a new life.

One hero who abandoned his own name, and whose legend Margery would have known well, was Yvain. In Chrétien de Troyes's version of the story, Yvain was a knight from the court of King Arthur whose misery stemmed from a crisis of middle-aged complacency. He had been happily married to his wife Laudine when he was lured away from home by his friends, who wanted him to join a campaign of tournaments and festivals.

He promised his wife he would be back before a year was gone, but Yvain had so much fun that he ended up staying away for twelve months and then several more. When he finally returned, Laudine disowned him. Pretending that he no longer existed, she removed her ring from his finger and sent a messenger to tell Yvain that the marriage was over.

Hating 'nothing so much as himself', Yvain now fell into a despair so acute that he 'ripped and tore at his clothing'. He ran off to live wild in a forest, desperate 'to flee entirely alone to a land so wild that no one could follow or find him', and survived by stalking wild animals and eating their raw flesh. Suicidal, he wept with despair. 'Truly', he said, anyone in his position 'should hate himself and seek to end his life'.[77]

Yvain's *acedia* only began to soften when he remembered how to do all the things he had once loved. An instinct deep in his body made him begin fighting and jousting again, overcoming tyrants and saving people from life-threatening danger. When he found a dragon attacking a lion he saved the lion's life, and it was only this creature's love that kept the grieving Yvain from plunging a sword through his own heart. From that moment he became the 'knight with the lion', and, suppressing his old name, he directed his whole soul to winning back the heart of his Laudine. And out of the ashes of his old life he built a new reputation as a mysterious hero, wandering across the land and defeating enemies of the public good wherever he found them.

Eventually Lunete, a friend of his wife's, stepped in to help him. Yvain had rescued Lunete when she was about to be burned at the stake for a crime she hadn't committed, so she repaid him by hatching a plan. Lunete arranged for the 'knight with the lion' to fight at a tournament, and made her friend Laudine swear that she would do everything in her power to reconcile this anonymous hero with his lost love. She agreed, persuaded by the good things she'd now heard about the 'knight with the lion'. When Yvain won a thrilling victory at the tournament, and removed his helmet to reveal to Laudine who he was and how he had changed, she was delighted to accept him back. The lesson, for the medieval audiences who enjoyed this tale, was clear. To have the bravery to find your heart again, sometimes you first have to strip yourself down to nothing.

Margery didn't consciously model her journey through depression on tales of Arthurian knighthood like Yvain's. But just like Chrétien's knights, what Margery was really searching for on her pilgrimage-quests – to Gdansk, to Norway, to Santiago de Compostela or to Jerusalem – was her own hidden heart. She was fleeing as far as she could from her darkest moments, from the time after her first child was born, when she had no kindness for anybody and wanted to rip off her own skin. In travel she found a way not only to fall in love with the world again, but also to fall in love with herself.

How we cry reflects how we think about ourselves. Catherine of Siena's 'lesser' tears are self-obsessed, or at least self-absorbed. When we cry her 'higher' tears, we see ourselves as sinners and even learn to hate ourselves. *Acedia*, clearly, can have a home on any of these levels. But with the highest kind of tears – the tears Catherine called the *tears of great peace* – we come to see ourselves in a more compassionate way. We accept ourselves as part of a community of humanity, and recognise that, in the eyes of goodness itself, we are all equal. We don't just see ourselves as 'Margery' or 'Peter' or 'Kim' any more. We see ourselves as another soul, a creature who deserves as much love and care as anybody else.

Sunrise was less than an hour ago. Instead of lying in bed for another sleepless morning, I've come out into the winter air to make an early start to the day. My legs are pumping through the snow in the tree-lined square to the south of our university building. Although my ankle is still sore, my mind feels sharp. Because rather than ruminating on things past, I'm thinking ahead to the day I need to live here in Tyumen.

Somewhere along the way, I know, I fell out of love with the things that brought me to Siberia. First I stopped caring about teaching and writing. Then I stopped caring about the world of King Richard, the world I had first seen through that window of oil and wood in the National Portrait Gallery when I was nine. I once cared, and cared so much. But *acedia* is cruel, and the heavier that care the heavier the avalanche when it comes. Augustine of Hippo once wrote that the power of memory is its infinity. That inside each of our past experiences are vast landscapes of desert and jungle, wildernesses and cities of endless horizons. Over the course of teaching this semester, I've felt myself swimming again in the infinity of the medieval lives I've seen; the libraries and archives and cathedrals and medical schools that showed me a world so distant but so close to my own. And so I see that I've been standing on my 'strong mountain' all along: the Middle Ages, teaching and writing about them. And to begin again – to begin to get out of my abyss – I need to find a way to carry on walking up that mountain.

Acedia is always a problem that stops the heart. But it also thrives on repetition. Dante, Juana and Margery all allowed themselves to obsess over hollow recreations of things that were dead and gone. Dante's crisis, lost in the forest of his midlife, came when he was caught in a loop; nursing an unrequited love for the dead Beatrice, and caught in a career deadlock he couldn't imagine his way through. Juana snagged her heart on her obsessions with her husband's corpse, her devotion to his memory jamming her in a holding pattern in the countryside around Valladolid. And Margery, despairing at her professional and social failures, tortured herself with memories of minor slip-ups that stretched back to her childhood. All three were suicidal, or at least driven to extreme self-harm. And all three of them admitted, in their moments of despair, that they no longer saw any light in the things that used to make their spirits move.

A misery like this can make every day feel the same: a sickly replica of a day that was once fun, free and spontaneous. The challenge, somehow, is to open up a space in these days for something new. William Peraldus was right when he said that fields lay fallow and curl up with thorns and then go on to give the sweetest fruit. The author of *The Pearl* was right to say, too, that even in a patch of earth where a dead child lies are spices and flowers that can grow to the fullest beauty. Out of Dante's abyss came the resurrected Beatrice, his guide through Paradise and his inspiration to fall in love with writing again. In Margery's deepest despair she saw a beautiful face, a set of flashing brown eyes, and the conviction to go further on the page than any English person had ever gone before.

Tyumen has no permafrost. Even this compacted snow I'm walking through now will melt in just a few months. I know this will not be the last time I feel the edges of depression through this winter in Siberia. But if I feel again like Juana, I can at least choose the better version of her *acedia* to follow. Instead of restaging a death over and over behind my eyes, I can reflect on the infinity that expands out of every memory. I can try to see myself not as a tortured soul who deserves the misery his mistakes have brought him, but as a person just like any other, deserving of compassion and alert to make something new out of the day. I can make space for my grief and my sadness and know that, aside from the black holes of interstellar space, there's no such thing as an abyss.

CHAPTER 5

Avarice

Outside I can see the golden rays of the sun, but I can't feel their warmth. All I can feel is a blast of temperature-controlled heat puffing up from beneath a plate glass window. Gudvin is a shopping mall fifteen minutes from my apartment, and I thought it would be a good place to spend the morning's break from teaching. Across two fluorescent floors it has a café decorated in a loosely French style, a bank of shops with suitcases and sports equipment, and an Italian fashion store that sells pleated formal trousers. I've tried on a few pairs in the last hour, not really liking the way they balloon around my waist, but still liking the idea of wearing them. And I just spent ten minutes holding a leather messenger bag while a sales assistant demonstrated each of its interior pockets and zips.

The strange rush I felt while buckling up the pleated trousers and running my hands across the surface of that smooth leather bag has a medieval name. Avarice, in treatises on the Deadly Sins, is a species of desire. It's the strain of 'immoderate love' that pushes you either 'to seek out, possess, or keep holding on to something'.[1] Any material object can be the focus of this love. It could be money (the love of which is 'the root of all evil', according to Saint Paul's letter[2]). Or it could be silks, or swords or trousers. But whatever it is, the thing that defines loving this object as 'avarice' is that it's essentially dead: a pile of mute threads or a slice of cold metal.

More than that, this sin is really about possession. It's about attaching ourselves to objects so tightly that we start to become the objects ourselves. Avarice is 'the service of idols' Paul said in another letter, because it compels us to make sacrifices and devote ourselves to something without any real spirit behind it. Avarice asks us to get on our knees and put our hopes into things – stacks of money, overpriced home decor, images of luxury – that have no soul.[3] Whenever we finally come to possess these objects we find, because they're empty on the inside, that they can't give us any real satisfaction.[4] Nevertheless they catch us in a loop of craving: a cycle of desire that casts us thirsting on the waves of an undrinkable sea.

It's true, life can throw harder tests of avarice at us than leather bags with gliding pockets and zips. The same capitalist system of profit and speculation that gave us Gudvin has also given us the scented bliss of a billionaire's hunting lodge, the cool bronze of a rococo clock, or the exhilaration of a premium economy flight to Banff. In the face of these greater temptations, a set of deeper medieval questions – *Which objects are worth desiring? When do our desires tip over from being social to antisocial?* – start to unfurl.

Why turn to medieval writers for wisdom when none of them had even heard of Banff, let alone premium economy upgrades? As it turns out, they thought about materialism more acutely than we might expect. Sitting at a marble bistro table on the first floor of this Siberian mall, with a caramel slice in front of me, I may feel I'm living at the apex of consumer culture. And in many ways I am. But people in the Middle Ages also knew a world of commodities that circled around the globe.[5] They lived in a time when the food you ate in the Netherlands was influenced by what was being grown in the Baltic, and when second-hand markets emerged to cater for people who wanted imported furs and tapestries.[6] They saw the birth of the first investment banks, and many were alive to witness the rise and fall of the richest person who ever lived. They existed, in other words, in times of economic complexity and material aspirations.

Was that complexity the thing we call 'capitalism'? It's true, this word is vague. Usually it implies the presence of a system where trade for private profit and the accumulation of wealth is backed by government support. But because that word 'system' is nebulous, it's impossible for historians to nail down precisely when something we can identify as capitalism arose. Still, a snapshot of society in the late 1300s and 1400s – a society where slaves from Africa were being bought and sold in Iberian port cities, where monarchs and city governments were investing in trade ships off the coasts of Italy – suggests capitalism was already present, at least in a nascent form.[7] As the historian Lester Little once argued, this was the moment when avarice (the sin of excessive greed and desire for money) was first coming to challenge pride (the sin of letting down a community) as the chief Deadly Sin in the popular imagination.[8] It was the era in European history when, as profit and wealth emerged as top social priorities, the evils of money first became something worth fighting.

So, although we may feel like avarice is our own special modern sin, people in the Middle Ages understood its thrill and novelty with an intensity that brought them to their own refreshing way of seeing objects. Not simply the puritan rejection of material things, but an alternative philosophy of accumulation. One where what matters is not how much or what we acquire, but whether or not these things possess a soul.

A Handful of Gold Dust

How did ordinary people spend their money in the Middle Ages? Were they 'consumers', able to go out and buy luxurious products? Or were most of them, after all, struggling to subsist?

A few years ago I travelled to Valencia for a conference. From the window of the plane that took me there I saw immaculate yellow beaches and the enormous park that flows through the heart of the city. I also caught sight of the cathedral's hexagonal dome, glinting in the late morning sun. According to the travel guide on my lap this was the home of the Holy Grail, although details were scant. I read something about a cup of agate stone, hidden in the Pyrenees for centuries. A secluded monastery, and the monks who sent the grail as a gift to the King of Aragon in the 1300s. I was sceptical. Why would a monastery give up the greatest Christian relic of them all? And if Valencia really had the Holy Grail, why had Indiana Jones battled through a rock temple in Jordan looking for it? All of which meant that the first thing I wanted to do, after landing, was visit the cathedral and see for myself.

But before that I had to attend the conference. It was a gathering of history professors studying the Western economy in the Middle Ages, and one of the key themes of the meeting was the 'commercial revolution' of the thirteenth century. This was a shift in the continent's history nearly as significant as the industrial revolution of the eighteenth and nineteenth centuries, or the agricultural revolution of the neolithic era. Before this commercial revolution, the theory goes, Europe had been a set of isolated peninsulas at the edge of the world's trading system. The economy was dominated by agriculture, and the average person spent their life working the same patch of land their family had occupied for generations.[9] With some exceptions, the road networks at this point were poor. Long-distance sea transport was unstable, and violent and erratic politics meant few wanted to invest in pushing trade up through the continent. And so commodities from the Silk Road (where all the real economic action was taking place) rarely connected with regions like France or England.

By the early 1200s, however, things were changing. Europe had now become a stable place to do business, with fewer civil wars and some robust new laws protecting against ambush, robbery, threats and murder. Agricultural abundance meant surpluses could be sold and profits reinvested in other areas.[10] Cities were expanding, trading markets were opening in towns from Troyes to Frankfurt, and secure roads were coming to connect every major town from the Baltic to the Adriatic.[11] Most people, it's true, still lived a rural life. Yet each year, thousands were moving to work in cities, picking up trades – like glass-blowing, university lecturing, cloth production, or accountancy – that paid all their wages in cash rather than in the old feudal arrangement of food, shelter and 'protection'.[12]

With its new combination of increased wealth and resources, this changing Europe became a more attractive prospect for traders in Egypt. And so these merchants, who were the real economic powerhouses of the 1200s, exploited their handy position as a pivot between the African, European and Asian markets and began investing in European commodities with confidence.[13] Alongside this flow of trade came a flow of the knowledge needed to process it. Before this time, merchants in Italian or French ports had still used Roman numerals. But the publication of the mathematician Fibonacci's *Liber abaci* in 1202 introduced the Arabic numeral system, which he'd learned while studying in Algeria. Along with this he brought some financial advice – about investment returns, about interest rates and about complex contracts – that Europeans had never been able to master until now.[14]

It was at this point that the sin of avarice began to change in the imagination of theologians.[15] Back in the 1100s, most of the sermons about this Deadly Sin railed against the top 1 per cent: the bishops who bribed their way into public office, or the kings who plundered cities. Now, amid the changes of the 1200s, the targets of these sermons shifted. Preachers talked about a new society of 'haves' and 'have nots', where everyone treated 'the rich with the utmost partiality, while only hearing half the case of the person in need'.[16] Storytellers described greed as commonplace, referencing piles of coins and bags of treasure as if these were things ordinary citizens carried around with them.

If anyone captured this new spirit best, it was the bishop Jacques de Vitry (d.1240). Jacques had travelled widely, going to Egypt in the 1210s to see its vast wealth and complex economy for himself. After he returned he wrote a sermon, telling a story full of anxiety about money, about profit and about the emerging culture of accumulation. Aside from revealing his own discomfort about Egyptian profit-making, Jacques's story reveals the double-edged nature of Europe's new economy.

There was once a 'poor man', Jacques said, who had worked and managed to earn 'a modest living'. He was extremely happy with his situation, and spent his evenings singing and laughing with his family before going to bed. But all of this was irritating to the man's neighbours, who unlike him were part of the city's new bourgeoisie. Why wasn't this man full of stress and anxiety, like them? So these neighbours decided to play a trick. They left 'a bag of money' on his doorstep and watched to see how he would react. Would the money change his life? Would he finally admit that he wanted more wealth, that he wanted to be just like the rest of them?

Coming home and seeing the sack, the poor man panicked. He hid the money in a cupboard, but still its presence tortured him. Terrified that the cash would be stolen, or that someone would turn up to accuse him of stealing it, he couldn't sleep, and his spirit began to fade away. He no longer sang songs with his family when he came home from work, and he no longer did much of anything. Eventually, the rich neighbours revealed their prank, hoping to make him even more miserable. But it turned out the joke was on them. Because instead of fighting or complaining, as they'd hoped, the poor man just gave them the money straight back. 'Now I can sing and laugh again,' he said, 'just like I used to.'[17]

Who were the thirteenth-century public supposed to sympathise with, when listening to a story like this? Although the poor man was meant to be the hero, wasn't the story really aimed at the newly wealthy 'stress balls' in the audience? In Paris, where Jacques had once lived, a new class of haberdashers, bankers and exporters were generating disposable incomes.[18] And yet this wealthy crowd was precarious, and still felt they had to struggle to secure their finances. Geoffroy de Saint-Laurent, a bourgeois citizen of Paris, is a case in point. Geoffroy started a business in the late 1200s, buying up properties and acting as a private legal consultant for a series of high-profile civic cases. Even though he was wealthy in his day, Geoffroy couldn't lay much of a cash foundation for his children, and within a generation or two the family fortune had dwindled.[19] When money was as vulnerable as this, the Geoffroys of this new economic landscape could hardly avoid the occasional sleepless night.

Still, there was a paradox. Even though people now enjoyed earning and spending money, and passed their evenings worrying about it, most of them still liked to pretend it was an alien concept. Some said that coins were *dirty*, or that money would 'rot' and 'putrefy' if it was hoarded.[20] Cash – because it was seen as something both disposable and toxic, rather than lasting and nourishing – was regularly compared to excrement. The marginal illustrations of manuscripts and the wooden misericords carved beneath church pews show coins flowing out of people's rectums.[21] The same connection made its way straight into the era's sermons. 'Has anyone handled gold or silver for any period of time,' the Dutch preacher Helinand of Froidmont asked around the year 1240, 'without soiling his fingers?'[22]

As well as being *dirty*, writers now claimed that money was *inhuman*. When the character of Avarice springs up in a fourteenth-century poem, Guillaume de Deguileville's *The Pilgrimage of Human Life*, it's a genuinely shocking moment. She's a hybrid being with six hands (made into a woman, most likely, as the Latin word for this sin – *avaritia* – is feminine). Several artists tried to capture what this being might have looked like, which is a difficult task. But the award goes to whoever illustrated the manuscript now kept in the Bibliothèque Sainte-Geneviève in Paris, a hypnotic vision standing in front of nausea-inducing wallpaper.

Avarice, in this Parisian manuscript, has had her real arms severed. Six new ones have grown in their place, and the symbolism of each is explained in the text. Avarice's highest two arms (which both have a set of feathered claws) are the hands she uses for 'plunder' and 'robbery'. Her two central arms represent the 'pests' that, Guillaume claimed, squeeze the most money out of ordinary citizens: 'the church' (the hand that holds the crooked stick); and 'beggars' (the hand holding the bowl). Finally, at the bottom is the pair of hands that signified the two groups that were corrupting the late-medieval financial industry. These are the traders or money-changers, signified by the hand that holds a file for clipping coins, and the money lenders, whose crime is represented by a set of scales.[23]

The Six-Handed Monster of Avarice.

It's easy to be bowled over by these arms. If we look closer though, exploring the full range of this image, we'll find an even bigger medieval myth about greed: the myth that the love of money is also, somehow, *foreign*. Because there, on Avarice's covered head, is a small white statue. As Guillaume explains, this is an idol of 'Mammon', who Avarice is in the act of worshipping as a god.

The name 'Mammon' appears only very briefly in the Bible, in the passage (repeated across two of the Gospels) when Jesus warns that it's impossible 'to serve both God and Mammon'. But medieval writers never agreed who or what this 'Mammon' actually was. Some said he was 'a demon who tempts people through wealth'.[24] Others explained (accurately, as it turns out)

AVARICE

that Mammon was simply another word for 'riches'.[25] Guillaume accelerated the debate in another direction, making Mammon into a fully-fledged god, complete with this statuette idol. 'You must submit to him,' his six-handed Avarice commands, because without Mammon 'nothing can be taken in the land of authority'. He was a deity, Guillaume wrote, 'who ensnares but who also wants to be tied down', and who seeks nothing more than 'to lie with the mice in the earth'.[26]

I was startled, when I first read *The Pilgrimage of Human Life*, to see the character of Avarice use the name 'Mammon' and 'Mahommet' interchangeably. Was this poet ignorant about Islam? Aside from the obvious overlap of the two names, there are other reasons for somebody writing in the 1300s to make this connection. When medieval writers imagined Mammon as a god, they usually decided he was native to lands under the control of Islamic rulers. Rupert of Deutz, the twelfth-century German preacher, believed Mammon was worshipped by the followers of 'an avenging king' in the Levant.[27] Some also identified the word 'Mammon' as native to the 'Assyrian' (or Aramaic) language, situating it firmly in what was then Muslim-controlled territory.[28]

Islam, generally, would have been synonymous with wealth for European Christians of this era. After all, the hundreds of thousands who went on crusades in the 1100s and 1200s all brought back confirmation that the societies of the Levant and Egypt were comfortably better off than their own. And yet the poet Guillaume would have had a more vivid reference point, and a better reason to conflate Mammon with Islam. Because at the time he was alive the world was still shaking from the impact of Mansa Musa, the Emperor of Mali from 1312 to 1337, and the richest person who has ever lived. Like Guillaume's Avarice, this was an individual who had been a turban-wearing

Muslim. And like that six-handed hoarder of 'the gold and silver denarius,' someone also renowned for his abundance of coins.

Measuring the net worth of Musa, who began ruling the Mali Empire when he was around thirty-two, would be impossible now. All we have to go on are some breathtaking ruins and a set of dubious legends. But a reasonable guess is that he amassed, by exploiting abundant gold mines to the south of his territory, and monopolising the salt trade to its north and west, a personal fortune equivalent to around $400 billion.[29] It's an absurd valuation, backed up by some absurd stories. On a state visit to Egypt in 1324, according to the Syrian historian al-Umari, Musa crashed the local economy.[30] Specifically, his 'abundant' gifts dropped the price of gold 'by two dirhams per mithkal' (*c.*12 per cent), creating a recession that didn't recover for over a decade.[31] And his troop of twelve thousand slaves, all wearing 'gowns of brocade and Yemeni silk,' carried with them eighty sacks of gold dust, scattered ahead to make the roads glitter and shine in front of Musa as they travelled.[32]

These more detailed legends didn't make it far enough north for a writer like Guillaume de Deguileville to hear about them. Instead, what most Europeans got was a version of the story that reduced Mansa Musa down to three basic characteristics. First, they were told that he was a *Muslim king*, and second, that he possessed an *extraordinary amount of gold*, something the two cartographers who made the Majorcan Catalan Atlas (*c.*1375) captured in their image of Musa, putting into his right hand a golden orb that sparkled on the map's vellum surface.[33] Already, from these two facts alone, Musa could have seemed like a fit for 'Mammon'. But people in the north were also told that he had a third, equally important characteristic. His *skin colour*. As the caption on the Catalan map described, Musa was a 'Black

AVARICE

lord' who was sometimes known as the 'lord of the Blacks of Geneua'.[34]

Would it be anachronistic to say this made him a natural target of racism? Dark skin didn't always have negative associations for medieval readers, as writers like Hugh of Saint Victor were keen to stress.[35] And while it's true that from the 1200s theologians were coming to conflate *blackness* with bad character, and artists were painting saints in paradise with a pure-white sheen,[36] communities were still enthusiastic about celebrating black-skinned saints or the black-skinned magus Balthazar.[37] That's not to say skin colour wasn't a big deal, or to defend exoticism as anything other than patronising. But for Europeans further north, who were unaccustomed to encountering Black Africans, their racism would have been of a different kind. Seeing Musa's appearance in the context of greed, they would have found it reassuringly distant from their own.[38] *Don't worry, his blackness would have said to them. The worst kind of avarice belongs to people who look quite different from you.*

If only writers like Guillaume de Deguileville had read the Arabic sources, they'd have found that Musa's avarice was never quite so full-throated as they imagined. At the height of his wealth he ploughed vast amounts of his personal money into public works, of which the dazzling spiked beehive Djinguereber Mosque in Timbuktu remains. He invested in justice, bringing the best Islamic lawyers into his empire.[39] Instead of hoarding his treasure, if anything he was too ready to give it all away. A man who worked in Musa's household told al-Umari that the king had been 'noble and generous', performing so many 'acts of kindness' that he even ran out of cash and had to secure private loans. Ibn Khaldūn, who called him 'an upright man', noted that he rewarded a builder named Abū Ishāq for constructing him a 'square building with a dome', covered with 'elegant' coloured patterns, by paying him 275 kilos of gold. At current market value, that's a personal wage of around 18.7 million dollars.[40]

So which was Musa? Was he the epitome of greed, loving riches so much that he stockpiled them away from his people? Or was he a classic case of prodigality, loving riches so little that he splashed his money indiscriminately, while failing to move it where it was really needed?[41] Whichever he may have been in reality, in the European imagination Musa became a lightning rod for their anxieties. And amid these projections was their deepest message about money. It seems the real crime of absurd wealth in the late medieval West wasn't the spending of it. Rather, it was its antisocial aspect: pursuing riches in a way that distracts people from doing things that would otherwise benefit the wider community. As Poggio Bracciolini put it in his treatise *On Avarice*, written in the early 1400s, greed is the impulse that ruins the social bond. 'Dedicated only to himself', the avaricious person 'not only deserts, but even opposes the public welfare'.[42]

Still, it would be unfair to level all these criticisms at Musa himself. Aside from one short speech recorded by al-Umari, nothing of the emperor's interior thought process survives. His 'palaces enclosed by circular walls' have all evaporated, and historians have been left to speculate over which strip of yellow land along the banks of the Niger River was once the capital city of his empire.[43] But even as his home was swamped by sand and dust, and his gold was scattered wide across the Sahara, Musa's legend remained. He became a convenient symbol – just as the Western capitalistic system was beginning to kick into life – of everything Europeans wanted to pretend they weren't.[44] Greed might feel like a social poison, or a tasteless fixation on having and holding. And yet it's much easier to pretend that greed goes on somewhere else – down in the street below, or along a river across the desert – than to stop and self-examine; to wonder just how far our own attitudes to spending and hoarding have led us away from other people, away from ourselves.

The Valencia Time Machine

In the Het Noordbrabants Museum in the southern Netherlands is a painting with a touch of vertigo about it (plate 9). Commissioned by the Cloth Sellers Guild of the town of 's-Hertogenbosch in around 1530, it's a late medieval street scene squeezed into an hourglass; Edvard Munch's *The Scream* reimagined as a CGI advert for a new shopping district. It was painted as a celebration of the hometown of the artist Hieronymus Bosch (d.1516), whose house is the seventh one from the right. Bosch, who liked to paint bodies being sliced by enormous knives as punishment for their envy, or hollowed out and used as furniture as retribution for their sloth, might have appreciated the psychedelic technique. Would he have appreciated its message about avarice, though?

When I first saw this painting, I was struck by all the evidence of the thriving late medieval economy. The bustling stalls, all tented against the rain threatened by those wispy cotton clouds, and the colourful range of late medieval fashions. All the same, I couldn't get away from the single premodern knot in the artwork; the detail that takes this painting to an even stranger place than the warped perspective. At the front is a saint with a halo, handing out free clothes to people who need them. He's a well-dressed dandy, in plum-coloured velvet and silk stockings. I was shocked to discover, reading the small plaque in the museum, that this was supposed to be Francis of Assisi. The Italian saint from the thirteenth century, and the man who has been called the most radical opponent of wealth in human history.

One problem is the outfit. As any medieval artist should have known, Francis stopped wearing expensive cloaks and stockings when he was still in his early twenties. Instead, he lived out his existence, between the roadways and doorways of Umbria, in pursuit of an impossible dream. The dream of living in total poverty.

Born Giovanni di Pietro di Bernardone in 1182, he had once been a typical member of Europe's new commercial class. Like many among this elite he had a father who traded commodities, and who took regular business trips over the Alps. As a child, Giovanni loved singing romantic French songs so much that his family began calling him Francis (or 'Frenchie'), and the name stuck. After a traumatic experience as a prisoner of war, though, Frenchie lost his *joie de vivre*. Stopping at a cave-like church to pray on his way home, a crucifix spoke to him – or at least, that's what he thought. Dazzled by this vision, he changed his life. First he gave away all his clothes, and then he began sleeping in an abandoned church on the road out of Assisi. Even though his father now began to shun Francis in public, a few followers joined him, and they became their own small team of builders and renovators, fixing the roofs of old churches and making them fit for communities again.

Fighting avarice was the motor of the young Francis's energies. He wanted to own nothing, not even a shirt or a pillow. And over the next two decades, his battle with avarice morphed into a titanic struggle against all seven of the Deadly Sins. Francis had to fight his pride, as Pope Innocent III made him the head of a great religious order. He sometimes envied the anonymous life he had lost, as new followers kept praising him as a type of messiah. He was angry that his companions kept demanding that he set up a system of rules. (Wasn't imitating the life of Jesus enough?) Gluttony was never much of a problem (he had a weak stomach), and neither was lust. But he suffered from terrible *acedia*, and grew depressed – until he died, after a severe eye infection, in October 1226 – at the thought that his experiment in poverty had never really gone far enough.[45]

Because what Francis and his early followers had wanted to achieve was something far more radical than that painting in 's-Hertogenbosch makes it seem. They had wanted to possess *nothing at all*. This meant never handling any money, a belief Francis once illustrated by making one of his brothers spit coins onto a pile of manure.[46] It also meant never owning any property. They would all live as lodgers, he decided, in buildings that otherwise had no use. But he also rejected the ownership of books, because this was the type of property that marked one person as 'better' than another. Anything that threatened to improve you materially was, for Francis, a strike against the only things that really mattered: love, honesty and living a life free from self-consciousness.[47] He believed in the total equality of all created beings, to the extent that one day when his trousers caught fire he let them burn, because nobody 'should hurt Brother Fire'.[48] Why should the needs of one being be more important than those of any other?[49]

It was a beautiful dream in principle. And in principle it seized on the ideas of some of the greatest critics of Europe's new economy. Just like Alain de Lille, whose *Complaint of Nature* was widely read in the early 1200s, Francis's followers believed that money would kill precisely the thing inside you that makes you who you really are. It would strip a Cicero of his 'eloquence', or an Orpheus of his music.[50] Like the wandering student Lothar of Segni (who later became Pope Innocent III), they felt that 'the wealth of this world' wouldn't 'remove need, but bring it'.[51] In Francis's philosophy, the minute you start to love your home or your clothes, your love gets sucked away from the things that matter (including other people but also, paradoxically, yourself). And this means you begin to lose your identity, too.

For the majority of medieval society, there were three problems with Francis's dream. First of all, it was hard to execute in practice. Surviving without money was nearly impossible in thirteenth-century Europe, when so many things now depended on a flow of cash transactions. Some contemporary commentators also felt his whole experiment in poverty was undermined after Francis died. When the Franciscan Order built an enormous painted basilica in Assisi, and allowed its members to become elite professors of theology in Paris and Oxford, didn't that mean that the spirit of total poverty was now gone for good?[52]

But the biggest problem with Francis's dream was actually much simpler. Many people, in the thriving world of the thirteenth-century 'commercial revolution', now thought that *a life of poverty sounded like a nightmare.* With new commodities sweeping through European towns, the lure of fashion and furniture was becoming too much to resist. For thousands of ordinary people, who now had access to cheaper spices and silks for the first time, building a richer material life was beginning to feel less like a way of losing personality, and more like a way of acquiring one.

Who could really afford these fashions, though? What was the economic landscape really like for the average person? Back at the conference in Valencia (where I was enjoying the academic talks, but also desperate to get outside to see the city's Holy Grail for myself), a series of papers debated the question of medieval monthly budgets. At the heart of the problem was the same question that occupies many of us today. How much did rent cost? What proportion of the average person's income – in a city like Valencia in the later Middle Ages – was given over to housing? And from this, can we infer how much might be left

A knight, in a thirteenth-century manuscript, prepares to combat the Seven Deadly Sins. Each sin is represented by a winged demon, with their 'children' and 'grandchildren' lined up behind them.

2 Hell, as imagined by the artist Herrad of Landsberg. This is a facsimile of the lost *Hortus Deliciarum* manuscript, made in the late 1100s and destroyed in 1870 during the Franco-Prussian War.

The reliquary of Saint Anthony of Padua, made in the 1340s. Anthony's green tongue is blocked from view here by his bottom row of teeth.

4 Giotto's fresco of Judas betraying Jesus in the Garden of Gethsemane. Wanting to blot out a rival is a classic symptom of envy.

A fifteenth-century panel showing Cain and Abel, the identical brothers, offering sacrifices to God. Abel's murder is shown on the left and Cain's exile on the right.

6 Thirty scenes from the Bible, painted on an enormous panel now kept in Verona. Judas still has a halo in panel number fourteen but has lost it by panel number sixteen.

7 One of the many stops on Juana of Castile's procession for her dead husband, as imagined by the nineteenth-century artist Francisco Pradilla y Ortiz. Looking at the faces gathered around Juana, is this the best depiction of boredom in the history of art?

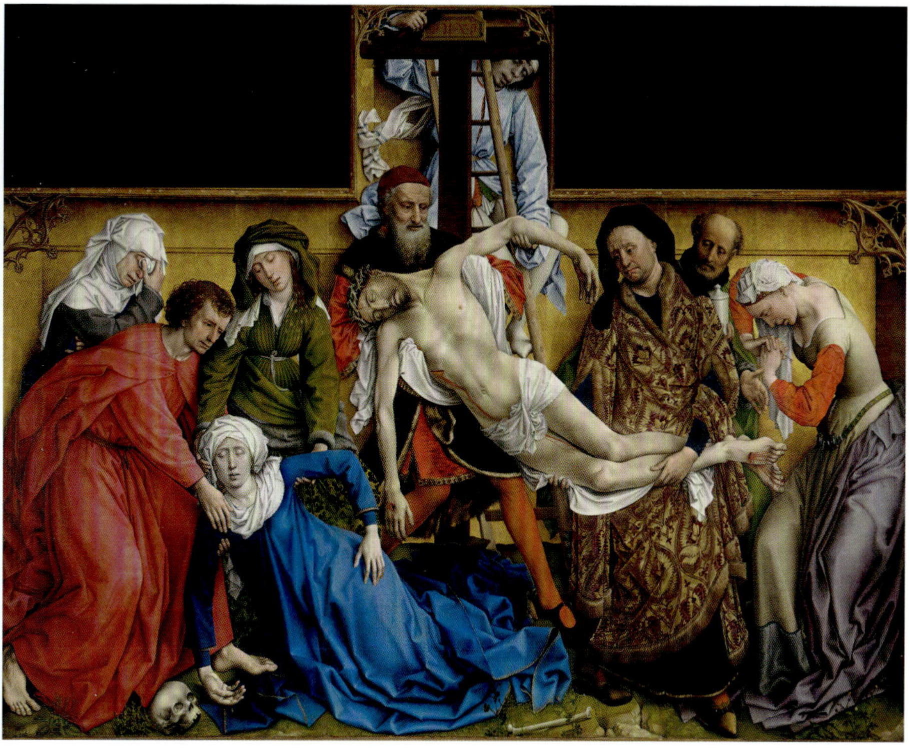

8 Rogier van der Weyden's *The Descent from the Cross* (c.1435), notable for the life-like tears, the rich fabrics and the swooning Virgin Mary.

9 A painting of the cloth market of 's-Hertogenbosch (*c*.1530). This is the birthplace of the artist Hieronymus Bosch, whose house is seventh from the right. At the front, Francis of Assisi, unlike the sellers behind him, is handing out clothes for free.

10 The Valencia Chalice (or the Holy Grail) from Valencia Cathedral. Although the gold parts are all later additions, the cup at the core dates from c.1 AD.

11 A page from the *Très Riches Heures du Duc de Berry* (1410s). This is the grape harvest, and at least one worker can't resist trying out this year's supply for himself.

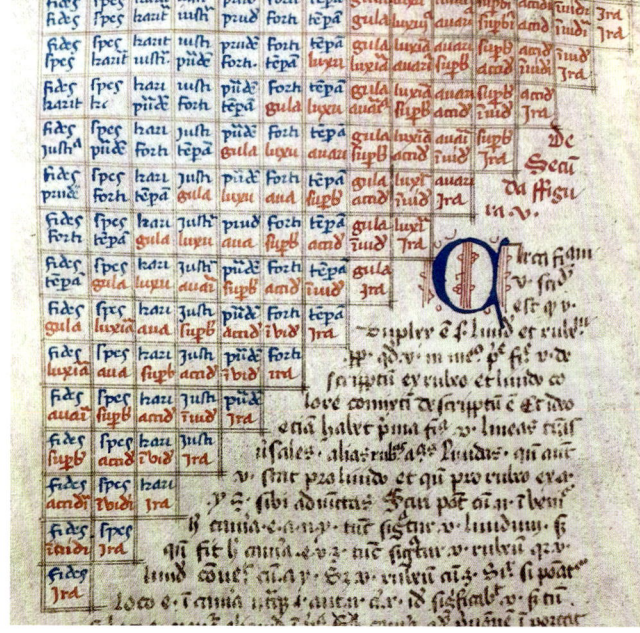

12 A grid from a fifteenth-century manuscript of Ramon Llull's *Ars demonstrativa*. The reader is meant to work through all the combinations of vice and virtue, reflecting on how one impulse can push the other in a new direction.

13 The central panel of Hieronymus Bosch's psychedelic masterpiece *The Garden of Earthly Delights* (c.1500). Is this paradise on earth? The world spun out of control? Or is it what humanity would have become if the idea of 'sin' had never existed?

over to invest in material pleasure, shopping for luxuries, or other species of avarice?

To answer this question, the historian Antonio Belenguer González had gone through the meticulous records of notaries. He'd combed hundreds of original rental contracts in Valencia's archives, and by cross-referencing these with the tenants' estimated salaries he said he could now give us an idea of how ordinary people coped with the price of housing. My pen hovered over my notepad, and I wondered what number I would write down. If the average Londoner today spends between 40–50 per cent of their income on rent, would the medieval percentage be much higher? When the number came, at first it was confusing. Rent in Valencia ranged between 200 and 400 *sous* per year, Antonio had discovered. As he explained, though, because the average annual salary was around 1100 *sous*, this meant that rent cost not much more than 25 per cent of a wage earner's outgoings.[53]

If housing was 25 per cent of income, what did people do with the other 75 per cent? Could they use it to spend on luxuries? Or did people have other crippling expenses lurking in the wings? Clicking through to another slide, Antonio rattled through a typical Valencian shopping basket, although this didn't necessarily clear things up. Buying a pillow was about a day's salary, he said. Only 40 per cent of homes had wooden chairs in the early 1400s, which seems impractical. And while a table would be three days' pay, it would take fifteen days to save up for a blanket. Children who soiled their bedclothes must have been in huge trouble.

Statistics and prices are useful, but they have their limitations. They tell us little about the texture of everyday life, and nothing about how these items were actually bought and used. To get a better picture, we need to look at the contents of individual homes themselves. Luckily, another researcher at the conference – Luis Almenar Fernández – gave a paper about the sources he'd been using to do this. And in the break between papers, he stopped to talk to me and explained these sources in detail.

Probate inventories, Luis explained over a tiny cup of coffee, are the closest thing we have to photographs of medieval home interiors. In single snapshots, they capture every item a medieval person left inside their homes when they died. They include tablecloths and bed linen, pet parrots and candelabras, as well as exhaustive lists of clothes and the wooden closets they were kept in. As Luis revealed, the average citizen of Valencia in the time of Mansa Musa owned around seventeen items of clothing. These included tunics – which had once been unisex but became tailored differently according to gender by the late 1300s – and more exotic garments – like ornamental Islamic headdresses, which became a sudden trend – that passed in and out of fashion.[54]

Luis's best snapshot, though, was the home interior of Jaume Suau, who lived in the early 1400s. Jaume worked as a textile craftsman, and his probate inventory lists all the needles and threads, the baskets and the pairs of scissors he left in his home when he died. But it also records his tasteful home decor: his three wooden chests, his two large wooden boxes, his two benches painted white and red, and his book of the Psalms (which, as all books were still copied by hand at this point, would have been an expensive luxury). On Jaume's table was a candelabra, a salt shaker, three glass cups and three ceramic plates designed to look metallic. And in his closet – alongside two red cloaks, some linen shirts and a belt made from white silk – was a black doublet with red sleeves.

What made Jaume's case such a surprise is that he was a

citizen who had once been a slave. As the inventory put it, he was *de llinatge d'etíops*, meaning that he had been brought from Ethiopia to Valencia, before becoming one of the few who managed to gain their freedom.[55] 'But there must have been quite a lot of social mobility,' Luis said, a band of light flashing across his glasses as we finished our coffees. 'He had so many wonderful possessions, even though he had once been a possession himself.'[56]

Did any of this behaviour – hunting down exotic doublets, cultivating a taste for fine silks – make somebody guilty of avarice? When he curated his home and upgraded his wardrobe, a worker like Jaume was riding a wave of consumerism that had changed significantly since Jacques de Vitry wrote those sermons for the stressed Parisian bourgeoisie in the 1200s. Up until then, European money had been concentrated in the hands of tight-knit urban families. So when Francis of Assisi had preached his radical message against money, he had mostly been rebelling against an emerging elite, a new fringe of society.

What changed everything was the second wave of the Black Death. When this pandemic hit in the 1360s it broke up old trade monopolies, freed-up housing and gave labourers the power to negotiate better wages.[57] As inequalities diminished, a whole new class of people could take advantage of falling costs, and buy commodities that had once been out of reach.[58] Even at the very bottom of the economic ladder, the poorest peasants could now expect to have smart homes, a choice of shirts and tunics and a fully equipped bed to sleep on. And maybe, if they could negotiate a cash bonus from their employer, they could even have a candelabra and a salt shaker on the table too.

Was this an epidemic of avarice? Francis of Assisi, at his most radical, would have said 'yes', and would have argued that any and all material acquisition is greed simply because it's another obstacle between you and raw existence; another shade to block out love's warmest rays. By the 1300s, a more forgiving angle had developed. Material desire will only turn into greed, according to a legal compendium of moral advice written around 1338, when it reaches for things that aren't 'necessary for your life, according to its conditions'.[59] All possessions are weights that drag us down, if we follow this doctrine, except for the ones we really need. And these ones will do the lifting for us, helping us to live a better, freer life.

Was every doublet in Jaume's wardrobe heavy or light? Did they liberate him or did they weigh him down? Ultimately, our judgement depends on how we understand that word 'necessary'. For a person with a fleet of doublets, adding one more with different coloured sleeves might be a push. But for Jaume – an ex-slave living in an Iberian world, in which people with dark skin would have often been assumed to be 'on the run' from their masters – buying a doublet with red sleeves to impress people in the street may have been a matter of urgency.[60] And who could call that a Deadly Sin?

In the modern world we no longer believe that material life should be reduced to mere survival.[61] By the same logic, if ordinary people in the early 1400s wanted to decorate their homes or participate in luxury, didn't this also fulfil a deeper 'need'? Lothar of Segni described how the love of money 'kills souls that do not die, and gives life to souls which do not live'.[62] With the help of Luis, I tried to see Jaume through Lothar's eyes. If he poured all his love and spirit into his wardrobe, never resting until he could buy his next cloak or candelabra, it would be like blood loss for his soul: a way of draining his spirit and pumping it directly into the lifeless objects around him. So long as Jaume was happy to 'put to use' everything he had, though, his accumulation would be not so much a process of soul killing as soul making.⁶³ It would become a way of expressing and enlarging his psychic life; enabling him to expand, not contract, his heart.

Face to Face with the Holy Grail

If Gudvin is where you go in Tyumen to hide, Galeria Voyage is where you go to be seen. Pulsing with neon lights, the mall is funnel-shaped (like New York's Guggenheim Museum), and occupies roughly the same ground space as the Eiffel Tower. Where Gudvin has its French café, Voyage has a Starbucks, and instead of Italian clothing stores it has more than a dozen major Western fashion chains. Although I know I haven't come here for any of those, I can't remember what it was I wanted. Baptised by the heat at the entrance way, I weave between other padded-coated shoppers and drift across the shiny floor. Before I know what I'm doing I find myself trying on a mustard-coloured woollen sweater in a shop on the second level. I stare into the mirror and wince at the coils of wool bunched up at my waist. I've often walked into a fitting room like this and felt an urgency; a sense that only this object, right now, can fill the need that's deep inside me. Then I get home with my bags and realise I feel just the same as before.

Was it so different on that day I finally got to see the Holy Grail?

Exiting the conference venue, that afternoon in Valencia, I made my way diagonally down through the city park and towards the cathedral. I trampled across a mottled grass lawn and twisted through rows of lime trees, moving in the direction of the misty sun. A shower of rain came as I began climbing a set of steps, so I ducked into a colonnade and opened up my city guidebook.

> Valencia Cathedral is also home to the Holy Grail, the chalice believed to have been used by Jesus at the Last Supper. While the golden handles and jewelled base were added in later centuries, the original cup, made of red agate stone, was dated by archaeologists to first-century Palestine.[64]

The book added a tale, uncredited, about how the goblet first came to the cathedral. Saint Lawrence (who had been working in Rome) found it and sent it back to his family in Huesca, Spain. From there the chalice was hidden in the Pyrenees for generations, until (according to 'a document in the archives') it turned up at the Monastery of San Juan de la Peña in the 1130s. These mountain monks then gave it as a gift to the King of Aragon in 1399, before a later king, Alfonso V, donated it to the cathedral to write off a debt.[65]

Shielded from the battering rain by a curtain of medieval stone, I wanted to believe every word of this story. But it turns out that no document from 'the archives' at San Juan de la Peña has ever listed the grail. In fact, the monastery doesn't have any archives. And according to a diligent Swiss scholar, no documentary evidence of the chalice exists from before the year 1437.[66]

Nevertheless, as I discovered later, the grail legend really did first emerge in the mountains of northern Spain.

'Grail', the word, comes from the archaic Catalan *gradal*, meaning bowl or dish. The earliest known image of a holy grail was made in 1123 in the small town of Taüll in the Pyrenees, on a wall painting from the church of Sant Climent.[67] It's a fresco showing the Virgin Mary on a burnished throne, her neck stretched like a chess piece, carrying a shallow bowl of flaming

AVARICE

tongues in her cloaked left hand. Although no story or song has survived to accompany this image, it must have been part of a local legend, because nearly a dozen wall paintings like this from the 1100s survive in the same cluster of mountain towns. All of them show Mary holding a chalice or bowl that seems to radiate its own kind of holy fire.[68]

The first known depiction of the Holy Grail: The Virgin Mary holding a dish of flames.

Did these artists in the Pyrenees inspire the world-famous legend? Or were they part of an offshoot grail tradition, now lost to history? No historian, so far, has unearthed any earlier evidence of the story. And so the first concrete evidence of the legend begins at the end of the 1100s, when a string of epic tales made the fiery grail into a parable about the nature of desire itself. While these writers disagreed over what this grail actually was – was it a chalice, or a dish, or a stone? – most agreed that it was a magical commodity just beyond human grasp. It was the one item that no money could buy, that no gold could outweigh, that no impurity could corrupt.

Usually, the legend of the Holy Grail centres on a Welshman named Parzival. It's a story of ignorance, courage and redemption. After Parzival's father died in combat his mother retreated to a remote forest. Terrified that the sins of the father would be visited on the son, she made sure Parzival never heard anything of knighthood – not even the word – throughout his entire childhood. Nevertheless, the boy somehow managed to stumble into a life of adventure. He first came upon the grail quest one day when he met an elderly fisherman who invited him to his castle. When Parzival arrived there for dinner later, though, he found that the fisherman (who was now revealed as the 'Fisher King') was suffering from a fatal wound.

What followed was a strange kind of test. Parzival watched as the king's servants walked in, parading magical objects in front of him. First they brought in a lance that dripped blood onto the floor. Then they brought the 'grail' itself, which shone with a ferocious light. Seeing this display, Parzival made a terrible mistake. Remembering some advice he had once heard about the danger of asking too many questions, he kept completely silent as the dazzling objects passed before his eyes. It was an error, he was later told, that prevented the Fisher King from healing, and it sent Parzival on a five-year spiral of depression and wandering dejection.

Clearly, Parzival's world was not a naturalistic one. But what on earth was going on here? What was the message of this moment? Why was the Fisher King wounded? And why was it supposed to be such a mistake to ask no questions when confronted with the grail?

Putting a train ticket in my guidebook to mark my page, I left the colonnade and began walking east. Now the rain had stopped and the sun had shaken its mist. After stepping along narrow street paths, skirting busy tobacco shops and bars with ashtrays full of olive stones, I came upon the cathedral almost by accident. The building itself is a fusion of architectural delights; like somebody has mixed up Lego sets of Notre-Dame de Paris and the Roman Colosseum. Walking through the dark entrance door under one of its wings, I entered to the immediate hush of cool stone and immense vertical space. A blocky typed sign, written in Catalan, Spanish and English, pointed the way to the 'Grail Chapel'. Was it really this easy? Did it really just take an EasyJet flight and a nine Euro donation to see human history's greatest lost relic?

Since the legend was first written down, writers have struggled to decode Parzival's mistake. Some have argued that he lacked the good taste to recognise something as special as the grail when he saw it. According to Chrétien de Troyes, the first writer to tell the story, Parzival's main problem was that he couldn't distinguish true brilliance from ordinary craftsmanship. 'Why did you not seize Fortune when you found her?' a woman shouts at him, in Chrétien's version, after he returns from the Fisher King's castle. Because although it should have been obvious that the grail was a miraculous object, Parzival treated it like any other piece of gold. The lesson of this was that we shouldn't treat everything that shimmers in the same way. Whereas avarice is indiscriminate, the desire we should show for objects like the Holy Grail involves deep discernment.[69] Greed sees every jewel as another temptation on a passing conveyor belt, but this desire stays alert for the unique treasures: those with a 'special light and brightness', brilliant enough to enlarge our souls.[70]

With this interpretation, an object is worth reaching for when it has real human value. In the classic version of the tale, written by the German writer Wolfram von Eschenbach in the early 1200s, the Holy Grail was a miraculous stone. Where Chrétien had said the grail was dazzlingly beautiful, Wolfram went deeper, giving it a subtle translucent quality.[71] The stone was an elixir of life, he said; a radiant nucleus of 'earth's perfection', first brought to the planet by a team of angels. And it had genuine transformative benefits for humanity. Anybody who looked at it was guaranteed to live for another week, no matter how old or sick they were. It brought youth to 'flesh and bone', so that its keeper would live for two hundred years or more without growing a single grey hair.[72] It also guaranteed freedom from hunger, conjuring any food a person desired, spontaneously at their command. So great was its power that it made people drop to their knees in worship, marvelling that there 'was nothing on earth so wealthy'.

Still, the beauty of the grail for Wolfram was also that it revealed the pointlessness of human riches. 'There are very few now alive', he complained, who 'would abandon earth's wealth for the sake of Heaven's fame'. Although the Queen of India believed she could buy the dazzling stone just like any other commodity, sending 'mountains of gold' and rivers of 'precious gems' to the castle to secure it, she failed. Instead the grail was a type of socialist tool. It selected its own keepers with no care for class or income, teleporting people from humbler backgrounds into positions of influence based on their bravery and moral virtue. Children's names would appear and then fade across the stone's surface, and these children – coming from 'poor and rich alike' – would then be catapulted into a world of elite castles and rituals.[73]

This was the case for Parzival, the boy raised in a forest who eventually attained the grail. After his humiliation at the castle he had to go through a stage of fear and depression, hiding from his mistakes and refusing to help people in distress. Then he had to go through a period of selfish desire, seeking to find the grail again, but only for his own personal gain. Things only turned around when he met a hermit, who taught him the meaning of existence. In a confessional encounter, the hermit helped Parzival confront his pride, his envy, his anger, his sadness, his lust, his gluttony and his greed. Then he instructed him to seek the grail again, but this time with a pure heart. 'Give your sins to me,' he said, 'and follow that course without fear.' Emboldened, and now aware that he was questing for a treasure that would help everybody and not just himself, Parzival's heroics won him the grail, and he ruled over the kingdom as its true guardian for ever more.[74]

What are we supposed to do, when we're finally in the presence of a beautiful object? Following the signs, I couldn't believe I had finally arrived at the end of my quest. All it took was a quick walk through the nave of Valencia Cathedral (I had to stop myself from breaking into a run) and I was standing right in front of the Holy Grail. At first, it's difficult to see it. Only seven inches tall, the goblet is set into an alcove in the back wall at a distance behind the altar, in a chapel with walls of cold, dark stone. But in its hexagonal glass case, the cup glows a plutonium yellow-gold, shining like the Neolithic fires that once lit up the caves of the Pyrenees (plate 10).

Many might be sceptical that this cup is the real historical grail; the actual cup used by Jesus at the Last Supper. What are the chances that somebody had the foresight to take this souvenir from the table, on that particular night that Jesus is supposed to have made a goodbye speech? More still, what are the chances that this one object could survive for over a thousand undocumented years without being lost or swapped or damaged? And yet the Valencia Chalice has a compelling case to be taken as the genuine item. It's made of red agate stone and chalcedony, two materials that were often used to make objects like this two thousand years ago. Although the two handles were obviously added later, archaeologists have identified the base vessel as being in the style of a Hebrew blessing cup, with indications that it was produced in a workshop in the era of Herod the Great (d.*c.*4 BCE).⁷⁵

On that day I'm not sure what I felt as I gazed up at the chalice. Looking back through my memories now, from the vantage of my Siberian mall life, I think I have a better idea. What I felt, really, was a tension between two types of desire. Two ways of desiring objects, only one of which can ever collapse into avarice.

The first type of desire is a desire for consumption. A desire to possess, to inhabit, to use, to use up. When I see things in the shops of Gudvin or Voyage, these items are all theoretically open to my possession. Every garment of clothing and every shoe appears as a consumable, something I can dream of buying or else absorbing into my life. Even if I don't go back to Gudvin to purchase that smooth leather bag, I can still desire it as something that could be mine to use, to scuff up, to exhaust altogether. And this type of desire is always open to avarice, lapsing into a hollow obsession with owning, with displaying, with possessing.

When I walk through an art gallery, though, I usually feel a different kind of desire. If I feel passion for an object, in this case it's a passion that lifts up my vision, and which resists any straightforward ambition to possess or consume. It would be absurd to stand in front of Van Gogh's *Sunflowers* and dream of owning it. There's something about that velvet guard rope, maybe, that prevents us from getting carried away by this simpler mechanism of desire, the impulse that can degenerate into avarice. So, instead, another type of desire kicks in. And this desire – as I understand it now – is the mechanism medieval writers called wonder.

Wonder, as the historian Caroline Walker Bynum defined it, is the experience of seeing something beautiful while understanding that we cannot 'incorporate, or consume, or encompass' it for ourselves. It's when we stop judging an object or hoping to control it and start to appreciate it for the mysterious, paradoxical, or spectacular thing that it is.[76] The Cistercian monk Bernard of Clairvaux explained this type of desire by pointing to a goblet of wine. We can look at the goblet, he said, and we can pick it up and drink down all its contents. But we can never absorb the goblet itself; we can never make this object become a part of us. All we can do with it is put it back on the table and admire it as it sparkles in the candlelight.[77] And this is how wonder – the non-avaricious way of seeing – works. It's allowing our eyes to adore without craving, to be assailed without needing to embrace. It's the desire that sets beauty free, precisely because it asks it for nothing in return.

All the same, we need to cultivate our eyes to appreciate what we see. As a visitor to Valencia Cathedral, on that final day of the conference, I admit I was a little underwhelmed by the chalice. To me, it looked like one of those trophies they give to children at karate tournaments. Maybe I should have got closer to it. Or maybe I missed its aura because I was squeezed in and peering over the shoulders of other visitors. Maybe, though, this awkward effect was also a sign that my gaze was moving in the right direction. That my eyes were still adjusting to the Gothic way of seeing.

Looking, in this mode, is like climbing a ladder of perception. According to Abbot Suger, the father of Gothic architecture, our eyes need to lead our minds, so that we 'rise towards truth through material things'. Then, 'once seeing this light,' we should 'rise above being immersed in them'.[78] Or, to put it another way, we have to train ourselves to see a multitude of meaning in a single object: to see the care and love of the people who made it and used it. As I gazed at the cup in its glowing glass case, I did feel my mind 'rising above it' in at least one sense. With curiosity, I wondered what had brought this object into existence. I wondered at how many people had passed it on, how many had cared for it. For Suger, the higher truth of the objects he valued was God, while for other viewers in other eras it has been geometry, or the evolution of the species, or the elements of the periodic table. For me, on that day in Valencia, that higher truth I saw in this chalice was the past: the legends and literatures and documents that led me to stand on that spot and wonder.

I suppose I've always looked for something eternal in objects. Now, I realise that what I was searching for was history itself. Whenever I've felt that exhilaration – the feeling that radiates from a great piece of human effort – it's been followed by a sense that there's a mystery attached to it. Something lying beyond my grasp that somehow connects that object to me and my life. What that mystery might be, I'm not sure I can say. But I've begun to think it has something to do with the ambitions and fantasies that conjured the object, the networks that brought the materials together, the skills that crafted it, the love that kept it safe over centuries, so that one day I could look at it too.

The truth I want is the sheer volume of human feeling, the thing that pulses in an artwork and makes it luminous to the human eye. It's the history, the naked history of it. So, now, this is what I think. That if I can stand in front of a chalice in Valencia, or even in front of a woollen sweater in Voyage, and train myself to see a matrix of adventure and daring and love, rather than a thing to have and hold, then maybe I can cure myself of this avarice. And then I'll no longer feel this thirst that even a grail couldn't quench.

*

AVARICE

I have to leave Gudvin in a hurry. Tangled up in yellow wool and lingering in the fitting rooms of a niche clothes shop, I'm hit by a wave of total boredom. Looking back over my shoulder as I walk (I'm already past Starbucks, the exit is in sight), I feel one kind of desire waning and another waxing.

Avarice was understood in the Middle Ages as the inordinate desire for more things; the fever-cycle of wanting objects, a cycle that can never be broken by owning those objects. In fact, the major problem is that in rushing to acquire we end up getting possessed by the objects, ourselves. As Europe commercialised in the 1200s, a wave of anxieties about avarice stalked the continent. Greed can make us lose our identities, Francis of Assisi warned, because focusing our love on the externals of our lives we neglect to love the inner person. Eventually, he believed, the weight of all those possessions would block us out altogether. Channel all our time and energy into accumulating clothes, and we risk reducing ourselves to mannequins. Emptier and emptier, we become little more than frames for displaying the prizes we've hoarded.

But as I discovered in Valencia, there was a space in the Middle Ages – especially after the first rush of guilt about the commercial revolution was over – for a more positive philosophy of material life. For every Francis of Assisi, advocating total poverty, there were now hundreds of Jaumes, enjoying the candelabras and smartly tailored doublets of Europe's new marketplaces. While preachers and poets condemned avarice, one of the best tricks this new consumer society played was pretending that the worst greed was always somewhere else. Lady Avarice was a monster with six hands. She was a pagan worshipping an idol, or a Muslim king in Africa hoarding his sacks of gold dust. All the while, readers in Europe could let themselves off the hook. Jaume could pick up his own elaborate book and read Psalm 15 – 'He that is greedy of gain troubles his own house, but he that hates gifts shall live' – and imagine this passage was really talking about somebody else, far away.

Having said that, Jaume doesn't strike me as avaricious. He seems to have lived an elegant life, one more comfortable, by its end, than the lives of most people who pay exorbitant rents for tiny apartments in London or Dublin or New York. More than that, it is only through the objects themselves – the things Jaume bought as a consumer – that historians like Luis have been able to sketch out who he was, how he felt, what he valued. Maybe there's a balance, after all. A way to purchase only the things that enlarge and express the soul; a way to hold wonder together with necessity, to calibrate desire without extinguishing it. No purchase can unlock depression, because (as the medieval preacher Vincent Ferrer once put it) 'temporal goods do not enter the heart.'[79] But wonder – the quirk of seeing, where you clash with an object and create a new way to encounter the world – just might.

CHAPTER 6

Gluttony

It's sunrise on Christmas Eve and the sky is a flaming orange. Today I have a long journey ahead of me. At the orders of our university's director I have to take a nine-hour train trip east across the steppe to the city of Omsk. Then tomorrow, on Christmas Day, which is an ordinary working day here, a taxi has been arranged to take me to a secondary school, where I have to give a lecture to students about why they should come to our university in Tyumen. Although it's earlier than my usual breakfast time, I've set myself up in the kitchen, angling my wicker chair towards the rising morning light. I've made my way through two slices of brioche and a cafetière of coffee, and I'm about to peel an overripe clementine. Physically, at least, I'm beginning to feel prepared for the challenge. But already, without leaving this patch of rising sun by the window, I'm guilty of a Deadly Sin. I've managed to commit all five strains of gluttony.

Gluttony Type number one, according to Pope Gregory the Great's enormous compendium of moral advice, the *Moralia in Job* (written c.578–595), is 'quantity'.[1] And never mind the brioche, I've covered this one with the cafetière. Drinking a litre of coffee in one sitting is excessive, even if you've recently had trouble sleeping and you're facing a day in a cramped train wagon. Equally straightforward is Type number two, which is 'haste', or wanting to eat or drink something when you're not actually hungry or thirsty. Without question, this applied to my fifth cup and probably my third and fourth as well. More complex is Type number three, which Gregory called 'the heat of desire'. As he explained it, this involves a burning ferocity to get the food or drink you want, precisely at the time you want it. When I snatched the kettle straight from the stove as it boiled, not worrying about scalding my hand, I committed gluttony in this way. But really I sowed the seeds for it last week, when I cut short a conversation with a student because I was desperate to get out and buy precisely this bag of coffee beans.

Although it's fun to apply gluttony to a cafetière, Gregory's first three types don't tell us much we didn't already know about food morality. We live in a society that counts calories and shames bodies that appear overweight. Although we may no longer act like aristocrats onboard the *Titanic*, eating tiny bites from a succession of delicate forks, we still raise our eyebrows when we see somebody rushing through their food too fast. I baulked, recently, when a colleague at the university canteen ordered a side of frankfurters to go with his pork burgers, and privately congratulated myself for avoiding choices like that. So, condemning excessive consumption as 'immoral' is a reflex that comes just as naturally now as it did for Pope Gregory, fourteen centuries ago.

The medieval label of gluttony was never just about flabbiness or clogged arteries, though. As it turns out, you could be guilty of it even with a 28-inch belt. Gregory's Type number four is what he called 'sumptuousness', meaning either connoisseurship or a devotional attitude to food. Maybe you only make your toast with ciabatta, or you refuse to eat tuna that isn't Bonito del Norte. Or maybe you shun anything that isn't 'simple' food, refusing an offer of croissants because you feel you should make a bowl of plain, salted porridge instead. But the point is, with this type of gluttony you have a level of obsession that makes you *go out of your way* to get what you want. When I spent my work time hiking between three different stores last Thursday, looking for the variety of Yirgacheffe Ethiopian coffee I prefer, I was a sinner firmly in this camp; cutting a hole in my teaching preparations just to follow my fixations.

For all that, my real shame is with how I've been committing Gluttony Type number five. Before I sat down in this wicker chair just now I performed a ritual I've been honing over the last several months. First I measured out the ground coffee, making sure its proportion was just less than 10 per cent of the cafetière's overall volume. Instead of pouring the boiling water directly onto the grounds, I deflected it off a cold spoon to bring the temperature down to 91°C. Then I stirred the liquid three times clockwise and three times anticlockwise, before setting a timer for four minutes and sliding down the plunger. For Pope Gregory, this would confirm that I am guilty of 'daintiness': a level of fuss over food or drink that takes the mind away from the things that really matter. I'm chasing what Gregory called the 'green thing': the ideal drink, doomed to turn the colour of pale straw in my bladder. And all the while I'm distracting myself from things that are 'evergreen': the real challenges of life at a Siberian liberal arts college.

Even though it's past time for me to pack my bag and set off on the long walk to Tyumen's railway station, I'm tempted to put another slice of brioche in the toaster. Why are the stomach's demands always so hard to resist? Some medieval thinkers used to claim that gluttony was really the pre-eminent Deadly Sin. It was the body's most immediate trigger of desire, John Cassian said, and so it will always be 'the first conflict we must enter upon'.[2] Wasn't it fruit that first led humans to their downfall in the Garden of Eden? And isn't this the first Deadly Sin that babies are guilty of, when they refuse to break away from their mother's breast? Gluttony is 'the origin of filth' and 'the mother of nausea', the twelfth-century writer Alain de Lille said.[3] It's the 'fever' that gives birth to 'all bodily infirmities and afflictions of the mind'.[4] Thinking of my digestion, I twist shut the plastic bag of brioche and head for the door. But already I'm making contingency plans to pick up a poppy seed bun on the way.

Soul Food

On a narrow street in the French city of Toulouse is a building called the Church of the Jacobins. It's a vast structure, a compact mini-mountain in tight rows of flat, red bricks. Walking inside it is like stepping into a forest of stone. Yellow and green stripes deck the walls, and several enormous palm-tree columns fan up into a breathtaking ribbed ceiling. When I arrived there on a winter morning a few years ago, the temperature was a little cool and the pace was sleepy, with only a few whispers echoing off the stone floor. It was strange to think that this was once the global headquarters of the Dominican Order, the network of preachers in black robes who stormed across Europe fighting heretics. Even more, that it was the final resting place of one of the liveliest minds the continent has ever produced.

No human being, I think, has ever held a pen in his hand as long as Thomas Aquinas. His *Summa Theologiae*, the masterwork that consumed him in the 1260s and 70s, ran to over two million words. Although this tackled many of the fundamental questions of what it means to be alive, it didn't exhaust his output. Thomas also wrote dozens of other treatises and books, investigating every corner of existence in his own tiny, unreadable, algebraic handwriting. Sitting for decades at his semicircular

GLUTTONY

desk, he dedicated himself to solving intellectual problems, and in the *Summa* he used the same relentless logical formula to tackle each one. First, he asked a question. Next, he found three or four potential answers. Then, he quoted the wisdom of an authority on the subject, either the Gospels or the Old Testament or the philosopher Aristotle. Next, he would reason through these elements to find a unique and nuanced conclusion. Finally, as a way to sharpen and secure that conclusion, he would move through and refute each of the three or four initial answers in turn.

Somewhere in the heart of this labyrinth of problem-solving, Thomas turned to the question of food. Why and how eating mattered, and what counted as 'too much'. Maybe it was because he wrestled so much with food temptation himself, or maybe it was just because he was meticulous with every topic he touched, but Thomas was able to throw himself into this question with a depth and intensity rarely achieved anywhere else in the history of philosophy.

Knowing I was going to visit Thomas's tomb, on my journey through Toulouse I carried with me the best biography still in print. *Friar Thomas d'Aquino: His Life, Thought, and Works* by James A. Weisheipl. It was a book, I discovered, that expanded my sense of Thomas completely. Up until then my understanding of him had only come through the things he wrote. As a student I'd read passages from his *Summa*, including his empirical proof of the existence of God. Later I'd read parts of his *Summa contra gentiles*, his *Disputed Questions on Evil*, and a handful of his sermons. The impression I had always got was of a mind both creative and forensic. He seemed like the most intelligent computer ever conceived, only more brilliant than that. He could glide through any subject with precision and a warmth that cut to the heart of why a problem mattered. I remember, once, reading his answer to the question 'Is hatred stronger than love?' Because 'every hatred arises from some love' he said, and because it was 'impossible for an effect to be stronger than its cause', then it would always be 'impossible for hatred to be stronger than love'.[5] And I suppose I fell in love with the mind that could think like that.

But Thomas was more than just a mind. He also had that body, the one now in the tomb in Toulouse. As well as causing him anxiety and irritation, this was a body that gave him great inspiration. His precise size – and by implication, the level of Thomas's own presumed gluttony – has been a matter of debate.[6] Nicholas of Priverno, who lived at the monastery of Fossanova 60 miles south-east of Rome, remembered meeting him as 'a big stout man, bald and with a dark complexion'.[7] A Dominican friar, who documented the exhumation of Thomas's coffin in 1368, described him as 'broad and robust'.[8] It's true also that medieval artists showed Thomas as a hulking figure. In the painting by Benozzo Gozzoli, now hanging in the Louvre, he's the shape of a large pear. His eyes are glazed, and his face frozen in what seems like pity. From his size, though, he also appears immovable. Unlike the crumpled philosopher Averroes at his feet, or the inclining Plato and Aristotle to his left and right, Thomas is a bulldozer; a man with a rock-steady body to mirror the concrete weight of his writing.

When I got the chance to read Weisheipl's book – which follows the philosopher's life from his birth in the mountain castle of Roccasecca, to his studies in Cologne and his teaching job in Paris – what came across most was how indifferent Thomas was to his bodily needs. He spent most of his days writing at a desk, Weisheipl says, and he swatted away bouts of tiredness or sickness as if they were flies. He was also so detached that even at a lunch with the King of France he ignored the conversation, remaining so absorbed in thought that he had to apologise ('I thought I was at my study').⁹ Yet, as Weisheipl also shows, Thomas's relationship with his body was always complex. He relied on it, after all, as the main tool of his philosophy. 'All human understanding begins with sense,' as he put it.¹⁰ He even produced a proof of God's existence based entirely on the evidence (or 'effects') that could be seen, heard, or touched in the world around him.¹¹

Beyond his reputation for girth – and beyond the nickname, the 'Dumb Ox', given to him by his teacher at Cologne – did Thomas have any kind of personal struggles with food? As useful as Weisheipl's book was, I later had to supplement it by looking at Thomas's *vitae* (the biographies of the saint, written in the medieval era), which gave me some new clues about Thomas's relationship to eating. From Bernard Gui's account I discovered that Thomas often needed help at meal times. Apparently he had a friend, whose name was Reginald, who always sat near him to make sure he avoided 'eating absent-mindedly what might have done him harm'.¹² And although the writer Bernard presented this as a story about the saint's heroic indifference to food, I wasn't so sure. Couldn't it equally have been a sign that Thomas needed safeguards against his own comfort eating?

What touched me most was a story recorded in William of Tocco's *vita*; a confession of one of Thomas's rare food fantasies. On his way to a council at Lyons he fell sick and soon became so unwell that he was unable to eat. His companions were distraught. Couldn't he try something? Just for the sake of his health? Only one thing might work, Thomas said. Could they maybe get some fresh herrings of the kind he used to eat while he had lived in Paris? This request caused some panic. Everyone wanted to please Thomas, but as they had stopped off at a castle in the mountain foothills, the idea of getting fresh herrings seemed ridiculous. Somehow, though, that evening a fishmonger came along the road who was able, miraculously, to sell them precisely the fish they wanted. And yet when Thomas was actually faced with the herrings his face fell. There was no way he could 'presume to eat of these fish', he said, because his intentions had been all wrong. He had proved himself a glutton, after all. He'd 'coveted' the herrings 'with a disordered desire', fixating and fussing rather than settling for the food that was already there.[13]

Whether or not Thomas actually struggled with food cravings like this all the time, he was at least conscious of the fight. His personal conflict over the herrings, also, matched his philosophical analysis of gluttony in the *Summa Theologiae*. Just like Gregory the Great, Thomas said gluttony came in five varieties, which he summarised as 'Hastily, sumptuously, too much, greedily, daintily'.[14] You could: 1) Eat too much between meals; or you could 2) Only take food that was exquisite or rich. Otherwise, you could 3) Eat too much; or 4) Eat with too frenzied an appetite. Alternatively, and finally, your meals could be dominated by 5) An overpowering fuss.

Thomas also went beyond this simple list. What tied these five types together, he said, was a deeper problem with the way we think about food itself. All these types of gluttony kick in when our relationship to eating slips beyond 'reason'. At this precise moment, Thomas said, it's no longer us eating the food, but the food eating us. And this isn't always a matter of overeating; it can also happen when we cultivate the kind of 'sensory appetite' in which our palate fixates on certain subtle tastes and qualities, to the exclusion of others.[15] So if we find that black olives are no longer enough because we need Kalamata, or we begin to shun Kenyan coffee because we must have Ethiopian, it means we've fallen down one of Thomas's rabbit holes.

GLUTTONY

On reflection, it seems Thomas was especially hard on himself, because herrings were at the tame end of the cookbooks of the medieval centuries – many of which were almost pornographic. It's hard to imagine him ever approving the earliest surviving menu in English history, a dinner that included 'the head of a boar, larded, with the snout well garlanded', as well as 'rabbits in gravy, all covered with sugar' and 'crisps and fritters... mixed with rosewater'.[16] The *Tractatus*, a French recipe book written around the time Thomas lay craving his herrings, was even more lavish. Pigs needed to be fed with pigeon fat to get the optimum taste, it said. When cooking a chicken, it was always best to throw in some white wine and 'a little almond milk, dashed with saffron'.[17] Tired of the pretentious trend among his colleagues for eating roast partridge, the Florentine politician Lapo Mazzei claimed he longed for something simpler. 'I like coarse foods,' he said. 'This year I would like to have, as I once had, a little barrel of salted anchovies.'[18]

Why was an anchovy 'coarser' than a partridge? Although Mazzei's inverse-snobbery seems like a joke, really there was a meticulous logic underneath. A grand architecture, which Mazzei must have been aware of, which ordered all medieval food by class and hierarchy. Birds in general were considered more 'suitable for noble, wealthy and peaceful people', according to the *Tractatus*, while mutton, pork, beef and venison were better for 'strong working people'.[19] Look closely at paintings of aristocratic banquets – like Botticelli's magnificent scene of a wedding feast, interrupted by a pair of ravenous dogs – and in theory we should only be able to find the traces of poultry bones, and never a single pork rib.

There was a concrete principle behind all of this. Medieval food hierarchy, according to one theory, was actually based on altitude.[20] The higher up something lived or grew, the more noble it was supposed to be to eat. In this typology chicken was superior to beef (as chickens could at least fly), and ham was superior to lobster.[21] While fruits were more refined than berries, root vegetables like onions sat right at the bottom of the medieval food pyramid. This didn't mean that finer tastes couldn't slip into an ordinary bowl of oats. A typical recipe for porridge, recorded in the English recipe book *Curye on Inglysch*, included rose petals, cinnamon and rice flour, as well as a dash of that ubiquitous favourite of medieval chefs: almond milk.[22]

Still, Thomas's herrings are poignant in other ways too. His anxieties also marked a philosophical shift that continues to define our relationship to food. This was the moment, in Western history, when food finally came to be associated with soul. It's true that body was always inseparable from soul in medieval thought, and that most thinkers believed people would be resurrected in paradise with the bodies they were currently walking around in. (Albeit, those bodies would be spun back to the ideal age of thirty-three, the same as Christ at his crucifixion, and slimmed down to the 'perfect' size and shape.)[23] But does this mean that the substance of the food we eat will also be a part of us for eternity? Before the thirteenth century, philosophers had always refused to accept this idea, and hated to think that the food we eat ever forms part of the body itself. As impossible as it may sound, a writer as sensitive and precise as Hugh of Saint Victor was even able to conclude that calorific energy had no role in making the human grow. Only God, Hugh argued, had the power to 'make something greater out of something' that was already there.[24]

How did this older theory of food work? What was supposed to happen to all the food that entered the body? An obscure manuscript in the British Library, the *Liber Pancrisis*, dealt with this question precisely. All the matter and nutrients from food were disposable energy, the *Liber* said, and nothing more. According to this theory, our digestive system processes everything we eat into four parts. It then sends those four parts to four different sections of our body. One part travels to the brain, one part is converted into black bile, one part becomes red bile and the other becomes our blood. But, according to the *Liber*, all this food energy doesn't stick around for long. After it has helped to sustain the body, the food's material substance is expelled and 'purgated'. So this means that the nutrients from a chicken sandwich or a bowl of olives never become a part of our 'true', essential selves. Just as a 'fire is nourished by wood', even though that wood never alters 'the essence of the fire', so our bodies are 'nourished by foods that are never converted' into the substance of our bodies.[25]

By the time Thomas was alive, consequently, there were two ideas about food and soul tugging in opposite directions. Recipe books from the 1200s were imagining that different foods had different essential qualities, with some being socially and morally 'better' than others. Scholarly works, though, were insisting that all food was transient, and that no digested particle would ever stay with or help build the growing body. But then, Thomas Aquinas – for all that he might have struggled with eating – formed part of the vanguard intellectual movement that flipped this position around. He attended a committee meeting at the University of Paris in 1250, convened to discuss this matter among others. And together with his colleagues, Thomas decided to reject the orthodox view. Nobody was allowed to argue, any more, 'that no ingredient in food is transformed into human nature'.[26] This position was to be prohibited. From now on, anything people ate was understood as contributing to the fabric of the human body. Which, for them, meant that food choices really could affect inner being.

Once people accepted this new doctrine, the implications spun off in some incredible directions. A few decades later the Franciscan writer Peter John Olivi took food philosophy to a new level. We come into the world in a near-perfect state, Peter said. As newborn babies, our bodies are as close to the divine template as we'll ever be, fresh out of the box with no wear and tear. The deterioration begins when we start to eat. We need food to replace the matter and energy we have worn out, but it can never quite bring us back to that original level. And this is where the quality of food becomes critical. 'Better' foods, Peter implied, can get us closer to that bodily ideal, while 'inferior' foods can only take us further and further away.[27] So, every bite matters. Every bite is a conscious choice to either improve or diminish our essential selves.

Thomas never went quite as far as Peter. He always remained a little uncomfortable with the idea that the substance of the things we eat – all the mollusc juices, the orange zest, the mashed-up herring flesh – would one day be resurrected with us. He wrangled over the question of food's transformation in the body in his *Summa Theologiae*, giving it one of his longest answers, with nearly a dozen subdivisions and qualifications. But he got there in the end. 'It must be said,' he conceded, that 'food really is changed into true human nature.'[28]

Back in the Jacobin church in Toulouse, I found that the only way to get a good look at Thomas's tomb is to squat right down. It's part submerged beneath a stone table altar, a sculpted arc behind an iron grill that glows like a fireplace. I did this, but only for half a minute or so before I felt awkward and stood up again, dizzy with the sudden drop in my blood pressure. According to Thomas's beliefs, any herrings that once made up the flesh of the body lying in that tomb are now with him up in paradise. Because this is the logic he accepted. That if the food we digest really *does* become part of our bodies, and if our body really *is* a part of our soul, then this means that molluscs and oranges really can become components of our eternal selves. And so, in terms of our souls, the maxim driving the sin of gluttony really is true. We are what we eat.[29]

Drinking at Heaven's Porches

Tyumen's railway station has a forbidding grey-brown exterior, like the headquarters of a mid-ranking plastics corporation. Out the back though, where gleaming freight trains slide across iron tracks, it hosts a festival of hissing engines. Bouncing my heavy overnight bag on one shoulder, and trying to disguise my run as a walk, I'm closing in on the 9 a.m. train to Omsk. The carriage door is so high off the snowy ground that, I think, nobody could climb it. But then I see the vertical steel steps and the slim handrail and I clamber up. This is the Trans-Siberian Railway, the country's oesophagus. And I'm nervous of being swallowed.

My compartment is just along the corridor to the left, past the kitchen area with its enormous tea urn. Opening the curtained door, the sudden change of colour makes me blink. In front of a glowing saffron window shade there's a narrow table, piled high with plastic bags and thermos flasks. Huddling behind it are two men, and the older one smiles straight up at me. 'I'm Anatoly,' he says, 'and this is my nephew Andrey.' I shake their cold hands. 'Would you like a drink?' Anatoly raises his flask and I take a plastic cup. But what he pours out is something much stronger than herbal tea. 'With this cognac,' he says, 'you need something salty', and he shuffles some dried fish out of a plastic wrapper and peels the flesh off its spine like sticky tape. Anatoly used to have a stressful job at a sweet factory, he tells me, but after two recent heart attacks he's decided to take life easy. So we make a toast: 'To easy living!' And, as I knock the rough liquid to the back of my throat, I can't believe that just over an hour ago I was fretting about taking a third slice of brioche.

Not everybody drank alcohol in the Middle Ages. Most people did, though; and to a staggering level. By the calculations of the historian Richard Unger the average English person drank around seven pints of beer every day, for a combination of reasons connected to abundance, nutrition and probably addiction too.[30] Wine was even more popular, and by the later 1200s grapevines were the second most cultivated crop, after wheat, in Western Europe.[31] Looking back from today, the whole culture can seem idyllic. On one of the pages of the *Très Riches Heures du Duc de Berry*, the sparkling private prayer book decorated by the Limbourg brothers in the early 1400s, a grape harvest is in full flow under a crystal blue sky (plate 11). Workers – whose heavy late-summer outfits confirm that the Medieval Warm Period was now over – are filtering bundles of deep purple grapes into a wooden wagon. One of them, his eyes glazed over, is pushing some of the stray pickings into his mouth. Is this the only taste he'll get before the landlord, watching from that high castle on the hill above him, claims all the bottles for himself?

Wine wasn't only for people who lived in Gothic turrets. Tax documents from the southern French commune of Arles reveal that 65 per cent of landowners produced their own personal wines in the early 1400s, using land from the surrounding countryside. Even poor shepherds purchased tiny vineyards, living in rented rooms and saving money to pay for them.[32] More than ten times as many wine grapes were cultivated in medieval Germany than today.[33] Because exports were limited, much of this wine was meant for immediate local consumption. Estimates of yearly grape harvests from the French commune of Carpentras indicate that there was enough wine in community circulation for the average person to drink around 300 litres per year, or just over a single standard-sized bottle of wine every day, all to themselves.[34]

All the same, there was a thorn in the side of all this drinking. Intoxication was a species of the sixth Deadly Sin, gluttony. And medieval preachers had a lot to say about it, numbering and subdividing its dangers in meticulous lists. One thirteenth-century manuscript, now kept in Lambeth Palace Library in London, describes drunkenness as having six varieties.[35] Although these six were originally modelled on the behaviour of medieval shepherds, or aristocrats in their high castles, it turns out that they make even more sense when applied to a modern context.

The first type is connoisseurship, or an obsession with the most exquisite kinds of drink. With this type, you're already 'drunk' if you're spending too long browsing the shelves of a craft beer store, or boring your friends with the details of IBVs, hop varieties, or Scottish barrel-ageing techniques. The second type is cultivation, the development of a sophisticated and discerning palate. While having good taste is not necessarily a problem in itself, this becomes disruptive and antisocial when it forces you to reject some drinks while craving others. The development of more 'hardcore' tastes is the third type of drunkenness, which is when you acquire a preference for only the strongest alcoholic drinks available. Anybody who has insisted on extra shots of tequila in their pint of stout is probably guilty of this one.

As well as capturing the mind, alcohol also takes over the body. According to the Lambeth Palace manuscript, the fourth kind of drunkenness is the simplest: excess, or drinking too much. The fifth is addiction, or the compulsive physical habit of putting a glass to your lips. Finally, the sixth type is superfluity, or the impulsive need for extra drinks in any situation.

This one covers regular beer garden lunches, sneaking a bottle of vermouth into the cinema, or ordering a pitcher of vodka and coke at a toddler's ball-pit birthday party. While some of these habits may seem benign, according to the text they all need to be struck out. Because beneath the six varieties of drunkenness the same manuscript page also lists a series of related crimes: 'theft', 'adultery' and 'murder'.

Despite these warnings, it's rare to find any text that recommended giving up drinking altogether.[36] While preachers often advised 'sobriety', this had a looser definition in medieval Latin. To be 'sober', according to one treatise, meant 'moderating the desire for drink', not extinguishing it.[37] After all, whatever the problems with excessive drinking, wine and beer remained essential to daily life. Families served alcohol at most meals, medics prescribed wine for all kinds of illnesses, and priests and parishioners shared chalices in communion. Wine was so essential to the fabric of community that even Muslims living in the grapevine-saturated landscape of Spain didn't reject alcohol outright. Although the Caliphs of Cordoba and Seville made attempts to impose total abstinence on Islamic Iberia from the 900s to the 1100s, all of them failed.[38]

So, instead of becoming teetotal, the usual medieval advice was to enjoy drinking with caution. To help you do this, there were different branches of ethics you could follow. Let's say you decide to put a wineglass to your lips. You tip it back and feel the dark liquid flowing down your throat. At this moment, depending on the writer you're listening to, you have three options, adjusted for how much pleasure or inebriation you want to allow yourself. The first is to remain hypervigilant and restrained. The second is to let the alcohol flow, and to push yourself through any embarrassment or regret while trying to reap some benefits from your inebriation. The third option is something more profound. And this, really, is the signature alcoholic policy of the Middle Ages. *To drink even more deeply, and in the process to touch on something divine.*

Although the hypervigilant option involves self-control, this is not as strict as might be imagined. Your drinking will be 'wise', the preacher Alain de Lille said, as long as you have only 'a little' at a time. Defining 'a little' involves listening closely to your body. If your sleep 'suffers', or if you feel 'fatigue' the next morning, you'll know you went too far.[39] Any 'vertigo of the brain' when you lie down after a night of drinking – or any waking up with 'a headache', or tasting 'the wine-ish-ness of your breath' at breakfast – will give you another clue.[40] But hypervigilance is not the same as abstinence. Knowing these limits is a practical measure only; a way to mark out the precise quantity you can drink next time. Learn to work with these new limits, Alain said, and your drinking will bring 'health to both body and soul'.

For those who can't stick to limits, things will be rockier. Your second option is to keep drinking until you get inebriated. Typically, medieval writers saw this as a form of gluttony: another variety of misdirected love. Excessive drinking shrinks the range of thought, one manuscript treatise said, so that even 'wise people fall away from their wisdom'.[41] Too much alcohol 'entangles words', Alain de Lille said, making you both 'dizzy' and boastful.[42] This doesn't mean there weren't caveats. If you didn't realise the drink in your glass was a strong one, your drunkenness could always be forgiven.[43] The problem with overstepping these limits, though, was that it made you more fragile, more likely to crack.[44] Just as 'a light touch will push the person who stands on a precipice over the edge,' wrote the twelfth-century intellectual John of Salisbury, so 'even a slight injury will excite the person drenched with wine into a fury.'[45]

On a good day, this kind of inebriation could still have its benefits. Some people, like the compulsive drinker in the thirteenth-century German poem *Der Weinschwelg*, can use alcohol to help them see the best in other people. As well as making everyone around him more 'attractive', a few glasses of wine gave the drinker in *Der Weinschwelg* bullet-proof levels of confidence.[46] Other advantages could include unlocking repression, or helping reconcile yourself to difficult truths. The poetry in the *Carmina Burana* manuscript, the thirteenth-century collection of romantic lyrics and drinking songs, puts it well. The more you drink, the more you can coax out the 'unheard words' you've stoppered up through the daytime.[47] Drink even more, and it's possible to blot out the horrors of death. 'When we are in the tavern,' one of these poems said, 'we don't think of the earth.'[48]

Right now I'm not in a tavern, I'm in a speeding train carriage. The windows beneath the saffron shade have clouded over with condensation, and we've drunk through several rounds of toasts, including one to Winston Churchill and another to the genius of Mikhail Gorbachev. Now, though, we've moved on to a subject much dearer to our hearts. The beauty of Siberia, the landscape but also the cold climate itself. 'This weather makes the heart stronger, the mind sharper,' Anatoly says, leaning forward and showing me a set of teeth too perfect for a man who used to spend his days in a sweet factory. 'When you go outside and it's minus 20°C, you have no choice. You have to take things slow.' I nod back, blinking at him. I see now that he's deadly serious. 'Sometimes we have to accept that nature is big, and that we are small.' Although I open my mouth to speak, somehow I can't find any of my own 'unheard words' to offload.

Could our conversation have got to this point without Anatoly's thermos full of cognac? For those who are willing, there's one final medieval way of drinking. Instead of restraining yourself

GLUTTONY

or leaping through drink's dangers, this method embraces alcohol for all its mind-altering potential. It means turning inebriation into a positive, even transcendent experience. It means drinking until you hit upon a strain of wisdom that only intoxication can unlock.

The medieval masters of this art were the countercultural poets known as the Goliards. Highly trained intellectuals, these were people who worked at the courts of great bishops or kings, and who grew frustrated by the constant pettiness of politics. So, they turned to writing poetry and drinking enormous amounts of wine and beer. The most famous Goliard was a writer known as the Archpoet, a bureaucrat who wrote in punchy Latin verse.[49] Although he worked at the very top level of German politics, his desk-based career crushed him completely. 'I'm constructed out of some light and weightless matter,' he wrote, 'like a leaf, an idle toy for the winds to scatter.'[50] Like so many of his generation he'd been born into a family where children were expected to grow up and become knights. But, caught in the wheels of twelfth-century social change, he was surprised to spend his life shuffling leaves of parchment and scratching with a pen instead. The whole experience left him feeling directionless: a 'masterless ship on the sea'.

Drinking was the Archpoet's lifeline, but it was also his philosophy. By soaking himself in 'good wine' he wanted to squeeze all the 'delights' out of life.[51] As well as releasing him from the drudgery of bureaucracy, alcohol drove him to new heights of intellectual inspiration. 'It's the fire that's in the cup', he said, that 'kindles the soul's torches', and 'the heart that's drenched in wine' that 'flies to heaven's porches'. What this meant in practice was drinking until he hit upon connections he might otherwise not have found. One of these was the realisation that it's impossible to express yourself if you haven't explored your own depths first. As the Archpoet believed, loosening the mind in drink was the best way to explore yourself precisely because it could reveal your own baseness, your own most vulnerable dimensions. 'Let them drink water,' he said, those who want to 'sit in quiet spots and think'. While they 'shun the tavern's portal', these sober people will 'write, and never having lived, die'.

For all the Archpoet's beautiful words, at heart he was still an entertainer. When he claimed that all his best ideas came at the bottom of a glass, he was also practising a type of exhibitionist humility, like a stand-up comedian making jokes about his own awkwardness. But there was a subculture of writers in the same decades who took this philosophy to a more intense level, living it far more seriously. These were the mystics, the love poets and the writers of obscure spiritual autobiographies, who made intoxication a pathway to the deepest kind of spiritual awareness.

Wine was always a powerful spiritual symbol in medieval Europe. After the doctrine of transubstantiation was formalised by Pope Innocent III in 1215, Christians believed wine was miraculously changed into Christ's blood during the communion. At a physical level, the drink had always already undergone its own magical transformation: from a barrel of water and mashed fruit to a strong and refined liquid with the power to alter the mind. So, wine also became a symbol for remaking a life, or for setting the mind on a new course. Dozens of mystics described their own experiences of revelation as like being 'intoxicated' with drink. Discovering God's love was like entering into a secret wine cellar, as the German writer Mechthild of Magdeburg put it. By drinking 'deeply' from this love, it was possible to become 'inebriated' with a powerful intellectual and bodily sense that, at least for Mechthild, felt higher than any book-based wisdom.[52]

For these mystics, alcohol also had a very real psychological power. As the abbot Bernard of Clairvaux explained, wine has a unique ability to clarify the mind. It can 'illuminate' us by taking us away from ourselves, detaching us through intoxication from our mundane daily concerns, or from our awkward self-consciousness. Bernard initially developed this idea as a metaphor, just like Mechthild's, with overflowing wine symbolising the overpowering feeling of a spiritual presence. But like the Archpoet, he couldn't help talking about alcohol as if it were also something divine itself. Drunkenness can 'overturn minds', Bernard said, making them 'entirely forgetful of themselves'.[53] While this could be a problem, it could also remove the fog that holds us back from reaching true self-awareness. Within our intoxication, he felt, we are able to take a strange and distant view of ourselves. We can see more sharply the wisdom we still lack, and, in drunken forgetting, prepare to become 'utterly unlike' what and who we were before.[54]

Our carriage is still rumbling on beneath the darkening Siberian sky. Anatoly and his nephew are snoozing in the bunks up above, and I'm rummaging in my bag for something to relieve the ache at my temples. Finding nothing, I fix my eyes on the window. In the dying light I can see pine trees and slim birches, and occasional plumes of smoke from chimney stacks. The sky is a misty orange and I'm surprised by the enormous patches of yellow steppe grass peeping out of the snow, and by how many trees are broken halfway up their trunks. Everything is silent except for the rush of steel against iron. If I wasn't drunk, could I be throwing myself further into this landscape? If I hadn't let Anatoly's poisoned thermos cloud my sight, could I be finding deeper shapes of my heart out there in this vision of birches? Or am I only straining to look at the world around me now because the clarity of drink has led me here?

Medieval mystics were not naïve. They knew that alcohol can often be a way of hiding: a way of running away from the reality of what's in front of us. Instead of drinking to avoid pain or frailties or thoughts of death, many of the best medieval writers drank to confront them. Alcohol, for Bernard or Alain de Lille or Mechthild, is only worth drinking if it can be a tool of self-awareness. It's useful if it helps process shortcomings, if it helps us recognise our own limitations, or if it helps us find greater clarity in the world around us. The picture becomes blurred when it comes to the Archpoet. Did he drink just to escape the bureaucratic job that was crushing him? Or did he drink to humble himself, to explore his own depths and realise his fullest self-expression? This is the thing about drinking, in the Middle Ages as much as today. It's always a game of hide and seek. But you'll know it's gluttony when you remain lost, and never really manage to find yourself.

Catherine's Herbs

Sometimes a food craving can be deadly, as one twelfth-century ruler found out the hard way. One night, while on a military campaign in Normandy, King Henry I of England wanted to relax with a treat. What he craved was a supple fish with beef-tone flavours; a snakelike creature with razor teeth and a mouth like the nozzle of a vacuum cleaner. What he wanted was lampreys, boiled in their own blood, and nothing else would do. Although Henry 'always loved' these space-alien fish, this time they made him ill. First he suffered 'violent' symptoms, including diarrhoea and vomiting. Next, the king slid into a sharp fever. Later that night, beneath the light of a half-moon, 'all power of resistance failed', and Henry died.[55]

In the aftermath a few contemporary writers said that Henry's death was a product of his gluttony.[56] And yet this wasn't because the king ate too much, or even because his gorging had led to his death.[57] Really, it didn't matter how many lampreys the king had eaten that night, because the real problem of Henry's gluttony was the way he had fussed. He had performed the sixth Deadly Sin by fixating, obsessively, on his favourite exotic food.

This morning I can't fixate on any food at all. It's 7.30 a.m. and I feel as clammy as a used plastic cup, as flaky as the spine of a smoked fish. Ideally I would skip at least one of today's high-school lectures to catch up on some sleep. But it's Christmas morning, and I can't let down Nastya, who is waiting at hotel reception. Nastya is my student, who grew up in Omsk, and who has agreed to be my chaperone and city guide. Thinking I should apologise straight away in case I'm sick in the taxi, I explain about Anatoly and his thermos. Nastya seems unfazed. 'How is your head?' she asks, before opening the hotel's thick door and gesturing to the cab that's idling in a slush puddle. It's now minus 27°C, my hands are stuffed deep into a pair of enormous orange gloves, and my left eye is streaming an icy trail down my face. 'Don't cry yet!' Nastya says, as I step down into the car. 'It will get even colder later, you can save your tears for then!'

Our first stop is a school somewhere near the bank of Omsk's main river, and my time there passes in a blur. I click through a dozen PowerPoint slides and stumble over the words 'opportunity', 'globalisation' and 'cosmopolitan', while the students look bored. Afterwards the headteacher ushers Nastya and me down a corridor into her office, where I see a table decked out with a platter of sandwiches and a pot of tea. Things are going to take a turn for the awkward, I can see, and not because of the conversation. All of the sandwiches are stuffed with slices of cheese, and regrettably this is something I cannot eat. Even the sight of it – the marbled, squidgy surfaces, the sickly shades of yellow – I find unbearable. The taste on my palette, whenever I try some by mistake, makes me panic like I'm trapped in a blazing elevator. How can I explain any of this? The headteacher is beaming, with her blow-dried hair and her rust-coloured dress suit, holding out the thoughtfully prepared lunch platter. So I have no choice but to smile and say 'Thank you.' Then I take one of the sandwiches in my hand and hold it near my mouth.

Really, am I not another kind of food obsessive? Another kind of glutton? According to medieval writers, you're just as likely to commit gluttony by leaving things untouched on the plate as you are by eating them.[58] A penitential manual written by John of Kent in the early 1200s warned people that cultivating highbrow food tastes was another strain of gluttony. 'Do you make a great attempt to salt and prepare foods with passion and delight?' the manual asked. 'Are you sometimes angry when they are not prepared in the optimum way?'[59] With this type of food fixation, the problem isn't really with the foods themselves. It's with you and the way you think about them. Because when you set 'the stomach as the lord' over the mind, you run the risk of being antisocial. Ignoring what's convenient for others while chasing your own preferences, you tend to put certain people – the ones struggling in a Norman river, late on a December night, to catch a snakelike fish – to more trouble than anybody needs to go.

Shunning cheese sandwiches and pursuing lampreys, though, are at the softest end of things. Further along the spectrum of medieval gluttony was a much deeper food-denial issue. Although this problem is familiar to the modern world, medieval writers also had a lot to say about it, because so many people in this era experienced it. It induced both horror and fascination in medieval commentators, and it's a problem that lies at the inverse of gluttony: a pattern of behaviour that forms its exact negative image. *The near-total refusal of all food.* Although

GLUTTONY

there are dozens of medieval accounts of people who practised this, arguably its most dedicated practitioner was a young Italian woman who died of starvation aged just thirty three.

Catherine of Siena's life would be incredible by any measure. While she was still in her twenties she attracted a group of disciples, sent policy guidance to the pope, founded her own monastery and spent years caring for infected plague patients. But her spiritual journey began at the age of just six, when, according to the biography written by her spiritual adviser Raymond of Capua, she had a series of mystical visions that gave her 'extraordinary wisdom'.[60] Catherine made a vow of lifelong virginity at the age of seven, and pledged to keep her body as 'pure' as possible. Even then, though, her campaign of purity had the denial of food at its heart. 'She determined to give up eating meat,' says Raymond, who claimed he got most of his information directly from Catherine's mother. 'And when she was obliged to sit down at table she usually either passed the meat to her brother Stefano or threw it to the cats on the sly.'[61]

All of this may have started as a curious experiment. Things got serious when Catherine was in her late teens. At fifteen she gave up wine (a decision that confirms the centrality of alcohol in the Italy she grew up in), and drank 'nothing but well water' for the rest of her life. Around this time her mother began fussing over her: combing her hair, decking her out in beautiful dresses and dropping hints about finding a husband. Although she later rejected this as a misguided phase, for the moment Catherine enjoyed looking good, even if she wasn't sure she wanted to marry anybody.[62] But then tragedy hit. Her elder sister Bonaventura – the sister who had joined her mother's campaign of grooming, and who had been the one to introduce Catherine to makeup – died in childbirth. And in grief Catherine's attitude hardened. First she 'seized a pair of scissors' and 'cut her hair off to the roots'. Then, although she had lapsed back into meat-eating before, she quit eating it for good.[63] Now, at the age of twenty, she transitioned to a totally raw diet. Rejecting even bread, Catherine survived on nothing but the scattering of herbs she managed to pick from the gardens near her home.

Was Catherine a medieval example of *anorexia nervosa*? Without doubt, her case matches most of the definitions used by modern specialists who have studied the condition. She definitely experienced 'self-inflicted starvation' in 'the midst of ample food', and whenever she needed to eat she felt both 'fear and anxiety'.[64] And yet, Catherine was part of a broader trend. The historian Caroline Walker Bynum has documented scores of similar food refusal cases, especially among younger women, across the later Middle Ages. Catherine was a little like the French woman Douceline of Digne, who starved herself until she collapsed, or the Belgian Marie d'Oignies, who only ate fruits and herbs, and felt intense nausea at the smell of meat frying.[65] As she sometimes 'had the habit of rejecting' food she'd swallowed, she was also similar to Walpurga from Devonshire, who 'if she ever tried to taste anything had to immediately vomit it out'.[66] Like these others, Catherine presaged the modern anorexics who, according to studies cited by Bynum, find food both 'degrading and self-defeating'.[67] As Catherine put it herself, anyone who eats 'the food of beasts' can only ever become an 'ugly soul'.[68]

Even so, Catherine's food fixation had a uniquely medieval twist: an element lacking from most modern discussions of anorexia or bulimia. One day, when she was tending to plague victims in a hospital, Catherine unwrapped a woman's bandages to wash one of her sores. Removing the pus with a cloth and then wringing it off into a bowl of water, she was hit by 'a stench so unbearable that her inside turned over'. In that moment she felt a strange compulsion. Holding the bowl of pus-water close to her face, she turned her back on the patient and moved a few steps away. Then she gulped the whole bowl down. Drinking pus-water became her secret new habit, and it soon escalated. Days later Catherine leaned over the same woman, who was now close to dying. She undid the wrappings of another putrefying wound, this one in her breast, and put her lips to the sore. Then she began licking and drained all the fluid into her mouth. 'Never in my life,' she whispered to Raymond of Capua much later, 'have I tasted any food or drink sweeter or more exquisite.'[69]

Just like her food denial, Catherine's pus fetish – if it's okay to call it that – was also part of a wider medieval pattern. The Italian mystic Angela of Foligno, decades earlier, also drank pus-filled water after washing the wounds of lepers. A century later the otherwise starving mystic Catherine of Genoa rubbed her nose in the seeping wounds of syphilitic patients, eating the lice she found in their hair.[70] What was this trend? As Bynum says, if we try to see these fixations as expressions of modern anorexia or bulimia we risk missing the point. Because really this desire for pus was a symptom of a distinctly medieval train of thought. It was part of a unique attempt to reprogramme the human relationship to food itself.

Catherine never tired of telling people that the food we eat reflects our souls. If you take 'the food of beasts', she wrote in a letter to her niece Eugenia, then 'would you not truly be a beast' yourself?'[71] When she complained about 'the wolfish shepherds who care for nothing but eating', or when she judged that anyone who couldn't control their eating would find it impossible to keep their 'innocence', Catherine was constructing her own philosophy of wellness, making food the primary measure of morality.[72] Drinking pus was the ultimate virtuous act, in her logic, because it combined two powerful principles: *service* and *suffering*. Not only did it convert eating into an act of kindness (cleaning the wounds of the sick), it also subverted gastronomic pleasure, making food into the kind of painful experience that confirmed it must be good for the soul. Carving out her own niche, Catherine was running with the ideas of Thomas Aquinas and taking them to their extreme. Because if you *are* what you eat, then doesn't this mean that eating anything other than 'soul food' makes you, somehow, a little bit soulless?

For some historians, Catherine was a kind of food crusader, denying food as a way to push back against the structures that contained her. But if it really was a crusade it only found a narrow appeal. Mainstream culture wasn't ready for extreme fasting, and Catherine received dozens of letters and complaints from people who felt her food denial was scandalous. Some said she was trying to outstrip Jesus, who although slim had no problems eating cooked food. Others complained that she was acting 'to excess', going beyond the confines of what was 'ordinary'.[73] Because mealtimes were social rituals, denying all food – like any of the other taboos of gluttony – was processed as another form of antisocial behaviour. Catherine was aware of this problem, and insisted that she didn't want to be disruptive. With all 'my power', she said, 'I have always forced myself once or twice a day to take food.'[74] As she put it in another letter, she had 'a special kind of illness'. 'I should like to be able to eat, but I can't.'[75]

So what, in this climate, did 'normal' look like? Balancing out Catherine's abstinence was a more popular model of medieval anti-gluttony, an approach that has been described as the 'Saint Francis Doctrine'.

Francis of Assisi is now famous in popular culture for his love of animals. Still, he was no vegetarian. Although he practised extreme self-denial – sleeping with a rock pillow at night – he didn't like excessive fasting. In fact, Francis saw abstinence as more troublesome than eating too much.[76] What made the 'Saint Francis Doctrine' unique was its adherence to a single, simple principle: *Never fuss about food*. The man from Assisi's only rule was that he would take whatever food he was given, whenever he was given it. It made no difference whether this was a bowl of cold porridge or a dish of 'crabcakes, honey and freshly-picked grapes': he would eat it without question.[77] Although he was drawn to the taste of 'delicacies and sweets', he fought this impulse, treating food as fuel for the things that make life worth living: talking, sharing and caring for other people.[78] Food fuss, consequently, is the only type of gluttony to worry about, and the master of all others: the impulse that wants us to reduce food to something that matters for itself alone.

Once you look for it, the 'Saint Francis Doctrine' can be found everywhere in later medieval texts. It's the unspoken assumption that seems to have guided many of Catherine's critics, as well as the principle that made Thomas Aquinas chastise himself for craving herrings. Perhaps because Francis wrote so little himself, the idea wasn't spelled out in too much detail until it appeared in a treatise called *The Mirror of Human Happiness* by Conrad of Megenberg, a German writer who died not long before Catherine. Eating and drinking should be governed by 'sobriety', Conrad said, although his idea of sobriety had more to do with discretion than denial. While it was wrong to snap after food with a 'wolfish mouth', it was equally bad to abstain from it. Instead, Conrad saw human happiness as existing in a state of what he called 'translucency'. Neither over-conscious nor under-conscious, this is a measured mentality where you approach any act of eating and drinking having already fully internalised your own limits. Guided by this habit, you'll find you're able to preserve the 'clarity of the eyes', without having to think too much about the food you eat.[79]

Old prejudices die hard, though. After holding the cheese sandwich for as long as I think I can get away with (a little less than ten minutes, judging by the clock on the wall), I lay it down, unbitten. The headteacher hardly seems to notice. She's too busy asking me about the British weather and the health of the queen. And yet, after I stand up and shake her hand and pull on my heavy jacket, I notice her looking down at the pristine triangle I've left on my plate. I know Francis would have been polite, eating whatever she offered, although Catherine would probably have been even more nauseous than me. Still, I'm wondering. Is there an order of food ethics that makes one of these medieval visionaries more 'right' than the other? Or are we all gluttons who've failed to learn, from Conrad, the translucent power of good taste?

Today, when we think about the dangers of food or drink, we tend to think about bodily health. But the interesting thing about the Middle Ages, and the advice of Thomas Aquinas or Alain de Lille or Catherine of Siena, is that they prioritised the health of the mind. Only one of the three 'Fs' of medieval gluttony concerned the body. *Fattening* yourself was certainly a problem for these thinkers, although more because it makes the mind pliable than because it inflates the waistline. The other two 'Fs' – *Fixating* and *Fussing* – were issues with thought and desire, and these were arguably even more important. Most writers advised that it wasn't *what* you ate that mattered, but *how far* you allowed your thoughts of eating it to take over the control centre of your mind. As Pope Gregory the Great put it, 'it is not the food' that is 'in fault'; it's 'the desire' for it.

In this crusade against fixation and fuss, Thomas Aquinas

GLUTTONY

and Catherine of Siena were fighters from opposite ends of the spectrum. Following the 'Saint Francis Doctrine', Thomas was always happy to eat whatever was put in front of him. Although he slipped up once when he was sick and craved for herrings, his principle was never to curate the dishes that came his way. In other words, he ate but he didn't fixate. Catherine was quite different. Although by starving herself and scrabbling around for herbs she hoped neither to fixate nor fuss about food, paradoxically the more she abstained the more she became the worst offender when it came to these two 'Fs'. When her critics complained that she stepped beyond what was reasonable or proportionate, they would have had the weight of a lot of theology and philosophy behind them, not least that of Thomas Aquinas.

Despite everything, medieval writers managed to find something transcendent in food and drink. It's tempting to believe, along with the Archpoet, that every glass can take us one step closer to 'heaven's porches'; to think that something like alcohol can help fix ourselves or even find ourselves. Even if it's often just another thing to hide behind, drinking was a part of the Archpoet's character, as much as herrings were a part of Thomas's and herbs a part of Catherine's. These were cravings around which they allowed that better, more beautiful part of themselves to grow. And this is the thing that makes gluttony, in Thomas's own words, a lesser sin than something like envy or sloth. Fussing and fixating can make you into a food snob, or a culinary bore, or an antisocial private diner. In the right measure, though, these 'Fs' can also add charm and character. More importantly, they can add soul.

CHAPTER 7

Lust

I'm lying on my back in a dark blue pool. Above me are thousands of stars, and when I exhale a fog of steam coils up to join them. I've been here swimming in the hot springs of Verkhniy Bor for so long that my fingertips have shrivelled like wet paper. Sweat is rolling down my eyelashes, even though the air temperature is nearly minus 30°C. I'm beginning to feel a little awkward. Just now I caught the eyes of a woman as she was stepping into the pool. She'd thrown off her bathrobe and her exposed body was shivering in the winter air. I didn't want to hold her gaze at that moment, but I couldn't help it. I'm not sure what I thought I saw. A flash of something new, a window into another life. Or a craving to be held by something other than hot water. Whatever it was, though, I snapped my eyes away and swam in the opposite direction.

Although lust was the least 'deadly' of the sins in the Middle Ages, today it's morphing into the opposite. The embodiment of the worst of our predatory instincts, with the power to make the flesh crawl. One of the reasons medieval writers considered it 'lighter' than the other Deadly Sins was its resemblance to love. Whereas with pride, envy or gluttony we want something for ourselves alone, with lust (or *luxuria*, as it was known in Latin) we want something shared: human contact and connection.[1] Still, this didn't stop writers describing it in incendiary ways.

LUST

Lust is an 'excessive' appetite for sex, according to William Peraldus's treatise, and brings a barrage of 'anxiety', 'embarrassment', 'stench' and 'infamy' along with it. 'Nothing is ever magnificent,' as he said, in the 'pleasure' of *luxuria*.[2] Although this may sound prudish, the point William was trying to make is that sexual desire can quickly morph into abuse. Unchecked, it can lead us to violate and neglect another person, to 'use them' like a toy.[3]

How do we identify lust in somebody's eyes? Whenever I've stood in front of the paintings of Cimabue or Giotto, or even Jan van Eyck or Robert Campin, I've always felt there's something missing. Where's the spark, the seductive qualities that made these people attractive to one another? Of all the Deadly Sins, lust is the hardest to see through medieval eyes. The self-righteous pride of Guillaume Bélibaste comes easily. The envious Giotto, the furious King Henry, the slothful Margery Kempe, the gluttonous Thomas: I can put myself in their shoes. But medieval passions and fantasies? Somehow these feel irretrievable. Because while beauty is timeless, sexiness only has seconds to live. Lust is always suspended in a precise moment; a glimpse, when light and mood and the flow of blood combine and explode in private craving. *Luxuria*, as Astesanus de Asti said, is a way of thinking defined by 'inconstancy', or by 'throwing yourself headlong' into something. It's also a dead end. Indifferent towards the future, lust cares nothing for the things that might carry on growing after the moment of passion is over.[4]

Depending on who you ask, the Middle Ages was a time of either extreme sexual denial or extreme sexual licence. At one end of the spectrum were dozens of medieval commentators who couldn't abide sex in any of its forms. If you can't help gazing at someone's body, a fifteenth-century manuscript advised, the remedy is to 'contemplate' how that same body will one day be eaten by 'horrible worms' (which seems unkind).[5] Some writers were even more sensationalist, telling stories of shapeshifting demons who sabotaged love affairs. These demons take on the appearance of your lover, they said, until you go in for a kiss. Then they reveal their true, monstrous form, and butcher your body into tiny pieces (even more unkind).[6]

Most sexual encounters didn't end this way. More typical is the true story of a widow named Beatrice, who lived in the countryside north of the Pyrenees. One day, while she was on her knees making her confession, she was seduced by a priest named Pierre. He bent down and wrapped her in his arms, and he whispered 'There's no woman in the world I love as much as you.' Over the following weeks Pierre began turning up at Beatrice's home, persuading her to adopt his own philosophy of lust. He told her that marriage is a sham, that life is short and this world is full of suffering. As long as they acted 'entirely according to pleasure', and as long as they confessed and made it up to God, why shouldn't they enjoy 'any sort of sin' now? Beatrice was surprised. 'How can you, as a priest, speak like that to a widow like me?' Against her better judgement she was won around, and the two of them began an affair that lasted eighteen months.[7]

When is lust a blessing and when is it a curse? Are these voyeurisms an unstoppable part of human nature, or do they corrupt us, leading us away from the most enduring connections? Stepping through the bank of steam at the poolside I climb up into the frozen air. I scrabble for my ice-coated flip-flops and walk towards the changing rooms. And yet even as I go I can't help glancing back, looking for the woman whose gaze I held earlier.

It's one thing to imagine somebody being 'corroded' by worms, but what about all the beauty and potential of our bodies? Nudged in the right direction, can't lust blossom into a connection, something beautiful and lasting? For many medieval thinkers, sexual urges were never just evil, and they were never just mundane or casual either. Lust, instead, was a raging fireball. Depending on how you handled it, it could either burn your body to dust or send you rocketing into the uncharted firmament.

Jump into the Freezing Lake

Anybody with a lust problem today might think it's ridiculous to take advice from a medieval monk. In many cases they would probably be correct. Monks had cloistered lives, shut away from society.[8] They lived in strict religious communities, wearing uniform robes, cutting their hair to look the same as each other and following codes of conduct that punished masturbation as an offence.[9] If they knew a lot about lust, we might assume they were experts in repressing it or keeping it under control. Would they know how to manage it in ordinary society, within the boundaries of a sexual relationship or a busy dating scene?

But to these people I would recommend one special medieval monk, one obsessed with lust. A writer who spent an entire career – a dazzling political, religious and literary career – attending not only to the problem but also to the power and the potential of the sexual drive. Bernard of Clairvaux, the Cistercian monk, was beset by anxieties in his younger life. He was a square peg in a round hole, although the kind of square that made everyone around him question why they weren't square-shaped too. Eventually he managed to face down all his demons, channelling his frustrated energy into radioactive texts: Latin works that glow at the fringes of Western culture. And so many of these texts throb with the power of lust.

The scene is a forested lake, just outside the town of

Châtillon-sur-Seine in Burgundy. It's the 1110s, a decade of winter sunshine and good wine harvests. Bernard is a shy boy in his teens with a terrible gastric complaint. Everybody who meets him gets the sense he must have been alive for centuries; he has a wisdom that seems out of time. But the same people also worry about the frailty of a body that can't keep down any food, a body that shudders and rattles inside ever-baggier tunics. Bernard's mother, a woman who had breastfed all seven of her children and always prepared and measured everything they ate, had died not long ago. Doesn't grief sometimes cast its spell on the stomach?[10]

At the lake Bernard is with his five brothers. They are doing what Bernard's biographer, William of Saint-Thierry, would later call 'larking around'. There are jokes, there are songs, there are thoughts of stalking back into the forest to catch a wild fox. Bernard is the group's phantom, half-in and half-out of every conversation. In a quiet moment he looks across the lake. On the bank he catches sight of a woman who seems just like him; a little bit lost, somehow broken. A fellow ghost on the shore. Bernard looks into her eyes and his response is slow, staggered, wounded. All we have to go on is William's account, which piles up apologies and repressions in the place of the lust he couldn't admit. Bernard's 'gaze falls on this woman', and he 'at once corrects himself, blushes deeply within, and blazes with self-annoyance'.[11]

And then Bernard throws himself into the lake. His brothers are stunned, the powerful swimmers among them caught off guard. It's a cold day, the water is icy, why is Bernard swimming? Is he trying to impress everybody? Or is he trying to escape from his feelings, from his family, from the suffocation of an aristocratic picnic? In a rare illustration of this scene from a manuscript in the Vatican Library in Rome, Bernard plunges through the translucent water with an athletic front crawl.

Although he swims away from his fantasy – the fantasy of himself pressing up against this woman's naked body under a sequined bedspread – he still can't help glancing back over his shoulder to look. By the time a long branch is found to drag Bernard out of the water he is almost frozen. But at least, as the writer William put it, the spell of his passion has been broken. 'By the power of grace, his lust had been cooled.'

Although William is our only source for this episode, it tallies with everything else we know. Every account we have of the young Bernard confirms that he had a roving eye. Not only was he extremely sensitive to beautiful faces, he loved to make an exhibition of himself. Around the time his mother became sick he began writing and performing his own erotic songs. Although none of these survive (did the older man destroy the manuscripts that held the younger man's fantasies?), one of his enemies left a critical review. 'In your adolescence you wrote little songs, so urbane,' Berengar of Poitiers, an intellectual from Paris, wrote to Bernard in a spiteful open letter. 'I would quote some of them but I don't want to dirty this page with filth.'[12]

What exactly was this 'filth'? Although it's difficult to be sure, Bernard's erotic songs were probably close in spirit to those of the Troubadours, the singers from the region of Toulouse who his brothers liked to imitate on their lakeside excursions. A verse from 'Lancan vei per mei la landa' by Bernart de Ventadorn, a poet who later became a favourite in Europe's highest political circles, captures precisely the sort of language people like Berengar were afraid to repeat.

> Evil she is if she doesn't call me
> To come where she undresses alone
> So that I can wait her bidding
> Beside the bed, along the edge,

Where I can pull off her close-fitting shoes
Down on my knees, my head bent down:
If only she'll offer me her foot.[13]

Facing a counterculture like this, it's easy to see why some theologians turned to a zero-lust policy. As the priest Andreas Capellanus described it, lust was a type of 'inborn suffering'; a hook that would 'get its claws' into you before draining you of all logic and reason.[14] Others felt the best way to deal with it was by policing speech. According to a thirteenth-century treatise from Oxford, while whatever happened in your mind could stay there, it was always 'shameless' to reveal your lust through 'exterior signs'.[15] Preachers like William Peraldus came up with an even more uncompromising solution. Because 'lust is fire', and humans are 'stubble or straw', the best answer was simple. *Don't let yourself catch fire in the first place.* Hide yourself away from anyone you find attractive. Duck into doorways to avoid faces that might tempt you. Flee society, if necessary. *Jump into the freezing lake.*[16]

In another life, Bernard might have become a predatory priest like Pierre from the Pyrenees. Or he might have become an Andreas Capellanus, satisfied to reject lust as 'suffering'. Bernard was a special case, though: he wanted to redeem the explosive power of the lust he felt inside him, even after his lake-jumping adventure. Joining the Cistercians, a little-known monastic order, Bernard used his exceptional energy and political instincts to make the organisation into a Europe-wide success. Thousands of young men were inspired to leave their families to follow him, including Bernard's own five brothers, and the shy young man from Burgundy became a household name across the continent. Now known as the Abbot of Clairvaux, he wrote penetrating works of philosophy and psychology, advised kings and queens on policy, and even elevated his protégé to the position of pope (Eugenius III). By the time he was in his early fifties, Bernard was de facto the most powerful man on the continent.[17]

Through all these achievements, Bernard never abandoned his lust. In fact, he made sexual desire the central pillar of his philosophy. Love is like a magnet, Bernard wrote in his treatise *De diligendo deo* ('On Loving God'). It's the biological mechanism that drives us to seek out larger meaning (or a 'consummation in the spirit'); the spark that draws the mind upwards to higher things. Because divine love always begins in the body, this sensation is virtually the same as sexual longing. 'We are born of lust,' he wrote, and 'our desire and love also begin in lust.' So the challenge of a good life was not to reject our sexual urges. Do that and we risk abandoning the most special capacity we have. Instead, the secret was to learn to work with our desires; to channel them in the right direction. With the correct discipline, even the most intense lust could become a tool for recognising the beauty and truth of the universe.[18]

How did this work, though? Bernard went into more detail in one of his sermons on the Song of Songs. Obsessing over the meaning of a single passage – 'Let him kiss me with the kiss of his mouth' – he described the process whereby lust crackles into divine love. It was the same as the magical possibility opened by two lips meeting, he said. The 'kiss' was many things for Bernard: 'a spring inside' him; the 'living, active word'; 'a marvellous mingling of the divine light'. Most of all, it was a symbol of enlightenment. Because unlike a text – or a dream, a vision, a parable, or an image – a kiss always comes straight to your senses without any filter. You feel it before you can process it.[19] And this made it the perfect conduit of mystical experience. Kisses make you feel the shock of realising something new, awakening your mind to something greater than yourself. When your blood surges at the touch of somebody else's lips, isn't it true that the experience can shatter you, opening up a new life, a new world?

This was elite theology: the kind of thing that could be debated by senior monks for dozens of hours, or fill the pages of university lecture notes. But over the next decades, Bernard's philosophy of love swept through Europe like a forest fire, and his sermons were translated into vernacular French, Dutch and German. A wave of new writers, a majority of them women, now began to crystallise Bernard's sermons into works of poetry with a staggering erotic power. One of these was a Belgian woman called Hadewijch, who took Bernard's idea of sacred lust to astonishing new heights.

All we know for sure about Hadewijch is that she grew up in a fairly wealthy urban family, and that for most of her life she was a member of a beguinage – a type of literate women-only commune – in the duchy of Brabant. These beguinages were radical spaces. The women who joined them were self-motivated, coming together because they wanted to live better lives, away from the world and away from men. Some of them were escaping forced or unhappy marriages. Others – like Yvette of Huy, who hated sex so much she fantasised about her husband dying – were simply tired of intimacy with men and were looking for female company.[20] Although these women were not nuns, the beguines all took informal vows of chastity. And although they had no hierarchies or official codes of conduct, they formed tight collectives, dedicating themselves to reading, prayer and work in the local community. Some trained as nurses, treating lepers or serving in nearby hospitals, and others worked giving poor relief to the homeless. Still others wrote magnificent works of poetry, shot through with the electricity of redirected sexual desire.[21]

Comfortable and full of poise, but restless, Hadewijch was a beguine who wrestled with the sense that she might be living in the wrong age. More melancholic than Bernard, she worried that no 'official' institution would ever really have her as a member. And yet when she started to write, she really wrote. Hadewijch's letters and poems are all written in a confessional style, interlaced with candid descriptions of her lust for Jesus, the 'handsome man' who haunted her waking dreams and visions.

One Pentecost Hadewijch had a vision of this phantom Christ. The 'passionate love' she felt was so intense that she 'imagined all [her] limbs breaking one by one and all [her] veins . . . separately in tortuous pain'. Having closed her eyes and contemplated Jesus's life, Hadewijch's desire only grew stronger. 'I wanted to consummate my Lover completely . . . to fulfil his humanity blissfully with mine.' More than that, 'I wished, inside me, that he would satisfy me with his Godhead in one spirit and he shall be all he is without restraint.'

This was no metaphor. As Hadewijch described it, her meeting with Jesus culminated in a ghostly rubbing of bodies. Like Margery Kempe did, she claimed that he came to her at night, 'in the appearance and the clothing of the man he was on that day when he first gave us his body'. Yet Hadewijch's encounter was far more sexual than Margery's. He looked into her eyes, she said, and showed to her 'his sweet and beautiful and sorrowful face'. First this spectral Jesus gave her a chalice full of his blood, and then he gave her his body itself. He 'took me completely in his arms and pressed me to him. And all my limbs felt his limbs, in the full satisfaction that my heart and my humanity desired.' Silent, she screamed in ecstasy. 'I was externally completely satisfied to the utmost satiation.'[22]

This category of medieval writing, which we could call 'holy lust', seems to have pushed the limits of Bernard's philosophy a little too far. Sometime after recording this vision (as far as historians have been able to piece together) Hadewijch was expelled by the other women in her beguinage.[23] Were they horrified by what she had written? Or were they divided, privately allured but publicly needing to enforce censorship? Regardless, it's an important detail that Hadewijch was never formally condemned. In fact, by all evidence it seems her works were allowed to spread, and generations of men and women were able to take her liaison with the phantom Christ as a blueprint. Following her lead, many lost souls looked down at their own bodies and wondered. Could they turbocharge those sexual cravings, and find a way to push them towards the 'higher' goals of spiritual wisdom or intellectual growth?

After Hadewijch, generations of erotic spiritual writers took 'holy lust' further and further. There was Mechthild of Magdeburg, the German woman who described how passion 'overwhelmed' her with 'great weakness' and 'trembling shame'.[24] 'O glowing spark!' she wrote in a poem directed at Jesus himself. 'Set me on fire! / How long must I endure this thirst? / One hour is already too long, / A day is as a thousand years / When you are absent!' And there was Angela of Foligno, an Umbrian woman who made a habit of stripping naked in front of the cross.[25] So hot was the inner fire Angela felt in these moments, she worried she was being deceived by 'a demon'. Deciding she had no choice but to overpower this burning lust with something stronger, one day she picked up a candle. And she held it steadily for a moment before putting it straight to her genitals.[26]

How do we know when a desire is healthy, and how can we tell if it's leading us down the wrong path? Lust is a fire so strong, William Peraldus wrote, that it can melt iron out of shape.[27] Maybe the real problem is imagining we're made of iron in the first place. Back when I was packing my bags to move to Tyumen, I thought I had a total grip on what I was doing. I was transfixed by the glimpse of Siberia I'd had, a glimpse of something that seemed dazzling. Like Hadewijch or the young Bernard, I thought I'd seen an exciting new world that I could fall in love with. The difference was that these medieval writers did much more than catch a glimpse. As Bernard put it – when he found the completion he'd always longed for, in a life of writing and contemplation – any fleeting 'love' worth following needs to be nurtured, until it becomes something wiser, something more social, more perceptive, more complete.[28] Because if lust is a glimpse, then love has the courage to hold the gaze.

Are These Genitals?

Medieval art can be divisive. While Renaissance paintings seem crystalline, lifelike and dazzling, Gothic ones often appear two-dimensional, monochrome, or suffocated by religious themes. It's true, Europe had no artists who could produce photorealistic images before around the time of Jan van Eyck, who had the advantage of working with oil paints. But does that matter? What the Middle Ages had over the Renaissance, the art historian Michael Camille said, was its sense of boundless play. The problem with pictures that look real is that they 'trick' the eye, 'capturing' you in whatever tiny world the artist has created. Instead, medieval paintings spin an enigma. Rather than seducing you, they compel you to stand there and wonder about an unseeable world just beyond the frame.[29]

With one picture in particular, the enigma is strong. It's an illumination from a fourteenth-century prayer book, and every time I see it I question myself at the deepest level. What exactly is this? Is it a gateway into another world? A medieval Rothko mural? A gaping void in the heart of all existence? Sometimes I see it as a wound. While Jesus was dying on the cross a Roman soldier punctured him just between his ribs with a lance, and this is assumed to be a picture of that injury: the wound, disembodied and floating in mid-air. Sometimes I see something more bizarre. *Are these genitals?* Is my mind playing tricks? Or is this a glimpse into the strangeness of medieval erotica?

A mandorla, from a fourteenth-century prayer book.

Although medieval clerics talked a lot about the 'filth' of lust, their millennium has left little in the way of pornography.[30] You can find exceptions, though, if you know where to look. One place is the *fabliaux*, the farcical and sometimes scandalous French poems written mostly in the 1200s. They include tales of peasants who steal from the market and beat each other up, wives who play tricks on their husbands, and confidence tricksters who swindle aristocrats. They also include graphic sex scenes, with 'panting' and 'screaming' lovers admiring each other's outsized body parts. If these poems weren't so funny, and if they didn't come with the occasional dose of magic, they might be obscene.

As it is, these *fabliaux* manage to stay within the boundaries of folk tale: revelling in sex in the most extreme ways, yet managing to wrap things up with a neat moral at the end.[31]

Digesting the *fabliaux* now can be a bit of a challenge. On the one hand, they depart from most of our modern expectations of genre. They rhymed and were usually performed aloud in public spaces. And because they were often hilariously funny, this pitches them somewhere between a sermon, a pantomime and a stand-up comedy show.[32] But the erotic and explicit content gave them an additional twist, to the extent that one critic has called them a type of public 'soft pornography'.[33] Which leads to another challenge: the erotic content itself. Many of these *fabliaux* blend couplets about throbbing penises and engrossing sex scenes along with esoteric religious parody, before throwing in a tragicomic ending. One tale, which is typical, features a lover who, to hide from a carpenter whose wife he has been having sex with, pretends to be a wooden Jesus on a life-size crucifix. Coming home suddenly, the carpenter claims he just needs to make a correction to one of his workshop items, and deliberately slices the man's penis off with a chisel. Was this pornography, with a side order of comedy? Or was it comedy, with a side order of pornography? Either way, it's a genre of lust that doesn't have much mainstream appeal in the modern world.

A good test case is the *fabliau* 'Saint Martin's Wishes'. Part fairy tale and part bawdy joke, there's no escaping the explicit surprises at its heart.

A peasant in Normandy is busy ploughing his field when, from nowhere, the legendary figure of Saint Martin appears. As a reward for years of devotion, the saint says, he wants to offer the peasant four wishes. The man runs home to tell his wife the good news, but she shouts at him for skipping work and demands the first wish for herself. Her wish is a strange one. 'I wish,' she says, 'that, in God's name, there spring up penises galore over your body, aft and fore. On face, arms, sides, from head to foot, may countless penises take root.'[34] Horrified with the erections now sprouting out of his face, the husband shoots back a revenge wish. So now his wife is covered in genitals (or *cons*) of her own, some 'large and small', some 'oval and round', some 'deep ones' and 'some raised on a mound'.

How can they get out of this mess? Mutually disgusted, the couple now call a truce. Their third wish to Saint Martin is that all the genitals should be removed. But the saint takes this literally, leaving their groins totally bare. So now there really is only one way the story can end. The wife sighs, and uses the final wish to get things back to normal. 'One prick for you, one *con* for me. We'll return to our former state no poorer off, at any rate.'

Was this *fabliau* supposed to be pornography? If so, how does it compare with the modern genre that, apparently, sucks up one in every seven internet searches?[35] If we boil 'Saint Martin's Wishes' down to its fundamental elements, the resemblance is striking. First of all, it plays with a fantasy at the heart of so much modern pornography: limitless sexual pleasure. Both husband and wife want more and more genitals, and more and more sex (even though this ultimately goes wrong). There's a kinky punishment element from the wife. And like in pornography, its characters seem to care more about people's bodies than they do about the people themselves.[36] Even so, there are so many strange elements here. The farcical comedy of castration, the grotesque way the genitals cover the entire bodies, the not-so-kinky arrival of the ghost of a magical saint. If these filters interrupted modern pornography, would it be so popular on the internet?

Yet there were more arousing *fabliaux* than this one. Another example, 'Le Foteor', seems on the surface to be much closer to a modern erotic story.

LUST

A handsome young man books into luxury lodgings in a new town and decides he'll pay the bill through a little sex work. So he begins lingering outside the house of the best-looking wealthy woman in town, until her servant comes out to ask him what he wants. 'I'm a professional fucker [*foteor*]', he says, and he gives her a breakdown of his tariffs and services. Scandalised, the servant reports him to the lady of the house. But, as her husband is away for the day, the lady finds herself intrigued. What *does* he charge? Which is where the young man's seduction kicks in. He tells the lady that, although he would have charged 100 shillings to the servant, for attractive women like her the fee is always less. She'll only have to pay 20 shillings, as long as she also provides him with a hot bath. For that, he promises, he'll 'serve' her 'with consummate skill'.

After all the anticipation, this *fabliau* tale now gives way to sexual frenzy. First the servant decides she wants in on the act, and – after negotiating a higher fee – the young *foteor* flips her 'on her back' and, 'quick as lightning', 'gives her double'. After that he gets into the bath with the lady, and the two of them lie drinking 'choice wines' and soaking in the piping-hot water. Now clean, they move to the bed, and the man honours his promise by taking the lady to a state of 'ecstasy'.

But then comes the sort of farce that anybody who remembers sitcoms from the 1970s might expect. The husband returns, out of the blue. While the lady manages to hide, the *foteor* is caught naked and dripping wet from head to foot. Only his quick thinking can save him. 'I'm a virtuoso sex worker,' he explains to the husband, and says his wife contracted him for 20 shillings to have sex with her. Because it was 'high time' to begin, could he just get out of the way so the 'pleasure session' could 'commence'? The husband, fooled and desperate, pays the *foteor* twice the original cost to break the contract. And so the 'hero' strolls back to his luxury lodgings, his extra coins jangling as he goes.

The sexual politics of 'Le Foteor' are shameful by modern standards. Even so, it feels more 'modern', a little less bizarre, than 'Saint Martin's Wishes', and has a stronger erotic element. Several pornographic hallmarks define the story, from the thrill of sexual prowess and 'ecstasy' to all the dirty talk. It also arouses a full spectrum of sexual desires simultaneously, offering the lure of an absent husband, endless erotic services and multiple male orgasms. Again, though, it's hard not to take this piece as comedy first, titillation second.

Pornography may or may not be the right word. But one thing that's certain in all this erotic play is that medieval writers didn't feel sex needed to be sanitised out of literature and life. This wasn't a Victorian world, where naked bodies were sequestered behind lace curtains. It was a world where sex was public, often crossing boundaries of genre and taste. A world where pornography could be smuggled into any other genre like the caffeine lurking in a hazelnut latte.

One glance at a fourteenth-century pilgrim's badge, unearthed in a Belgian riverbed, shows just how far this idea could go in medieval culture. Because the reward for whichever pilgrim bought this souvenir was a pewter badge showing three erect penises, all with arms and legs and carrying a crowned vulva on a bier.[37] Although this badge seems surprising now, it was hardly unique. In the margins of sacred texts, such as a thirteenth-century Bible made in Hainaut, there are images of people masturbating.[38] In other explicitly Christian works, like a book of hours now held in New York's Pierpont Morgan Library, people perform cunnilingus above lines of solemn prayer.[39]

Scholars have come up with two competing theories to explain these sexualised images, which floated into so much medieval art and literature. First, some have argued that these genitals were a way of framing and defining 'holiness'. Like gargoyles on cathedral walls, they were there to mark the boundaries and to enforce the idea that dirty things belonged *outside* and holy things *inside*.[40] A badge like this, according to this theory, would have been quite a conservative object. If you wore sex organs on your tunic, this was mostly as a reminder of what your pilgrimage *wasn't*. If people laughed at this souvenir, it was because of the sharp contrast between pornography and their own act of self-sacrifice.

The other explanation takes a far more left-field approach, challenging us to see medieval sex as radically different to the sex we know today. By putting genitals on a pilgrim's badge, or by drawing cunnilingus in a book of hours, medieval artists were deliberately combining two powerful impulses: the force of sexual desire and the soul's quest for enlightenment. In this theory, these objects are extensions of Bernard of Clairvaux's connection between kissing and mystical wisdom. Inspired by the *Roman de la Rose* (the epic thirteenth-century poem of seduction and romance) or the love songs of the Troubadours, they imagine carnal love as a major step on the journey to wisdom and happiness. Sexual impulses, in this explanation, should be taken as sparks of something much brighter. The genitals are more than just genitals. *They are symbols of eternal wisdom.*

Where does this leave the status of sexual fantasy? If the genitals are really 'symbols of eternal wisdom', does this mean we no longer 'see' them for the physical things they are? One of the inescapable messages of 'Saint Martin's Wishes' is that our arousal can misdirect us. We may think we're aroused by one thing – the penis itself, and the more of them the better – the story seems to say. But really, this isn't the thing that actually pushes our buttons. What we're looking for is the *something else* that lies beyond the penis, beyond the genitals, beyond the touch of flesh that seems to consummate desire but never quite does. Even if a medieval audience enjoyed this story as 'pornography', they would have taken one basic lesson from it. That only by getting our fantasies off our chests – only by finding out how the world would really look if everything became an erotic prop – can we leave them behind and return to a relationship that might get us closer to that *something else* that we sometimes glimpse in arousal.[41]

So, medieval lust wasn't our lust, and medieval pornography wasn't our pornography. And if these erotic stories were anything they were capacious, bringing multiple sympathies and tonal registers and spiritual philosophies into tales of organs and orgasms. In the process, they – and the sexual badges or marginal drawings from manuscripts just like them – did something more subtle than either smuggling lust in or blocking lust out. Without banishing sex from the conversation, they were trying to filter the antisocial element out of it. They were critiquing lust without censoring it, confronting it without giving into it. If we make sex organs totally taboo they acquire a deeper power and attraction. But if we make them too central and ever-present, they have no power left to excite us. The magic of the *fabliaux* is that they managed to stay poised between these two poles, celebrating sex as a social relation rather than as a fantasy where (as Andreas Capellanus complained) men and women treat each other like toys.[42]

Nudity in Paradise

I'm taking my time, in the half hour before class, to walk through Tyumen's city centre. Crunching through the snow, I enter

Svetnaya Boulevar park, with its colourful sculptures and fairground rides, and walk towards the circus on the opposite side. Instead of taking the straight path, I step to the right and crunch a new route through a bank of pine trees. As I fight through the branches I'm hit by a set of images. The wonder of this city as I first found it. The restaurants, humid with garlic and barbecued meat. The coiling Tura river, with its iron lamp posts lighting up the promenade. The lover's bridge, reaching out to the wooden houses on the opposite bank. Making new friends, toasting them with vodka in grey apartment blocks. Visiting the countryside, kneeling down in wooden mosques heated by networks of thin water pipes. Accordion music, fresh tarragon, iced fish, helium balloons, tiny vanilla ice creams wrapped in paper. My heart deadened when all of these lost their colour for me. Today I'm feeling the courage to make them colourful again.

Lust, like envy, is a sin of the eyes. Rather than clouding the vision with poison, it clouds it with fragrances, fantasies and desires. In medieval Latin the word *luxuria* meant indulgence and extravagance, especially – although not exclusively – relating to sex. It also meant taking a more general delight in the surface of things. As Hugh of Saint Victor described it, *luxuria* is a power that first captures the eyes with pleasure, and then tricks the brain to plunge after it. Under this spell you come to believe that nothing else matters: that 'there's a long time left for repentance'; that 'the torments of hell are either tiny or non-existent'; and that the universe will always be 'merciful', no matter what you do.[43] *Luxuria* sustains your gaze in an eternal present and lulls you into believing that the past and future do not exist.

But they do exist. And unlike their Renaissance counterparts (who tended to paint scenes in a single time and space), medieval artists were masters of jumbling different portions of time together. Only rarely did they show the present moment. More often, the subject – whether a saint, the Virgin Mary, or the King of England – was painted alongside events from the past that shaped them, as well as the consequences of their actions, which lay in the future. In the Wilton Diptych, a twin set of oak panels painted in the late 1300s, King Richard II is surrounded by two holy kings from England's past, Edmund Martyr and Edward the Confessor, as he kneels in supplication before the angels who await him in paradise.[44] On the Hereford *Mappa Mundi*, created in the late 1200s, the map's recently built castles and cities appear next to the Tower of Babel and the mythical Labyrinth of ancient Crete, with Christ presiding over the Last Judgement at the top.[45]

But no medieval artist jumbled the time codes quite like Hieronymus Bosch. Born in the Dutch town of 's-Hertogenbosch sometime around 1450, his works radiate anxiety, horror, trauma and a surreal humour. Although he was almost an exact contemporary of Leonardo da Vinci, Bosch's style and subject matter make him firmly medieval. In fact, as his life ended one year before the onset of the Reformation in 1517, there are grounds to argue that the Middle Ages died with him.

Most of Bosch's works are otherworldly, as if a modern surrealist had travelled back to the medieval era to play a prank on the art world. His *Adoration of the Magi* showed time, typically, in three registers: the past (the birth of Jesus, in a rundown shack in the wilderness); the future (the Antichrist, lingering in a doorway); and the present (the contemporary city of Antwerp, gleaming in the distance).[46] But his works are not always so easy to decipher. His greatest masterpiece was also his greatest enigma, a work so complex that Erwin Panofsky, the supreme art historian of the twentieth century, declined to analyse it, saying it was 'too high for my wit'.[47]

LUST

It's impossible to describe *The Garden of Earthly Delights*, Bosch's enormous three-panel painting, without already interpreting it. Some of its parts are less controversial than others. On the far left is the Garden of Eden, with pools of crystal water, flocks of birds and grazing animals surrounding the figures of Christ, Eve and Adam. On the right panel is a psychedelic image of Hell, showing hundreds of naked souls being sliced, frozen, raped, tortured and burned by reptilian demons. What about the largest panel (plate 13), the central image? All that can be said of this, in neutral terms, is that it's a collection of bodies. It shows hundreds of naked people writhing around with outsized animals in a fantastical green pasture that appears similar to the landscape of Eden.

Are these bodies enjoying themselves, or are they suffering? Are they free or unfree? Are they in the past, the present, or the future? Or are they outside of time altogether?

All these puzzles, which Bosch himself never helped to solve, have divided people since the day the painting was finished. The writer Antonio de Beatis, who saw the work in July 1517, believed it was a commentary on 'nature'. With enthusiasm, he noted that it contained 'white and black' men and women dancing with 'birds and animals of every sort', as well as other 'things so pleasant and fantastic, that to those with no knowledge of them they could not be well described'.[48] More guarded was José de Sigüenza, who called this '*el quadro del madroño*',[49] or 'the *madroño* painting', after the enormous fruit that's being cradled by a woman near the bottom of the central panel. It's extraordinary that, in this great sea of bodies and creatures, this is what stood out to him. Still, for Sigüenza this fruit was more than a superficial detail. Because although the *madroño* looks almost exactly like a strawberry, when you bite into it the taste is bitter not sweet. And, in the same way, the seductions of Bosch's landscape are not all that they seem.

For my part, I've always taken *The Garden of Earthly Delights* to be a type of Rorschach test. If you look into its central panel and describe what you see, you'll always pick out some combination of details unique to you: *the* madroño; *the animals; the bodies; the pools of clear water.* And in this process of looking and describing, you'll find the painting tells you what it is you *really* feel about lust, about nudity, about the possibility of finding real freedom in the human body. This is a painting with the power to stir the prejudices and fantasies that lie dormant inside us all, half-hidden and half-known even to ourselves.

Scholars who've taken this Rorschach test have mostly fallen into three different camps. Those in camp number one see it as a garden of sexual liberation, and they usually pick out the sheer freedom of the bodies. Bosch painted a world 'before civilization', the art historian Margaret Carroll wrote. A world before the corrupting influence of cities or economies.[50] A world where the people are 'peaceful and egalitarian', 'endowed with a natural capacity for friendship', going around naked because they're liberated from any 'nuptial or political bonds'.[51] Hans Belting, in the same spirit, has described the garden as a 'sumptuous' place where 'no discordance disturbs the idyll', and where men and women play in 'sunny meadows' and 'move freely in the shimmering waters'. What really makes this a paradise for Belting is that it's a place without self-consciousness. Like 'the animals that frolic with them', the people here accept themselves, fully and unquestioningly, as parts of the natural world. And because they have this knowledge they feel neither shame nor any unquenchable desire. They just feel free.[52]

All of this can seem a little optimistic, and conveniently close to a modern ecological viewpoint. But members of camp number one have insisted that it's compatible with Bosch's worldview. For Margaret Carroll, the idea of a moral pleasure garden echoed the thirteenth-century poet Jean de Meun's descriptions of 'the golden age' of earth: a time when 'love was loyal and true' and 'free from covetousness and rapine'.[53] For Hans Belting, Bosch's garden matched the *paradisum voluptatis*, the 'paradise of lust' mentioned in the Book of Genesis, where sex was enjoyed without lust and its corrupting selfishness.[54] Describing the coming paradise, the twelfth-century bishop Otto of Freising wrote that humans would acquire 'new bodies', configured 'for a new use'.[55] When Bosch painted naked people burrowing into clam shells or dancing with owls on their heads, was he imagining what this 'new use' might look like?

Arguments like this will never wash with the members of camp number two. Picking out scenes of misery, hollow pleasure and sexual harassment, this camp sees Bosch's garden as a world spinning out of control. For Ernst Gombrich it was a snapshot of the earth before the flood, a time of gigantic vegetation when men 'abused the wives of their brothers' and 'lusted after' their friends.[56] For Nils Büttner, Bosch's garden is a 'flat' world where the naked souls are deliberately 'abstract' and drained of any warmth or life. Remarking on a chilling absence – there are no children and no elderly people in the central panel – Büttner reads it as an adult-only space, an orgy of 'moral decay'.[57] Remove all ethical codes, all preaching, all confession and all moral accountability, and this is what life would become. A hollow sex party, with more groping than anybody could ever want.

It's clear that there really is a lot of groping in this panel. What isn't so clear is whether the people are supposed to be enjoying it. Drifting on an enormous sprouting bud, a couple are cocooned in a bubble and caressing each other. But even as she grabs him, just above his knee, there's something unsettled in her body language. Is there a deadness in her eyes? A resignation, a disgust? More obviously upset is the woman just behind her, who is standing thigh-deep in water and whose partner has seized her wrist. Most poignant is the victim at the top of the panel, inside the dark blue sphere which makes up the painting's centrepiece. She's a naked woman in shadow, looking out from the canvas. And her face is a painful blank as a man's hand reaches between her thighs. Of all the souls in this garden, she's the only one who holds the gaze of the viewer. It's as if she's pleading with us to put ourselves in her place. To contemplate how it might feel if your body had to be open to anybody who wanted it all of the time.

No moral judgements about lust are required for those in camp number three. Seeing this panel as a window into an alternative reality, these take Bosch as an artist of the virtual world. They often pick out a tiny detail – not in the centre but on the left, in the panel showing the original Garden of Eden. Neither Adam nor Eve has a leaf over their genitals, meaning only one thing: Bosch was giving us a rare glimpse of the first couple *before* the moment of original sin. And so it follows, people in this camp say, that this central panel is a continuation of that moment. It's Bosch's way of imagining what the world would have looked like if humans had never eaten the forbidden fruit in the Tree of Knowledge, if they had never discovered shame.

How did this work? For scholars such as Jos Koldeweij, the central panel is not a painting of life without sin. It's a painting of life without the concept of sin.[58] The beauty of this theory is that it can also explain all those outsized animals in the landscape, all the vast birds and dancing owls. They're there because this is a planet where humans didn't develop as we know them, as oppressive exploiters of the natural landscape. Instead, they lived just like other animals, free from shame or ambition or moral choice. So, the naked people in the painting are also unburdened by the one thing that makes us most human: the constant struggle to be good.

I often look at pictures of this painting on my laptop screen while I'm sitting in my office in Siberia. I zoom in to small details in the digital reproduction, taking in close-ups of tortured souls and bodies relaxing in shining water. Most of them seem so warm, which is one of the reasons I keep coming back. But all of this zooming in to the details of the painting misses the message of the piece as a whole. Really, the only way to really see *The Garden of Earthly Delights* – to take it all in, in its expansiveness – is to visit it in person, in the Prado Museum in Madrid, a few corridors along from the grieving Juana of Castile and the weeping Joseph of Arimathea.

At some point on my medieval journey, between my encounter with Richard III's portrait as a nine-year-old boy and this current moment in Tyumen, I did exactly this. I stood for thirty minutes looking, in that room surrounded by Bosch's other masterpieces, and I performed my own Rorschach test. And what I saw revealed to me something new about medieval lust, and how we can tell when desire is leading us along a dangerous path.

I saw the bubbles. Once I began to look for them, they unlocked the whole sweep of Bosch's painting. Everywhere in *The Garden of Earthly Delights* are people trying to isolate themselves in their own bubbles, or private booths or spheres. There's the pair of lovers in the hollowed-out floating apple, who we assume are enjoying a private moment until we notice another leg, poking out of a hole to the right. There's the trio sheltering under a translucent, umbrella-like half bubble. There's the crowd of people crammed together in a conical red pouch. Then there are the bodies clambering into clam shells, or burrowing into enormous berries, or prising their way inside the buds of enormous flowers, or poking their heads into crystal tubes. It's odd, because the garden seems to be a place of great freedom and expression. So why are all its inhabitants so desperate to shut themselves away?

The clue, as always with Bosch, involves scrambling across the time codes. Because he also projected these isolating bubbles back onto the past and forward onto the future. At the painting's left, in Eden, the only creatures who are seeking privacy in a cave are the scuttling reptiles. At the centre of that panel is the brooding owl – whose nocturnal life and predatory behaviour made him, for Bosch, a symbol of the devil – occupying his own hollow pink disk.[59] Over in Hell the same logic is twisted further, with souls forced into horrifying capsules and traps. As well as the bodies being defecated into a droplet by a giant bird, there are the ones cramped into a phone box-style torture chamber. At the heart of them all, gazing back towards the owl in Eden, is the tree man. Housing a band of recluses in his hollowed-out torso, this sad figure has become the bubble himself. An empty shell, resigned to his eternal isolation.

Standing in the Prado, I realised that, for the world that died with Hieronymus Bosch, this was really the biggest problem with lust. The violent nowness of it. It's always beautiful to be captured by a glance, to sigh at the grace of a body as it moves. Who could blame someone who gets transfixed by beauty and then wants to dive into it? But the deadly trick of *luxuria* is the trick of tunnel vision. It's when our desire traps us inside a bubble, where nothing other than that beauty – no other lives, no other possibilities – seems to exist. It's being enthralled by a surface while denying the existence of its depth.

So it turns out that the problem of lust is also a problem of history. Anyone we find attractive is always constituted by a past (their story, where they've been, how they've come to be the person they are in this moment), and is always waiting to jump into a future (the life they're yet to build or shape for themselves). But *luxuria*, in all its suspended desire, pays no respect to the passing of time or the duration of a human life. While lust wants you to rip the person you desire out of time, real love is historical. Love wants you to take people as they are, as they have been, as they will come to be, flowing always from past to future.

Back in my apartment in Tyumen, my wet swimming things drying on the radiator, I stand looking out of the window again. Outside I can see the same smoke stacks, the same pink sky that I gazed at back when the winter was just beginning. I imagine painted bodies from a fifteenth-century canvas, writhing in circles through the ice. My heart heaves in my chest, and I turn back to my books and my notes; to the adventure of doing history, which can never be over, can never be exhausted.

Lust was the least deadly of the seven sins because it was the impulse closest to love. As Bernard of Clairvaux said, lust was a power that could lead in two directions. It could go down, to a superficial fixation on bodies, but also up, to the eternal mysteries of the universe. And yet whichever way it went, lust was always something you felt and experienced through the body, a point Hadewijch of Brabant or Angela of Foligno made in the most powerful ways. The challenge was to tip lust in the right direction. If we can nudge it towards something beyond the self – the service of others, or a total engagement with another person – then, according to these writers, it won't just enable the 'preservation of the whole human race'. It will be divine.[60]

Undirected, or pointed the wrong way, the dangers of medieval *luxuria* were usually antisocial ones. Give ourselves over to a fantasy, like the wife who wants a dozen penises sprouting from her husband's flesh, and we substitute the living person for a sex toy. Or bind ourselves in a bubble, like the lovers in Bosch's garden, and we absorb ourselves in a cocoon, blocking out past and future as well as the depths of the lives around us. Lust is moving to a place, or taking a job, and never letting it into our hearts. Lust is infatuation with an image, a dream, a glimpse held in a single moment. Love, by contrast, is opening the heart up. It's allowing that conversation to develop over time. Love is having the courage to be naked and vulnerable in the places where lust wants us to be an alluring nude.

The Seven, Again

How do we escape the Siberia we sometimes make for ourselves?

Self-help from the Middle Ages shouldn't make sense. But although our struggles today seem distant from those who lived eight hundred years ago, maybe we've been looking through the telescope from the wrong end. And although we're speeding away from the Middle Ages, the place we're rushing to isn't necessarily a better understanding of ourselves. When we listen to the voices in medieval manuscripts it's obvious that they're still alive; that they have messages to give us about the most intimate struggles of our lives. Messages about fear and compulsion, about grieving and wonder, about ego and ecstasy. Compassionate messages about what it means to be ourselves, and how to live with all this selfishness and desire.

When Pride, Envy, Anger, Sloth, Avarice, Gluttony and Lust overwhelm us, we stop perceiving the world around us clearly. With pride we're no longer sensitive to events and details, everything's blocked by our absorption in ourselves. In envy, our hatred obscures our vision, reducing the lives of others to a commentary on ourselves. With anger, we only see one side of an argument, and with sloth, we no longer have the will to notice much at all. With avarice we obsess, with gluttony we fixate and with lust we fantasise, and in each case we find that we're ripped away from the reality and variety of the world. If the Deadly Sins share one thing in common, it's how they alienate us from our environment.

So what to do? How can we make ourselves at home wherever

we are? There aren't any easy solutions for this, either in the wisdom of the Middle Ages or in that of any other era. But I've learned that one answer is to follow that warning at the heart of Bosch's mysterious painting, *The Garden of Earthly Delights*. If each of the sins is an impulse that wants us to shut ourselves away, then the remedy is to open up. It's to get out of those bubbles. To fight the temptation to burrow and hide, and find the courage to show our real faces. To live in the world, and not inside our heads.

Sometimes over the past few years I've felt the power of this idea surging through me. I've woken up and thrown myself into all the hours of the day, living every experience like today is the only one that will ever exist. But whenever I think I've mastered this, a day or two later I slip up. And then I'm hit by the Seven, again.

Is this really so bad?

In the library at Trinity College Cambridge I once found a small book. It hadn't been digitised, and the description in the catalogue was evasive. The manuscript was grey and fragile, but when I opened it the pages were full of mysterious grids in bright colours. They were charts, with sets of words boxed together in cells. And there, on the thirteenth folio, I found a grid with the names of the Seven Deadly Sins, coloured red, matched with seven positive qualities in blue (plate 12). They were grouped in combinations, so that in one square 'lust' was together with 'justice' and in another 'pride' was with 'charity'.[1] For whoever made this slim book, the system of the sins really was a type of Periodic Table. Just like that tool of modern chemistry, it could help us recognise the combinations – of virtues and vices, of strengths and weaknesses – that make us who we are.

What I saw that day, I realise now, was a more endurable remedy for the sins. To accept the force of our desires, and by matching them with virtues compound them into something better. When we combine pride with humility it becomes self-belief, and the confidence to use our talents for the benefit of others. When we balance the watchfulness of envy with an open heart it can become compassion, sympathy and care. Anger matched with perspective knows its limits, recognising when something is worth fighting against, and knowing what that rage can achieve. Avarice in moderation helps us find the objects that express our personalities, that build soul, that create wonder. A restrained gluttony takes food or drink as something social and character-building, and a modified lust can give us the courage to reach out to others, looking beyond the surfaces of the lives we see. Finally, if we can find a way to get through our sloth with courage, we can come to recognise that, from fields that bristle over with dead thorns, the most incredible flowers can grow.

It's been several years now since I stood by that apartment window looking out at a pink Siberian sky. So much has changed in my life and in the world. I chose to leave Russia sometime between the Covid-19 pandemic and the invasion of Ukraine, and I haven't been able to go back. It was heartbreaking and abrupt, although unlike moving there it was a choice I made with no illusions of glamour. Now I live in a city that's much warmer, although every time I eat beetroot or feel a rush of cold air in my lungs my mind is back in Tyumen. But I also go back there in my thoughts all the time, as I keep struggling to live with my failings and weaknesses. Because Siberia now reminds me of something that will stay with me until the day my heart stops beating; the final lesson of this journey through the Deadly Sins.

Self-forgiveness is one of the most valuable moves the mind can make, though also one of the hardest. Bosch's *Garden of Earthly Delights* shows us that a world without sin is pure fantasy, and wouldn't be much fun anyway. At their best, the Seven Deadly Sins were never really about making us 'pure'. They were supposed to be a way of mapping the mind, of revealing ourselves for what we are. Instead of blotting out our vulnerabilities, or torturing ourselves for our failings, these maps were supposed to help us work with our envy or anger or sloth, and learn to push them in a better direction. Only by dissolving the two phantoms inside us, the monster and the angel, can we make space for the real person to live in their place.

Acknowledgements

So much talk about the sins. What about the virtues? One way or another I've spent twenty years circling around the topics and questions of this book, and I'd like to thank everyone who has helped me with their fortitude, prudence, diligence, patience, charity, faith and hope.

Writing wasn't always a simple process. But everything felt easier with the encouragement of Zoë Waldie, a literary agent who possesses all seven of the capital virtues and more. Working with the incredible team at Rogers, Coleridge & White has been a pleasure, and I want to thank Phoebe Wyatt, Sam Coates, Stephen Edwards, Katharina Volckmer, Tristan Kendrick, Aanya Davé, Sampurna Ganguly, Maddie Luke and Chris Bentley-Smith.

Helen Conford's editing saved the manuscript from way too much vice, while pushing the ideas further than I thought they could go. She and the team at Hutchinson Heinemann have been amazing, and I want to thank Emily Fish, Laura Brooke, Ania Gordon, Cameron Watson and Vanessa Phan for making the publication process a dream. At Doubleday it was a privilege to work with Kris Puopolo, who grounded the project when it was spinning away, and I'm grateful for the brilliant work of Faith Griffiths, Sara Hayet, and Anne Jaconette. Thanks, also, to Josh Ireland for the exceptional copy-editing and Laurie Ip Fung Chun for managing the editorial process.

So many academic friends and mentors have helped me over the course of this project, it would be impossible to name everyone. But thanks especially to Brigitte Bedos-Rezak, Bill Jordan, Maryanne Kowaleski, James Robertson, Nick Vincent, John Gillingham, Martin Aurell, John Sabapathy, David d'Avray, Sophie Page, Chloë

ACKNOWLEDGEMENTS

Ireton, Yves Mausen, Gregory Lippiatt, María Asenjo González, María Ángeles Martín Romera, Carolina Obradors Suazo and Luis Almenar Fernández. My medieval journey started at the University of Bristol with the teaching of Anke Holdenried, Marcus Bull, Ian Wei, Pam King and Kenneth Austin, and I'm lucky to have kept up a historical dialogue with the friends I met there, especially the players in the annual Medievalists vs Modernists cricket match.

Working at the School of Advanced Studies at the University of Tyumen was a life-defining experience, and I want to thank the colleagues who made living in Siberia so much fun: duskin drum, Evgeny Grishin, John Tangney, Zach Reyna, Svetlana Erpyleva, Natalya Savalyeva, Oleg Zhuravlev, Maxim Alyukov, Elena Arbatskaya, Louis Vervoort, Giacomo Andreoletti, Fabio Grazioso, Tomasz Blusiewicz, Erika Wolf, David Melbye, Corinne Doria, Jay Silverstein, Anna Varfolomeeva, Brian Smith, Arlyce Menzies, Matvey Lomonsov, Krishna Muthukumarappan, Juliet Colinas, Julie Resche, Shakhlo Makhmudova, Valeria Savina, Ekaterina Selikhovkina, Lyudmila Malyogina, Alyona Bunkova, Anastasia Roussakova, Elina Samokhvalova, Fedor Gook, Daniel Kontowski, Gulnara Bayazitova and Gulyusa Zinnatulina. Also, I want to thank the school's students, especially those in my Seven Deadly Sins class of Q1 2020/2021, who inspired this book. Our school's founder and director, Andrey Shcherbenok, gave advice at the earliest stages of writing, and his loss is devastating.

It's impossible to find a way through any project without the kindness of friends, and I want to thank Edmund Caldecott and Charles and Sasha Knox-Vydmanov for reading versions of the text in its earliest stages, offering so many ideas and so much support. Mike Firman, Michael Marshall, Lee Bulmer and Thom Davies talked me through all seven of the sins, in the most imaginative ways. The writing was supported, at all stages, by the hospitality and good spirit of Margaret Mulhall and family, Fra, Baya and Audi. In Dublin, thanks to Sarah O'Connell and Peadar Melhorn for providing our family with a home when we had nowhere to live, and to Eimear Clowry Delaney at Notre Dame, who did the same for me professionally. For their encouragement, I want to thank Lillie Rage

ACKNOWLEDGEMENTS

and Sara Sjölund, who believed in this project from the beginning, and Evgeny Lebedev too, for his art-historical advice. Finally, Ben Dark offered support and consolation throughout; it was a pleasure to share experiences with him at all stages of the writing process.

As I finished this book, I was lucky to have some family members who made writing a joy. My brother, Mike, has shown me how to never give up. Tony Clark has been a rock of support for our family. My mother, Kim, read every word and gave me feedback on how to shape the material, and this book is dedicated to her. Todd Foley and Sharon Ostfeld-Johns, my other family, showed their infinite patience, infinite generosity and infinite humour, guiding me not only on how to write large parts of this, but also on how to live with my own deadly sins.

But there's no point writing anything without hope. And as long as I live with Anne Mulhall, there will always be that. Thanks not just for the reading, but for all of it. Our lives are chaos, but if I had to live the thousand years of the Middle Ages with anyone, it would be with you. And with Frida and Frank, too!

Notes

THE SEVEN

1. Vatican Library MS Vat.Lat. 671. The *Liber Arcis Sapientiae* is on fols.93r–255r. Alongside this text, this Vatican manuscript contains three of Bernard of Clairvaux's works, as well as his complete *Sermons on the Canticles*. I would like to acknowledge that this project has received funding from the European Union's Horizon 2020 research and innovation programme under the Marie Skłodowska-Curie grant agreement no. 847635.
2. Vatican Library MS Vat.Lat. 671, fols.106r., 101r., 141r. Extensive work on the *Liber Arcis Sapientiae* – a vast compendium that includes excerpts from other texts and treatises on the sins, as well as unique material – remains to be done, although the manuscript as a whole is discussed in Chiara Azzolini, 'Spigolature sulla biblioteca gerolamina del Castellazzo', in *I manoscritti della Biblioteca del Capitolo Metropolitano di Milano: studi e ricerche*, edited by Milvia Bollati (Rome: Viella, 2023), pp.77–88.
3. John Cassian, *The Institutes*, translated by Boniface Ramsey (New York: Paulist Press, 2000), Book 5.
4. The best academic introductions to the sins as they were understood in medieval Europe are: Morton W. Bloomfield, *The Seven Deadly Sins: An Introduction to the History of a Religious Concept, with Special Reference to Medieval English Literature* (East Lansing, MI: Michigan State College Press, 1952); Siegfried Wenzel, 'The Seven Deadly Sins: Some Problems of Research', *Speculum*, 43 (1968); Richard Newhauser, *The Early History of Greed: The Sin of Avarice in Early Medieval Thought and Literature* (Cambridge: Cambridge University Press, 2000); *In the Garden of Evil: The Vices and Culture in the Middle Ages*, edited by Richard Newhauser (Toronto: Pontifical

Institute of Mediaeval Studies, 2005); *The Seven Deadly Sins: From Communities to Individuals*, edited by Richard Newhauser (Leiden: Brill, 2007).
5. I. M. Berwian, H. Walter, E. Seifritz and Q. J. M. Huys, 'Predicting Relapse after Antidepressant Withdrawal: A Systematic Review', *Psychological Medicine*, 47:3 (2017), pp.426–437. As the authors make clear, relapse rates vary by age and gender, race and ethnicity, age of onset, number of prior episodes, severity at onset, episode length, drug response, depression subtypes and comorbidities.
6. For example Byung-Chul Han, *The Burnout Society*, translated by Erik Butler (Stanford, CA: Stanford University Press, 2015).
7. On the career ambitions of the first university graduates, see Ian P. Wei, *Intellectual Culture in Medieval Paris: Theologians and the University, c.1100–1330* (Cambridge: Cambridge University Press, 2012).
8. 'Parens scientiarum', in *Chartularium Universitatis Parisiensis*, edited by H. Denifle and A. Chatelain (Paris: Delalain Frères, 1889), 1, no. 79. See also the discussion of the centrality of pastoral theology in the early University of Paris in Wei, *Intellectual Culture*, e.g., pp.107–108.
9. The Fourth Lateran Council, Canon 21, in *Conciliorum oecumenicorum decreta*, edited by Joseph Alberigo, Joseph A. Dossetti, Pericles Joannou, Claude Leonardi and Paul Prodi (Basel: Herder, 1972), p.221.
10. Julia Barrow, *The Clergy in the Medieval World: Secular Clerics, Their Families and Careers in North-Western Europe c.800–c.1200* (Cambridge: Cambridge University Press, 2015), pp.236–268.
11. Beth Allison Barr, 'Three's a Crowd: Wives, Husbands, and Priests in the Late Medieval Confessional', in *A Companion to Pastoral Care in the Late Middle Ages (1200–1500)*, edited by Ronald J. Stansbury (Leiden: Brill, 2010), pp.213–234.
12. This process is described in detail in Nicholas Orme, *Going to Church in Medieval England* (New Haven: Yale University Press, 2021), pp.69–71, 264–274.
13. Alexander Murray, 'Counselling in Medieval Confession', in *Handling Sin: Confession in the Middle Ages*, edited by Peter Biller and Alastair J. Minnis (York: York Medieval Press, 1998), pp.63–77.

14. The story of Everard is recorded in Caesarius of Heisterbach, *Dialogus miraculorum*, 4:98, vol.1, pp.266–267. This is cited and discussed in relation to confession in Murray, 'Counselling', at pp.72–73.
15. Joseph Goering, 'The Internal Forum and the Literature of Penance and Confession', *Traditio*, 59 (2004), pp.175–227.
16. For penances, see for example the selection in *Medieval Handbooks of Penance: A translation of the principal* libri poenitentiales *and selections from related documents*, edited and translated by John T. McNeill and Helena M. Gamer (New York: Columbia University Press, 1990 [1938]).
17. An example of one of these trees of vices is in Biblioteca Vaticana MS Reg.Lat. 399, fol.65v.
18. Dublin, Trinity College Dublin MS 306, fol.46r. The thorns passage is: 'Plus amatur ager qui post spinas et tribulos fructus uberes reddit quam ille qui spinas et tribulos nunquam tulit et semper sterilis extitit.'
19. Dublin, Trinity College Dublin MS 306, fol.47r. 'Homo vero in vita est similem illi qui est in flumine impetuoso, qui in uno loco stare non potest, et nisi ad summa conetur, ad ima dilabitur.'
20. Dublin, Trinity College Dublin MS 306, fol.47r. 'Velis nolis intra fines tuos habitat Iebusaeus, qui subiugari potest sed non exterminari.'
21. For resources on the life and writings of Evagrius, see *Guide to Evagrius Ponticus*, edited by Joel Kalvesmaki (2025), https://evagriusponticus.net/life.htm [Accessed July 2025]. For selections of Evagrius's work in English, see *Evagrius Ponticus*, edited by Augustine Casiday (London: Routledge, 2006).
22. David Brakke, 'Holy Men and Women of the Desert', in *The Oxford Handbook of Christian Monasticism*, edited by Bernice M. Kaczynski (Oxford: Oxford University Press, 2020), pp.35–50.
23. Athanasius, *The Life of Saint Antony*, translated by Robert T. Meyer (Westminster, MD: The Newman Press, 1950), ch.85, p.90.
24. John Wortley, *An Introduction to the Desert Fathers* (Cambridge: Cambridge University Press, 2019).
25. *The Lives of the Desert Fathers: The Historia Monachorum in Aegypto*, edited and translated by Norman Russell (Kalamazoo: Cistercian Publications, 1981), ch.20:7.

26. On this aspect, see Rowan Williams, *Silence and Honey Cakes: The Wisdom of the Desert* (Oxford: Lion Hudson, 2003).
27. On Evagrius's challenges, see David T. Bradford, 'Brain and Psyche in Early Christian Asceticism', *Psychological Reports*, 109, no. 2 (2011), pp.461–520.
28. Evagrius Ponticus, *Talking Back [Antirrhêtikos]: A Monastic Handbook for Combating Demons*, translated by David Brakke (Collegeville, MI: Liturgical Press, 2009). Greek text here: *Evagrius Ponticus*, Abhandlung der Königlichen Gesellschaft der Wissenschaften zu Göttingen, Philologisch-Historische Klasse, Neue Folge, Band xiii, no. 2 (Berlin, 1912), pp.472–544.
29. Evagrius, *Talking Back*, Prologue.
30. *The Devils and Evil Spirits of Babylonia*, vol.1: '*Evil Spirits*', edited and translated by R. Campbell Thompson (London: Luzac and Co., 1903), pp.xlii–xliii, xlv–xlvi.
31. For Mithras, see Bloomfield, *The Seven Deadly Sins*, pp.22–23. See also Dan-Tudor Ionescu, 'Mithras, Neoplatonism and the Stars', *Acta Classica Universitatis Scientiarum Debreceniensis*, 54 (2018), pp.161–180.
32. *Testament of Reuben*, translated by Marinus de Jonge in *The Apocryphal Old Testament*, edited by H. F. D. Sparks (Oxford: Clarendon Press, 1984), pp.515–521.
33. Virgil, *The Aeneid*, translated by David West (London: Penguin, 2003), vi: 714.
34. Origen, *Homily V in Psalmos*, in Origen, *Opera omnia quae graece vel latine tantum exstant et ejus nomine circumferuntur*, vol.XII: *Origenis: Selectorum in Psalmos, Pars II*, edited by Carl Heinrich Eduard Lommatzsch (Rome: Berolini, 1841), p.233.
35. Seneca, *On the Shortness of Life*, in Seneca, *Dialogues and Letters*, translated and edited by C. D. N. Costa (London: Penguin, 1997), pp.59–86; Epictetus, *The Enchiridion*, in Epictetus, *Discourses and Selected Writings*, translated and edited by Robert Dobbin (London: Penguin, 2008), pp.219–245: ch.5.
36. On this, see Columba Stewart, 'Evagrius Ponticus and the Eastern Monastic Tradition on the Intellect and the Passions', *Modern Theology*, 27:2 (2011), pp.263–275.

37. John Cassian, *De Coenobiorum Institutis*, Book 5, chapter 19. Latin from *Patrologia Latina*, edited by J.-P. Migne [hereafter *PL*], vol.49, cols.235–236.
38. Gregory the Great, *Moralia in Job: or Morals on the Book of Job*, translated by James Bliss and Charles Marriott (Oxford: Parker and Rivington, 1850), vol.3, part 6, book 31, pp.424ff. Note that, contemporary to Gregory was Isidore of Seville, who also seized upon Cassian's system, and also trimmed them down to seven. But Isidore's seven were gluttony (*gastrimargia*), lust (*fornicatione*), avarice (*philargyria*), anger (*ira*), sadness (*tristicia*), sloth (*accidia*) and vainglory (*cenodoxia*). He made pride (*superbia*), along with envy (*invidia*), part of an ancillary set of symptoms of these seven vices that, he said, would cease when they were exterminated. Isidore of Seville, *Quaestiones in vetus testamentum*, 'In Deuteronomium', Q.16, *PL* vol.83, cols.366B–367B.
39. On the theological adoption of the seven sins in the 1100s and 1200s, see Spencer E. Young, *Scholarly Community at the Early University of Paris* (Cambridge: Cambridge University Press, 2014), ch.5, pp.168–207.
40. Hugh of Saint Victor's *De quinque septenis* (*On the Five Sevens*) and its Versification in Samuel Presbiter's *De oratione dominica* (*On the Lord's Prayer*), edited by Andrew Dunning, *Scholarly Editing*, 37 (2016). Available online: at http://scholarlyediting.org/2016/editions/intro.dunning.html. On Hugh's view of the sins, see Boyd Taylor Coolman, *The Theology of Hugh of St. Victor: An Interpretation* (Cambridge: Cambridge University Press, 2010), pp.192–224.
41. For this section of Robert Pullen's sermons, see Lambeth Palace MS 4776, f.12v. Geoffrey Babio, 'De civitate sancta Jerusalem secundum sensum tropologicum', *PL*, vol.177, 999A–1003A. This sermon was once attributed to Hugh of Saint Victor, although was attributed to Geoffrey in Jan Bistřický, 'K Tak Zvanému Zdikívu Homiliári', *Listy filologické / Folia philologica*, 84:1 (1961), pp.66–84 at p.73.
42. For a nuanced and realistic reassessment of the impact of Lateran IV, see Jeffrey M. Wayno, 'Rethinking the Fourth Lateran Council of 1215', *Speculum*, 93: 3 (2018), pp.611–637.
43. For example, Lambeth Palace MS 477, fols.32rff. In this manuscript, the directory for *avarice* is by far the longest (running to thirteen

folios). For comparison, *gluttony* has seven folios, *pride* has just over four, *lust* just short of two, *sloth* a page and a half, *envy* one folio and *anger* and *sadness* less than one. See also Oxford, Bodleian Library MS Laud Misc. 345.

44. Biblioteca Vaticana MS Reg.Lat. 630, fol.22r.
45. To give two examples of this: Oxford, Bodleian Library MS Lat. th.e.22, inside upper board; Biblioteca Vaticana MS Borgh. 56, fol.140v.
46. Peter Damian, *Die Briefe des Petrus Damiani*, edited by Kurt Reindel (Munich: Monumenta Germaniae Historica, 1989), pp.156–157. For another, later example of a harsh treatment of the sins, demanding sinners make retribution for them as with a debt, see Cambridge, Corpus Christi College MS 136, fol.108v.
47. Paris, Bibliothèque Nationale de France MS Lat. 16417, fol.113r–113v.
48. At the time of writing, an edition is in the process of being prepared by Siegfried Wenzel, Richard Newhauser, Bridget K. Balint and Edwin Craun, among other contributors. The challenges of producing this edition are colossal, given the number of extant manuscripts of the work and also its considerable length.
49. See George Corbett, 'Peraldus and Aquinas: Two Dominican Approaches to the Seven Capital Vices and the Christian Moral Life', *The Thomist: A Speculative Quarterly Review*, 79:3 (2015), pp.383–406.
50. On these virtues as applied to the Seven Deadly Sins, in works known as *remedia*, see Siegfried Wenzel, 'The Source for the "Remedia" of the Parson's Tale', *Traditio*, 27 (1971), pp.433–453.
51. Dante Alighieri, *Inferno*, translated by Robert Hollander and Jean Hollander (New York: Doubleday, 2000); Dante Alighieri, *Purgatorio*, translated by Robert Hollander and Jean Hollander (New York: Doubleday, 2003); Dante Alighieri, *Paradiso*, translated by Robert Hollander and Jean Hollander (New York: Doubleday, 2007). My interpretations of Dante are guided by the notes in the Hollander English editions of the text.
52. Siegfried Wenzel, *The Sin of Sloth:* Acedia *in Medieval Thought and Literature* (Chapel Hill: University of North Carolina Press, 1967), pp.164–190.

53. Jonathan Willis, '"Moral Arithmetic" or Creative Accounting? (Re-)-defining Sin through the Ten Commandments', in *Sin and Salvation in Reformation England*, edited by Jonathan Willis (Farnham: Ashgate, 2016), pp.69–86. For an alternative view, which acknowledges how the Deadly Sins lost their centrality as a meaningful framework for Christian European life after the Reformation, while emphasising how the schema remained valuable in the Renaissance literary arena, see Dana Lynn Key, 'From Medieval Morality Play to Jacobean City Comedy: The Afterlives of the Seven Deadly Sins' (PhD Thesis, University College London, 2021).
54. This point is made in Carol Jamison, 'The New Seven Deadly Sins', in *Studies in Medievalism XVIII: Defining Medievalism(s) II*, edited by Karl Fugelso (Woodbridge: Boydell and Brewer, 2009), pp.265–288.
55. This original speech documented in 'Reid Hoffman: The venture capitalist on how to hit a fast-moving target in the second-wave Web boom,' *Wall Street Journal*, 23 June 2011. For Tim Chang, see https://techcrunch.com/2012/03/24/worlds-a-game/ [Accessed July 2025].
56. Reid Hoffman has talked about this idea in several places, notably a podcast interview he did with Axios: https://www.axios.com/2019/02/26/reid-hoffman-masters-of-scale-seven-deadly-sins [Accessed June 2025].

1. PRIDE

1. Biblioteca Vaticana, MS Reg.Lat. 150, fol.156r.
2. Lisa A. Williams and David DeSteno, 'Pride: Adaptive Social Emotion or Seventh Sin?', *Psychological Science*, 20:3 (2009).
3. Gregory the Great, *Moralia in Job*, vol.3, book 31, pp.489–490.
4. John Cassian, *The Institutes*, book 12, ch.3.
5. London, Lambeth Palace MS Sion L40.2/L12, fol.78r: 'Cetera qui super memet, transcendere spero.'
6. Biblioteca Vaticana MS Vat.Lat. 671, fols.98v–99r.
7. James Given, 'The Inquisitors of Languedoc and the Medieval Technology of Power', *American Historical Review*, 94:2 (1989), pp.336–359.

8. On this manuscript, and the intellectual life of Herrad, see Fiona J. Griffiths, *The Garden of Delights: Reform and Renaissance for Women in the Twelfth Century* (Philadelphia: University of Pennsylvania Press, 2007).
9. Danielle Joyner, 'All That Is Evil: Images of Reality and Figments of Imagination in the *Hortus Deliciarum*', in *Imagination und Deixis: Studien zur Wahrnehmung im Mittelalter*, ed. Kathryn Starkey and Horst Wenzel (Stuttgart: Hirzel, 2007), pp.105–25. See also Danielle Joyner, *Painting the* Hortus Deliciarum*: Medieval Women, Wisdom, and Time* (University Park: Pennsylvania State University Press, 2016), pp.28–29.
10. Gerald B. Guest, 'The Beautiful Lucifer as an Object of Aesthetic Contemplation in the Central Middle Ages', *Studies in Iconography*, 38 (2017), pp.107–141. Guest also analyses each of the pre-fall Lucifers I discuss in this chapter, alongside other examples. And although he doesn't emphasise the question of *superbia* in the same way, his article was valuable in driving my own analysis forward.
11. Dionysius the Areopagite, *The Celestial and Ecclesiastical Hierarchy*, translated by John Parker (London: Skeffington & Son, 1894), pp.39–42.
12. This is from Ezekiel, 28:13.
13. Mechthild of Magdeburg, *The Revelations of Mechthild of Magdeburg (1210–1297), or The Flowing Light of the Godhead*, translated by Lucy Menzies (London: Longmans, Green and Co., 1955), 3:1, p.64.
14. This is from the description of Lucifer in Dante, *Inferno*, cantos 33–34.
15. Peter of Poitiers, *Sententiae*, book 2, ch.18, *PL*, vol.211, cols.1013B–1014A.
16. Hugh of Saint Victor's *De quinque septenis* (*On the Five Sevens*) and its Versification in Samuel Presbiter's *De oratione dominica* (*On the Lord's Prayer*), edited by Andrew Dunning, *Scholarly Editing*, 37 (2016). Available online: at http://scholarlyediting.org/2016/editions/intro.dunning.html [Accessed July 2025].
17. This point is made in Griffiths, *The Garden of Delights*, p.112.
18. Paris, Bibliothèque Nationale MS Lat. 16417, fol.87v.

19. Hildegard of Bingen, *Scivias*, translated by Mother Columba Hart and Jane Bishop (New York: Paulist Press, 1990), pp.309–324.
20. Thomas Aquinas, *Summa Theologiae*, 2a 2ae, Q.162, Art.1. All translations of the *Summa* are taken from *The Summa Theologiæ of St. Thomas Aquinas*, second and revised edition, 4 vols., translated by Fathers of the English Dominican Province (London: Burns, Oates and Washbourne Ltd, 1920), which is available online at https://www.newadvent.org/summa/ [Accessed July 2025].
21. This story was first brought to the attention of a popular audience in Emmanuel Le Roy Ladurie, *Montaillou: village Occitan de 1294 à 1324* (Paris: Éditions Gallimard, 1975).
22. *Le registre d'inquisition de Jacques Fournier 1318–1325*, edited by Jean Duvernoy (Toulouse: Privat, 1965), vol.2, p.179. For all major passages, I have corroborated Duvernoy's edition by checking against the original manuscript, Biblioteca Vaticana MS Vat.Lat. 4030.
23. Mark Gregory Pegg, for example, has argued that the Cathars did not exist in any meaningful way before the systematic persecutions of the 1200s, and is sceptical that the group ever had a coherent organisational structure after that. See *The Corruption of Angels: The Great Inquisition of 1245–1246* (Princeton: Princeton University Press, 2001). For the other side of the debate, see Peter Biller, 'Goodbye to Catharism?', in *Cathars in Question: Heresy and Inquisition in the Middle Ages*, vol.4, edited by Antonio Sennis (York: York Medieval Press, 2016), pp.274–313; and Claire Taylor, 'Looking for the "Good Men" in the Languedoc: An Alternative to "Cathars"?', in *Cathars in Question*, pp.242–256.
24. *Sacrorum conciliorum nova et amplissima collectio*, edited by Giovanni Domenico Mansi, 54 vols. (Paris, 1901–27), vol.23, pp.569–75: Innocent IV, *Ad extirpanda*, 15 May 1252.
25. Given, 'The Inquisitors of Languedoc and the Medieval Technology of Power', pp.336–359.
26. Gauthier Langlois, 'Note sur quelques documents inédits concernant le parfait Guilhem Bélibaste et sa famille', *Heresis*, 25 (1995), pp.130–134. Langlois notes that the Archbishop of Narbonne had initiated proceedings against Bélibaste for the murder by 1307, which is likely the trigger that made him flee across the Pyrenees.

27. This community and its beliefs are discussed in Christine Caldwell Ames, 'Understanding the Good: Medieval Inquisitions and Modern Religion', *Church History*, 93 (2024), pp.239–262.
28. This ritual is described in *Heresies of the High Middle Ages*, edited and translated by Walter L. Wakefield and Austin P. Evans (New York: Columbia University Press, 1991), pp.465–493.
29. On the use of this term 'perfecti' or 'perfected spirits', which may have only been a category imposed by inquisitors, see Peter Biller, 'Christians and Heretics', in *Christianity in Western Europe, c.1100–c.1500*, edited by M. Rubin and W. Simons (Cambridge: Cambridge University Press, 2009), pp.170–86.
30. *Le registre d'inquisition*, vol.3, pp.120–124.
31. *Le registre d'inquisition*, vol.3, pp.120–124.
32. *Le registre d'inquisition*, vol.3, p.167.
33. *Le registre d'inquisition*, vol.3, p.198.
34. See Constantine Sedikides, 'In Search of Narcissus', *Trends in Cognitive Science*, 25:1 (2021), pp.67–80.
35. John Gower, *Confessio Amantis*, translated by Terence Tiller (London: Penguin, 1963), pp.82–84, ll.2274–2342.
36. On the 'understanding of the good', see Ames, 'Understanding the Good'.
37. *Le registre d'inquisition*, vol.2, p.23.
38. *Le registre d'inquisition*, vol.2, p.23.
39. *Le registre d'inquisition*, vol.2, pp.76–77.
40. This story is recounted in *Le registre d'inquisition*, vol.2, p.20.
41. *Dits et Contes de Baudouin de Condé et de son fils Jean de Condé*, edited by Auguste Scheler (Brussels: Victor Devaux, 1866), pp.91–95.
42. On literacy in the Middle Ages, I rely on Michael T. Clanchy, *From Memory to Written Record: England 1066–1307*, second edition (Oxford: Blackwell, 1993).
43. Vincent Ferrer labels Simon Magus an exemplar of *superbia*. See Alberto Ferreiro, *Simon Magus in Patristic, Medieval and Early Modern Traditions* (Leiden: Brill, 2005), pp.241–260.
44. Jacobus of Voragine, *The Golden Legend: Readings on the Saints*, translated by William Granger Ryan, with an introduction by

Eamon Duffy (Princeton: Princeton University Press, 2012), pp.340–350.

45. Simon's book is quoted at length in Hippolytus, *Philosophumena: or The Refutation of All Heresies*, translated by F. Legge (New York: The Macmillan Company, 1921), vol.2, Book VI, pp.2–17.

46. Bernard of Clairvaux, *The Twelve Degrees of Humility and Pride*, translated by Barton R. V. Mills (London: Society for Promoting Christian Knowledge, 1929). Latin from Bernard of Clairvaux, *De gradibus humilitatis et superbiae*, in *Sancti Bernardi Opera*, vol.3, edited by Jean Leclercq and H. M. Rochais (Rome: Editiones Cistercienses, 1963), pp.13–59.

47. On this tendency, see Richard of Saint Victor, *Adnotationes mysticae in Psalmos*, Adnotatio in Psalmus 28, *PL*, vol.196, cols.293B–293C.

48. On Simon's flapping wings, see Lynn Thorndike, *A History of Magic and Experimental Science*, I (New York: Columbia University Press, 1923), p.426, n.1: 'Et statim in voce Petri implicatis remigiis alarum quas sumserat, corruit.'

49. Lynn White, Jr., 'Eilmer of Malmesbury, an Eleventh-Century Aviator: A Case Study of Technological Innovation, Its Context and Tradition', *Technology and Culture*, 2: 2 (1961), pp.97–111.

50. Roger Bacon, *Opus Tertium, Opus Minus, Compendium Philosophiae*, edited by John Sherren Brewer (London: Longman, 1859), pp.532–535.

51. On Roger's ambitions, see Amanda Power, *Roger Bacon and the Defence of Christendom* (Cambridge: Cambridge University Press, 2013).

2. ENVY

1. This idea of envy as the 'hatred of all good things' appears, alongside nineteen other reasons why envy is to be detested, in both Chaucer's *The Parson's Tale* and in its proposed source material, Peraldus's *Summa of Virtues and Vices*, as well as the series of English abbreviated manuscript editions related to it. See Siegfried Wenzel, 'The Source of Chaucer's Seven Deadly Sins', *Traditio*, 30 (1974), pp.351–378, at pp.356–357.

2. Adrian Meier and Benjamin K. Johnson, 'Social Comparison and Envy on Social Media: A Critical Review', *Current Opinion in Psychology*, 45 (2022). Note that Meier and Johnson also stress the potential positive effects of 'benign envy', and treat social media use as highly differentiated, making no simple statement about whether platforms either improve or harm mental health overall. See also M. Burke, J. Cheng and B. de Gant, 'Social comparison and Facebook: feedback, positivity, and opportunities for comparison', *Proceedings of the 2020 CHI conference on human factors in computing systems, Honolulu HI USA* (2020), Article 355, which makes the point that social comparison is more of an issue for users who have more friends, who are younger, who spend more time on social media platforms, and who regularly encounter more highly liked account activity and posts.
3. Frank John Ninivaggi, *Envy Theory: Perspectives on the Psychology of Envy* (Lanham, MD: Rowman and Littlefield, 2010), pp.43–72.
4. Alain de Lille, *The Complaint of Nature*, translated by Douglas M. Moffat (Hamden, CT: Archon Books, 1972), pp.71–73.
5. Paris, Bibliothèque Nationale de France, MS Lat. 16417, fol.113r–v.
6. Bonaventure, *Breviloquium*, translated by Erwin Esser Nemmers (London: Herder, 1947), part 3, chapter 9, pp.98–100.
7. Alain de Lille, *The Complaint of Nature*, p.72.
8. Cambridge, Corpus Christi College MS 063, fols.133v–134r.
9. On the Medieval Warm Period, see Richard C. Hoffmann, *An Environmental History of Medieval Europe* (Cambridge: Cambridge University Press, 2014), pp.320–323; Christian Rohr, Chantal Camenisch and Kathleen Pribyl, 'The European Middle Ages', in *The Palgrave Handbook of Climate History*, edited by Sam White, Christian Pfister and Franz Mauelshagen (London: Palgrave, 2018), pp.247–264; Fredrik Charpentier Ljungqvist, 'A regional approach to the medieval warm period and the little ice age', in *Climate Change and Variability*, edited by Suzanne Simard (2010). For the specific Black Sea example, see Elena Teodoreanu, 'The Little Climactic Optimum in Romania', *Publishing House of the Romanian Academy* (2013). For wine grapes in Scotland, see Hoffmann, pp.322–323. One analysis shows, for example, that the tongue of the Great Aletsch glacier in

Valais retreated by between two and three kilometres from the period *c.*900–1300. As Hoffmann says, 'In 1250 the glacier's front stood at an altitude higher than it would again occupy until after 1950.' (p.321).

10. R. S. Bradley, M. K. Hughes and H. F. Diaz, 'Climate in Medieval Time', *Science*, 302 (2003), pp.404–405. On causes, see Michael E. Mann, Zhihua Zhang, Scott Rutherford, Raymond S. Bradley, Malcolm K. Hughes, Drew Shindell, Caspar Ammann, Greg Faluvegi and Fenbiao Ni, 'Global Signatures and Dynamical Origins of the Little Ice Age and the Medieval Climate Anomaly', *Science*, 326 (2009), pp.1256–1260.
11. William Chester Jordan, *The Great Famine: Northern Europe in the Early Fourteenth Century* (Princeton, NJ: Princeton University Press, 1996).
12. Paul C. Buckland et al., 'Norsemen at Nipáitsoq, Greenland: A Paleoecological Investigation', *Norwegian Archaeological Review*, 16:2 (1983), pp.86–98.
13. For the accounts of Giotto in this paragraph and the next, see Giorgio Vasari, *Lives of the Most Eminent Painters, Sculptors and Architects*, translated by Gaston Duc de Vere (London: Macmillan, 1912–14), 10 volumes, vol.1, pp.69–94.
14. Similar observations about Giotto are made in Pier Paolo Tamburelli, 'Giotto: Or, Beauty in Space', *San Rocco*, 13 (2016), pp.32–53. The styles of Cimabue and Giotto are compared also by Joseph Polzer, 'Cimabue Reconsidered', *Arte medieval*, 5 (2015), pp.197–224, who rejects the view that the two actively collaborated on paintings, insisting they belong to separate generations of art.
15. An extensive study of *invidia* in the Arena Chapel is Matthew G. Shoaf, 'Eyeing Envy in the Arena Chapel', *Studies in Iconography*, 30 (2009), pp.126–167. Shoaf's exceptional analysis of the chapel was inspirational to me in crafting this chapter, and without it I wouldn't have noticed the envious figures in the background of several of the frescoes' scenes.
16. This description of the envious face is in London, Lambeth Palace MS 388, fol.199v: 'aspectis pallor, in facie tremor, in labiis stridor, in dentibus verba rabida . . .'
17. Ovid, *Metamorphoses*, translated by Mary M. Innes (London: Penguin, 1955), Book 2, pp.70–71.

18. *Bestiary: Being an English Version of the Bodleian Library, Oxford MS Bodley 764 with all the Original Miniatures Reproduced in Facsimile*, translated by Richard W. Barber (Woodbridge: Boydell, 1993), pp.184–185. For Bernard's discussion of the Basilisk and envy, see Jonah Wharff, 'Bernard of Clairvaux and René Girard on Desire and Envy', *Cistercian Studies Quarterly*, 42:2 (2007), pp.183–207.
19. Bernard of Clairvaux, *Pro Dominica I Novembris*, Sermon 5: 6, 1, 3, 10, *PL* vol.183, cols.359A–359B.
20. William Peraldus, *Summa de virtutibus et vitiis* (Lyons: Nicolaus de Benedictis, 1500), fol.154v. The quote here is from Shoaf, 'Eyeing Envy', p.130.
21. London, Lambeth Palace MS 388, fol.199v.
22. Roger Bacon, *Opus Majus*, 3:5:5.
23. Cambridge, Corpus Christi College MS 136, fol.108r.
24. Baldwin of Canterbury, *Tractatus divesrsi*, *PL*, vol.204, cols.497A–B.
25. Exodus 34:29–30. This is discussed in Jonathan Kirsch, *Moses: A Life* (New York: Ballantine Books, 1998), p.5.
26. London, National Archives, E 401/1565.
27. Anthony of Padua, 'A sermon against those beset by the devil while living on earth', Sixth Sunday after Easter; and 'A sermon on the blindness of the sinner,' Third Sunday of Lent, *Sermons for Sundays and Festivals*, translated by Paul Spilsbury, https://www.documentacatholicaomnia.eu/03d/1195-1231,_Antonius_Patavinus,_Sermones,_EN.pdf.
28. Anthony of Padua, 'A sermon on the seven vices', First Sunday of Lent, *Sermons for Sundays and Festivals,* translated by Paul Spilsbury, https://www.documentacatholicaomnia.eu/03d/1195-1231,_Antonius_Patavinus,_Sermones,_EN.pdf.
29. Robert of Cricklade, *Speculum fidei*, Corpus Christi College Cambridge MS 380, fols.4v–5r. On Robert, see Andrew N. J. Dunning, 'St Frideswide's Priory as a Centre of Learning in Early Oxford', *Mediaeval Studies*, 80 (2018), pp.253–96.
30. Cambridge, Corpus Christi College MS 136, fol.108r.
31. This image is discussed in Tom Nickson, 'The First Murder: Picturing Polemic c.1391', in *The Hebrew Bible in Fifteenth-Century Spain: Exegesis, Literature, Philosophy, and the Arts*, edited by Jonathan Decter and Arturo Prats (Leiden: Brill, 2012), pp.41–59.

32. Cambridge Corpus Christi College MS 067, fol.31v.
33. Brian O. Murdoch, *The Apocryphal Adam and Eve in Medieval Europe: Vernacular Translations and Adaptations of the Vita Adae et Evae* (Oxford: Oxford University Press, 2009), p.151.
34. Augustine of Hippo, *City of God*, translated by Henry Bettenson (London: Penguin, 2003), book 15, ch.7.
35. Claudio Bellinati, *Iconographic Atlas of Giotto's Chapel, 1300–1305* (Ponzano: Vianello, 2003), pp.104–105.
36. Jacobus of Voragine, *The Golden Legend*, pp.166–171.
37. Papias of Hierapolis, *Fragments*, in *The Apostolic Fathers*, vol.2, edited and translated by Bart D. Ehrman (Cambridge, MA: Harvard University Press, 2003), p.105.
38. *The Book of the Resurrection of Christ by Bartholomew the Apostle* is discussed in John W. Welch, 'The Apocryphal Judas Revisited', *BYU Studies Quarterly*, 45:2 (2006), pp.45–53.
39. These four 'friends' are identified in the margins of two manuscripts of this work: Leonardo Dandolo, the son of the Venetian Doge Andrea Dandolo (r.1343–54); Tommaso Talenti, a silk merchant; Zaccaria Contarini, a lawyer from an illustrious Venetian family; and Guido da Bagnolo, a physician who studied medicine in Bologna. On this episode, see David Marsh, 'Petrarch's adversaries: the *Invectives*', in *The Cambridge Companion to Petrarch*, edited by Albert Russell Ascoli and Unn Falkeid (Cambridge: Cambridge University Press, 2015), pp.167–178.
40. Petrarch, Letter to Donato, 'On His Own Ignorance and That of Many Others, II', in *The Renaissance Philosophy of Man*, edited and translated by Ernst Cassirer, Paul Oskar Kristeller and John Herman Randall (Chicago: The University of Chicago Press, 1948), pp.47ff.
41. *The Letters of Arnulf of Lisieux*, edited by Frank Barlow, Camden Society, Third Series, vol.61 (London: The Royal Historical Society, 1939), Letter 10, pp.13–14. Translation from: Carolyn Poling Schriber, *The Letter Collections of Arnulf of Lisieux* (Lewiston: The Edwin Mellen Press, 1997), 3:02, pp.190–191.
42. Wei, *Intellectual Culture*. On student numbers, see David C. Lindberg, *The Beginnings of Western Science: The European Scientific Tradition in Philosophical, Religious, and Institutional Context, Prehistory to AD*

1450, second edition (Chicago: University of Chicago Press, 2007), p.211.
43. All of these passages are taken from Peter Abelard, *Historia Calamitatum*, translated by Betty Radice (London: Penguin, 1974).
44. This quote is from Petrarch, Letter to Donato, 'On His Own Ignorance and That of Many Others, II', in *The Renaissance Philosophy of Man*, pp.47ff.
45. Petrarch, Letter to Boccaccio, 'Petrarch Disclaims all Jealousy of Dante', in *Petrarch: The First Modern Scholar and Man of Letters*, edited and translated by James Harvey Robinson (New York: G. P. Putnam, 1898), pp.178–190.
46. Petrarch, Letter to Boccaccio, 'On the Italian Language and Literature', in *Petrarch: The First Modern Scholar and Man of Letters*, pp.197–214.
47. Petrarch, *De remediis utriusque fortunae*, Book 2:35, in *Petrarch's Remedies for Fortune Fair and Foul: A Modern English Translation of* De remediis utriusque fortune, edited and translated by Conrad H. Rawski (Bloomington, IN: Indiana University Press, 1991), vol.3, pp.93–94.
48. This quotation from Petrarch, 'On the Italian Language and Literature', p.204.
49. Cambridge, Corpus Christi College MS 136, fol.111r.
50. This metaphor is from John Climacus (d.649), *The Ladder of Divine Ascent*, translated by Archimandrite Lazarus Moore (New York: Harper & Brothers, 1959), Step 10, ch.16.

3. ANGER

1. Iolie Nicolaidou, Federica Tozzi and Athos Antoniades, 'A gamified app on emotion recognition and anger management for pre-school children', *International Journal of Child-Computer Interaction*, 31 (2022).
2. See, for example, Kathleen O'Bannon, *The Anger Cure: A Step-by-Step Program to Reduce Anger, Rage, Negativity, Violence, and Depression in Your Life* (Laguna Beach, CA: Basic Health, 2009).

3. William Davies, *Overcoming Anger and Irritability: A Self-Help Guide Using Cognitive Behavioural Techniques*, second edition (London: Little, Brown, 2009).
4. Laura Silva, 'Anger and Its Desires', *European Journal of Philosophy*, 29 (2021), pp.1115–1135.
5. As Erin Matson writes, '*Anger Management Issues* were invented as a mechanism for abusers to save face, to give them an out for which there is learning and functioning and the bland speak of corporatese.' https://erintothemax.com/2023/05/15/anger-management-issues-are-abuse-just-say-that/
6. Thomas Aquinas, *Summa Theologiae*, 1a 2ae, Q47, Article 2.
7. *Constantini Liber de coitu. El tratado de andrología de Constantino el Africano*, edited by Enrique Montero Cartelle (Santiago de Compostela: Universidad de Santiago de Compostela, 1983), pp.76–184. Translated by Faith Wallis in *Medieval Medicine: A Reader* (Toronto: University of Toronto Press, 2010), pp.517–518.
8. Alexander Neckam, *Commentarium in Martiani Capellae De nuptiis Mercurii et Philologiae I–II*, ed. C. J. McDonough (Florence: SISMEL, Edizioni del Galluzzo, 2006), pp.81–82.
9. Albertanus of Brescia, *Liber consolationis et consilii*, edited by Thor Sundby (Paris: A. Franck, 1873), ch.12, pp.33–35.
10. Bartholomaei Anglici, *De genuinis rerum coelestium, terrestrium et infer[n]arum proprietatibus* (Frankfurt: Wolfgang Richter, 1601), pp. 276–367. Here I have adapted and spliced parts of the translation by Faith Wallis in *Medieval Medicine: A Reader*, from the section 'Frenzy: Its Causes, Signs, and Remedies', pp.252–253. The final line, 'The feeling of being once again alive', is my own paraphrase of some of the symptoms described.
11. John of Fonte, *Auctoritates Aristotelis*, edited by Jacqueline Hamesse (Louvain: Louvain Publications Universitaires, 1974), p.265, '*Ad omnem iram sequitur delectatio propter spem puniendi, unde dicit Homerus quod ira est dulcior melle stillante.*' Note that this is a florilegium from the 1200s, here compiling aphorisms on anger taken from Aristotle. Aristotle's idea that anger can be 'sweeter than dripping honey' comes originally from Homer, *The Iliad*, 18.107–111.

12. Paris, Bibliothèque Nationale de France MS Lat 10401, fol.66v. 'De Ira: Inquinat infatutit condempnat...'
13. Augustine of Hippo, Letter 38, translated by J. G. Cunningham in *Nicene and Post-Nicene Fathers*, First Series, vol.1, edited by Philip Schaff (Buffalo, NY: Christian Literature Publishing Co., 1887), pp.271–272.
14. Bonaventure, *Breviloquium*, part 3, ch.9.
15. Albertanus of Brescia, *Liber consolationis et consilii*, ch.12, pp.33–35.
16. Cambridge, Trinity College MS B.14.4., fol.95r. Ayton here seems to be alluding to Aristotle's 'difficult anger', or the insatiable thirst to keep finding new things that will make you angry every day. Aristotle, *Nicomachean Ethics*, book 4, ch.5. On Ayton, see J. H. Baker, 'Famous English Canonists: III: John Ayton (or Acton) U.J.D. (d.1349), Professor of Law, Cambridge University, Canon of Lincoln', *Ecclesiastical Law Journal*, 2:8 (1991), pp.159–163.
17. François-Olivier Touati, 'How is a University Born? Montpellier before Montpellier', *CIAN: Revista de Historia de las Universidades*, 21:2 (2018), pp.41–78. See also Sonoma Cooper, 'The Medical School of Montpellier in the Fourteenth Century', *Annals of Medical History*, 2:2 (1930), pp.164–195.
18. On the medical university at Montpellier more generally, see Daniel Le Blévec (ed.), *L'université de médecine de Montpellier et son rayonnement (XIIIe–XVe siècles)* (Turnhout: Brepols, 2004).
19. *Cartulaire de l'université de Montpellier*, ed. Alexandre Germain, vol.1: *1181–1400* (Montpellier: Ricard Frères, 1890), pp.179–180, no. 1; Marcel Fournier, *Les statuts et privilèges des universités françaises depuis leur fondation jusqu'en 1789* (Paris: Larose et Forcel, 1891), II, 3, no. 879. Cited and translated in Touati, 'How is a University Born?', p.67.
20. Michael McVaugh, 'Theriac at Montpellier 1285–1325 (with an edition of the "Questiones de tyriaca" of William of Brescia)', *Sudhoffs Archiv*, 56:2 (1972), pp.113–144.
21. On Arnaud, see Michael McVaugh, 'Arnau de Vilanova and Paris: One Embassy or Two?', *Archives d'histoire doctrinale et littéraire du Moyen Âge*, 73 (2006), pp.29–42.
22. On Arnaud's apocalypticism and the course of these condemnations, see Clifford R. Backman, 'Arnau de Vilanova and the Body at the End

of the World', in *Last Things: Death and the Apocalypse in the Middle Ages*, edited by Caroline Walker Bynum and Paul Freedman (Philadelphia: University of Pennsylvania Press, 2000), pp.140–155.
23. Arnaud de Vilanova, *Tractatus de tempore adventus Antichristi*, in 'El text primitiu del *De mysterio cymbalorum ecclesiae* d'Arnau de Vilanova. En apèndix, el seu *Tractatus de tempore adventus Antichristi*', edited by Josep Perarnau i Espelt, *Arxiu de Textos Catalans Antics*, 7–8 (1988–9), 7–169. This passage appears on p.164. Further discussion appears in Joseph Ziegler, *Medicine and Religion c.1300: The Case of Arnau de Vilanova* (Oxford: Clarendon Press, 1998), pp.21–5.
24. Arnaud de Vilanova, *De regimine sanitatis*, in *Arnaldi de Villanova Opera Medica Omnia*, vol.10, edited by Luis García-Ballester and Michael R. McVaugh (Barcelona: Publicacions i Edicions de la Universitat de Barcelona, 2000), pp.359–361. Also cited in Elena Carrera, 'The uses of anger in medieval and early modern medicine', https://emotionsblog.history.qmul.ac.uk/2012/06/the-uses-of-anger-in-medieval-and-early-modern-medicine/ [Accessed July 2025].
25. The distinction is made in *De regimine sanitatis*, ch.9, p.76.
26. Irene Meekes - van Toer, '*Als die maen is inden weder*: Practical Advice in a Late-Fifteenth-Century Astrological Calendar Manuscript Amsterdam UB MS XXIII A 8' (MA Thesis, Utrecht University, 2013), p.45.
27. Meekes - van Toer, '*Als die maen*', p.36.
28. Scott E. Hendrix, 'Albertus Magnus and Rational Astrology', *Religions*, 11 (2020), p.481.
29. I consulted the astrological treatises and tables in Oxford, Bodleian Library MS Laud Misc. 594. For a thorough and breathtaking look at medieval astrology, see Seb Falk, *The Light Ages: A Medieval Journey of Discovery* (London: Penguin, 2020).
30. Honorius Augustodunensis, *De imagine mundi*, book 2, ch.59, *PL* vol.172, col.158B.
31. Arnaud de Vilanova, *De consideracionibus operis medicine sive de flebotomia*, in *Arnaldi de Villanova Opera Medica Omnia*, vol.4, edited by Luke Demaitre (Barcelona: Publicacions i Edicions de la Universitat de Barcelona, 1988), p.199.
32. Arnaud de Vilanova, *De consideracionibus*, pp.144–55.

33. See also Honorius Augustodunensis, *De imagine mundi*, book 2, ch.59, *PL* vol.172, col.154D.
34. *The Earliest Printed Book on Wine, by Arnald of Villanova [Liber de vinis]*, translated by Henry E. Sigerist (New York: Schuman's, 1943), pp.33–34.
35. A moving description of medieval treatment of cancer in Montpellier can be found in *Acta Sanctorum Julii Tomus Primus* (Paris: Victor Palme, 1867), pp.525–27, translated in *Medieval Medicine: A Reader*, pp.345–8.
36. Dosage is listed in McVaugh, 'Theriac,' pp.128–129. Note that I have converted measurements into metric.
37. Arnaud de Vilanova, *Antidotarium*, in *Opera Arnaldi de Villa Nova*, edited by Petrus Salius (Venice: Heirs of Octavian Scotus, 1527), pp.288–289.
38. Arnaud de Vilanova, *Epistola de dosi tyriacalium medicinarum*, in *Arnaldi de Villanova Opera Medica Omnia*, vol.3, edited by Michael R. McVaugh (Barcelona: Publicacions i Edicions de la Universitat de Barcelona, 1985), p.86.
39. Arnaud de Vilanova, *Antidotarium*, pp.288–289.
40. The Latin of the treatise is printed in McVaugh, 'Theriac,' pp.113–144.
41. Arnaud de Vilanova, *De consideracionibus*, pp.198–9.
42. Arnaud de Vilanova, *De regimine sanitatis*, ch.9, p.76. 'In ira quidem movetur calor et spiritus subito et impetuose ad cor, non totaliter relinquens radicem, sed in radice primo accenditur, et postea movetur ad extra et iterdum totaliter radix, puta cor relinquitur denudatum.'
43. Paris, Bibliothèque Nationale de France MS Lat. 3143, fol.38v.
44. Cambridge, Trinity College MS B.14.4, fol.88r–88v.
45. All references to the Warburg refer to the layout of the building before the renovations, which were completed in 2024. Since then the photographic collection has moved to the basement.
46. This original story is from the Old Testament Book of Judith. Medieval accounts, which I have cited below, include passages within the work of Christine de Pizan and the Old English poem from the Beowulf manuscript.
47. Christine de Pizan, *The Book of the City of Ladies*, translated by Rosalind Brown-Grant (London: Penguin, 1999), ch.31.

48. Peter Damian, *Die Briefe des Petrus Damiani*, edited by Kurt Reindel (Munich: Monumenta Germaniae Historica, 1989), pp.156–157.
49. This poem of the Judith and Holofernes story was preserved in the same manuscript as Beowulf, the Nowell Codex (*c*.975–1025). The text can be found on the website of the Old English Poetry Project, https://oldenglishpoetry.camden.rutgers.edu/judith/ [Accessed July 2025].
50. On Cranach's painting in context, see Helen Watanabe-O'Kelly, 'The Eroticization of Judith in Early Modern German Art', *Gender Matters: Discourses of Violence in Early Modern Literature and the Arts*, edited by Mara R. Wade (Amsterdam: Rodopi, 2014), pp.81–100. In particular, Watanabe-O'Kelly draws out some of the sexual ambiguity in this tale, suggesting that Cranach channelled this tension through Judith's charged expression.
51. Here Judith is modelling the philosophy of patience that would have been exemplified for medieval readers by Seneca. See Seneca, *De Ira*, book 3, ch.38, in *Seneca: Moral Essays*, vol.1, translated by John W. Basore (Cambridge, MA: Harvard University Press, 1928), pp.107ff.
52. Cambridge, Queens' College MS 19, fol.31r.
53. Jacobus of Voragine, *Sermones Quadragesimales*, edited by Giovanni Paolo Maggioni (Florence: SISMEL, Edizioni del Galluzzo, 2005), Feria Tertia Sermo I.
54. Boethius, *Consolation of Philosophy*, translated by David R. Slavitt (Cambridge, MA: Harvard University Press, 2008), met.4, pp.9–10.
55. On patience in medieval romances, see Corey Alec Owen, 'The Passions of Sir Gawain: Patience and the Idiom of Medieval Romance in England' (PhD dissertation, Dalhousie University, 2007), with reference to Guigemar on pp.80–82. For Saint Lawrence, see Catherine Conybeare, 'The Ambiguous Laughter of Saint Laurence', *Journal of Early Christian Studies*, 10 (2002), pp.175–202.
56. Guido da Pisa, *Expositiones et glose super Comediam Dantis*, edited by Vincenzo Cioffari (New York: State University of New York Press, 1974), *Inferno* V, Expositio lictere, vv.37–39.
57. John Climacus, *The Ladder of Divine Ascent*, translated by Archimandrite Lazarus Moore (New York: Harper & Brothers, 1959), Step 8.

58. Lactantius, *De ira dei*, 5:13. In *Lactancio, Sobre la Ira de Dios*, edited and translated into Spanish by Marcela Islas Jacinto (Mexico City: Universidad Nacional Autónoma de México, 2020), p.50.
59. Christine de Pizan, *The Book of the City of Ladies*. The Amazons episode appears in ch.18, while Judith is in ch.31.
60. On Thomas's work, see Catherine Cavadini, 'An Ardent Embrace: Thomas the Cistercian's *In cantica canticorum*', *Cistercian Studies Quarterly*, 47:3 (2012), pp.297–311.
61. Thomas of Perseigne, *Commentary on the Canticles*, PL vol.206, book 3, ch.2, cols.159–160. 'Ego flos campi et illium convallium.'
62. On these shifts, see Clanchy, *From Memory to Written Record*; John Gillingham, *The Angevin Empire* (London: Arnold, 2001). I have also covered this process in my own book, *Laughter and Power in the Twelfth Century* (Oxford: Oxford University Press, 2019), esp. ch.5.
63. For an account that emphasises the king's fury in the moment of ordering the murder, see London, British Library MS Cotton Julius D. III, *Vita beati Thome martiris Archiepiscopi Cantuariensis*, fols.188v–189r. 'Dixit ut est moris concepti verba furoris / Indicom quorum coniecit mens aliorum / Quod causaretur quia non interficeretur / Thomas trahator regni suus insidiator.'
64. Hugh of Saint Victor, *De fructibus carnis et spiritus*, PL vol.176, col.1000D.
65. On Henry, see W. L. Warren, *Henry II* (Berkeley: University of California Press, 1973); Nicholas Vincent, 'The Court of Henry II', in *Henry II: New Interpretations*, edited by Christopher Harper-Bill and Nicholas Vincent (Woodbridge: The Boydell Press, 2007). On Henry's new laws, see John Hudson, *The Formation of the English Common Law: Law and Society in England from King Alfred to Magna Carta*, second edition (London: Routledge, 2014), chapter 6; Paul Brand, 'Henry II and the Creation of the English Common Law', in *Henry II: New Interpretations*, pp.215–41. On his financial reforms, see G. L. Harriss, *King, Parliament and Public Finance in Medieval England to 1369* (Oxford: Clarendon Press, 1975), pp.188–193.

66. Gerald of Wales, *Speculum Duorum, or A Mirror of Two Men*, edited by Yves Lefèvre and R. B. C. Huygens, translated by Brian Dawson (Cardiff: University of Wales Press, 1974), pp.16–17.
67. *The Chronicle of Battle Abbey*, edited and translated by Eleanor Searle (Oxford: Clarendon Press, 1980), p.186.
68. See *The Lives of Thomas Becket*, selected and translated by Michael Staunton (Manchester: Manchester University Press, 2001), p.88.
69. *The Correspondence of Thomas Becket*, edited and translated by Anne Duggan (Oxford: Oxford University Press, 2000), vol.1, Letter 112, p.543.
70. The phrase comes from Ralph V. Turner, *Men Raised from the Dust: Administrative Service and Upward Mobility in Angevin England* (Philadelphia: University of Pennsylvania Press, 1988).
71. R. I. Moore, *The Formation of a Persecuting Society: Authority and Deviance in Western Europe 950–1250*, second edition (Oxford: Blackwell, 2007).
72. Gilbert Foliot, *Gilberti ex abbate Glocestriae episcopi primum Herefordiensis deinde Londoniensis epistolae*, edited by J. A. Giles (Oxford: J. H. Parker, 1845), pp.266–267.
73. *Materials for the History of Thomas Becket, Archbishop of Canterbury*, edited by James Craigie Robertson (London: Longman & Co., 1877, 1879), vol.3, pp.180–181; and vol.4, pp.85–88. Translated in *The Lives of Thomas Becket*, edited and translated by Michael Staunton, pp.59–61.
74. *The Correspondence of Thomas Becket*, vol.2, Letter 200, pp.864–865.
75. *The Correspondence of Thomas Becket*, vol.1, Letter 36, pp.142–3.
76. This passage is from *The Lives of Thomas Becket*, pp.191–192.
77. London, British Library MS Cotton Julius D. III, f.190r.
78. Cambridge, Trinity College MS B.5.4., fols.12v–13r. 'Nam ira dei motus est . . .'
79. London, British Library MS Egerton 2951, fol.8r.
80. Peter of Blois, *Dialogus inter regem Henricum et abbatem Bonevallis*, reprinted in *Serta Mediaevalia: Textus Varii Saeculorum X–XIII, Tractatus et Epistulae*, edited by R. B. C. Huygens (Turnhout: Brepols, 2000), pp.375–408. Dating of the writing is estimated at c.1187–9.
81. Peter of Blois, *Dialogus*, pp.388ff.
82. John of Fonte, *Auctoritates Aristotelis*, p.265.

4. SLOTH

1. Siegfried Wenzel, *The Sin of Sloth:* Acedia *in Medieval Thought and Literature* (Chapel Hill, NC: University of North Carolina Press, 1967), pp.164–190.
2. *The Desert Fathers: Sayings of the Early Christian Monks*, translated by Benedicta Ward (London: Penguin, 2003), ch.7, pp.27–28.
3. Evagrius Ponticus, *Antirrhêtikos*, Book 6, translated by Luke Dysinger: http://www.ldysinger.com/Evagrius/07_Antirrhet/00a_start.htm [Accessed July 2025]. Dysinger's translation is based on Evagrius Ponticus, *Antirrheticus* (Selections), in *Ascetic Behavior in Greco-Roman Antiquity: A Sourcebook*, edited by Vincent Wimbush (Minneapolis: Fortress Press, 1990), pp.243–262.
4. William Peraldus, *Summa de virtutibus et vitiis*, fol.78r.
5. Alain de Lille, *Summa de arte praedicatoria*, ch.7: 'haec est acedia quae Christiani manum ab aratro retrahit.'
6. These incorporate several of the definitions of *acedia* in William Peraldus's *Summa*, including *mollities*, *dilation* and *ignavia*. For a summary of these, see Wenzel, *The Sin of Sloth*, pp.195–196.
7. Bernard of Clairvaux, *Sermons on the Song of Songs*, 21:5.
8. Conrad of Hirsau, *De fructibus carnis et spiritus*, ch.7: 'De tristitia seu acedia et comitatu ejus', *PL* vol.176, cols.1001A–B. 'rei bonae bene gerendae taedium.' Note, this text was previously ascribed to Hugh of Saint Victor. See R. Bultot, 'L'auteur et la fonction littéraire du "De fructibus carnis et spiritus"', *Recherches de Théologie Ancienne et Médiévale*, 30 (1963), pp.148–54.
9. The quotation about despairing and hating your own life is from a checklist of *acedia* written *c*.1385 in John de Burgo, *Pupilla oculi* (Paris, 1510), book 5, ch.8. Reproduced in Wenzel, *The Sin of Sloth*, p.197.
10. Yan Wang, Haibo Yang, Christian Montag and Jon D. Elhai, 'Boredom proneness and rumination mediate relationships between depression and anxiety with problematic smartphone use severity', *Current Psychology*, 41 (2022), pp.5287–5297.
11. Annette Brose, Florian Schmiedek, Peter Koval and Peter Kuppens, 'Emotional inertia contributes to depressive symptoms beyond perseverative thinking', *Cognition and Emotion*, 29:3 (2015), pp.527–538.

12. Andrew Solomon, *The Noonday Demon: An Anatomy of Depression* (London: Vintage, 2001).
13. *Elisabeth of Schönau: The Complete Works*, translated and introduced by Anne L. Clark (New York: Paulist Press, 2000), pp.44–45.
14. *Elisabeth of Schönau: The Complete Works*, pp.45–66.
15. William Peraldus, *Summa de virtutibus et vitiis*, fol.94r.
16. Dante Alighieri, *La Vita Nuova*, translated by David R. Slavitt (Cambridge, MA: Harvard University Press, 2010), ch.2, pp.28–29.
17. Marco Santagata, *Dante: The Story of His Life* (Cambridge, MA: Harvard University Press, 2016), pp.41–42.
18. *La Vita Nuova*, ch.14, pp.59–60.
19. Dante, *Rime* 25, in *Dante's Lyric Poetry*, translated by K. Foster and P. Boyde (Oxford: Clarendon, 1967). On this poem and the sequence that surrounds it, see Tristan Kay, 'Dante's Cavalcantian Relapse: The "Pargoletta" Sequence and the *Commedia*', *Dante Studies*, 131 (2013), pp.73–97.
20. Dante, *Il Convivio (The Banquet)*, translated by Richard H. Lansing (New York: Garland Library of Medieval Literature, 1990), 2:12: 1–10, p.66.
21. *La Vita Nuova*, ch.31, pp.116–117.
22. Boccaccio, *Life of Dante*, translated by George Rice Carpenter (New York: Grolier Club, 1900), ch.3, pp.48–49.
23. Details of Dante's life and exile from Alessandro Barbero, *Dante*, translated by Allan Cameron (London: Profile Books, 2021), pp.143–165. The reference to Boniface in *Inferno* is from Canto 19.
24. Dante, *Inferno*, 1, ll.10–12.
25. Dante, *Purgatorio*, 1, ll.58–66.
26. Dante, *Inferno*, 13.
27. Cambridge, Queens' College MS 18, fol.92v.
28. On Ralph, see Samu Niskanen, 'The Treatises of Ralph of Battle', *Journal of Medieval Latin*, 26 (2016), pp.199–226.
29. Oxford, Bodleian Library MS Laud. Misc. 363, fol.3v.
30. Oxford, Bodleian Library MS Laud. Misc. 363, fol.4r.
31. Dante, *Purgatorio*, 19, ll.7–33.
32. On Dante's dismissal of his wife, Gemma, Barbero affirms the idea, circulated first by Boccaccio, that after Dante left Florence in 1302

'he never wanted to go back where [Gemma] was, nor could he suffer her ever to come where he was' (p.166). Santagata disputes this claim, arguing that it is 'most likely' that Gemma joined Dante with their daughter Antonia in Ravenna late in his life (although he provides no concrete evidence that Gemma and Dante ever reunited). Santagata, *Dante*, pp.53–54.

33. This passage is analysed in Reinhard C. Kuhn, *The Demon of Noontide: Ennui in Western Literature* (Princeton: Princeton University Press, 1976), pp.58–59. Note that this interpretation, following Kuhn, differs from that of many other Dante scholars, who have read this as a vision of Lust or else as solely referring to the awaiting sins of Avarice, Gluttony and Lust on the terraces above.
34. This interpretation of the poem is inspired by the analysis of Robert Hollander, as expressed in his notes throughout the three volumes of the *Commedia*.
35. Robert Frost, 'A Servant to Servants', in *Early Poems* (London: Penguin, 1998), pp.86–92.
36. Núria Silleras-Fernández, *The Politics of Emotion: Love, Grief, and Madness in Medieval and Early Modern Iberia* (Ithaca, NY: Cornell University Press, 2024), pp.49–81.
37. Philippe Aries, *The Hour of Our Death*, translated by Helen Weaver (New York: Knopf, 1981), p.143.
38. Carol Lansing, *Passion and Order: Restraint of Grief in the Medieval Italian Communes* (Ithaca, NY: Cornell University Press, 2018).
39. On the question of expected time limit, see Emma L. Penman, Lauren J. Breen, Lauren Y. Hewitt and Holly G. Prigerson, 'Public Attitudes about Normal and Pathological Grief', *Death Studies*, 38:8 (2014), pp.510–516.
40. On this decision by the World Health Organization, see Maarten C. Eisma, Bishakha te Riele, Marleen Overgaauw, Bettina K. Doering, 'Does prolonged grief or suicide bereavement cause public stigma? A vignette-based experiment', *Psychiatry Research*, 272 (2019), pp.784–789.
41. ICD-11 for Mortality and Morbidity Statistics, Section 6, Part 6B42, https://icd.who.int/browse/2025-01/mms/en#1183832314 [Accessed June 2025].

42. Origen, commentary on Psalm 118:28. Cited in Wenzel, *The Sin of Sloth*, p.8.
43. While countless historians have diagnosed Juana with insanity, the argument for Juana as 'depressed' was made most strongly in Manuel Fernández Álvarez, *Juana la Loca: La Cautiva de Tordesillas* (Madrid: Espasa, 2002). A recent argument for Juana as the victim of family manipulation is Gillian Fleming, *Juana I: Legitimacy and Conflict in Sixteenth-Century Castile* (London: Palgrave Macmillan, 2018), ch.9.
44. See Fernando's letter dated 28 October 1504, where he sends the Bishop of Cordoba to the ambassador of Flanders, Gutierre Gómez de Fuensalida, saying he will speak to him about 'algunas cosas que el dyra'. Gómez de Fuensalida, *Correspondencia*, edited on behalf of Jacobo Fitz-James Stuart y Falcó (Madrid: Duque de Berwick y de Alba, Conde de Siruela, 1907), p.296.
45. Pedro Mártir de Anglería, *Epistolario*, edited by José López de Toro (Madrid: Documentos Inéditos para la Historia de España, 1953–1957), 4 vols, vol.2, b.15, doc.253 (4 January 1502), p.41.
46. Gómez de Fuensalida, *Correspondencia*, pp.195–198, at p.197; Silleras-Fernández, *The Politics of Emotion*, ch.8, pp.255–297.
47. Pedro Mártir de Anglería, *Epistolario*, vol.2, b.17, doc.272 (6 July 1504).
48. Quoted in Silleras-Fernández, *The Politics of Emotion*, ch.8, p.214.
49. Fleming, *Juana I*, pp.132–137.
50. Anonymous, *Notice sur le relation manuscrite de deuxième voyage de Philippe le Beau en Espagne*, cited in Javier Manso, *Breve Historia de Juana I de Castilla: Juana la Loca* (Madrid: Nowtilus, 2019), pp.169–170.
51. William Peraldus, *Summa de virtutibus et vitiis*, fols.91v–92r.
52. Cited in Silleras-Fernández, *The Politics of Emotion*, ch.8, p.219.
53. Gómez de Fuensalida, *Correspondencia*, pp.460–461.
54. I have calculated the distance of 105 miles by putting the route of the cortège into Google Maps. Notably, by the time Fernando terminated the journey the procession was looping back round towards Burgos.
55. Archivo General de Simancas, AGS/PTR, LEG, 50, 36.

56. Silleras-Fernández, *The Politics of Emotion*, ch.8; Bethany Aram, *La reina Juana: Gobierno, piedad y dinastía* (Madrid: Marcial Pons Historia, 2016), ch.3; Fleming, *Juana I*, p.156.
57. Aram, *La reina Juana*, p.128.
58. *The Pearl*, translated by Simon Armitage (London: Faber, 2016).
59. *The Pearl*, chs.1–5.
60. *The Pearl*, ch.81.
61. Juan Luis González García, 'Saturno y la reina "impía". El oscuro retiro de Juana I en Tordesillas', in *Juana I en Tordesillas: su mundo, su entorno*, edited by Miguel Ángel Zalama Rodríguez (Valladolid: Ayuntamiento de Tordesillas, 2010), at pp.163–184, at pp.164–166.
62. Lesley K. Twomey, 'Juana of Castile's Book of Hours: An Archduchess at Prayer', *Religions*, 11, 201 (2020).
63. Ben Lerner, *Leaving the Atocha Station* (Minneapolis, MN: Coffee House Press, 2011), ch.1.
64. Catherine of Siena, *The Dialogue of Saint Catherine of Siena*, translated by Algar Thorold (London: Kegan Paul, 1907), pp.178–204. On Catherine's tears, see Heather Webb, '*Lacrime cordiali*: Catherine of Siena on the Value of Tears', in *A Companion to Catherine of Siena*, edited by Carolyn Muessig, George Ferzoco and Beverly Mayne Kienzle (Leiden: Brill, 2012), pp.99–112.
65. On this economic trend, see Judith M. Bennett, *Ale, Beer, and Brewsters in England: Women's Work in a Changing World, 1300–1600* (Oxford: Oxford University Press, 1996), esp. chs.3 and 8.
66. *The Book of Margery Kempe*, translated and edited by B.A. Windeatt (London: Penguin, 1985), book 1, ch.2. On Margery's economic life, see Kathleen Ashley, 'Historicizing Margery: *The Book of Margery Kempe* as Social Text', *Journal of Medieval and Early Modern Studies*, 28 (1998), pp.375–392.
67. *The Book of Margery Kempe*, book 1, ch.1.
68. *The Book of Margery Kempe*, book 1, ch.7.
69. *The Book of Margery Kempe*, book 1, ch.57.
70. *The Book of Margery Kempe*, book 1, ch.3.
71. *The Book of Margery Kempe*, book 1, ch.61.
72. *The Book of Margery Kempe*, book 1, ch.22.

73. Demonstrating the scale of this exchange, englandsimmigrants.com is a fantastic resource. This is a database containing more than 64,000 names of people who migrated to England in the period between *c.*1300 and 1600.
74. William Peraldus, *Summa de virtutibus et vitiis*, fol.119r (https://books.google.es/books?id=uWzQqjx6oqUC&printsec=frontcover&hl=es#v=onepage&q&f=true).
75. Cambridge, Queens' College MS 18, fols.22v–23r. 'Non timebis a negotio perambulante in tenebris, id est a gravi temptatione quae fit nescienter peccantibus.'
76. *The Book of Margery Kempe*, book 2, chs.2 and 3.
77. *Yvain*, in Chrétien de Troyes, *Arthurian Romances*, translated with an introduction and notes by William W. Kibler (London: Penguin, 1991).

5. AVARICE

1. Oxford, Bodleian Library MS Laud Misc. 345, fol.212r. 'Avaritia est imoderatus amor ad quaerendi vel possidendi vel retinendi aliquid.'
2. 1 Timothy 6.10.
3. Colossians 3:5. For two representative medieval scholastic commentaries on this passage, see Hugh of Saint Victor, *Quaestiones et Decisiones in Epistolas D. Pauli, In Epistolam ad Colossenses*, PL vol.175, cols.584D–585A; and Lothar of Segni (Pope Innocent III), *On the Misery of the Human Condition*, edited by Donald R. Howard, translated by Margaret Mary Dietz (Indianapolis: Bobbs-Merrill, 1969), Book 2:15, p.44.
4. On this question of idols, see Hugh of Saint Victor, *In Epistolam ad Colossenses*, PL vol.175, cols.584D–585A.
5. On the state of the economy in later medieval Europe, see Jessica Dijkman, *Shaping Medieval Markets: The Organisation of Commodity Markets in Holland, c.1200–c.1450* (Leiden: Brill, 2011); and Maryanne Kowaleski, 'A Consumer Economy', in *A Social History of England, 1200–1500*, edited by Rosemary Horrox and W. Mark Ormrod (Cambridge: Cambridge University Press, 2006), pp.238–259.

6. James Davis and Richard H. Britnell, 'Introduction', in *A Cultural History of Shopping in the Middle Ages*, edited by James Davis (London: Bloomsbury, 2022), pp.1–26.
7. On slavery, see Debra Blumenthal, *Enemies and Familiars: Slavery and Mastery in Fifteenth-Century Valencia* (Ithaca, NY: Cornell University Press, 2009).
8. Lester K. Little, 'Pride Goes before Avarice: Social Change and the Vices in Latin Christendom', *American Historical Review*, 76:1 (1971), pp.16–49.
9. This form of economic organisation was traditionally called 'feudalism', although this is a term medieval historians often avoid as it implies an overly simplistic set of social and economic relations. See the critiques in Elizabeth A. R. Brown, 'The Tyranny of a Construct: Feudalism and Historians of Medieval Europe', *American Historical Review*, 79:4 (1974), pp.1063–1088; Suzanne Reynolds, *Fiefs and Vassals: The Medieval Evidence Reinterpreted* (Oxford: Clarendon Press, 1994). Prior to these, the classic work on this topic was always Marc Bloch, *La société féodale*, 2 vols. (Paris: Albin Michel, 1949).
10. The *locus classicus* for the commercial revolution is Roberto S. Lopez, *The Commercial Revolution of the Middle Ages, 950–1350* (Cambridge: Cambridge University Press, 1976). But see the challenge to this thesis in Michael McCormick, *Origins of the European Economy: Communications and Commerce, A.D. 300–900* (Cambridge: Cambridge University Press, 2001), which undermines Lopez's assumption of a stagnant economy in the earlier medieval period; and more recently, Chris Wickham, *The Donkey and the Boat: Reinterpreting the Mediterranean Economy, 950–1180* (Oxford: Oxford University Press, 2023), which gives a spectacular and far more fine-grained analysis of this transformation.
11. Alan Cooper, 'Once a Highway, Always a Highway: Roads and English Law, c.1150–1300', in *Roadworks: Medieval Britain, Medieval Roads*, edited by Valerie Allen and Ruth Evans (Manchester: Manchester University Press, 2016), pp.50–73.
12. For city population data, see Eltjo Buringh, *European urban population, 700–2000* (Data Archiving and Networked Services,

2020), https://doi.org/10.17026/dans-xzy-u62q [Accessed July 2025].

13. On the value of Egypt, see Wickham, *The Donkey and the Boat*. According to Wickham, 'without Egypt there could hardly have been a Mediterranean-wide network of any type' (p.25). But this argument also extends back at least to the work of Janet L. Abu-Lughod, *Before European Hegemony: The World System A.D. 1250–1350* (Oxford: Oxford University Press, 1989), e.g., pp.227–236.
14. William N. Goetzmann, 'Fibonacci and the Financial Revolution', NBER Working Paper, no. 10352 (2004).
15. Little, 'Pride Goes before Avarice'.
16. Lothar of Segni (Pope Innocent III), *On the Misery of the Human Condition*, p.35.
17. *The Exempla or Illustrative Stories from the Sermones Vulgares of Jacques de Vitry*, edited and translated by Thomas Frederick Crane (London: The Folk-lore Society, 1890), Sermon 66, pp.162–163.
18. Simone Roux, *Paris in the Middle Ages*, translated by Jo Ann McNamara (Philadelphia: University of Pennsylvania Press, 2009), pp.67–82.
19. Anne Terroine, *Un bourgeois parisien du XIIIe siècle: Geoffroy de Saint-Laurent, 1245?–1290*, edited by Lucie Fossier (Paris: CNRS Éditions, 1992).
20. For example, Peter of Blois, Letter 129 to Archdeacon R. Aurelianensem, *PL* vol.207, col.382C: 'Tu vero sordes avaritiae, et immunditias Simoniae ab Ecclesia Dei non ejicis, sed inducis'; Guido Faba, *Ars dictaminis*, in Augusto Gaudenzi, 'Guidonis Fabe *Summa dictaminis*', in *Il Propugnatore*, N S 3 (1890), ii, p.347: 'Qui doctori mercedem non exhibet, avaritie tenacitate sordescit.' The rotting piles example is from Martin of Liege, *Expositio in epistolam B. Jacobi apostoli*, *PL* vol.209, col.206D. 'Aurum et argentum vestrum . . . aerugo eorum, superflua videlicet congregatio eorum, quae cum non erant necessaria, congregata putrescebat.'
21. Elaine C. Block, *Corpus of Medieval Misericords: Belgium (B) - Netherlands (NL)*, vol.3 (Turnhout: Brepols, 2010).
22. Helinandus Frigidi Montis, *Sermones*, Sermon 25 'In Festo Omnium Sanctorum III', *PL* vol.212, col.690D.

23. Guillaume de Deguileville, *Le pelerinage de vie humaine*, edited by J. J. Stürzinger (London: Nichols and Sons, 1893), pp.316–317. For these descriptions, see *The Brussels Horloge de Sapience: Iconography and Text of Brussels, Bibliothèque Royale, MS. IV 111*, edited by Peter Rolfe Monks (Leiden: Brill, 1990), p.163; Hilary Maddocks, 'Vile Bodies in Guillaume de Deguileville's *Pelèrinage de la vie humaine*', *Australian and New Zealand Journal of Art*, 22:1 (2022), pp.6–19.
24. Paris, Bibliothèque Nationale de France MS Lat. 3570, fol.127r: 'Mammon interpretaur divicie, et est nomen demonis qui per divicias temptat.'
25. The earliest example I could find of a Christian writer explaining that Mammon is the Syrian word for 'riches' is Luculentus, *Comentarii* (*c.*550). I: Lectio Sancti Evangelii secundum Matthaeum, *PL* vol.72, col.803B.
26. Guillaume de Deguileville, *Le pelerinage de vie humaine*, pp.316–317.
27. Rupert of Deutz, *Commentaria in duodecim prophetas minores* (1129): Book 4, *PL* vol.168, cols.160A–160B. Note, though, that Rupert here believed that Mammon was worshipped by Assyria's Jewish population.
28. See for example Lothar of Segni (Pope Innocent III), *Sermones de tempore*, Sermo 26: Dominica Nona Post Octavam Pentecostes, *PL* vol.10, col.432B.
29. François-Xavier Fauvelle, *The Golden Rhinoceros: Histories of the African Middle Ages*, translated by Troy Tice (Princeton, NJ: Princeton University Press, 2018), pp.191–197. The figure of 400 billion dollars is given in Charlie Harris, 'Mansa Musa I of Mali: Gold, Salt, and Storytelling in Medieval West Africa', Oxford Centre for Global History: Global History of Capitalism Project (April 2020): https://globalcapitalism.history.ox.ac.uk/files/ghocmansamusainmalipdf. Note, however, that Harris gives no citation for this estimate of Musa's wealth.
30. *Corpus of Early Arabic Sources for West African History*, edited by Nehemia Levtzion and J. F. P. Hopkins (Princeton, NJ: Markus Wiener, 2000), p.271. Note that the Mamluk writer Ibn Taghribirdi, observing from a century or so later, recorded this drop in the price

of gold around the same time, but explained it as the product of other factors, unconnected to Musa's visit. See Nawal Morcos Bell, 'The Age of Mansa Musa of Mali: Problems in Succession and Chronology', in *Papers Presented to the International Conference of Manding Studies, SOAS* (London: SOAS, 1972), p.224.

31. *Recueil des sources arabes concernant l'Afrique occidentale du VIIIe au XVIe siècles*, edited by Joseph M. Cuoq (Paris: Éditions du CNRS, 1985), p.327.
32. Ibn Khaldūn, in *Corpus of Early Arabic Sources for West African History*, edited by Nehemia Levtzion and J. F. P. Hopkins (Princeton, NJ: Markus Wiener, 2000), p.335.
33. On the Catalan Atlas, see Clara Estow, 'Mapping Central Europe: The Catalan Atlas and the European Imagination', *Mediterranean Studies*, 13 (2004), pp.1–16.
34. Translation of this in Fauvelle, *Golden Rhinoceros*, p.192.
35. Hugh of Saint Victor, *De sacramentis*, II: 11, *PL* vol.176, col.404A.
36. Madeline Caviness, 'From the Self-Invention of the Whiteman in the Thirteenth Century to *The Good, The Bad, and The Ugly*', *Different Visions: New Perspectives on Medieval Art*, 1 (2008).
37. Geraldine Heng, *The Invention of Race in the European Middle Ages* (Cambridge: Cambridge University Press, 2018), pp.181–256.
38. On European encounters with people from Ethiopia in these decades, see Matteo Salvadore, *The African Prester John and the Birth of Ethiopian-European Relations, 1402–1555* (London: Routledge, 2017), pp.1–18; and Heng, *The Invention of Race*, pp.135–150.
39. Al-Umari, ch.10, 26a, in *Corpus of Early Arabic Sources for West African History*, p.261.
40. Ibn Khaldūn, in *Corpus of Early Arabic Sources for West African History*, p.335.
41. Astesanus de Asti, *Summa de casibus conscientiae*, edited by Bartolomeo Bellati and Gomes de Lisboa (Nuremberg: Anton Koberger, 1482), book 2, ch.30.
42. Poggio Bracciolini, *On Avarice*, in *The Earthly Republic: Italian Humanists on Government and Society*, edited by Benjamin G. Kohl, Ronald G. Witt and Elizabeth B. Welles (Philadelphia: University of Pennsylvania Press, 1978), pp.241–292.

43. The quotation about the several palaces is from al-Umari, 27a, in *Corpus of Early Arabic Sources*, p.262. See also J. O. Hunwick, 'The Mid-Fourteenth Century Capital of Mali', *Journal of African History*, 14:2 (1973), pp.195–206. Hunwick locates the capital between Segu and Bamako.
44. On the anxieties surrounding money at the birth of capitalistic desire, see Eugene McCarraher, *The Enchantments of Mammon: How Capitalism Became the Religion of Modernity* (Cambridge, MA: Belknap Press, 2019), ch.1.
45. My sense of Francis's character comes from the narrative of his life in Augustine Thompson, *Francis of Assisi: A New Biography* (Ithaca, NY: Cornell University Press, 2012). For an account of Francis through the lens of disability, see Donna Tremblinski, *Illness and Authority: Disability in the Life and Lives of Francis of Assisi* (Toronto: University of Toronto Press, 2020).
46. *The Assisi Compilation*, ch.27, in *Francis of Assisi: Early Documents*, vol.2, edited by Regis J. Armstrong, J. A. Wayne Hellmann and William J. Short (New York: New City Press, 2000), p.137. Also, Anonymous of Perugia, ch.6, in *Francis of Assisi: Early Documents*, vol.2, pp.47–8.
47. On Francis's attitude towards animals in this way, see Nigel Harris, *The Thirteenth-Century Animal Turn: Medieval and Twenty-First-Century Perspectives* (London: Palgrave Macmillan, 2020), pp.87–108.
48. *The Assisi Compilation*, ch.86, in *Francis of Assisi: Early Documents*, vol.2, pp.189–191.
49. I have written two articles that reflect on Francis of Assisi in this way: Peter J. A. Jones, 'Humility & Humiliation: The Transformation of Franciscan Humour, c.1210–1310', *Cultural and Social History*, 15: 2 (2018), pp.155–175; and 'Bones, Fire, and Falcons: Loving Things in Medieval Europe,' *Journal of Material Culture*, 26:4 (2021), pp.433–450.
50. Alain de Lille, *The Complaint of Nature*, translated by Douglas M. Moffat (Hamden, CT: Archon Press, 1908), p.64.
51. Lothar of Segni (Pope Innocent III), *De Miseria Condicionis Humane*, edited by Robert E. Lewis (Athens, GA: University of Georgia Press, 1978), pp.38–9.

52. This is referred to as 'Francis's Second Death' in André Vauchez, *Francis of Assisi: The Life and Afterlife of a Medieval Saint* (New Haven: Yale University Press, 2012), pp.156–181.
53. Antonio Belenguer González, '*Quasdam domos nostras*: El mercado inmobiliario en Valencia a principios del siglo xv', in *Espacios de Vida: Casa, Hogar y Cultura Material en la Europa Medieval*, edited by Juan Vicente García Marsilla (Valencia: Universitat de València, 2022), pp.131–162.
54. Luis Almenar Fernández, 'Los inventarios *post mortem* de la Valencia medieval: Una fuente para el estudio del consumo doméstico y los niveles de vida', *Anuario de Estudios Medievales*, 47:2 (2017), pp.533–566. On fashions, see Juan Vicente García Marsilla and Luis Almenar Fernández, 'Fashion, emulation and social classes in late medieval Valencia. Exploring textile consumption through probate inventories', in *La moda come motore economico*, edited by Giampiero Nigro (Florence: Firenze University Press, 2022), pp.341–366. For similar records surviving from late medieval England, see Chris Briggs, Alice Forward, Ben Jervis and Matthew Tompkins, 'People, Possessions and Domestic Space in Late Medieval Escheators' Records', *Journal of Medieval History*, 45: 2 (2019), pp.145–161.
55. Debra Blumenthal, *Enemies and Familiars: Slavery and Mastery in Fifteenth-Century Valencia* (Ithaca, NY: Cornell University Press, 2009), pp.194–238.
56. Luis Almenar Fernández, 'La cultura material de los pobres en la Valencia bajomedieval', in *Économies de la pauvreté au Moyen Âge*, edited by Pere Benito, Sandro Carocci and Laurent Feller (Madrid: Open Edition Books, 2023), pp.341–354, at p.353.
57. Mark Bailey, *After the Black Death: Economy, Society, and the Law in Fourteenth-Century England* (Oxford: Oxford University Press, 2021); Samuel Cohn, Jr., 'The Black Death and Consequences for Labor', *Labor: Studies in Working-Class History*, 20:2 (2023), pp.14–29; Sam Geens, *A Golden Age for Labour? Income and Wealth before and after the Black Death in the Southern Low Countries and the Republic of Florence, 1275–1550* (University of Antwerp, PhD thesis, 2023).
58. Bailey, *After the Black Death*, pp.135–185.

59. London, Lambeth Palace MS 205, fol.12v: 'bonum hominis contra exteriora de quae consistat in quandam mensura scilicet ut quaerat habere exteriores divitias prout fiunt as vitam eius necessariae secundum suam condicionum' (Bartholomaeus, *De Casibus Conscienciae*).
60. These kinds of decisions are documented in Blumenthal, *Enemies and Familiars*, pp.194–238.
61. On this point, see Daniel Miller, *Stuff* (Cambridge: Polity Press, 2010).
62. Lothar of Segni (Pope Innocent III), *On the Misery of the Human Condition*, p.35.
63. Lothar of Segni (Pope Innocent III), *On the Misery of the Human Condition*, pp.37–39.
64. The Valencia chalice's history is discussed in Antonio Beltrán, *Estudio sobre el Santo Cáliz de la Catedral de Valencia* (Valencia: Instituto Diocesano Valentino 'Roque Chabás', 1960).
65. This story of the grail can be found in Janice Bennett, *St. Laurence & the Holy Grail: The Story of the Holy Chalice of Valencia* (San Francisco: Ignatius Press, 2004).
66. André de Mandach, *Le 'Roman du Graal' Originaire* (Göppingen: Kümmerle, 1992), p.42. Note that, nevertheless, Mandach believes the chalice was kept in the monastery of San Juan de la Peña.
67. Joseph Goering, *The Virgin and the Grail: Origins of a Legend* (New Haven: Yale University Press, 2005), pp.71–111.
68. Several of these frescoes are now kept in the Museu Nacional d'Art de Catalunya in Barcelona. See Goering, *The Virgin and the Grail*, pp.71–111.
69. Chrétien de Troyes, *Erec et Enide*, in *Arthurian Romances*, translated by William W. Kibler and Carleton W. Carroll (London: Penguin, 1991), ll.2925–3085: 'Male chose a an coveitise.'
70. Chrétien de Troyes, *Cligès*, in *Arthurian Romances*.
71. For this observation, see G. Ronald Murphy, *Gemstone of Paradise: The Holy Grail in Wolfram's Parzival* (Oxford: Oxford University Press, 2006), p.42.
72. Wolfram von Eschenbach, *Parzival*, translated by A. T. Hatto (London: Penguin, 1980). The first glimpse of the grail comes in Book 5, pp.120–146. The description of the stone's youth-giving power is Book 9, pp.222–255.

73. Wolfram von Eschenbach, *Parzival*, Book 9. On Wolfram's literacy, see his own words in *Parzival*, Book 2, pp.41–67.
74. Wolfram von Eschenbach, *Parzival*, Book 9, p.255.
75. Ana Mafé García, *El Santo Grial: un estudio que nos desvela dónde se encuentra la copa de la última cena* (Valencia: Editorial Sargantana, 2020).
76. Caroline Walker Bynum, 'Wonder', *American Historical Review*, 102:1 (1997), pp.1–26.
77. Bernard of Clairvaux, *Third Sermon for the Vigil of the Nativity*, Sancti Bernardi Opera, vol.4, pp.211–19.
78. *Selected Works of Abbot Suger of Saint-Denis*, translated with an introduction by Richard Cusimano and Eric Whitmore (Washington, DC: The Catholic University of America Press, 2018), pp.97–98.
79. Vincent Ferrer, 'Sermon for the Third Sunday of Lent', https://www.svfsermons.org/A561_Lent3%20Samaritan%20Woman.htm [Accessed July 2025].

6. GLUTTONY

1. Gregory the Great, *Moralia in Job*, XXX, xviii.
2. John Cassian, *The Institutes*, book 5, ch.3.
3. Alain de Lille, *Liber sententiarum, De Sancta Maria*, PL vol.210, cols.249A–C.
4. Alain de Lille, *Summa de Arte Praedicatoria*, ch.4, PL vol.210, cols.120A–B.
5. Thomas Aquinas, *Summa Theologiae*, Prima Secundae, Q.29, 3.
6. Weisheipl (cited below) doesn't make any comment on Thomas's body. But Denys Turner calls him 'fat Thomas, the man as gross in girth as an ox', and says he was somebody 'as vast in output of words as he was in girth'. Denys Turner, *Thomas Aquinas: A Portrait* (New Haven: Yale University Press, 2013), p.269.
7. *From the First Canonization Enquiry*, XIX (Nicholas of Priverno), in *The Life of Saint Thomas Aquinas: Biographical Documents*, edited and translated by Kenelm Foster (London: Longmans, Green and Co., 1959), p.88.

8. *Vita B. Thomae de Aquino*, in *Acta Sanctorum der Bollandisten*, Band März, ch.11., https://www.heiligenlexikon.de/ActaSanctorum/7.Maerz.html [Accessed July 2025].
9. James A. Weisheipl, *Friar Thomas d'Aquino: His Life, Thought, and Works* (Washington, DC: Catholic University of America Press, 1983), p.236.
10. Weisheipl, *Friar Thomas*, p.202.
11. Thomas Aquinas, *Summa Theologiae*, Prima Pars, Q.2, 3. Weisheipl deals with this on pp.225–230.
12. Bernard Gui, *The Life of St. Thomas Aquinas*, in *The Life of Saint Thomas Aquinas: Biographical Documents*, ch.41, p.57.
13. William of Tocco, *The Life of St. Thomas Aquinas*, translated by David M. Foley (St Mary's, KA: Angelus Press, 2023), ch.56, pp.185–186. Latin edition: Guillaume de Tocco, *Ystoria sancti Thome de Aquino*, edited by Claire le Brun-Gouanvic (Toronto: PIMS, 1996).
14. Thomas Aquinas, *Summa Theologiae*, Secunda Secundae, Q.148, 4.
15. Thomas Aquinas, *Summa Theologiae*, Secunda Secundae, Q.148, 1.
16. *The Treatise of Walter of Bibbesworth*, translated by Andrew Dalby (Totnes: Prospect Books, 2012), pp.38–39.
17. *Tractatus de modo preparandi et condiendi omnia cibaria*, in Marianne Mulon, 'Deux traités inédits d'art culinaire médiéval', *Bulletin philologique et historique (jusqu'à 1610) du Comité des travaux historiques et scientifiques* (1971), pp.369–435: pp.380–395, part 2, section 10, p.387; and part 2, section 4, p.385.
18. Allen J. Grieco, 'Food and Social Classes in Late Medieval and Renaissance Italy', in *Food: A Culinary History from Antiquity to the Present*, edited by Jean-Louis Flandrin and Massimo Montanari (New York: Columbia University Press, 1999), pp.302–312.
19. *Tractatus de modo preparandi*, part 2, section 1, p.384.
20. The hierarchy theory – also known as the 'great chain of being' approach to food – was identified in Allen J. Grieco, 'Les utilisations sociales des fruits et légumes dans l'Italie médiévale', in *Le Grand Livre des fruits et légumes: histoire, culture et usage*, edited by D. Meiller and P. Vannier (Paris: La Manufacture, 1991). Grieco derives this hierarchy from texts produced by doctors and works by

other medical writers, such as the treatise by Corniolo della Cornia, *La Divina Villa*, edited by L. Bonelli Conenna (Siena: Accademia delle Scienze di Siena, 1982). Grieco's examples are largely intellectual and Italian, though, and caution should be applied when extending this theory out across Europe in the medieval centuries.

21. In medieval England, for example, wild birds were reserved for elite banquets. Christian M. Woolgar, 'Food and the Middle Ages', *Journal of Medieval History*, 36:1 (2010), pp.1–19, at p.16. But note that Chris Dyer concluded that 'poultry . . . contributed to the quality, if not greatly to the quantity, of aristocratic meals'. Chris Dyer, *Standards of Living in the Later Middle Ages: Social Change in England, c.1200–1520* (Cambridge: Cambridge University Press, 1989), p.60.

22. *Curye on Inglysch: English Culinary Manuscripts of the Fourteenth Century (Including the Forme of Cury)*, edited by Constance B. Hieatt and Sharon Butler (Oxford: Oxford University Press, 1985), p.46.

23. On this complex question, see Caroline Walker Bynum, *The Resurrection of the Body in Western Christianity, 200–1336*, expanded edition (New York: Columbia University Press, 2017).

24. Hugh of Saint Victor, *De sacramentis*, 1.6: 37, *PL* vol.176, cols. 285A–B.

25. London, British Library Harley MS 3098, fol.86r–86v. Bynum also engages with this passage, and includes the quote about firewood in her *Resurrection of the Body*, p.138, although she omits some details I have included here.

26. The original position they overturned had been argued in Peter Lombard, *Sentences*, dist. 30. For Thomas's approval of the committee's decision, see Weisheipl, pp.74–75.

27. Philip Lyndon Reynolds, *Food and the Body: Some Peculiar Questions in High Medieval Theology* (Leiden: Brill, 1999), pp.432–434.

28. Thomas Aquinas, *Summa Theologiae*, Prima pars, Q.119, Article 1.

29. Reynolds, *Food and the Body*, pp.431–432. But for more detail on Thomas's complex view, see Bynum, *The Resurrection of the Body*, ch.6.

30. Richard W. Unger, *Beer in the Middle Ages and the Renaissance* (Philadelphia: University of Pennsylvania Press, 2004), p.127.

31. Louis Stouff, *Ravitaillement et alimentation en Provence aux XIVe et XVe siècles* (Berlin: De Gruyter Mouton, 1970).

32. Stouff, *Ravitaillement et alimentation*, p.90. Stouff cites Les Archives Communales d'Arles, CC 4–CC 7.
33. Tom Scott, 'Medieval Viticulture in the German-Speaking Lands', *German History*, 20:1 (2002).
34. Stouff, *Ravitaillement et alimentation*, p.92. Here he draws on Les Archives Communal Carpentras, CC 83–95.
35. London, Lambeth Palace MS 477, fol.247r.
36. Albrecht Classen, 'Alcohol, Drunkenness, and Excess: Consumption and Transgression in European Medieval and Early Modern Literature,' *Neophilologus*, 106 (2022), pp.589–610.
37. Parts of this treatise are reproduced in Siegfried Wenzel, 'The Source for the "Remedia" of the Parson's Tale', *Traditio*, 27 (1971), pp.433–453; this quotation from p.446. I am grateful to Yves Mausen for alerting me to this article.
38. Rudi Matthee, *Angels Tapping at the Wine-Shop's Door: A History of Alcohol in the Islamic World* (Oxford: Oxford University Press, 2023), pp.58–61.
39. Alain de Lille, *Summa de Arte Praedicatoria*, ch.4, *PL* vol.210, cols.119A–119C.
40. Samuel J. Klumpenhouwer, 'The *Summa de penitencia* of John of Kent: Study and Critical Edition' (PhD dissertation, University of Toronto, 2018), Book 3, p.211.
41. London, Lambeth Palace MS 497, fol.77r.
42. Alain de Lille, *Summa de Arte Praedicatoria*, ch.4, *PL* vol.210, cols.119A–119C.
43. Thomas Aquinas, *Summa Theologiae*, 2a 2ae, Q.150, Article 1.
44. Classen, 'Alcohol, Drunkenness, and Excess', p.598–604.
45. John of Salisbury, *Policraticus: The Statesman's Book of John of Salisbury*, translated by John Dickinson (New York: Knopf, 1927), Book VII, 25, p.330. I have adapted Dickinson's translation, referring to the Latin edition.
46. Der Stricker, *Fünfzehn kleine Verserzählungen mit einem Anhang: Der Weinschwelg*, edited by Hanns Fischer (Tübingen: Max Niemeyer, 1960), translation by Kathryn Starkey, Björn K. Buschbeck, Robert Forke, Mae Velloso-Lyons, Mareike E. Reisch and Kathleen Smith, in *Global Medieval Sourcebook: A Digital*

Repository of Medieval Texts, https://www.sourcebook.stanford.edu/ [Accessed July 2025].

47. The idea that drink releases 'unheard words' is expressed in the poem 'Potores exquisiti' from the *Carmina Burana* MS, poem number 202: 'non dormiant, et sermones inauditi prosiliant.' *Carmina Burana. I. Band: Text, 3: Die Trink- und Spielerlieder; Die geistlichen Dramen Nachträge*, edited by Otto Schumann and Bernhard Bischoff (Heidelberg: Carl Winter Universitätsverlag, 1970), p.44.
48. 'In taberna quando sumus.' *Carmina Burana. I. Band: Text, 3*, poem number 196, p.35.
49. A. G. Rigg, 'Golias and Other Pseudonyms', *Studi Medievali*, 3rd Series, 18 (1977), pp.65–109, at p.70.
50. *Hugh Primas and the Archpoet*, edited and translated by Fleur Adcock (Cambridge: Cambridge University Press, 1994), pp.114–119.
51. *Hugh Primas and the Archpoet*, especially pp.78–81.
52. Mechthild of Magdeburg, *The Revelations of Mechthild of Magdeburg*, pp.70–71.
53. Bernard of Clairvaux, *De diligendo deo*, in *Sancti Bernardi Opera*, vol.3, edited by Jean Leclercq and H. M. Rochais (Rome: Editiones Cistercienses, 1963), pp.119–154, ch.11: 32.
54. Bernard of Clairvaux, *De diligendo deo*, ch.11: 32.
55. Henry of Huntingdon, *Historia Anglorum: The History of the English People*, edited and translated by Diana Greenway (Oxford: Clarendon Press, 1996), Book 7, pp.259–260.
56. Andrzej K. Kuropatnicki, 'A Surfeit of Lampreys – A True Story or a Myth?' *Food, Culture & Society* (2024), pp.1–18.
57. Matthew D. Turner, ' "Forbidden Fish": Did King Henry I Die of Lamprey Poisoning?', *Cureus*, 15:5 (2023).
58. Aelred of Rievaulx, *Sermones de oneribus*, Sermon 25, *PL* vol.195, cols.463B–463D.
59. Klumpenhouwer, 'The *Summa de penitencia* of John of Kent', p.213. These quotations, which I have translated from Klumpenhouwer's edition, are from Book 3 of John's *Summa*.
60. Raymond of Capua, *The Life of Catherine of Siena*, translated by George Lamb, updated edition (Charlotte, NC: TAN Books, 2011), Part 1, ch.2, pp.6–14.

61. Raymond of Capua, *The Life of Catherine of Siena*, Part 1, ch.3, pp.14–20.
62. Raymond of Capua, *The Life of Catherine of Siena*, Part 1, ch.4, pp.20–30.
63. Raymond of Capua, *The Life of Catherine of Siena*, Part 1, ch.6, pp.34–43.
64. Caroline Walker Bynum, *Holy Feast and Holy Fast: The Religious Significance of Food to Medieval Women* (Berkeley, CA: University of California Press, 1987), p.201.
65. Jacques de Vitry, *The Life of Marie d'Oignies* (Toronto: Peregrina Publishing Company, 1987), pp.23–24. A similar case is Douceline of Digne, see Philippine de Porcellet, *La Vie de Sainte Douceline, fondatrice des Béguines de Marseille, composée au treizième siècle en langue provençale*, edited and translated into French by Joseph-Hyacinthe Albanès (Marseille: É. Camoin, 1879), pp.106–107.
66. Adelboldus Trajectensis, *Vita S. Walburgis*, PL vol.140, ch.2, 8, cols.1095D–1096B.
67. Bynum, *Holy Feast*, p.201. Here Bynum quotes the clinical definition from Mara Selvini Palazzoli, *Self-Starvation: From Individual to Family Therapy in the Treatment of Anorexia Nervosa*, translated by A. Pomerans (New York: Aronson, 1978), p.86.
68. Catherine of Siena, 'A Treatise on Discretion', in *Dialog of Catherine of Siena*, translated by Algar Thorold (London: Kegan Paul, 1907), p.58.
69. Raymond of Capua, *The Life of Catherine of Siena*, Part 2, ch.4, pp.111–130.
70. Bynum, *Holy Feast*, pp.144–145. Catherine of Genoa, *Purgation and Purgatory: The Spiritual Dialogue*, translated by Serge Hughes (New York: Paulist Press, 1979), p.131.
71. Catherine of Siena, *Epistolae*, 'To Sister Eugenia, her Niece at the Convent of Saint Agnes of Montepulciano', http://www.domcentral.org/trad/cathletters.htm#personstable [Accessed July 2025].
72. Catherine of Siena, *Epistolae*, 'To Gregory XI', and 'To Messer Ristoro Canigiani', http://www.domcentral.org/trad/cathletters.htm#personstable [Accessed July 2025].

73. Raymond of Capua, *The Life of Catherine of Siena*, Part 2, ch.5, pp.130–143.
74. Catherine of Siena, *Epistolae*, 'To a religious man in Florence', http://www.domcentral.org/trad/cathletters.htm#personstable [Accessed July 2025].
75. Raymond of Capua, *The Life of Catherine of Siena*, Part 2, ch.5, pp.130–143.
76. For example, *The Assisi Compilation*, ch.50, quotes Francis as telling his companions: 'Just as we must beware of overindulgence in eating, which harms body and soul, so we must beware of excessive abstinence even more, because the Lord desires mercy and not sacrifice.' *Francis of Assisi: Early Documents*, vol.2, edited and translated by Regis J. Armstrong, J.A. Wayne Hellmann and William J. Short (New York: New City Press, 2000), p.149.
77. The crabcakes story is from *The Assisi Compilation*, ch.68, in *Francis of Assisi: Early Documents*, vol.2, p.171.
78. The *Legend of Three Companions* suggests that Francis went on a transformative journey from loving 'delicacies and sweets' to sometimes sprinkling ashes in his food, if it tasted especially good, to make sure he didn't get excess pleasure from eating. *Francis of Assisi: Early Documents*, vol.2, pp.82–83.
79. Conrad of Megenberg, *Speculum felicitates humanae*, edited by Sabine Krüger (Stuttgart: Hiersemann, 1992), pp.165–167.

7. LUST

1. Paris, Bibliothèque Nationale de France, MS Lat. 16417, fol.113r–113v. 'Inordinatio amoris boni inferioris scilicet carnis secundum actum generationie est luxuria.'
2. William Peraldus, *Summa de virtutibus et vitiis*, fol.12r.
3. See the seven stages described in Cambridge, Corpus Christi College MS 063, fol.134v.
4. Astesanus de Asti, *Summa de casibus conscientiae*, edited by Bartolomeo Bellati and Gomes de Lisboa (Nuremberg: Anton Koberger, 1482), book 2, ch.46

5. London, Lambeth Palace MS 78, fol.93r.
6. London, Lambeth Palace MS 78, fols.50v–51r.
7. See Jean Duvernoy, *Le registre d'inquisition de Jacques Fournier 1318–1325* (Toulouse: Privat, 1965), vol.1, pp.241–243.
8. A useful introduction to monasteries is C. H. Lawrence and Janet Burton, *Medieval Monasticism: Forms of Religious Life in Western Europe in the Middle Ages*, fifth edition (London: Routledge, 2023). The most inspiring works I have read on these institutions and their radical ideals are Jean Leclercq, *The Love of Learning and the Desire for God: A Study of Monastic Culture*, translated by Catharine Misrahi (New York: Fordham University Press, 1961); and Bernard McGinn, *The Growth of Mysticism* (New York: Crossroad, 1994).
9. James A. Brundage, *Law, Sex, and Christian Society in Medieval Europe* (Chicago: University of Chicago Press, 1987), pp.165–168. Brundage analyses a series of penitentials, including the reforms made by Theodore of Canterbury as Archbishop of Canterbury in the later 600s. For monks in particular, see Jacqueline Murray, 'Men's Bodies, Men's Minds: Seminal Emissions and Sexual Anxiety in the Middle Ages', *Annual Review of Sex Research*, 8:1 (1997), pp.1–26.
10. For these details, I have drawn on William of Saint-Thierry, *Vita Prima*, edited by Paul Verdeyen (Turnhout: Brepols, 2010), 1: 3, 4 and 5. Also Brian Patrick McGuire, *Bernard of Clairvaux: An Inner Life* (Ithaca, NY: Cornell University Press, 2020), ch.2.
11. William of Saint-Thierry, *Vita Prima*, 1: 6. This translation is from William of Saint-Thierry, Arnold of Bonneval and Geoffrey of Auxerre, *The First Life of Bernard of Clairvaux*, translated by Hilary Costello (Collegeville, MN: Cistercian Publications and Liturgical Press, 2015), p.9.
12. *For and Against Abelard: The Invective of Bernard of Clairvaux and Berengar of Poitiers*, edited and translated by Rodney M. Thomson and Michael Winterbottom (Woodbridge: Boydell Medieval Texts, 2020), pp.41–61.
13. 'Lancan vei per mei la landa', in *The Songs of Bernart de Ventadorn*, edited by Stephen G. Nichols, John A. Galm and A. Bartlett Giamatti (Chapel Hill, NC: UNC Department of Romance Studies, 1962), no. 26.

14. Andreas Capellanus, *The Art of Courtly Love*, translated by John Jay Parry (New York: Norton, 1969), pp.28–32.
15. Oxford, Bodleian Library MS Auct. D.5.5., f.250. 'Inpudentia est exterioribus signis luxueriam anime de monstrare . . .'
16. William Peraldus, *Summa de virtutibus et vitiis*, fol.20v.
17. This narrative is handled by McGuire, *Bernard of Clairvaux: An Inner Life*, chs.3–8.
18. Bernard of Clairvaux, *De diligendo deo*.
19. Bernard of Clairvaux, *Sermons on the Canticles*, Sermon 2, in *Sancti Bernardi Opera*, edited by Jean Mabillon (Paris: Gaume Fratres, 1839), vol.1, cols.2671–2672.
20. Yvette is discussed in Walter Simons, *Cities of Ladies: Beguine Communities in the Medieval Low Countries, 1200–1565* (Philadelphia: University of Pennsylvania Press, 2001), p.70.
21. On the beguines, Simons, *Cities of Ladies*; Tanya Stabler Miller, *The Beguines of Medieval Paris: Gender, Patronage, and Spiritual Authority* (Philadelphia: University of Pennsylvania Press, 2014).
22. Hadewijch of Brabant, Vision 7, in *The Essential Writings of Christian Mysticism*, edited by Bernard McGinn (New York: Modern Library, 2006), pp.102–104.
23. On Hadewijch's life, see Elizabeth A. Dreyer, *Passionate Spirituality: Hildegard of Bingen and Hadewijch of Brabant* (New Jersey: Paulist Press, 2005).
24. Mechthild of Magdeburg, *The Revelations of Mechthild of Magdeburg*, pp.78, 28.
25. On Angela's stripping naked, see *Angela of Foligno: Complete Works*, edited and translated by Paul Lachance (New York: Paulist Press, 1993), p.126. On Angela generally, see Michael Hahn, 'Angela of Foligno', in *The Palgrave Encyclopedia of Medieval Women's Writing in the Global Middle Ages*, edited by Michelle M. Sauer, Diane Watt, Liz Herbert McAvoy (Cham: Springer International Publishing, 2022).
26. *Angela of Foligno: Complete Works*, p.198. Note that the historian and theologian Michael Hahn has disputed this reading, arguing – through a study of the manuscript tradition – that the original text specified that Angela did 'not' put a candle to her genitals.
27. William Peraldus, *Summa de virtutibus et vitiis*, fol.20v.

28. Bernard expresses this view throughout his *De diligendo deo*.
29. Michael Camille, *Image on the Edge: The Margins of Medieval Art* (Cambridge, MA: Harvard University Press, 1992), p.157.
30. Observations about masturbation made in Ruth Mazo Karras, *Sexuality in Medieval Europe: Doing Unto Others*, third edition (London: Routledge, 2017), pp.111–112. See also Jacqueline Murray, '"The Law of Sin That Is in My Members": The Problem of Male Embodiment', in *Gender and Holiness: Men, Women, and Saints in Late Medieval Europe*, edited by Samantha J. E. Riches and Sarah Salih (London: Routledge, 2002), pp.9–22.
31. This last point is made in Thomas D. Cooke, 'Pornography, the Comic Spirit, and the Fabliaux', in *The Humor of the Fabliaux*, edited by Thomas D. Cooke and Benjamin L. Honeycutt (Columbia: University of Missouri Press, 1974), pp.137–162.
32. Brian Levy, 'Performing Fabliaux', in *Performing Medieval Narrative*, edited by Evelyn Birge Vitz, Nancy Freeman Regalado and Marilyn Lawrence (Woodbridge: Boydell and Brewer, 2005), pp.123–140.
33. Evelyn Birge Vitz, 'Erotic Reading in the Middle Ages: Performance and Re-performance of Romance', in *Performing Medieval Narrative*, pp.73–88.
34. 'Saint Martin's Wishes', from *The Fabliaux: A New Verse Translation*, edited and translated by Nathaniel E. Dubin (New York: Liveright, 2013), pp.885–894.
35. https://www.bbc.co.uk/news/technology-23030090 [Accessed June 2025].
36. This view, again, is taken from Cooke, 'Pornography, the Comic Spirit, and the Fabliaux'.
37. For a description and discussion of this badge, see Jos Koldeweij, '"Shameless and Naked Images": Obscene Badges as Parodies of Popular Devotion', in *Art and Architecture of Late Medieval Pilgrimage in Northern Europe and the British Isles*, edited by Sarah Blick and Rita Tekippe (Leiden: Brill, 2005), pp.493–510. I have written about this badge in my own article, Peter J. A. Jones, 'Laughing with Sacred Things: A History in Four Objects', *Church History*, 89:4 (2021), pp.759–778.
38. This is New York Public Library MS MA 4, fol.24r.

39. Marguerite's Hours, New York, Pierpont Morgan Library MS M.754, fol.16v.
40. This argument is treated at length, with a nuanced critique, in Camille, *Image on the Edge*. It is also rejected, beautifully, in Martha Bayless, *Parody in the Middle Ages: The Latin Tradition* (Ann Arbor, MI: University of Michigan Press, 1996).
41. Cooke, 'Pornography, the Comic Spirit, and the Fabliaux'.
42. This view emerges across Andreas Capellanus, *The Art of Courtly Love*, but appears most specifically on p.33 and pp.148–149.
43. Hugh of Saint Victor, *Adnotatiunculae elucidatoriae in threnos Jeremiae*, PL vol.175, cols.295B–C.
44. Dillian Gordon, 'The Wilton Diptych: An Introduction', in *The Regal Image of Richard II and the Wilton Diptych*, with an introduction by Caroline Barron, edited by Dillian Gordon, Lisa Monnas and Caroline Elam (London: Harvey Miller, 1997), pp.189–196.
45. For a novel interpretation of time on the Hereford map, comparing its layout with that of a sundial, see Maria Magdalena Morawiecka, 'In a Circle: The Hereford Map as a "Cosmic Clock"', *Imago Mundi*, 75:1 (2023), pp.90–98.
46. On this work and its fusing of temporalities generally, see Debra Higgs Strickland, *The Epiphany of Hieronymus Bosch: Imagining Antichrist and Others from the Middle Ages to the Reformation* (London: Harvey Miller, 2016). Note that Higgs Strickland's identification of this character as Antichrist follows the interpretation made earlier by Lotte Brand Philip, 'The Prado Epiphany of Jerome Bosch', *Art Bulletin*, 35:4 (1953), pp.267–293.
47. Erwin Panofsky, *Early Netherlandish Painting: Its Origins and Character* (New York: Harper and Row, 1953), p.358.
48. Antonio de Beatis, *Die Reise des Kardinals Luigi d'Aragona durch Deutschland, die Niederlande, Frankreich und Oberitalien, 1517–1518*, edited by Ludwig Pastor (Freiburg im Breisgau: Herder, 1905), vol.4: 4, p.116. See also E. H. Gombrich, 'The Earliest Description of Bosch's *Garden of Delight*', *Journal of the Warburg and Courtauld Institutes*, 30 (1967), pp.403–406.
49. José de Sigüenza, *Tercera parte de la Historia de la Orden de San Geronimo* (Madrid: Imprenta Real, 1605), reproduced in Godfried

Christian Maria van Dijk, *Op zoek naar Jheronimus van Aken alias Bosch: De feiten* (Zaltbommel: Europese Bibliotheek, 2001), pp.116ff.

50. Margaret D. Carroll, *Hieronymus Bosch: Time and Transformation in the Garden of Earthly Delights* (New Haven: Yale University Press, 2022), pp.94–95, 97. The sexual-liberation thesis began with Wilhelm Fraenger, *Hieronymus Bosch: Das Tausendjährige Reich* (Coburg: Winkler-Verlag, 1947). See also Jean Wirth, *Hieronymus Bosch: Der Garten der Lüste. Das Paradies als Utopie* (Frankfurt: S. Fischer, 2000), p.90.
51. Carroll, *Hieronymus Bosch*, pp.94–95, 97.
52. Hans Belting, *Garden of Earthly Delights* (Munich: Prestel, 2005), p.47.
53. Carroll, *Hieronymus Bosch*, p.95.
54. Belting, *Garden*, pp.87–88.
55. Otto of Freising, *Chronica sive Historia de duabus civitatibus* [*Two Cities*], edited by Adolf Hofmeister (Munich: Monumenta Germaniae Historica, 1912), 8: 9, pp.437–438.
56. E. H. Gombrich, 'Bosch's "*Garden of Earthly Delights*": A Progress Report', *Journal of the Warburg and Courtauld Institutes*, vol.32 (1969), pp.162–170.
57. Nils Büttner, 'No Flesh in *The Garden of Earthly Delights*', in *Aesthetics of the Flesh*, edited by Felix Ensslin and Charlotte Klink (Berlin, 2014), pp.272–299.
58. Matthijs Ilsink and Jos Koldeweij, *Hieronymus Bosch: Visions of Genius* (New Haven, CT: Yale University Press, 2016), pp.55–56.
59. On the owl as a symbol of evil for Bosch, see Nils Büttner, *Hieronymus Bosch: Visions and Nightmares* (London: Reaktion Books, 2016), pp.90–91.
60. Antonius of Bitonto, *Sermones dominicales per totum annum*, edited by Philippus de Rotingo (Strassburg: Johann Grüninger, 1496), fol.125v.

THE SEVEN, AGAIN

1. Cambridge, Trinity College MS R.1.66, fol.131r. Note that the figures from this manuscript are drawn from Ramon Llull's *Ars demonstrativa* (*c*.1283).

Bibliography

MANUSCRIPTS & ARCHIVAL SOURCES

Archivo General de Simancas, AGS/PTR, LEG, 50, 36.
Cambridge, Corpus Christi College MS 063.
Cambridge, Corpus Christi College MS 067.
Cambridge, Corpus Christi College MS 136.
Cambridge, Corpus Christi College MS 380.
Cambridge, Queens' College MS 18.
Cambridge, Queens' College MS 19.
Cambridge, Trinity College MS B.5.4.
Cambridge, Trinity College MS B.14.4.
Cambridge, Trinity College MS R.1.66.
Dublin, Trinity College Dublin MS 306.
London, Lambeth Palace MS 78.
London, Lambeth Palace MS 205.
London, Lambeth Palace MS 388.
London, Lambeth Palace MS 477.
London, Lambeth Palace MS 497.
London, Lambeth Palace MS 4776.
London, Lambeth Palace MS Sion L40.2/L12.
London, British Library MS Cotton Julius D. III.
London, British Library MS Egerton 2951.
London, British Library MS Harley 3098.
London, National Archives, E 401/1565.
New York, New York Public Library MS MA 4.
New York, Pierpont Morgan Library MS M.754.
Oxford, Bodleian Library MS Auct. D.5.5.

Oxford, Bodleian Library MS Lat.th.e. 22.
Oxford, Bodleian Library MS Laud Misc. 345.
Oxford, Bodleian Library Laud Misc. 363.
Oxford, Bodleian Library MS Laud Misc. 594.
Paris, Bibliothèque Nationale de France MS Lat. 3143.
Paris, Bibliothèque Nationale de France MS Lat. 3570.
Paris, Bibliothèque Nationale de France MS Lat. 10401.
Paris, Bibliothèque Nationale de France, MS Lat. 16417.
Vatican City, Biblioteca Vaticana MS Borgh. 56.
Vatican City, Biblioteca Vaticana MS Reg.Lat. 150.
Vatican City, Biblioteca Vaticana MS Reg.Lat. 399.
Vatican City, Biblioteca Vaticana MS Reg.Lat. 630.
Vatican City, Biblioteca Vaticana MS Vat.Lat. 671.
Vatican City, Biblioteca Vaticana MS Vat.Lat. 4030.

PRIMARY SOURCES

Acta Sanctorum Julii Tomus Primus. Paris: Victor Palme, 1867.
Aelred of Rievaulx. *Sermones de oneribus*. Sermon 25. *Patrologia Latina*, vol. 195.
Alain de Lille. *The Complaint of Nature*. Translated by Douglas M. Moffat. Hamden, CT: Archon Books, 1972.
—*Liber sententiarum, De Sancta Maria*. *Patrologia Latina*, vol. 210.
—*Summa de Arte Praedicatoria*. *Patrologia Latina*, vol. 210.
Albert of Brescia. *Liber consolationis et consilii*. Edited by Thor Sundby. Paris: A. Franck, 1873.
Alexander Neckam, *Commentarium in Martiani Capellae De nuptiis Mercurii et Philologiae I–II*. Edited by C. J. McDonough. Florence: SISMEL, Edizioni del Galluzzo, 2006.
Angela of Foligno. *Angela of Foligno: Complete Works*. Edited and translated by Paul Lachance. New York: Paulist Press, 1993.
Anglería, Pedro Mártir de. *Epistolario*. Edited by José López de Toro. 4 vols. Madrid: Documentos Inéditos para la Historia de España, 1953–1957.
Anthony of Padua. *Sermons for Sundays and Festivals*. Translated by Paul Spilsbury. https://www.documentacatholicaomnia. eu/03d/1195-1231,_Antonius_Patavinus,_Sermones,_EN.pdf.

BIBLIOGRAPHY

Antonio de Beatis, *Die Reise des Kardinals Luigi d'Aragona durch Deutschland, die Niederlande, Frankreich und Oberitalien, 1517–1518*, edited by Ludwig Pastor. Freiburg im Breisgau: Herder, 1905.

Antonius of Bitonto. *Sermones dominicales per totum annum*. Edited by Philippus de Rotingo. Strassburg: Johann Grüninger, 1496.

The Apocryphal Old Testament. Edited by Hedley F. D. Sparks. Oxford: Clarendon Press, 1984.

The Apostolic Fathers, vol. 2. Edited and translated by Bart D. Ehrman. Cambridge, MA: Harvard University Press, 2003.

Arnaud de Vilanova. *Antidotarium*. In *Opera Arnaldi de Villa Nova*, edited by Petrus Salius. Venice: Heirs of Octavian Scotus, 1527.

—*De consideracionibus operis medicine sive de flebotomia*. In *Arnaldi de Villanova Opera Medica Omnia*, vol. 4, edited by Luke Demaitre. Barcelona: Publicacions i Edicions de la Universitat de Barcelona, 1988.

—*De regimine sanitatis*. In *Arnaldi de Villanova Opera Medica Omnia*, vol. 10, edited by Luis García-Ballester and Michael R. McVaugh. Barcelona: Publicacions i Edicions de la Universitat de Barcelona, 2000.

—*Epistola de dosi tyriacalium medicinarum*. In *Arnaldi de Villanova Opera Medica Omnia*, vol. 3, edited by Michael R. McVaugh. Barcelona: Publicacions i Edicions de la Universitat de Barcelona, 1985.

—*The Earliest Printed Book on Wine, by Arnald of Villanova* [*Liber de vinis*]. Translated by Henry E. Sigerist. New York: Schuman's, 1943.

—*Tractatus de tempore adventus Antichristi*. In 'El text primitiu del *De mysterio cymbalorum ecclesiae* d'Arnau de Vilanova. En apèndix, el seu *Tractatus de tempore adventus Antichristi*', edited by Josep Perarnau i Espelt. *Arxiu de Textos Catalans Antics* 7–8 (1988–9).

Astesanus of Asti. *Summa de casibus conscientiae*. Edited by Bartolomeo Bellati and Gomes de Lisboa. Nuremberg: Anton Koberger, 1482.

Athanasius. *The Life of Saint Antony*. Translated by Robert T. Meyer. Westminster, MD: The Newman Press, 1950.

Augustine of Hippo. *City of God*. Translated by Henry Bettenson. London: Penguin, 2003.

—Letter 38. Translated by J. G. Cunningham. In *Nicene and Post-Nicene Fathers*, First Series, vol. 1, edited by Philip Schaff. Buffalo, NY: Christian Literature Publishing Co., 1887.

BIBLIOGRAPHY

Bacon, Roger. *Opus Tertium, Opus Minus, Compendium Philosophiae.* Edited by John Sherren Brewer. London: Longman, 1859.

Baldwin of Canterbury. *Tractatus diversi. Patrologia Latina*, vol. 204.

Bartholomaei Anglici. *De genuinis rerum coelestium, terrestrium et infer[n]arum proprietatibus.* Frankfurt: Wolfgang Richter, 1601.

Bestiary: Being an English Version of the Bodleian Library, Oxford MS Bodley 764 with all the Original Miniatures Reproduced in Facsimile. Translated by Richard W. Barber. Woodbridge: Boydell, 1993.

Bernard of Clairvaux. *De diligendo deo.* In *Sancti Bernardi Opera*, vol. 3, edited by Jean Leclercq and H. M. Rochais. Rome. Editiones Cistercienses, 1963.

—*De gradibus humilitatis et superbiae.* In *Sancti Bernardi Opera*, vol. 3, edited by Jean Leclercq and H. M. Rochais. Rome: Editiones Cistercienses, 1963.

—*Pro Dominica I Novembris*, Sermon 5. *Patrologia Latina*, vol. 183.

—*Sancti Bernardi Opera.* Edited by Jean Mabillon. Paris: Gaume Fratres, 1839.

—*Sermons on the Canticles.* In *Sancti Bernardi Opera*, vol. 1. Edited by Jean Mabillon. Paris: Gaume Fratres, 1839.

—*Third Sermon for the Vigil of the Nativity.* In *Sancti Bernardi Opera*, vol. 4. Edited by Jean Leclercq and H. M. Rochais. Rome: Editiones Cistercienses, 1966.

—*The Twelve Degrees of Humility and Pride.* Translated by Barton R. V. Mills. London: Society for Promoting Christian Knowledge, 1929.

Boccaccio, Giovanni. *Life of Dante.* Translated by George Rice Carpenter. New York: Grolier Club, 1900.

Boethius. *The Consolation of Philosophy.* Translated by David R. Slavitt. Cambridge, MA: Harvard University Press, 2008.

Bonaventure. *Breviloquium.* Translated by Erwin Esser Nemmers. London: Herder, 1947.

The Book of Margery Kempe. Translated and edited by B.A. Windeatt. London: Penguin, 1985.

The Book of the Resurrection of Christ by Bartholomew the Apostle. Discussed in John W. Welch, 'The Apocryphal Judas Revisited'. *BYU Studies Quarterly* 45, no. 2 (2006): 45–53.

Bracciolini, Poggio. *On Avarice.* In *The Earthly Republic: Italian*

Humanists on Government and Society, edited by Benjamin G. Kohl, Ronald G. Witt and Elizabeth B. Welles. Philadelphia: University of Pennsylvania Press, 1978.

The Brussels Horloge de Sapience: Iconography and Text of Brussels, Bibliothèque Royale, MS. IV 111. Edited by Peter Rolfe Monks. Leiden: Brill, 1990.

Caesarius of Heisterbach. *Dialogus Miraculorum*. Edited by Joseph Strange. Cologne: Sumptibus J. M. Heberle. 1851.

Capellanus, Andreas. *The Art of Courtly Love*. Translated by John Jay Parry. New York: Norton, 1969.

Carmina Burana. I. Band: Text, 3: Die Trink- und Spielerlieder; Die geistlichen Dramen Nachträge. Edited by Otto Schumann and Bernhard Bischoff. Heidelberg: Carl Winter Universitätsverlag, 1970.

Cartulaire de l'université de Montpellier. Edited by Alexandre Germain. Vol. 1: *1181–1400*. Montpellier: Ricard Frères, 1890.

Cassian, John. *De Coenobiorum Institutis. Patrologia Latina*, vol. 49.

—*The Institutes*. Translated by Boniface Ramsey. New York: Paulist Press, 2000.

Catherine of Genoa. *Purgation and Purgatory: The Spiritual Dialogue*. Translated by Serge Hughes. New York: Paulist Press, 1979.

Catherine of Siena. *The Dialogue of Saint Catherine of Siena*. Translated by Algar Thorold. London: Kegan Paul, 1907.

—*Epistolae*. http://www.domcentral.org/trad/cathletters.htm#personstable.

Chartularium Universitatis Parisiensis. Edited by H. Denifle and A. Chatelain. Paris: Delalain Frères, 1889.

Chrétien de Troyes. *Arthurian Romances*. Translated by William W. Kibler and Carleton W. Carroll. London: Penguin, 1991.

Christine de Pizan. *The Book of the City of Ladies*. Translated by Rosalind Brown-Grant. London: Penguin, 1999.

The Chronicle of Battle Abbey. Edited and translated by Eleanor Searle. Oxford: Clarendon Press, 1980.

Climacus, John. *The Ladder of Divine Ascent*. Translated by Archimandrite Lazarus Moore. New York: Harper & Brothers, 1959.

Conciliorum oecumenicorum decreta. Edited by Joseph Alberigo, Joseph

A. Dossetti, Pericles Joannou, Claude Leonardi and Paul Prodi. Basel: Herder, 1972.

Corpus of Early Arabic Sources for West African History. Edited by Nehemia Levtzion and J. F. P. Hopkins. Princeton, NJ: Markus Wiener, 2000.

The Correspondence of Thomas Becket. Edited and translated by Anne Duggan. Oxford: Oxford University Press, 2000.

Curye on Inglysch: English Culinary Manuscripts of the Fourteenth Century (Including the Forme of Cury). Edited by Constance B. Hieatt and Sharon Butler. Oxford: Oxford University Press, 1985.

Dante Alighieri. *Il Convivio (The Banquet).* Translated by Richard H. Lansing. New York: Garland Library of Medieval Literature, 1990.

—*Dante's Lyric Poetry.* Translated by K. Foster and P. Boyde. Oxford: Clarendon, 1967.

—*Inferno.* Translated by Robert Hollander and Jean Hollander. New York: Doubleday, 2000.

—*Paradiso.* Translated by Robert Hollander and Jean Hollander. New York: Doubleday, 2007.

—*Purgatorio.* Translated by Robert Hollander and Jean Hollander. New York: Doubleday, 2003.

—*La Vita Nuova.* Translated by David R. Slavitt. Cambridge, MA: Harvard University Press, 2010.

De Miseria Condicionis Humane. Edited by Robert E. Lewis. Athens, Georgia 1978.

Der Stricker. *Fünfzehn kleine Verserzählungen mit einem Anhang: Der Weinschwelg.* Edited by Hanns Fischer. Tübingen: Max Niemeyer, 1960.

The Desert Fathers: Sayings of the Early Christian Monks. Translated by Benedicta Ward. London: Penguin, 2003.

The Devils and Evil Spirits of Babylonia, vol. 1: 'Evil Spirits'. Edited and translated by R. Campbell Thompson. London: Luzac and Co., 1903.

Dionysius the Areopagite. *The Celestial and Ecclesiastical Hierarchy.* Translated by John Parker. London: Skeffington & Son, 1894.

Dits et Contes de Baudouin de Condé et de son fils Jean de Condé. Edited by Auguste Scheler. Brussels: Victor Devaux, 1866.

BIBLIOGRAPHY

Elisabeth of Schönau: The Complete Works. Translated and introduced by Anne L. Clark. New York: Paulist Press, 2000.

Epictetus. *The Enchiridion*. In Epictetus, *Discourses and Selected Writings*, translated and edited by Robert Dobbin. London: Penguin, 2008.

The Essential Writings of Christian Mysticism. Edited by Bernard McGinn. New York: Modern Library, 2006.

Evagrius Ponticus. Abhandlung der Königlichen Gesellschaft der Wissenschaften zu Göttingen, Philologisch-Historische Klasse, Neue Folge, Band xiii, no. 2. Berlin, 1912.

Evagrius Ponticus. *Antirrheticus (Selections)*. In *Ascetic Behavior in Greco-Roman Antiquity: A Sourcebook*, edited by Vincent Wimbush. Minneapolis: Fortress Press, 1990.

—*Talking Back [Antirrhêtikos]: A Monastic Handbook for Combating Demons*. Translated by David Brakke. Collegeville, MI: Liturgical Press, 2009.

Evagrius Ponticus. Edited by Augustine Casiday. London: Routledge, 2006.

Faba, Guido. *Ars dictaminis*. In Augusto Gaudenzi, 'Guidonis Fabe Summa dictaminis'. *Il Propugnatore* N S 3 (1890).

The Fabliaux: A New Verse Translation. Edited and translated by Nathaniel E. Dubin. New York: Liveright, 2013.

Francis of Assisi: Early Documents, vol. 2. Edited by Regis J. Armstrong, J. A. Wayne Hellmann and William J. Short. New York: New City Press, 2000.

Frost, Robert. 'A Servant to Servants'. In *Early Poems*. London: Penguin, 1998.

Gerald of Wales. *Speculum Duorum, or A Mirror of Two Men*. Edited by Yves Lefèvre and R. B. C. Huygens, translated by Brian Dawson. Cardiff: University of Wales Press, 1974.

Gilbert Foliot. *Gilberti ex abbate Glocestriae episcopi primum Herefordiensis deinde Londoniensis epistolae*. Edited by J. A. Giles. Oxford: J. H. Parker, 1845.

Gómez de Fuensalida, Gutierre. *Correspondencia*. Edited on behalf of Jacobo Fitz-James Stuart y Falcó. Madrid: Duque de Berwick y de Alba, Conde de Siruela, 1907.

Gower, John. *Confessio Amantis*. Translated by Terence Tiller. London: Penguin, 1963.

Gregory the Great. *Moralia in Job: or Morals on the Book of Job*. Translated by James Bliss and Charles Marriott. Oxford: Parker and Rivington, 1850.

Guido da Pisa. *Expositiones et Glose super Comediam Dantis*. Edited by Vincenzo Cioffari. New York: State University of New York Press, 1974.

Guillaume de Deguileville. *Le pelerinage de vie humaine*. Edited by J. J. Stürzinger. London: Nichols and Sons, 1893.

Guillaume de Tocco. *Ystoria sancti Thome de Aquino*. Edited by Claire le Brun-Gouanvic. Toronto: PIMS, 1996.

Hadewijch of Brabant. Vision 7. In *The Essential Writings of Christian Mysticism*, edited by Bernard McGinn. New York: Modern Library, 2006.

Henry of Huntingdon. *Historia Anglorum: The History of the English People*. Edited and translated by Diana Greenway. Oxford: Clarendon Press, 1996.

Heresies of the High Middle Ages. Edited and translated by Walter L. Wakefield and Austin P. Evans. New York: Columbia University Press, 1991.

Hildegard of Bingen. *Scivias*. Translated by Mother Columba Hart and Jane Bishop. New York: Paulist Press, 1990.

Hippolytus. *Philosophumena: or The Refutation of All Heresies*. Translated by Francis Legge. New York: The Macmillan Company, 1921.

Honorius Augustodunensis. *De imagine mundi*. Patrologia Latina, vol. 172.

Hugh Primas and the Archpoet. Edited and translated by Fleur Adcock. Cambridge: Cambridge University Press, 1994.

Hugh of Saint Victor. *Adnotatiunculae elucidatoriae in threnos Jeremiae*, PL vol.175, cols.295B–C.

Hugh of Saint Victor. *De quinque septenis (On the Five Sevens) and its Versification in Samuel Presbiter's De oratione dominica (On the Lord's Prayer)*, edited by Andrew Dunning. *Scholarly Editing* 37 (2016). Available online: http://scholarlyediting.org/2016/editions/intro.dunning.html.

—*De sacramentis*. Patrologia Latina, vol. 176.

—*Quaestiones et Decisiones in Epistolas D. Pauli, In Epistolam ad Colossenses*. Patrologia Latina, vol. 175.

—*Sermones de tempore*, Sermo 26. Patrologia Latina, vol. 10.

Isidore of Seville. *Quaestiones in vetus testamentum*, 'In Deuteronomium', Patrologia Latina, vol. 83.

Jacobus of Voragine. *The Golden Legend: Readings on the Saints*. Translated by William Granger Ryan, with an introduction by Eamon Duffy. Princeton: Princeton University Press, 2012.

—*Sermones Quadragesimales*. Edited by Giovanni Paolo Maggioni. Florence: SISMEL, Edizioni del Galluzzo, 2005.

Jacques de Vitry, *The Exempla or Illustrative Stories from the Sermones Vulgares of Jacques de Vitry*. Edited by Thomas Frederick Crane. London: The Folk-lore Society, 1890.

—*The Life of Marie d'Oignies*. Toronto: Peregrina Publishing Company, 1987.

John of Kent. *Summa de penitencia*. Edited by Samuel J. Klumpenhouwer. PhD dissertation, University of Toronto, 2018.

John of Salisbury. *Policraticus: The Statesman's Book*. Translated by John Dickinson. New York: Knopf, 1927.

Lactantius. *De ira dei*. In *Lactancio, Sobre la Ira de Dios*, edited and translated into Spanish by Marcela Islas Jacinto. Mexico City: Universidad Nacional Autónoma de México, 2020.

Lothar of Segni (Pope Innocent III). *On the Misery of the Human Condition*. Edited by Donald R. Howard, translated by Margaret Mary Dietz. Indianapolis: Bobbs-Merrill, 1969.

—*De Miseria Condicionis Humane*. Edited by Robert E. Lewis. Athens, GA: University of Georgia Press, 1978.

The Letter Collections of Arnulf of Lisieux. Edited and translated by Carolyn Poling Schriber. Lewiston: The Edwin Mellen Press, 1997.

The Letters of Arnulf of Lisieux. Edited by Frank Barlow. Camden Society, Third Series, vol. 61. London: The Royal Historical Society, 1939.

The Life of Saint Thomas Aquinas: Biographical Documents. Edited and translated by Kenelm Foster. London: Longmans, Green and Co., 1959.

BIBLIOGRAPHY

The Lives of the Desert Fathers: The Historia Monachorum in Aegypto. Edited and translated by Norman Russell. Kalamazoo: Cistercian Publications, 1981.

The Lives of Thomas Becket. Selected and translated by Michael Staunton. Manchester: Manchester University Press, 2001.

Mechthild of Magdeburg. *The Flowing Light of the Godhead.* Translated by Lucy Menzies. London: Longmans, Green, and Co., 1955.

Medieval Handbooks of Penance: A translation of the principal libri poenitentiales and selections from related documents. Edited and translated by John T. McNeill and Helena M. Gamer. New York: Columbia University Press, 1990.

Medieval Medicine: A Reader. Edited by Faith Wallis. Toronto: University of Toronto Press, 2010.

McVaugh, Michael R. 'Theriac at Montpellier 1285–1325 (with an edition of the "Questionesde tyriaca" of William of Brescia)'. *Sudhoffs Archiv* 56:2 (1972).

Otto of Freising. *Chronica sive Historia de duabus civitatibus [Two Cities].* Edited by Adolf Hofmeister. Munich: Monumenta Germaniae Historica, 1912.

Ovid. *Metamorphoses.* Translated by Mary M. Innes. London: Penguin, 1955.

Papias of Hierapolis. *Fragments.* In *The Apostolic Fathers*, vol. 2, edited and translated by Bart D. Ehrman. Cambridge, MA: Harvard University Press, 2003.

The Pearl. Translated by Simon Armitage. London: Faber, 2016.

Peraldus, William. *Summa de virtutibus et vitiis.* Lyons: Nicolaus de Benedictis, 1500.

Peter Abelard. *Historia Calamitatum.* Translated by Betty Radice. London: Penguin, 1974.

Peter Damian. *Die Briefe des Petrus Damiani.* Edited by Kurt Reindel. Munich: Monumenta Germaniae Historica, 1989.

Peter of Blois. *Dialogus inter regem Henricum et abbatem Bonevallis.* In *Serta Mediaevalia: Textus Varii Saeculorum X–XIII, Tractatus et Epistulae*, edited by R. B. C. Huygens. Turnhout: Brepols, 2000.

Peter Lombard, *Magistri Petri Lombardi Parisiensis episcopi Sententiae in IV libris distinctae*, a revised edition by I. C. Brady (Grottaferrata, Editiones Collegii S. Bonaventurae, 1971), Book 2, Dist.30.

Peter of Poitiers. *Sententiae. Patrologia Latina*, vol. 211.

Petrarch. *De remediis utriusque fortunae*. In *Petrarch's Remedies for Fortune Fair and Foul: A Modern English Translation*, edited and translated by Conrad H. Rawski. Bloomington, IN: Indiana University Press, 1991.

—Letters. In *Petrarch: The First Modern Scholar and Man of Letters*, edited and translated by James Harvey Robinson. New York: G. P. Putnam, 1898.

de Porcellet, Philippine. *La Vie de Sainte Douceline, fondatrice des Béguines de Marseille, composée au treizième siècle en langue provençale*. Edited and translated into French by Joseph-Hyacinthe Albanès. Marseille: É. Camoin, 1879.

de Sigüenza, José. *Tercera parte de la Historia de la Orden de San Geronimo*. Madrid: Imprenta Real, 1605.

Raymond of Capua. *The Life of Catherine of Siena*. Translated by George Lamb, updated edition. Charlotte, NC: TAN Books, 2011.

Recueil des sources arabes concernant l'Afrique occidentale du VIIIe au XVIe siècles. Edited by Joseph M. Cuoq. Paris: Éditions du CNRS, 1985.

Le registre d'inquisition de Jacques Fournier 1318–1325. Edited by Jean Duvernoy. 3 vols. Toulouse: Privat, 1965.

The Renaissance Philosophy of Man. Edited and translated by Ernst Cassirer, Paul Oskar Kristeller and John Herman Randall. Chicago: The University of Chicago Press, 1948.

Richard of Saint Victor. *Adnotationes mysticae in Psalmos*, Adnotatio in Psalmum 28. *Patrologia Latina*, vol. 196.

Rupert of Deutz. *Commentaria in duodecim prophetas minores* (1129). *Patrologia Latina*, vol. 168.

Sacrorum conciliorum nova et amplissima collectio. Edited by Giovanni Domenico Mansi. 54 vols. Paris, 1901–27.

Selected Works of Abbot Suger of Saint-Denis. Translated with an introduction by Richard Cusimano and Eric Whitmore. Washington, DC: The Catholic University of America Press, 2018.

Seneca. *De Ira*. In *Seneca: Moral Essays*, vol. 1. Translated by John W. Basore. Cambridge, MA: Harvard University Press, 1928.

—*On the Shortness of Life*, in Seneca, *Dialogues and Letters*. Translated and edited by C. D. N. Costa. London: Penguin, 1997.

BIBLIOGRAPHY

The Songs of Bernart de Ventadorn. Edited by Stephen G. Nichols, John A. Galm and A. Bartlett Giamatti. Chapel Hill, NC: UNC Department of Romance Studies, 1962.
The Treatise of Walter of Bibbesworth. Translated by Andrew Dalby. Totnes: Prospect Books, 2012.
Virgil. *The Aeneid*. Translated by David West. London: Penguin, 2003.
William of Saint-Thierry, Arnold of Bonneval and Geoffrey of Auxerre. *The First Life of Bernard of Clairvaux*. Translated by Hilary Costello. Collegeville, MN: Cistercian Publications and Liturgical Press, 2015.
William of Tocco. *William of Tocco, The Life of St. Thomas Aquinas*. Translated by David M. Foley. St Mary's, KA: Angelus Press, 2023.
Wolfram von Eschenbach. *Parzival*. Translated by A. T. Hatto. London: Penguin, 1980.

SECONDARY SOURCES

Abu-Lughod, Janet L. *Before European Hegemony: The World System A.D. 1250–1350*. Oxford: Oxford University Press, 1989.
Almenar Fernández, Luis. 'La cultura material de los pobres en la Valencia bajomedieval'. In *Économies de la pauvreté au Moyen Âge*, edited by Pere Benito, Sandro Carocci and Laurent Feller. Madrid: Open Edition Books, 2023.
—'Los inventarios *post mortem* de la Valencia medieval: Una fuente para el estudio del consumo doméstico y los niveles de vida'. *Anuario de Estudios Medievales* 47, no. 2 (2017): 533–566.
Ames, Christine Caldwell. 'Understanding the Good: Medieval Inquisitions and Modern Religion'. *Church History* 93 (2024): 239–262.
Aram, Bethany. *La reina Juana: Gobierno, piedad y dinastía*. Madrid: Marcial Pons Historia, 2016.
Aries, Philippe. *The Hour of Our Death*. Translated by Helen Weaver. New York: Knopf, 1981.
Ashley, Kathleen. 'Historicizing Margery: *The Book of Margery Kempe* as Social Text'. *Journal of Medieval and Early Modern Studies* 28 (1998): 375–392.
Azzolini, Chiara. 'Spigolature sulla biblioteca gerolamina del Castellazzo'. In *I manoscritti della Biblioteca del Capitolo Metropolitano*

di Milano: studi e ricerche, edited by Milvia Bollati. Rome: Viella, 2023.

Backman, Clifford R. 'Arnau de Vilanova and the Body at the End of the World'. In *Last Things: Death and the Apocalypse in the Middle Ages*, edited by Caroline Walker Bynum and Paul Freedman. Philadelphia: University of Pennsylvania Press, 2000.

Bailey, Mark. *After the Black Death: Economy, Society, and the Law in Fourteenth-Century England*. Oxford: Oxford University Press, 2021.

Baker, J. H. 'Famous English Canonists: III: John Ayton (or Acton) U.J.D. (d.1349), Professor of Law, Cambridge University, Canon of Lincoln'. *Ecclesiastical Law Journal* 2, no. 8 (1991): 159–163.

Barbero, Alessandro. *Dante*. Translated by Allan Cameron. London: Profile Books, 2021.

Barr, Beth Allison. 'Three's a Crowd: Wives, Husbands, and Priests in the Late Medieval Confessional'. In *A Companion to Pastoral Care in the Late Middle Ages (1200–1500)*, edited by Ronald J. Stansbury. Leiden: Brill, 2010.

Barrow, Julia. *The Clergy in the Medieval World: Secular Clerics, Their Families and Careers in North-Western Europe c.800–c.1200*. Cambridge: Cambridge University Press, 2015.

Bayless, Martha. *Parody in the Middle Ages: The Latin Tradition*. Ann Arbor, MI: University of Michigan Press, 1996.

Belenguer González, Antonio. '*Quasdam domos nostras*: El mercado inmobiliario en Valencia a principios del siglo xv'. In *Espacios de Vida: Casa, Hogar y Cultura Material en la Europa Medieval*, edited by Juan Vicente García Marsilla. Valencia: Universitat de València, 2022.

Bell, Nawal Morcos. 'The Age of Mansa Musa of Mali: Problems in Succession and Chronology'. In *Papers Presented to the International Conference of Manding Studies, SOAS*. London: SOAS, 1972.

Bellinati, Claudio. *Iconographic Atlas of Giotto's Chapel, 1300–1305*. Ponzano: Vianello, 2003.

Belting, Hans. *Hieronymus Bosch: Garden of Earthly Delights*. Munich: Prestel, 2005.

Beltrán, Antonio. *Estudio sobre el Santo Cáliz de la Catedral de Valencia*. Valencia: Instituto Diocesano Valentino 'Roque Chabás', 1960.

BIBLIOGRAPHY

Bennett, Janice. *St. Laurence & the Holy Grail: The Story of the Holy Chalice of Valencia*. San Francisco: Ignatius Press, 2004.

Bennett, Judith M. *Ale, Beer, and Brewsters in England: Women's Work in a Changing World, 1300–1600*. Oxford: Oxford University Press, 1996.

Berwian, I. M., H. Walter, E. Seifritz and Q. J. M. Huys. 'Predicting Relapse after Antidepressant Withdrawal: A Systematic Review'. *Psychological Medicine* 47, no. 3 (2017): 426–437.

Biller, Peter. 'Christians and Heretics'. In *Christianity in Western Europe, c.1100–c.1500*, edited by M. Rubin and W. Simons. Cambridge: Cambridge University Press, 2009.

Bloch, Marc. *La société féodale*. 2 vols. Paris: Albin Michel, 1949.

Block, Elaine C. *Corpus of Medieval Misericords: Belgium (B) - Netherlands (NL)*, vol. 3. Turnhout: Brepols, 2010.

Bloomfield, Morton W. *The Seven Deadly Sins: An Introduction to the History of a Religious Concept, with Special Reference to Medieval English Literature*. East Lansing, MI: Michigan State College Press, 1952.

Blumenthal, Debra. *Enemies and Familiars: Slavery and Mastery in Fifteenth-Century Valencia*. Ithaca, NY: Cornell University Press, 2009.

Bradford, David T. 'Brain and Psyche in Early Christian Asceticism'. *Psychological Reports* 109, no. 2 (2011): 461–520.

Bradley, R. S., M. K. Hughes and H. F. Diaz. 'Climate in Medieval Time'. *Science* 302 (2003): 404–405.

Brakke, David. 'Holy Men and Women of the Desert'. In *The Oxford Handbook of Christian Monasticism*, edited by Bernice M. Kaczynski. Oxford: Oxford University Press, 2020.

Brand, Paul. 'Henry II and the Creation of the English Common Law'. In *Henry II: New Interpretations*, edited by Christopher Harper-Bill and Nicholas Vincent. Woodbridge: The Boydell Press, 2007.

Briggs, Chris, Alice Forward, Ben Jervis and Matthew Tompkins. 'People, Possessions and Domestic Space in Late Medieval Escheators' Records'. *Journal of Medieval History* 45, no. 2 (2019): 145–161.

Britnell, Richard H., and James Davis. 'Introduction'. In *A Cultural*

History of Shopping in the Middle Ages, edited by James Davis. London: Bloomsbury, 2022.

Brose, Annette, Florian Schmiedek, Peter Koval and Peter Kuppens. 'Emotional inertia contributes to depressive symptoms beyond perseverative thinking'. *Cognition and Emotion* 29, no. 3 (2015): 527–538.

Brown, Elizabeth A. R. 'The Tyranny of a Construct: Feudalism and Historians of Medieval Europe'. *American Historical Review* 79, no. 4 (1974): 1063–1088.

Brundage, James A. *Law, Sex, and Christian Society in Medieval Europe.* Chicago: University of Chicago Press, 1987.

Buckland, Paul C., Gudrún Sveinbjarnardóttir, Diane Savory, Tom H. McGovern, Peter Skidmore and Claus Andreasen. 'Norsemen at Nipáitsoq, Greenland: A Paleoecological Investigation'. *Norwegian Archaeological Review* 16, no. 2 (1983): 86–98.

Bultot, R. 'L'auteur et la fonction littéraire du "De fructibus carnis et spiritus"'. *Recherches de Théologie Ancienne et Médiévale* 30 (1963): 148–54.

Buringh, Eltjo. *European urban population, 700–2000.* Data Archiving and Networked Services, 2020. https://doi.org/10.17026/dans-xzy-u62q.

Burke, M., J. Cheng and B. de Gant. 'Social comparison and Facebook: feedback, positivity, and opportunities for comparison'. *Proceedings of the 2020 CHI conference on human factors in computing systems*, Honolulu HI USA (2020), Article 355.

Büttner, Nils. *Hieronymus Bosch: Visions and Nightmares.* London: Reaktion Books, 2016.

—'No Flesh in *The Garden of Earthly Delights*'. In *Aesthetics of the Flesh*, edited by Felix Ensslin and Charlotte Klink. Berlin, 2014.

Bynum, Caroline Walker. *Holy Feast and Holy Fast: The Religious Significance of Food to Medieval Women.* Berkeley, CA: University of California Press, 1987.

—*The Resurrection of the Body in Western Christianity, 200–1336*, expanded edition. New York: Columbia University Press, 2017.

—'Wonder'. *American Historical Review* 102, no. 1 (1997): 1–26.

Camille, Michael. *Image on the Edge: The Margins of Medieval Art.* Cambridge, MA: Harvard University Press, 1992.

Carrera, Elena. 'The uses of anger in medieval and early modern medicine'. https://emotionsblog.history.qmul.ac.uk/2012/06/the-uses-of-anger-in-medieval-and-early-modern-medicine/.

Carroll, Margaret D. *Hieronymus Bosch: Time and Transformation in the Garden of Earthly Delights.* New Haven: Yale University Press, 2022.

Cavadini, Catherine. 'An Ardent Embrace: Thomas the Cistercian's *In cantica canticorum*'. *Cistercian Studies Quarterly* 47, no. 3 (2012): 297–311.

Caviness, Madeline. 'From the Self-Invention of the Whiteman in the Thirteenth Century to *The Good, The Bad, and The Ugly*'. *Different Visions: New Perspectives on Medieval Art* 1 (2008).

Clanchy, Michael T. *From Memory to Written Record: England 1066–1307*, second edition. Oxford: Blackwell, 1993.

Classen, Albrecht. 'Alcohol, Drunkenness, and Excess: Consumption and Transgression in European Medieval and Early Modern Literature'. *Neophilologus* 106 (2022): 589–610.

Cohn, Samuel, Jr. 'The Black Death and Consequences for Labor'. *Labor: Studies in Working-Class History* 20, no. 2 (2023): 14–29.

Conenna, L. Bonelli, ed. *La Divina Villa*. Siena: Accademia delle Scienze di Siena, 1982.

Conybeare, Catherine. 'The Ambiguous Laughter of St. Laurence'. *Journal of Early Christian Studies* 10 (2002): 175–202.

Cooke, Thomas D. 'Pornography, the Comic Spirit, and the Fabliaux'. In *The Humour of the Fabliaux*, edited by Thomas D. Cooke and Benjamin L. Honeycutt. Columbia: University of Missouri Press, 1974.

Coolman, Boyd Taylor. *The Theology of Hugh of St. Victor: An Interpretation.* Cambridge: Cambridge University Press, 2010.

Cooper, Alan. 'Once a Highway, Always a Highway: Roads and English Law, c.1150–1300'. In *Roadworks: Medieval Britain, Medieval Roads*, edited by Valerie Allen and Ruth Evans. Manchester: Manchester University Press, 2016.

Cooper, Sonoma. 'The Medical School of Montpellier in the Fourteenth Century'. *Annals of Medical History* 2, no. 2 (1930): 164–195.

Corbett, George. 'Peraldus and Aquinas: Two Dominican Approaches to the Seven Capital Vices and the Christian Moral Life'. *The Thomist: A Speculative Quarterly Review* 79, no. 3 (2015): 383–406.

Davies, William. *Overcoming Anger and Irritability: A Self-Help Guide Using Cognitive Behavioural Techniques*, second edition. London: Little, Brown, 2009.

Dijkman, Jessica. *Shaping Medieval Markets: The Organisation of Commodity Markets in Holland, c.1200–c.1450*. Leiden: Brill, 2011.

Dreyer, Elizabeth A. *Passionate Spirituality: Hildegard of Bingen and Hadewijch of Brabant*. New Jersey: Paulist Press, 2005.

Dunning, Andrew. 'St Frideswide's Priory as a Centre of Learning in Early Oxford'. *Mediaeval Studies* 80 (2018): 253–96.

Dyer, Chris. *Standards of Living in the Later Middle Ages: Social Change in England, c.1200–1520*. Cambridge: Cambridge University Press, 1989.

Eisma, Maarten C., Bishakha te Riele, Marleen Overgaauw and Bettina K. Doering. 'Does prolonged grief or suicide bereavement cause public stigma? A vignette-based experiment'. *Psychiatry Research* 272 (2019): 784–789.

Elhai, Jon D., Y. Wang, H. Yang and C. Montag. 'Boredom proneness and rumination mediate relationships between depression and anxiety with problematic smartphone use severity'. *Current Psychology* 41 (2022): 5287–5297.

Estow, Clara. 'Mapping Central Europe: The Catalan Atlas and the European Imagination'. *Mediterranean Studies* 13 (2004): 1–16.

Falk, Seb. *The Light Ages: A Medieval Journey of Discovery*. London: Penguin, 2020.

Fauvelle, François-Xavier. *The Golden Rhinoceros: Histories of the African Middle Ages*. Translated by Troy Tice. Princeton, NJ: Princeton University Press, 2018.

Fernández Álvarez, Manuel. *Juana la Loca: La Cautiva de Tordesillas*. Madrid: Espasa, 2002.

Ferreiro, Alberto. *Simon Magus in Patristic, Medieval and Early Modern Traditions*. Leiden: Brill, 2005.

Fleming, Gillian. *Juana I: Legitimacy and Conflict in Sixteenth-Century Castile*. London: Palgrave Macmillan, 2018.

Fournier, Marcel. *Les statuts et privilèges des universités françaises depuis leur fondation jusqu'en 1789*. Paris: Larose et Forcel, 1891.

Fraenger, Wilhelm. *Hieronymus Bosch: Das Tausendjährige Reich*. Coburg: Winkler-Verlag, 1947.

García Marsilla, Juan Vicente and Luis Almenar Fernández. 'Fashion, emulation and social classes in late medieval Valencia. Exploring textile consumption through probate inventories'. In *La moda come motore economico*, edited by Giampiero Nigro. Florence: Firenze University Press, 2022.

Geens, Sam. *A Golden Age for Labour? Income and Wealth before and after the Black Death in the Southern Low Countries and the Republic of Florence, 1275–1550*. University of Antwerp, PhD thesis, 2023.

Gillingham, John. *The Angevin Empire*. London: Arnold, 2001.

Given, James. 'The Inquisitors of Languedoc and the Medieval Technology of Power'. *American Historical Review* 94, no. 2 (1989): 336–359.

Goering, Joseph. 'The Internal Forum and the Literature of Penance and Confession'. *Traditio* 59 (2004): 175–227.

—*The Virgin and the Grail: Origins of a Legend*. New Haven: Yale University Press, 2005.

Goetzmann, William N. 'Fibonacci and the Financial Revolution'. NBER Working Paper, no. 10352 (2004).

Gombrich, E. H. 'Bosch's "*Garden of Earthly Delights*": A Progress Report'. *Journal of the Warburg and Courtauld Institutes* 32 (1969): 162–170.

—'The Earliest Description of Bosch's *Garden of Delight*'. *Journal of the Warburg and Courtauld Institutes* 30 (1967): 403–406.

González García, Juan Luis. 'Saturno y la reina "impía". El oscuro retiro de Juana I en Tordesillas'. In *Juana I en Tordesillas: su mundo, su entorno*, edited by Miguel Ángel Zalama Rodríguez. Valladolid: Ayuntamiento de Tordesillas, 2010.

Gordon, Dillian. 'The Wilton Diptych: An Introduction'. In *The Regal Image of Richard II and the Wilton Diptych*, with an introduction by Caroline Barron, edited by Dillian Gordon, Lisa Monnas and Caroline Elam. London: Harvey Miller, 1997.

BIBLIOGRAPHY

Grieco, Allen J. 'Food and Social Classes in Late Medieval and Renaissance Italy'. In *Food: A Culinary History from Antiquity to the Present*, edited by Jean-Louis Flandrin and Massimo Montanari. New York: Columbia University Press, 1999.

—'Les utilisations sociales des fruits et légumes dans l'Italie médiévale'. In *Le Grand Livre des fruits et légumes: histoire, culture et usage*, edited by D. Meiller and P. Vannier. Paris: La Manufacture, 1991.

Griffiths, Fiona J. *The Garden of Delights: Reform and Renaissance for Women in the Twelfth Century*. Philadelphia: University of Pennsylvania Press, 2007.

Guest, Gerald B. 'The Beautiful Lucifer as an Object of Aesthetic Contemplation in the Central Middle Ages'. *Studies in Iconography* 38 (2017): 107–141.

Hahn, Michael. 'Angela of Foligno'. In *The Palgrave Encyclopedia of Medieval Women's Writing in the Global Middle Ages*, edited by Michelle M. Sauer, Diane Watt, Liz Herbert McAvoy. Cham: Springer International Publishing, 2022.

Han, Byung-Chul. *The Burnout Society*, translated by Erik Butler. Stanford, CA: Stanford University Press, 2015.

Harris, Charlie. 'Mansa Musa I of Mali: Gold, Salt, and Storytelling in Medieval West Africa'. Oxford Centre for Global History: Global History of Capitalism Project (April 2020). https://globalcapitalism.history.ox.ac.uk/files/ghocmansamusainmalipdf.

Harris, Nigel. *The Thirteenth-Century Animal Turn: Medieval and Twenty-First-Century Perspectives*. London: Palgrave Macmillan, 2020.

Harriss, G. L. *King, Parliament and Public Finance in Medieval England to 1369*. Oxford: Clarendon Press, 1975.

Hendrix, Scott E. 'Albertus Magnus and Rational Astrology'. *Religions* 11 (2020): 481.

Heng, Geraldine. *The Invention of Race in the European Middle Ages*. Cambridge: Cambridge University Press, 2018.

Higgs Strickland, Debra. *The Epiphany of Hieronymus Bosch: Imagining Antichrist and Others from the Middle Ages to the Reformation*. London: Harvey Miller, 2016.

Hoffmann, Richard C. *An Environmental History of Medieval Europe*. Cambridge: Cambridge University Press, 2014.

Hudson, John. *The Formation of the English Common Law: Law and Society in England from King Alfred to Magna Carta*, second edition. London: Routledge, 2014.

Hunwick, J. O. 'The Mid-Fourteenth Century Capital of Mali'. *The Journal of African History* 14, no. 2 (1973): 195–206.

Ilsink, Matthijs and Jos Koldeweij. *Hieronymus Bosch: Visions of Genius*. New Haven, CT: Yale University Press, 2016.

Ionescu, Dan-Tudor. 'Mithras, Neoplatonism and the Stars'. *Acta Classica Universitatis Scientiarum Debreceniensis* 54 (2018): 161–180.

Jamison, Carol. 'The New Seven Deadly Sins'. In *Studies in Medievalism XVIII: Defining Medievalism(s) II*, edited by Karl Fugelso. Woodbridge: Boydell and Brewer, 2009.

Jones, Peter J. A. 'Bones, Fire, and Falcons: Loving Things in Medieval Europe'. *Journal of Material Culture* 26, no. 4 (2021): 433–450.

—'Humility & Humiliation: The Transformation of Franciscan Humour, c.1210–1310'. *Cultural and Social History* 15, no. 2 (2018): 155–175.

—*Laughter and Power in the Twelfth Century*. Oxford: Oxford University Press, 2019.

—'Laughing with Sacred Things: A History in Four Objects'. *Church History* 89, no. 4 (2021): 759–778.

Jordan, William Chester. *The Great Famine: Northern Europe in the Early Fourteenth Century*. Princeton, NJ: Princeton University Press, 1996.

Joyner, Danielle. 'All That Is Evil: Images of Reality and Figments of the Imagination in the *Hortus Deliciarum*'. In *Imagination und Deixis: Studien zur Wahrnehmung im Mittelalter*, edited by Kathryn Starkey and Horst Wenzel. Stuttgart: Hirzel, 2007.

—*Painting the Hortus Deliciarum: Medieval Women, Wisdom, and Time*. University Park: Pennsylvania State University Press, 2016.

Kalvesmaki, Joel, ed. *A Guide to Evagrius Ponticus* (2025). https://evagriusponticus.net/life.htm.

Karras, Ruth Mazo. *Sexuality in Medieval Europe: Doing Unto Others*, third edition. London: Routledge, 2017.

Kay, Tristan. 'Dante's Cavalcantian Relapse: The "Pargoletta" Sequence and the *Commedia*'. *Dante Studies* 131 (2013): 73–97.

Key, Dana Lynn. 'From Medieval Morality Play to Jacobean City Comedy: The Afterlives of the Seven Deadly Sins', PhD Thesis, University College London, 2021.

Kirsch, Jonathan. *Moses: A Life*. New York: Ballantine Books, 1998.

Klumpenhouwer, Samuel J. 'The *Summa de penitencia* of John of Kent: Study and Critical Edition'. PhD dissertation, University of Toronto, 2018.

Koldeweij, Jos. ' "Shameless and Naked Images": Obscene Badges as Parodies of Popular Devotion'. In *Art and Architecture of Late Medieval Pilgrimage in Northern Europe and the British Isles*, edited by Sarah Blick and Rita Tekippe. Leiden: Brill, 2005.

Kowaleski, Maryanne. 'A Consumer Economy'. In *A Social History of England, 1200–1500*, edited by Rosemary Horrox and W. Mark Ormrod. Cambridge: Cambridge University Press, 2006.

Kuhn, Reinhard C. *The Demon of Noontide: Ennui in Western Literature*. Princeton: Princeton University Press, 1976.

Kuropatnicki, Andrzej K. 'A Surfeit of Lampreys – A True Story or a Myth?' *Food, Culture & Society* (2024): 1–18.

Ladurie, Emmanuel Le Roy. *Montaillou: village Occitan de 1294 à 1324*. Paris: Éditions Gallimard, 1975.

Langlois, Gauthier. 'Note sur quelques documents inédits concernant le parfait Guilhem Bélibaste et sa famille'. *Heresis* 25 (1995): 130–134.

Lansing, Carol. *Passion and Order: Restraint of Grief in the Medieval Italian Communes*. Ithaca, NY: Cornell University Press, 2018.

Lawrence, C. H. and Janet Burton. *Medieval Monasticism: Forms of Religious Life in Western Europe in the Middle Ages*, fifth edition. London: Routledge, 2023.

Le Blévec, Daniel, ed. *L'université de médecine de Montpellier et son rayonnement (XIIIe–XVe siècles)*. Turnhout: Brepols, 2004.

Leclercq, Jean. *The Love of Learning and the Desire for God: A Study of Monastic Culture*, translated by Catharine Misrahi. New York: Fordham University Press, 1961.

Lerner, Ben. *Leaving the Atocha Station*. Minneapolis, MN: Coffee House Press, 2011.

Levy, Brian. 'Performing Fabliaux'. In *Performing Medieval Narrative*, edited by Evelyn Birge Vitz, Nancy Freeman Regalado and Marilyn Lawrence. Woodbridge: Boydell and Brewer, 2005.

Lindberg, David C. *The Beginnings of Western Science: The European Scientific Tradition in Philosophical, Religious, and Institutional Context, Prehistory to AD 1450*, second edition. Chicago: University of Chicago Press, 2007.

Little, Lester K. 'Pride Goes before Avarice: Social Change and the Vices in Latin Christendom'. *American Historical Review* 76, no. 1 (1971): 16–49.

Ljungqvist, Fredrik Charpentier. 'A regional approach to the medieval warm period and the little ice age'. In *Climate Change and Variability*, edited by Suzanne Simard (2010).

Lopez, Robert S. *The Commercial Revolution of the Middle Ages, 950–1350*. Cambridge: Cambridge University Press, 1976.

Maddocks, Hilary. 'Vile Bodies in Guillaume de Deguileville's *Pelèrinage de la vie humaine*'. *Australian and New Zealand Journal of Art* 22, no. 1 (2022): 6–19.

Mafé García, Ana. *El Santo Grial: un estudio que nos desvela dónde se encuentra la copa de la última cena*. Valencia: Editorial Sargantana, 2020.

Mandach, André de. *Le 'Roman du Graal' Originaire*. Göppingen: Kümmerle, 1992.

Mann, Michael E., Zhihua Zhang, Scott Rutherford, Raymond S. Bradley, Malcolm K. Hughes, Drew Shindell, Caspar Ammann, Greg Faluvegi and Fenbiao Ni. 'Global Signatures and Dynamical Origins of the Little Ice Age and the Medieval Climate Anomaly'. *Science* 326 (2009): 1256–1260.

Manso, Javier. *Breve Historia de Juana I de Castilla: Juana la Loca*. Madrid: Nowtilus, 2019.

Marsh, David. 'Petrarch's adversaries: the *Invectives*'. In *The Cambridge Companion to Petrarch*, edited by Albert Russell Ascoli and Unn Falkeid. Cambridge: Cambridge University Press, 2015.

Matthee, Rudi. *Angels Tapping at the Wine-Shop's Door: A History of Alcohol in the Islamic World*. Oxford: Oxford University Press, 2023.

BIBLIOGRAPHY

McCarraher, Eugene. *The Enchantments of Mammon: How Capitalism Became the Religion of Modernity*. Cambridge, MA: Belknap Press, 2019.

McCormick, Michael. *Origins of the European Economy: Communications and Commerce, A.D. 300–900*. Cambridge: Cambridge University Press, 2001.

McGinn, Bernard. *The Growth of Mysticism*. New York: Crossroad, 1994.

McGuire, Brian Patrick. *Bernard of Clairvaux: An Inner Life*. Ithaca, NY: Cornell University Press, 2020.

McVaugh, Michael R. 'Arnau de Vilanova and Paris: One Embassy or Two?' *Archives d'histoire doctrinale et littéraire du Moyen Âge* 73 (2006): 29–42.

— 'Theriac at Montpellier 1285–1325 (with an edition of the "Questiones de tyriaca" of William of Brescia)'. *Sudhoffs Archiv* 56, no. 2 (1972): 113–144.

Meekes - van Toer, Irene. '*Als die maen is inden weder*: Practical Advice in a Late-Fifteenth-Century Astrological Calendar Manuscript Amsterdam UB MS XXIII A 8'. MA Thesis, Utrecht University, 2013.

Meier, Adrian and Benjamin K. Johnson. 'Social Comparison and Envy on Social Media: A Critical Review'. *Current Opinion in Psychology* 45 (2022).

Miller, Daniel. *Stuff*. Cambridge: Polity Press, 2010.

Miller, Tanya Stabler. *The Beguines of Medieval Paris: Gender, Patronage, and Spiritual Authority*. Philadelphia: University of Pennsylvania Press, 2014.

Moore, R. I. *The Formation of a Persecuting Society: Authority and Deviance in Western Europe 950–1250*, second edition. Oxford: Blackwell, 2007.

Morawiecka, Maria Magdalena. 'In a Circle: The Hereford Map as a "Cosmic Clock"'. *Imago Mundi* 75, no. 1 (2023): 90–98.

Mulon, Marianne. 'Deux traités inédits d'art culinaire médiéval'. *Bulletin philologique et historique (jusqu'à 1610) du Comité des travaux historiques et scientifiques* (1971): 369–435.

Murdoch, Brian O. *The Apocryphal Adam and Eve in Medieval Europe: Vernacular Translations and Adaptations of the Vita Adae et Evae*. Oxford: Oxford University Press, 2009.

Murphy, G. Ronald. *Gemstone of Paradise: The Holy Grail in Wolfram's Parzival*. Oxford: Oxford University Press, 2006.

Murray, Alexander. 'Counselling in Medieval Confession'. In *Handling Sin: Confession in the Middle Ages*, edited by Peter Biller and Alastair J. Minnis. York: York Medieval Press, 1998.

Murray, Jacqueline. '"The Law of Sin That Is in My Members": The Problem of Male Embodiment'. In *Gender and Holiness: Men, Women, and Saints in Late Medieval Europe*, edited by Samantha J. E. Riches and Sarah Salih. London: Routledge, 2002.

—'Men's Bodies, Men's Minds: Seminal Emissions and Sexual Anxiety in the Middle Ages'. *Annual Review of Sex Research* 8, no. 1 (1997): 1–26.

Newhauser, Richard. *The Early History of Greed: The Sin of Avarice in Early Medieval Thought and Literature*. Cambridge: Cambridge University Press, 2000.

—, ed. *In the Garden of Evil: The Vices and Culture in the Middle Ages*. Toronto: Pontifical Institute of Mediaeval Studies, 2005.

—, ed. *The Seven Deadly Sins: From Communities to Individuals*. Leiden: Brill, 2007.

Nickson, Tom. 'The First Murder: Picturing Polemic c.1391'. In *The Hebrew Bible in Fifteenth-Century Spain: Exegesis, Literature, Philosophy, and the Arts*, edited by Jonathan Decter and Arturo Prats. Leiden: Brill, 2012.

Nicolaidou, Iolie, Federica Tozzi and Athos Antoniades. 'A gamified app on emotion recognition and anger management for pre-school children'. *International Journal of Child-Computer Interaction* 31 (2022).

Ninivaggi, Frank John. *Envy Theory: Perspectives on the Psychology of Envy*. Lanham, MD: Rowman and Littlefield, 2010.

Niskanen, Samu. 'The Treatises of Ralph of Battle'. *Journal of Medieval Latin* 26 (2016): 199–226.

O'Bannon, Kathleen. *The Anger Cure: A Step-by-Step Program to Reduce Anger, Rage, Negativity, Violence, and Depression in Your Life*. Laguna Beach, CA: Basic Health, 2009.

Orme, Nicholas. *Going to Church in Medieval England*. New Haven: Yale University Press, 2021.

BIBLIOGRAPHY

Owen, Corey Alec. 'The Passions of Sir Gawain: Patience and the Idiom of Medieval Romance in England'. PhD dissertation, Dalhousie University, 2007.

Panofsky, Erwin. *Early Netherlandish Painting: Its Origins and Character*. New York: Harper and Row, 1953.

Pegg, Mark Gregory. *The Corruption of Angels: The Great Inquisition of 1245–1246*. Princeton: Princeton University Press, 2001.

Penman, Emma L., Lauren J. Breen, Lauren Y. Hewitt and Holly G. Prigerson. 'Public Attitudes about Normal and Pathological Grief'. *Death Studies* 38, no. 8 (2014): 510–516.

Philip, Lotte Brand. 'The Prado Epiphany of Jerome Bosch'. *Art Bulletin* 35, no. 4 (1953): 267–293.

Polzer, Joseph. 'Cimabue Reconsidered'. *Arte medievale* 5 (2015): 197–224.

Power, Amanda. *Roger Bacon and the Defence of Christendom*. Cambridge: Cambridge University Press, 2013.

Reynolds, Philip Lyndon. *Food and the Body: Some Peculiar Questions in High Medieval Theology*. Leiden: Brill, 1999.

Reynolds, Suzanne. *Fiefs and Vassals: The Medieval Evidence Reinterpreted*. Oxford: Clarendon Press, 1994.

Rigg, A. G. 'Golias and Other Pseudonyms'. *Studi Medievali*, 3rd Series, 18 (1977): 65–109.

Robinson, James Harvey, ed. and trans. *Petrarch: The First Modern Scholar and Man of Letters*. New York: G. P. Putnam, 1898.

Rohr, Christian, Chantal Camenisch and Kathleen Pribyl. 'The European Middle Ages'. In *The Palgrave Handbook of Climate History*, edited by Sam White, Christian Pfister and Franz Mauelshagen. London: Palgrave, 2018.

Roux, Simone. *Paris in the Middle Ages*, translated by Jo Ann McNamara. Philadelphia: University of Pennsylvania Press, 2009.

Salvadore, Matteo. *The African Prester John and the Birth of Ethiopian-European Relations, 1402–1555*. London: Routledge, 2017.

Santagata, Marco. *Dante: The Story of His Life*. Cambridge, MA: Harvard University Press, 2016.

Scott, Tom. 'Medieval Viticulture in the German-Speaking Lands'. *German History* 20, no. 1 (2002).

Sedikides, Constantine. 'In Search of Narcissus'. *Trends in Cognitive Science* 25, no. 1 (2021): 67–80.

Selvini Palazzoli, Mara. *Self-Starvation: From Individual to Family Therapy in the Treatment of Anorexia Nervosa*. Translated by A. Pomerans. New York: Aronson, 1978.

Sennis, Antonio, ed. *Cathars in Question: Heresy and Inquisition in the Middle Ages*, vol. 4. York: York Medieval Press, 2016.

Shoaf, Matthew G. 'Eyeing Envy in the Arena Chapel'. *Studies in Iconography* 30 (2009): 126–167.

Silleras-Fernández, Núria. *The Politics of Emotion: Love, Grief, and Madness in Medieval and Early Modern Iberia*. Ithaca, NY: Cornell University Press, 2024.

Silva, Laura. 'Anger and Its Desires'. *European Journal of Philosophy* 29 (2021): 1115–1135.

Simons, Walter. *Cities of Ladies: Beguine Communities in the Medieval Low Countries, 1200–1565*. Philadelphia: University of Pennsylvania Press, 2001.

Solomon, Andrew. *The Noonday Demon: An Anatomy of Depression*. London: Vintage, 2001.

Stewart, Columba. 'Evagrius Ponticus and the Eastern Monastic Tradition on the Intellect and the Passions'. *Modern Theology* 27, no. 2 (2011): 263–275.

Stouff, Louis. *Ravitaillement et alimentation en Provence aux XIVe et XVe siècles*. Berlin: De Gruyter Mouton, 1970.

Strickland, Debra Higgs. *The Epiphany of Hieronymus Bosch: Imagining Antichrist and Others from the Middle Ages to the Reformation*. London: Harvey Miller, 2016.

Thompson, Augustine. *Francis of Assisi: A New Biography*. Ithaca, NY: Cornell University Press, 2012.

Thomson, Rodney M. and Michael Winterbottom, eds. and trans. *For and Against Abelard: The Invective of Bernard of Clairvaux and Berengar of Poitiers*. Woodbridge: Boydell Medieval Texts, 2020.

Thorndike, Lynn. *A History of Magic and Experimental Science*, I. New York: Columbia University Press, 1923.

Touati, François-Olivier. 'How is a University Born? Montpellier before Montpellier'. *CIAN: Revista de Historia de las Universidades* 21, no. 2 (2018): 41–78.

Tremblinski, Donna. *Illness and Authority: Disability in the Life and Lives of Francis of Assisi*. Toronto: University of Toronto Press, 2020.

Turner, Denys. *Thomas Aquinas: A Portrait*. New Haven: Yale University Press, 2013.

Turner, Matthew D. '"Forbidden Fish": Did King Henry I Die of Lamprey Poisoning?' *Cureus* 15, no. 5 (2023).

Turner, Ralph V. *Men Raised from the Dust: Administrative Service and Upward Mobility in Angevin England*. Philadelphia: University of Pennsylvania Press, 1988.

Twomey, Lesley K. 'Juana of Castile's Book of Hours: An Archduchess at Prayer'. *Religions* 11, 201 (2020).

Unger, Richard W. *Beer in the Middle Ages and the Renaissance*. Philadelphia: University of Pennsylvania Press, 2004.

van Dijk, Godfried Christian Maria. *Op zoek naar Jheronimus van Aken alias Bosch: De feiten*. Zaltbommel: Europese Bibliotheek, 2001.

Vasari, Giorgio. *Lives of the Most Eminent Painters, Sculptors and Architects*. Translated by Gaston Duc de Vere. London: Macmillan, 1912–14. 10 volumes, vol. 1.

Vauchez, André. *Francis of Assisi: The Life and Afterlife of a Medieval Saint*. New Haven: Yale University Press, 2012.

Vitz, Evelyn Birge, Nancy Freeman Regalado and Marilyn Lawrence, eds. *Performing Medieval Narrative*. Woodbridge: Boydell and Brewer, 2005.

Wang, Yan, Haibo Yang, Christian Montag and Jon D. Elhai. 'Boredom proneness and rumination mediate relationships between depression and anxiety with problematic smartphone use severity'. *Current Psychology* 41 (2022): 5287–5297.

Warren, W. L. *Henry II*. Berkeley: University of California Press, 1973.

Watanabe-O'Kelly, Helen. 'The Eroticization of Judith in Early Modern German Art'. In *Gender Matters: Discourses of Violence in Early Modern Literature and the Arts*, edited by Mara R. Wade. Amsterdam: Rodopi, 2014.

Wayno, Jeffrey M. 'Rethinking the Fourth Lateran Council of 1215'. *Speculum* 93, no. 3 (2018): 611–637.

Webb, Heather. '*Lacrime cordiali*: Catherine of Siena on the Value of Tears'. In *A Companion to Catherine of Siena*, edited by Carolyn Muessig, George Ferzoco and Beverly Mayne Kienzle. Leiden: Brill, 2012.

Wei, Ian P. *Intellectual Culture in Medieval Paris: Theologians and the University, c.1100–1330*. Cambridge: Cambridge University Press, 2012.

Weisheipl, James A. *Friar Thomas d'Aquino: His Life, Thought, and Works*. Washington, DC: Catholic University of America Press, 1983.

Welch, John W. 'The Apocryphal Judas Revisited'. *BYU Studies Quarterly* 45, no. 2 (2006): 45–53.

Wenzel, Siegfried. 'The Seven Deadly Sins: Some Problems of Research'. *Speculum* 43 (1968).

—*The Sin of Sloth: Acedia in Medieval Thought and Literature*. Chapel Hill: University of North Carolina Press, 1967.

—'The Source for the "Remedia" of the Parson's Tale'. *Traditio* 27 (1971): 433–453.

—'The Source of Chaucer's Seven Deadly Sins'. *Traditio* 30 (1974): 351–378.

Wharff, Jonah. 'Bernard of Clairvaux and René Girard on Desire and Envy'. *Cistercian Studies Quarterly* 42, no. 2 (2007): 183–207.

White, Lynn, Jr. 'Eilmer of Malmesbury, an Eleventh-Century Aviator: A Case Study of Technological Innovation, Its Context and Tradition'. *Technology and Culture* 2, no. 2 (1961): 97–111.

Wickham, Chris. *The Donkey and the Boat: Reinterpreting the Mediterranean Economy, 950–1180*. Oxford: Oxford University Press, 2023.

Williams, Lisa A. and David DeSteno. 'Pride: Adaptive Social Emotion or Seventh Sin?' *Psychological Science* 20, no. 3 (2009).

Williams, Rowan. *Silence and Honey Cakes: The Wisdom of the Desert* (Oxford: Lion Hudson, 2003).

Willis, Jonathan. '"Moral Arithmetic" or Creative Accounting? (Re-)-defining Sin through the Ten Commandments'. In *Sin and Salvation in Reformation England*, edited by Jonathan Willis. Farnham: Ashgate, 2016.

BIBLIOGRAPHY

Wirth, Jean. *Hieronymus Bosch: Der Garten der Lüste. Das Paradies als Utopie.* Frankfurt: S. Fischer, 2000.

Woolgar, Christian M. 'Food and the Middle Ages', *Journal of Medieval History* 36, no. 1 (2010): 1–19.

Wortley, John. *An Introduction to the Desert Fathers.* Cambridge: Cambridge University Press, 2019.

Young, Spencer E. *Scholarly Community at the Early University of Paris.* Cambridge: Cambridge University Press, 2014.

Ziegler, Joseph. *Medicine and Religion c.1300: The Case of Arnau de Vilanova.* Oxford: Clarendon Press, 1998.

WEB SOURCES

https://erintothemax.com/2023/05/15/anger-management-issues-are-abuse-just-say-that/ [Accessed July 2025].

https://evagriusponticus.net/life.htm [Accessed July 2025].

Global Medieval Sourcebook. https://www.sourcebook.stanford.edu/ [Accessed July 2025].

ICD-11 for Mortality and Morbidity Statistics, Section 6, Part 6B42. https://icd.who.int/browse/2025-01/mms/en#1183832314 [Accessed June 2025].

https://techcrunch.com/2012/03/24/worlds-a-game/ [Accessed July 2025].

https://www.axios.com/2019/02/26/reid-hoffman-masters-of-scale-seven-deadly-sins [Accessed June 2025].

https://www.bbc.co.uk/news/technology-23030090 [Accessed June 2025].

Picture Credits

INTEGRATED IMAGES

p.34 *Hortus Deliciarum*, fol.3r. Reproduced by Comte Auguste de Bastard d'Estang (*c*.1832–1869), in R. Green, *Herrad of Hohenbourg: Hortus Deliciarum*, pl. I. Photo courtesy of the Bibliothèque nationale de France.

p.36 Munich, Bayerische Staatsbibliothek, Clm. 14399, fol.iv (*c*.1160s). Image courtesy of the Bayerische Staatsbibliothek.

p.39 Bamberg Book of Hours, Morgan Library, MS M.739 fol.9r (*c*.1204–1219). Image courtesy of the Morgan Library and Museum, New York.

p.40 Holkham Bible, London, British Library, Add. MS 47682, fol.2r (*c*.1327–1335). Image provided by Science Photo Library.

p.71 Cimabue, *Santa Trinità Maestà*, Uffizi Gallery, Florence (*c*.1280). Giotto, *Virgin and Child Enthroned*, Uffizi Gallery, Florence (*c*.1300). Images courtesy of Wikimedia Commons.

p.72 Giotto, *Annunciation to St Anne* (detail), Arena Chapel, Padua (*c*.1305). Image courtesy of Wikimedia Commons.

p.73 Giotto, *Meeting at the Golden Gate* (detail), Arena Chapel, Padua (*c*.1305). Image courtesy of Wikimedia Commons.

p.74 Giotto, *Invidia*, Arena Chapel, Padua (*c*.1305). Image courtesy of Wikimedia Commons.

p.113 From top left to bottom right: 1. Prague Bible, Morgan Library, MS M.833, fol.190v (*c*.1391). Image courtesy of the Morgan Library and Museum, New York; 2. Stephen Harding's Bible, Burgundy, Dijon, MS 14, fol.158r (*c*.1109). Image courtesy of the Bibliothèque municipale de Dijon; 3. National Library of Russia, St Petersburg, MS Lat. Q.v.I. 126, fol.47r. Image provided by the Bridgeman Image Library, with permission from the National Library of

PICTURE CREDITS

Russia; 4. Denstone Bible, Bologna, Morgan Library, MS G.38, fol.205v (*c.*1270). Image courtesy of the Morgan Library and Museum, New York; 5. *Speculum Humanae Salvationis*, Morgan Library, MS M.140, fol.32v (*c.*1380–1399). Image courtesy of the Morgan Library and Museum, New York; 6. Northern French Bible, Morgan Library, MS M.163, fol.159v (*c.*1229). Image courtesy of the Morgan Library and Museum, New York.

p.126　Cambridge, Trinity College, MS B. 5. 4, fol.11v. Image reproduced with permission from Trinity College Cambridge.

p.138　Albrecht Dürer, *Melencolia I* (*c.*1514). Image courtesy of Wikimedia Commons.

p.156　Rogier van der Weyden, *Descent from the Cross* (detail), Prado Museum, Madrid. Image courtesy of Wikimedia Commons.

p.176　Paris, Bibliothèque Sainte-Geneviève, MS 1130, fol.60v. Image reproduced from the public domain digital archive of the Bibliothèque Sainte-Geneviève.

p.191　The St Clement Master, *The Virgin with Grail*, Museu Nacional d'Art de Catalunya (*c.*1123). Image reproduced from the public domain digital archive of the Museu Nacional d'Art de Catalunya.

p.244　*Psalter and Prayer Book of Bonne de Luxembourg*, Metropolitan Museum of Art, New York, Cloisters Collection (*c.*1349). Image reproduced from the public domain digital archive of the Metropolitan Museum of Art, New York.

PLATE SECTION

1. London, British Library, Harleian MS. 3244, fols.27–28. Image courtesy of Wikimedia Commons.
2. *Hortus Deliciarum*, fol.255r. Reproduced by Comte Auguste de Bastard (*c.*1832–1869). Image courtesy of Wikimedia Commons.
3. Reliquary of Saint Anthony of Padua, Basilica di San Antonio, Padua (*c.*1349). Photo: Richard Mortel. Image reproduced under Creative Commons license 2.0.
4. Giotto, *The Garden of Gethsemane*, Arena Chapel, Padua (*c.*1305). Image courtesy of Wikimedia Commons.

PICTURE CREDITS

5. *Scene from the Life of Cain*, Nelson-Atkins Museum, Kansas City, Missouri (*c.*1400s). Image courtesy of the Nelson-Atkins Museum.
6. *Trenta storie della Bibbia*, Museo di Castelvecchio, Verona (*c.*1340–1360). Musei Civici di Verona, Archivio fotográfico (Gardaphoto, Salò). Image courtesy of the Museo di Castelvecchio.
7. Francisco Pradilla y Ortiz, *Juana la Loca*, Prado Museum, Madrid (1877). Image courtesy of Wikimedia Commons.
8. Rogier van der Weyden, *Descent from the Cross*, Prado Museum, Madrid (*c.*1435). Image courtesy of Wikimedia Commons.
9. Anonymous, *De Lakenmarkt van's-Hertogenbosch*, Het Noordbrabants Museum (*c.*1530). Image courtesy of Wikimedia Commons.
10. The Valencia Chalice, Valencia Cathedral. Photo: Fernando Pascullo. Image reproduced under Creative Commons license 4.0.
11. *Les Très Riches Heures du Duc de Berry*, Chantilly, Musée Condé (*c.*1412–1416), MS 65, fol.9v. Photo: R.M.N. / R.-G. Ojéda. Image courtesy of Wikimedia Commons.
12. Cambridge, Trinity College, MS R.1.66, fol.13r. Photo by the author. Reproduced with the permission of Trinity College Library.
13. Hieronymus Bosch, *The Garden of Earthly Delights*, Prado Museum, Madrid (*c.*1500). Image courtesy of Wikimedia Commons.

Index

Aaron (biblical figure) 137
Abelard, Peter 5, 91, 284*n*43
Abū Ishāq 179–80
acedia 12–14, 21, 25, 132–67, 183, 292*n*6, 292*n*9
Adalbert of Metz 115
Adam and Eve 81, 203, 253, 256
AI (Artificial Intelligence) 27–8
Alain de Lille 66, 183, 204, 217, 222, 230
Alba Bible 82–3
Albertanus of Brescia 97, 98
alcohol 3, 213–22, 225, 229–30, 231, 309*n*47; as antiseptic 101; *see also* beer; wine
Alfonso V, King of Aragon 190
Alighieri, Antonia 141, 294*n*32
Almenar Fernández, Luis 186, 200
altarpieces 85–6
al-Umari 178, 179, 180, 302*n*43
Amazons (mythical warriors) 116–17, 290*n*59
ambition 20, 30, 42, 79, 84, 93, 95, 196, 256
American colonies 7, 9
Angela of Foligno 227, 242, 259, 313*n*25–6
Anglería, Pedro Mártir de 149, 150
Anne (mother of Virgin Mary) 72–3, 73
anorexia nervosa 226, 227, 310*n*67
Anthony of Egypt 16–17
Anthony of Padua 79–81, 83, 86, 88, 94
Antichrist 102, 252, 315*n*46
antidepressants 7, 99, 107, 270*n*5

anti-Semitism 77–8
Antonio de Beatis 253
Antwerp 252
apatheia 21
Apollo (god) 20
Arabic science 8, 101, 106, 172
Archpoet (anonymous Latin poet) 219–20, 221, 222, 231
Aries (zodiac sign) 104
Aristotle 88, 205, 206, 285*n*11, 286*n*16; *Nicomachean Ethics* 20
Ark of Wisdom 1–3, 12, 32, 269*n*1
Arles (France) 214
Arnaud de Vilanova 101–3, 104–8, 286*n*21–22, 287*n*23–5
Arqua' Parcheggio (Italy) 88
Artemis (goddess) 20
Arthurian romances 8, 147, 163–5; *see also* Parzival
Artificial Intelligence (AI) 27–8
Assisi (Italy) 184
Astesanus de Asti 233
astrology 103–4, 108, 287*n*29
Athena (goddess) 20
Augustine of Hippo 83, 86, 97, 166
Averroes 206
aviation 59–61, 169
Avicenna 106
Ayton, John, *Septuplum* 99, 286*n*16

Babylonians 19–20, 110
Bacon, Roger 59–60, 77, 279*n*51
badges, pilgrim 248, 249, 314*n*37

INDEX

Baldwin of Canterbury 77
Balthazar (magus) 179
Bamberg (Bavaria) 39
Banff (Canada) 169
Barbero, Alessandro, *Dante* 293*n*23, 293*n*32
Barcelona, Museu Nacional d'Art de Catalunya 304*n*68
Bardi, Simone de' 140
basilisks 75, 282*n*18
Beatles: *Abbey Road* 9; *The Beatles* ('White Album') 8–9; *Revolver* 8; *Sgt Pepper's Lonely Hearts Club Band* 8
beer 159, 214, 215, 216, 296*n*65
beguine communities 240–1, 242, 313*n*21
Belenguer González, Antonio 185
Bélibaste, Guillaume 46–53, 54, 55, 56, 57, 58, 61–2, 233, 277*n*26
Bellinati, Claudio 84
Belting, Hans 254, 255
Beowulf (poem) 288*n*46, 289*n*49
Berengar of Poitiers 237
Bernard de Gordon 106
Bernard of Clairvaux 76, 197, 220–1, 222, 235–40, 241, 243, 249, 259, 282*n*18, 314*n*28; *The Steps of Humility and Pride* 57–9
Bernart de Ventadorn 237–8
Bethulia (biblical city) 110, 112
Black Death 187
blindness 62, 66–7, 75–6, 77, 86
boastfulness 19, 56, 58, 60, 217
Boccaccio, Giovanni 88, 92, 140, 293*n*32
Boethius, *The Consolation of Philosophy* 10, 115–16
Bologna University 8, 90–1, 283*n*39
Boniface VIII, Pope 141
books of hours *see* prayer books
boredom 57, 133, 134, 135, 137, *138*, 144
Bosch, Hieronymus 26, 181, 252–8; *Adoration of the Magi* 252; *The Garden of Earthly Delights* 253–8, 260, 262, 263, 315*n*46, 316*n*50
Bosworth Field, Battle of (1485) 5
Botticelli, Sandro, *The Banquet in the Forest* 209
Bracciolini, Poggio, *On Avarice* 180
Brexit (British exit from European Union) 120
Bristol 34–5, 146
Brundage, James A. 312*n*9
bulimia 226, 227
Burgos (Spain) 151, 295*n*54
burnout 6–7
Büttner, Nils 255, 316*n*59
Bynum, Caroline Walker 197, 226, 227, 307*n*25, 307*n*29, 310*n*67

Caesarius of Heisterbach, *Dialogus* 271*n*14
Cain and Abel 81–3, 84, 87, 92, 93–4, 95
Cambridge University *see* Corpus Christi College; Trinity College
Camille, Michael, *Image on the Edge* 243, 315*n*40
Campin, Robert 233
Cancer (zodiac sign) 103
cancer, treatment of 101, 105–6, 107, 288*n*35
Canterbury Cathedral 119–20, 124–5
Capellanus, Andreas 238, 250, 315*n*42
capitalism 169–70, 180, 302*n*44; *see also* trade and commerce
Caravaggio, *Judith Beheading Holofernes* 111
Carcassonne (France) 46, 52
Carmina Burana (manuscript) 218, 309*n*47
Carpentras (France) 215
Carroll, Margaret 254, 255
Cassian, John 2, 21–2, 27, 31, 203, 273*n*38
Catalan Atlas 178–9, 301*n*33
Cathars 46, 277*n*23

INDEX

Catherine of Genoa 227
Catherine of Siena 225–8, 229, 230, 231;
  five types of tears 157–9, 161, 165,
  296*n*64
Chang, Tim 27, 275*n*55
Chartres (France) 90
Châtillon-sur-Seine (France) 236
Chaucer, Geoffrey 153; *The Canterbury
  Tales* 8–9, 26, 279*n*1
Chrétien de Troyes 163, 165, 193, 194
Christine de Pizan 116–17, 288*n*46,
  290*n*59
Churchill, Sir Winston 218
Cicero 24, 88, 183
Cimabue, Giovanni 69–71, 233, 281*n*14;
  Santa Trinita Maestà 70–1, *71*
Cisneros, Francisco Jiménez de 150
Cistercian Order 117, 197, 235, 238–9
Climacus, John 94, 116, 284*n*50
climate change 68–9, 214, 280*n*9
coffee 201, 202, 203, 208
coldness, emotional 6, 11–15, 134
Cologne 10–11, 206, 207
commerce *see* trade and commerce
communion, holy 136, 216, 220
confession (religion) 10–11
Conrad of Megenberg, *The Mirror of
  Human Happiness* 229–30
Constantinople 16
Contarini, Zaccaria 89, 283*n*39
cookbooks 209, 210, 211
cooperation, refusal of 41–2, 58
Cordoba (Spain) 216
Corpus Christi College, Cambridge 93,
  274*n*46
Council of Vienna (1267) 78
Covid-19 pandemic 263
Cranach, Lucas the Elder, *Judith with
  the Head of Holofernes* 114,
  289*n*50
crusades 8, 177
crying 28, 156–65, 296*n*64

Dallas (Texas), Dealey Plaza 119
Dandolo, Andrea 283*n*39
Damian, Peter 24, 111
Dandolo, Leonardo 89, 283*n*39
Dante Alighieri 88, 92, 138–42, 144–5,
  160, 166, 167, 293*n*32; *Commedia* 8–9,
  25–6, 38, 92, 138–9, 141–2, 143, 144,
  274*n*51, 276*n*14, 293*n*23, 294*n*33–4;
  Rime 25 140, 293*n*19; *La Vita Nuova*
  130–40
Deadly Sins: definitions of 2–3, 18–20,
  22, 44, 262–3; evolution of 2, 15–28,
  273*n*38–9, 273*n*43, 275*n*53; and
  medieval handbooks and literary
  works 12–15, 23–6, 28, 57–9, 93; order
  and ranking of 2–3, 18, 22, 97, 135, 262
depression 2, 6–7, 134–5, 149, 165, 167,
  183, 192, 200, 270*n*5, 295*n*43
DeSteno, David 31
devil *see* Lucifer
Dionysus (god) 20
Dominican Order 204, 206
Donatello, *Judith and Holofernes* 111
Donati, Gemma 140, 293*n*32
Douceline of Digne 226, 310*n*65
Downs, Gerry 44–5, 48, 61
dragons 19, 81, 164
dress codes, ignoring 37–8, 41, 43, 49
drinking *see* alcohol; beer; wine
Dublin, Trinity College library 12–15
Dürer, Albrecht, *Melancholia* 137, *138*
Dyer, Chris, *Standards of Living in the
  Later Middle Ages* 307*n*21

eating *see* food
Eden, Garden of 203, 253, 256, 258
Edmund the Martyr 252
Edward the Confessor 252
Egypt 16–21, 132, 172, 173, 177, 178, 299*n*13
Eilmer of Malmesbury 59, 60
Elisabeth of Schönau 135–8, 142, 144,
  145, 160

353

INDEX

Epictetus 21, 115
Ethiopia 187, 301*n*38; coffee 203, 208
Eugenius III, Pope 239
European Union, British exit 120
Evagrius Ponticus 16–21, 26, 271*n*21, 272*n*27; *Antirrhêtikos* 18, 292*n*3
Everard (Cologne priest) 10–11, 271*n*14

fabliaux (poems) 244–8, 250, 314*n*31
fashion 162, 168, 181–2, 184, 186, 187, 188, 189, 199, 303*n*54
Fernando, King of Spain 148, 151–2, 295*n*44, 295*n*54
feudalism 172, 298*n*9
Fibonacci, *Liber abaci* 172–3
Fisher King (legendary figure) 192, 193
Fitzstephen, William 124
Fitzurse, Sir Reginald 124, 125
Florence 69, 70, 88, 139, 141, 209; Uffizi Gallery 70
flying 59–61, 169
food 3, 17, 46, 170, 194, 201–13, 222–31, 263, 306*n*20–21, 311*n*76
fortitude 25, 108, 162–3
Fossanova Monastery (Italy) 206
'Foteor, Le' (*fabliau*) 246–8
four humours 104–5, 106, 108
Fournier, Jacques 51–2; Fournier Register 45–6, 48, 277*n*22
Francis of Assisi 181–4, 187–8, 199, 302*n*45, 302*n*47, 302*n*49, 303*n*52; 'Saint Francis Doctrine' 228–30, 231, 311*n*76–78
Franciscan Order 182–3, 184, 212
Franco-Prussian War 35
Frankfurt 172
fraudsters and tricksters 55–7, 62, 244
Freeman, Morgan 2
Frost, Robert, 'A Servant to Servants' 145

Gagarin, Yuri 6
Galen 106

Garden of Delights (*Hortus Deliciarum*) 34, 35–6, 39, 42
Garden of Eden 203, 253, 256, 258
Gawain (legendary knight) 147
Gdansk 159, 161, 162, 163, 165
genitals 242, 243–50, 256, 259–60
Geoffrey Babio 273*n*41
Geoffroy de Saint-Laurent 174
Gilbert Foliot, Bishop of London 122, 123
Gilbert of Poitiers 142
Gilyovskaya Roscha (Siberia) 132, 146
Giotto di Bondone 69–79, 88, 139, 233, 281*n*13–14; Arena Chapel frescoes 69, 71–9, *72*, *74*, 84, 85, 88, 94, 281*n*15–16; *Ognissanti Madonna* 70–1, *71*
Gods, Olympian 20
golden calf (Book of Exodus) 126–7
Goliards 219; *see also* Archpoet
Gombrich, Sir Ernst 255
Gómez de Fuensalida, Gutierre 295*n*44
'good people' (14th-century France) 46–54, 277*n*23
Gorbachev, Mikhail 218
Gower, John, *Confessio Amantis* 50
Gozzoli, Benozzo, *The Triumph of St. Thomas Aquinas* 206
Granada (Spain) 151, 152, 153
Great Plague (1665–6) 8
Greece, Ancient 20, 116–17
Greenland 68; 'Viking Pompeii' 68–9
Gregory the Great, Pope 22, 27, 201, 202, 208, 230, 273*n*38
Gregory IX, Pope 9, 46
Grieco, Allen J. 306*n*20
grief 140, 146–55, 162, 167, 225–6, 236, 294*n*39–40
Guelphs 141
Guest, Gerald B. 276*n*10
Gui, Bernard, *The Life of St. Thomas Aquinas* 207

354

INDEX

Guido da Bagnolo 89, 283*n*39
Guido da Pisa 116
Guigemar (legendary knight) 116, 289*n*55
Guillaume de Deguileville, *The Pilgrimage of Human Life* 175–6, *176*, 177, 178, 179

Hadewijch of Brabant 240–2, 243, 259, 313*n*23
Hahn, Michael 313*n*25–6
handwriting, medieval 54–5, 204
Helinand of Froidmont 175
Heloïse d'Argenteuil 5
Henry I, King 222–3, 224
Henry II, King 119–21, 122–4, 128–30, 233, 290*n*63, 290*n*65
Henry VII, King 152
Hera (goddess) 20
Heracles (mythological figure) 117
Herbert of Bosham 125–6, *126*, 127, 128
Hereford 54–5; *Mappa Mundi* 252, 315*n*45
Hermes (god) 20
Herod the Great 196
Herrad of Landsberg *34*, 35–6, 276*n*8
Hildegard of Bingen 43
Hippolyta (Amazon warrior) 116–17
Hoffman, Reid 27–8, 275*n*55–6
Hoffmann, Richard C. 280*n*9
Holkham Bible *40*, 41, 43
Hollander, Robert 274*n*51, 294*n*34
Holofernes (biblical figure) 110–12, 115, 129, 131, 289*n*49
Holy Grail 171, 184, 189–98, *191*, 304*n*64–6, 304*n*72
Homer, *The Iliad* 116, 285*n*11
Horace 88
horns 19, 37, 42, 73, 77–8
Hortus Deliciarum see *Garden of Delights*
housing costs 184–5, 200

Huesca (Spain) 190
Hugh de Morville 124, 125
Hugh of Saint Victor 23, 41–2, 179, 210, 251, 273*n*40–1, 292*n*8, 297*n*3; seven types of anger 120–4, 127
humility 25, 263
humours, four 104–5, *106*, 108
Hundred Years' War 9

Ibn Khaldūn 179–80
Ibn Taghribirdi 300*n*30
Ibora 21
ice cream 2, 27–8
idols 169, 176, 177, 297*n*4
immigration 101, 162, 297*n*73
Indiana Jones (film series) 171
inertia 7, 133–4, 135
Innocent III, Pope (Lothar of Segni) 10, 23, 182, 183, 188–9, 220, 297*n*3, 300*n*28
inquisitions (Catholic Church) 46, 47, 51–2, 278*n*29
invidia 65–95, 281*n*15; personification of 73–9, *74*, 88
ira 109–31
Isabella, Queen of Spain 148, 149, 151
Isidore of Seville 273*n*38
Islam 8, 177–8, 179, 186, 216

Jacobus of Voragine 56, 84
Jacques de Vitry 173–4, 187
Jean de Condé, *Li dis dou miroir* 52, 53
Jean de la Rochelle 24, 67
Jebusites (tribe) 14
Jerome, Saint 78
Jerusalem 14, 159, 165; Golden Gate 72–3, *73*
Jews 20, 78, 101, 300*n*27
Joachim (father of Virgin Mary) 71, 72–3, *73*
John of Fonte 129–30, 285*n*11
John of Kent 224

INDEX

John of Salisbury 122, 217, 308n45
Joseph of Arimathea 156–7, *156*, 257
Jove/Jupiter 20, 104
Joyner, Danielle 35–6
Juana, Queen of Castile and Léon 148–53, 155, 166–7, 257, 295n43
Judas Iscariot 83–6, 87, 92, 93–4, 95
Judith (biblical figure) 110–15, *113*, 116–17, 118, 129, 130, 131, 288n46, 289n49–51, 290n59
Julius Caesar 119
Jupiter/Jove 20, 104

Kempe, Margery 159–62, 163, 165, 166, 167, 233, 241, 296n66
Kennedy, John F. 119
Kent, University of 128
King's Lynn, Norfolk 160, 161, 163
kissing 72–3, *73*, 83, 84, 150, 153, 234, 239–40, 249
Klimt, Gustav 114
Koldeweij, Jos 256, 314n37
Kuhn, Reinhard C. 294n33

La Mota Castle (Spain) 149
Lactantius 116
Ladurie, Emmanuel Le Roy, *Montaillou* 277n21
Lais of Marie de France (narrative poems) 116
Lambeth Palace Library 77, 215
Langlois, Gauthier 277n26
Last Supper 190, 195
Lateran Council, Fourth (1215) 10, 23, 273n42
Lawrence, Saint 116, 190, 289n55
Lenin, Vladimir 64, 65, 88, 146
Leo (zodiac sign) 104
Leonardo da Vinci 60, 252
leprosy 227, 240
Lerner, Ben, *Leaving the Atocha Station* 156–7

Liber Arcis Sapientiae 1–2, 269n2
Liber Pancrisis 210–11
Limbourg brothers 214
listening 41, 61, 95
literacy 7, 55, 278n42
Little, Lester K. 170
Lombard, Peter, *Sentences* 307n26
London 68, 185; Lambeth Palace Library 77, 215; National Portrait Gallery 4–5; Warburg Institute 16, 109–10, 111, 112, 114–15, 125, 288n45
Lorris, Guillaume de 115–16
Lothar of Segni *see* Innocent III, Pope
Lucifer 5, 12, 34–44, *34*, *36*, *39*, *40*, 49, 55, 56, 57, 58, 61–2, 276n10, 276n14
luxuria 232–3, 251–60

Madrid, Prado Museum 148, 156–7, 257, 258
Magna Carta 119, 129
Mali Empire 178–80
Malmesbury, Wiltshire 59
Mammon 176–7, 178, 300n25, 300n27
Mandach, André de 304n66
Manuel I, King of Portugal 152
Mappa Mundi 252, 315n45
Marie d'Oignies 226
Mars (planet) 20, 104
Martin, Saint 245–6
Mary, Virgin 70–1, *71*, 72, 142, 190–1, *191*, 252
masturbation 235, 242, 248, 314n30
Matson, Erin 285n5
Maury, Pierre 46–53, 62
Mazzei, Lapo 209
Mechthild of Magdeburg 38, 220, 221, 222, 242
Medieval Warm Period/Climate Anomaly 68, 214, 280n9
Menalippe (Amazon warrior) 116–17
Mercury (planet) 20
Metz 90

INDEX

Meun, Jean de 10, 255
Michael, Saint *36*, 37, 38
'Middle Ages': coinage of term 88; definition of 7–9, 252
Mithras (god) 19–20, 272n31
monasteries and monasticism 90, 123, 132, 133, 135–6, 171, 190, 225, 235, 273n41, 312n8–9; *see also* Cistercian Order; Dominican Order; Franciscan Order
money 77, 95, 170, 171, 173–6, 183–6, 187, 302n44; *see also* Mammon
Montefalco, Francesco 64–5, 87, 95
Montpellier (France) 100–1, 103–8, 123, 130, 286n18, 288n35
Moore, R.I. 122
Moscow 32
Moses 78, 126–7, 128, 137
mourning 110, 147–55, 225–6, 236, 294n39–40
Munch, Edvard, *The Scream* 181
Munich 37
Musa, Mansa (Emperor of Mali) 177–81, 186, 300n29, 302n43
Muslims 101, 177–81, 199, 216; *see also* Islam

nakedness *see* nudity
narcissism 31, 49–50, 56–7
National Portrait Gallery, London 4–5
Nebuchadnezzar, King of Babylon 110, 112
Nero, Roman Emperor 56
New York, Guggenheim Museum 189; Pierpont Morgan Library 248
New York University 5, 44–5, 65
Newton, Sir Isaac 83
Nicholas of Priverno 206
Noordbrabants Museum (Netherlands) 181
Nowell Codex 289n49
nudity 16, 237, 242, 247–8, 253–7, 260

Olivi, Peter John 212
Olympian Gods 20
Omsk (Russia) 201, 213, 223–4, 230
Origen 20–1, 148
Orme, Nicholas, *Going to Church in Medieval England* 270n12
Orvieto (Italy) 147
Otto of Freising 255
Ovid, *Metamorphoses* 75
Oxford University 9, 23, 59, 90–1, 184, 238; Weston Library 143

Padua 27–8, 69, 70, 79, 82, 88, 91; Arena Chapel 69, 71–9, *72*, *74*, *84*, *85*, 88, 94, 281n15–16; Basilica di Sant'Antonio 79–81
Panofsky, Erwin 252
Paris 174, 187, 206; Bibliothèque Sainte-Geneviève 175; Louvre 206; Saint-Denis 8
Paris, University of 8, 9, 90–1, 184, 211
Parzival (legendary figure) 192, 193, 194–5, 304n72
patience 25, 116, 127, 137, 289n51, 289n55
Paul, Saint 78, 168, 169
Pavia (Italy) 115
Pearl, The (poem) 153–5, 167
Peasants' Revolt (1381) 8
Pegg, Mark Gregory 277n23
penances 11, 271n16
Peraldus, William, *Summa of Virtues and Vices* 24–5, 76, 137, 150–1, 162, 167, 233, 238, 242, 274n48, 279n1, 292n6
Peréz de Almazán, Miguel 151
Peter, Saint 56
Peter of Blois 299n20; *Dialogus inter regem Henricum et abbatem Bonevallis* 128–9
Peter of Poitiers 40
Petrarch, Francesco 88–90, 91–3, 283n39, 284n44

INDEX

Philip III, King of France 78
Philippe 'the Handsome', Archduke of Burgundy 149–51, 152–3
pilgrimages 119, 162, 248, 249, 314*n*37
Piquier, Raymonde 48–9
Pisces (zodiac sign) 103
Pitt, Brad 2
plague 8, 187, 225, 226–7
Plato 206
pogroms, anti-Jewish 78
Pontigny (France) 123
pornography 28, 244–5, 246–9, 250
Portinari, Beatrice 139–40, 141, 145, 166, 167
Poseidon (god) 20
Pradillo y Ortiz, Francisco, *Doña Juana la Loca* 148, 156, 257
prayer books 39, *39*, 114, 155, 214, 243–4, *244*, 248, 249
printing press, invention of 7, 68
procrastination 133, 144
Prolonged Grief Disorder 147, 155, 294*n*40
Property of Things, The (encyclopaedia) 97
Psalms 186, 199–200; commentaries on 125–6, *126*, 128, 142
Pullen, Robert 23, 273*n*41
puritanism 123, 170
Putin, Vladimir 6

Quran 8

race and racism 178–9, 188, 301*n*38
Ralph of Battle 143, 293*n*28
Ravenna 294*n*32
Raymond of Capua 225, 227
recipe books 209, 210, 211
Reformation 7, 26, 119–20, 252, 275*n*53
Reims (France) 90

relics and reliquaries 80; Anthony of Padua's tongue 79–81, 86; *see also* Holy Grail
Renaissance 26, 68, 69, 111, 243, 251, 275*n*53
restlessness 57, 66, 77, 129, 131, 133, 134, 139, 240
Richard II, King 252
Richard III, King 4–5, 7, 166, 257
Richard le Breton 124, 125
Richard of Saint Victor 279*n*47
rixa 99, 129, 131
Robert, King of Sicily 89
Robert of Cricklade 82, 83
Roccasecca (Italy) 206
Roger of Pontigny 121
Rolls Series (Chronicles and Memorials of Great Britain and Ireland) 44–5
Roman de la Rose (poem) 249
Roman Empire 55–7, 88; end of 7
Romance of the Rose (poem) 10
Rome 55–6, 162; Capitoline Hill 55, 59, 60; Palazzo Barberini 111; Theatre of Pompey 119; Vatican Library 1, 3, 236, 269*n*1
Rupert of Deutz 177, 300*n*27

Sagittarius (zodiac sign) 104
'Saint Francis Doctrine' 228–30, 231, 311*n*76–8
'Saint Martin's Wishes' (*fabliau*) 245–6, 248, 249
Saint Petersburg 114
San Juan de la Peña Monastery (Spain) 190, 304*n*66
San Mateo (Spain) 47–52
Santagata, Marco, *Dante* 294*n*32
Satan *see* Lucifer
Saturn (planet) 20, 104
Schönau (Germany) 135–6
Scorpio (zodiac sign) 103, 104
self-awareness 9, 53–5, 96, 157–8, 221–2

INDEX

Seneca 21, 24, 115, 289n51
Sens Cathedral 8
serpents *see* snakes and serpents
Se7en (film; 1995) 2
Seven Deadly Sins *see* Deadly Sins
Seville (Spain) 216
sex and sexuality 31, 46, 49, 233–5, 239, 240–2, 244–51, 254, 255, 260, 289n50, 312n9, 316n50
Shakespeare, William, *Hamlet* 143
's-Hertogenbosch (Netherlands) 181, 183, 252
'shit sandwich' (feedback technique) 13
Siberia 4, 5–6, 15, 29, 30, 87–8, 132, 166, 167, 168, 169, 201, 213, 218, 221, 242–3, 263; *see also* Omsk; Tyumen
Sicily 107–8
Sicre, Arnaud 50–2
Sigüenza, José 253–4
Silicon Valley (California) 27–8
Silk Road 172
Simancas, Archivo General de 152
Simon Magus 55–7, 59–62, 278n43, 279n45, 279n48
slavery 170, 178, 187, 298n7
smugness 34, 39–41, *39*, 49
snakes and serpents 19, 73, 74, *74*, 75, 79, 85, 94; viper's flesh 106
sobriety 216, 229
social media 27–8, 66, 76, 77, 280n2
Solomon, Andrew, *The Noonday Demon* 134
Song of Songs, commentaries on 117, 239
Speculum astronomiae (13th-century astrological text) 103–4
starvation, self-inflicted 21, 224–6, 227, 231
Stoicism 21, 115–16, 117, 131
Strickland, Debra Higgs, *The Epiphany of Hieronymus Bosch* 315n46
Suau, Jaume 186–7, 188–9, 199–200
Suger, Abbot of Saint-Denis 197–8

suicide 25, 84, 141, 164, 167
superbia 31–63

Talentini, Tommaso 89, 283n39
Taüll (Spain) 190–1
Taurus (zodiac sign) 103
teams, working in 41–2, 43
tears *see* crying
tech companies 27–8; *see also* social media
Testament of Reuben (Hebrew text) 20
Theobald of Bec, Archbishop of Canterbury 122, 123
Theodore of Canterbury 312n9
Theriac (drug) 105–7, 108, 131, 288n36
Theseus (mythological figure) 117
Thomas Aquinas 44, 53, 97, 204–11, 228, 229, 230–1, 277n20, 305n6, 307n26
Thomas Becket, Archbishop of Canterbury 119–20, 121–5, 126, 127, 129, 130, 131
Thomas of Perseigne 117, 118, 131, 290n60
Timbuktu (Mali), Djinguereber Mosque 179
Titanic, RMS 202
Toledo (Spain) 82, 149
Tordesillas (Spain) 152
Toronto 146
Toulouse (France) 205, 206, 237; Church of the Jacobins 204, 212–13
trade and commerce 27, 139, 169–70, 171–3, 176, 178, 182, 184, 187, 199, 297n5, 298n9–10
Trans-Siberian Railway 213, 218, 221
transubstantiation 220
Très Riches Heures du Duc de Berry (illuminated manuscript) 214
tricksters *see* fraudsters and tricksters
Trinity College, Cambridge, Wren Library 125, 262

INDEX

Trinity College, Dublin 12–15
Troubadours 237, 249
Troyes (France) 172
Turner, Denys, *Thomas Aquinas* 305*n*6
Tyumen (Siberia) 5–6, 33, 167, 250–1, 259, 263; forests and parks 6, 132, 133, 251; hot springs 232; railway station 213; shopping malls 168, 189, 196, 199
Tyumen University 4, 5–6, 15, 29, 30, 32–4, 64, 87–8, 95, 96, 98, 166, 167, 201

Ukraine, Russian invasion (2022) 263
Unger, Richard W., *Beer in the Middle Ages* 214
universities, development and role of 8, 9, 24, 90–1, 100–1, 184, 270*n*7–8, 286*n*18
university teaching 13, 15, 30, 32–4, 54, 61, 62–3, 64–5, 90–1, 96, 98, 166, 201
'upward contrast' 66
urbanisation 172, 298*n*12

Valencia (Spain) 171, 184–7, 303*n*54, 304*n*64–6; Cathedral 171, 189–90, 192–3, 195–6, 197, 198
Valladolid (Spain) 149, 151, 152, 167
van der Weyden, Rogier 9; *The Descent from the Cross* 156–7, *156*
van Eyck, Jan 9, 233, 243
Van Gogh, Vincent, *Sunflowers* 196
Vasari, Giorgio 69–70, 281*n*13
Vatican Library 1, 3, 236, 269*n*1
vegetarianism 46, 228
Venice 88, 159
Ventoux, Mont (France) 91
Venus (planet) 20, 104
Verona, Museo di Castelvecchio 85–6
Verona University 64–5, 87
Vienna, Council of (1267) 78
Vincent Ferrer 200, 278*n*43
Virgil 88, 141–2, 144, 145; *Aeneid* 20

Virgo (zodiac sign) 104
virtues, capital 25, 26–7, 262–3, 274*n*50

Walpurga (saint) 226
Warburg, Aby 109
Warburg Institute, London 109–10, 111, 112, 114–15, 116, 125, 288*n*45
Watanabe-O'Kelly, Helen 289*n*50
Weinschwelg, Der (poem) 218
Weisheipl, James A., *Friar Thomas d'Aquino* 205, 206–7, 305*n*6, 306*n*11, 307*n*26
WHO *see* World Health Organization
William VIII, Lord of Montpellier 101
William de Tracy 124, 125
William of Brescia 107
William of Champeaux 91
William of Malmesbury 59
William of Saint-Thierry 236, 237, 312*n*10–11
William of Tocco, *The Life of St. Thomas Aquinas* 207–8
Williams, Lisa 31
Wilton Diptych (panel painting) 252
wine 47, 51, 68, 94, 107, 111, 214–15, 216, 220–1, 225, 280*n*9; oxtongue wine 105, 131
Wolfram von Eschenbach, *Parzival* 193–4, 304*n*72, 305*n*73
wonder 196–8, 200, 263
World Health Organization (WHO), guidance on period of grieving 147, 148, 152, 155, 294*n*40
Wright brothers (aviators) 59
Würzburg 90

Yvain (legendary knight) 163–5
Yvette of Huy 240, 313*n*20

Zagreb 98
Zeus (god) 20
zodiac 103–4, 108, 287*n*29